Critical Acclaim for
James Wilson's *The Earth Shall Weep*

"Carefully researched and a wide-ranging narrative . . . both a survey of the disastrous impact of white conquest on indigenous cultures and a dissection of the stubborn and contradictory myths . . . generated by the conquerors."
—Richard E. Nicholls, *The New York Times Book Review*

"The long history of 'Native America' . . . is overwhelmingly complex, elusive, and hugely misunderstood, as James Wilson reminds us. Untangling it and giving it coherence on a broad scale is the considerable accomplishment of Wilson's absorbing and powerful synthetic history."
—William R. Handley, *Boston Review of Books*

"A wonderful new history of the Indians of the United States—thoroughly informed, thoughtful, and compellingly written."
—Alvin M. Josephy, Jr., author of *500 Nations*

"Wilson chronicles the past five centuries with an unflinching narrative. . . . Even when brutal and honest, *The Earth Shall Weep* is not a tragedy. It carries the story of Native Americans forward toward the future."
—Mark Trahant, *The Seattle Times*

"Employing elegiac prose and steady narrative momentum, Wilson has written a richly informative history that places Native Americans at the center of the historical stage."—*Publishers Weekly* (starred review)

"Wilson's book draws on traditional historical texts, on archaeology, ethnography, and written and oral accounts from the Indians themselves. The result is an unusually rich, credible and readable history."
—Kristen Lillegard, *Chicago Tribune*

"Wilson includes many Indian voices—defiant, betrayed, frustrated, resilient— that reveal what it felt like to be on the receiving end of countless lies and of an often brutal regime of cultural subordination. These eyewitness accounts, often missing from the standard work in the field, heighten the emotional punch of an intrinsically powerful narrative."
—Edward Lazarus, *Los Angeles Times Book Review*

"Wilson has grasped the core issues in developing an understanding of the Native American experience. All books about Native peoples should start with stories of how each tribe was created."
—Mace J. Delorme, Paiute/Pit River/Cree/Dakota Nations

"Perhaps writing of this nature will allow the start of a healing, the Indigenous soul."—Loren Bommelyn, Tolowa Nation

"The most balanced account of the taking of the American continent I've ever seen. . . . Wilson's words are riveting."
—David Pego, *The Austin American-Statesman*

"Wilson's clear and convincing account not only gives the sweep of events from the past, but allows us to put the present in a larger perspective. *The Earth Shall Weep* is a history that allows for a future, and for that reason alone it is a story worth reading."—Steven Harvey, *The Atlanta Journal Constitution*

"[Wilson] presents a comprehensive, imaginative overview of Native American history that is exceptional in its concept: Wilson has gathered information not only from historical sources but from ethnographic and archaeological works as well as oral histories. . . . Because it encompasses so many facets of the Native American situation, this volume will appeal to a broad spectrum of readers."
—*Library Journal*

"A sweeping, well-written, long-view history of American Indian societies . . . a trustworthy telling of a sad epic of misunderstanding, mayhem, and massacre."
—*Kirkus Reviews*

"*The Earth Shall Weep* is a very different history of Native America. James Wilson has written a fresh and lively account of Native American relations with Europeans and settlers. By placing Native American ideas of the world at the forefront and using native testimony and writings as well as conventional history, Wilson avoids the sense of tragic victimhood and academic ponderousness that so much of the writing on the subject is mired in. Taking us through the very diverse experiences of Native Americans in New England, the Northeast, the Southeast, the Southwest, the Great Plains, and the Far West, the book is a wonderfully sympathetic introduction to native predicaments from the first encounters to the casinos."
—Colin Samson, director of Native American Studies, University of Essex

"Wilson is constantly seeking fresh insights. . . . First-rate history . . . intellectually sophisticated, lucid, nuanced, fair and judicious, this is an outstanding addition to the literature on the subject."
—Frank McLynn, *The Independent Saturday Magazine* (London)

The Earth Shall Weep

A History of Native America

JAMES WILSON

GROVE PRESS
New York

First published in 1998 by Picador, an imprint of Macmillan Publishers Ltd., London
Published simultaneously in Canada
Printed in the United States of America

FIRST GROVE PRESS EDITION

 A proportion of the proceeds from this book will go to Survival, the worldwide movement to support tribal peoples, 11–15 Emerald Street, London WC1N 3QL, England. Tel: +44 (0)171-242-1441; Fax: +44 (0)171-242-1771; E-mail: www.survival.org.uk.

A proportion of the proceeds from this book will go to Native American Rights Fund, 1506 Broadway, Boulder, Colorado 80302-6296. Tel: 303-447-8760; Fax: 303-443-7776; E-mail: www.narf.org.

The maps entitled "Culture Areas and Approximate Locations of Native American Groups at Time of Contact" and "Land Losses" were created by Sanderson Associates and are reproduced by permission from *Encyclopedia of North American Indians*, copyright © 1996 by Houghton Mifflin Company.

Library of Congress Cataloging-in-Publication Data

Wilson, James, 1949–
    The earth shall weep : the history of Native Americans / James
Wilson.
        p. cm.
    Includes bibliographical references.
    ISBN 0-8021-3680-X (pbk.)
    1. Indians of North America—History. 2. Indians, Treatment of—North
America. 3. Indians of North America—Government policy.

    I. Title.
    E77.W54   1999
    970.004'97—dc21   99-13098

Grove Press
841 Broadway
New York, NY 10003

00 01 02 03   10 9 8 7 6 5 4 3 2 1

For Paula
and for Tom, Kit and my Mother
with love and gratitude

Some day the earth will weep, she will beg for her life, she will cry with tears of blood. You will make a choice, if you will help her or let her die, and when she dies, you too will die.

John Hollow Horn, Oglala Lakota, 1932

**CULTURE AREAS AND APPROXIMATE LOCATIONS OF
NATIVE AMERICAN GROUPS AT TIME OF CONTACT**

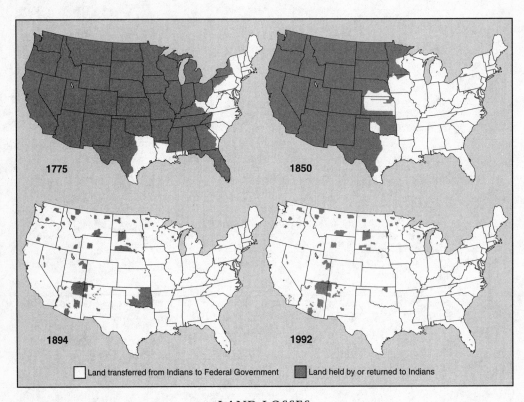

1775

1850

1894

1992

Land transferred from Indians to Federal Government

Land held by or returned to Indians

LAND LOSSES

Contents

Acknowledgements

This book is the fruit of more than twenty years' involvement with native North Americans, and many people have contributed, wittingly or unwittingly, to its final shape. Most important of all, of course, are the hundreds of Native Americans themselves who have generously given me the benefit of their knowledge and understanding. Although it would be impossible to mention them all by name, I want to acknowledge my immense gratitude for all the guidance, hospitality and friendship I have received over the years.

For quotes used in the text, or for material which helped me to write specific sections, I am especially indebted to: N. Scott Momaday; the late Nanepashemet; Wayne Newell and Dwayne Sockabasin of the Passama-quoddy Tribe of Maine; Irving Powless Jr. of the Onondaga Nation; Tom Porter and Harold Tarbell of the Mohawk Nation; Alex O. Shepherd of the Paiute Indian Tribe of Utah; Gloria B. Benson of the Kaibab Paiute Tribe, Arizona; Eleanor Whittier and Gilbert C. Innis of the Gila River Indian Community, Arizona; Governor Robert E. Lewis and Andrew L. Othole of the Pueblo of Zuñi; Roy Montoya of Santa Ana Pueblo; Rosilda Lopez-Manuel of the Tohono O'odham Tribe, Arizona; Ronnie Lupe of the White Mountain Apache Tribe, Arizona; Lauren Bomellyn of the Tolowa Tribe of California; Faith Mayhew, Chuck Kimbol, Mary Gentry and Gordon Bettles of the Klamath Tribes of Oregon; the late Joe Redthunder, his son Soy and daughter Jeannie Moon, of the Joseph band, Colville Reservation, Washington; Horace Axtel and Elsie Franks of the Nez Perce Tribe of Idaho; Gordon Watters and Fermore and Priscilla Craig, of Pendleton, Oregon; Ben Black Bear Jr. and Albert White Hat of the Rosebud Sioux Tribe; Charlotte Black Elk, Gerald Clifford, John Haas, Johnson Holy Rock, Claudia Iron Hawk, Birgil Killstraight, Celene Not Help Him, Marie Not Help Him, Gerald One Feather, Leola One Feather, Matt Two Bulls, Alex and Debbie White Plume, Harry Bird and James

Bad Wound of the Oglala Sioux Tribe; Grace Jameson and Ron McNeil of the Standing Rock Sioux Tribe; and Harry Charger of the Lower Brule Sioux Tribe. I would also like to thank the Innu people of Utshimassit and Sheshatshiu in Labrador, especially Pien and Matthew Penashue and their families, Ben Andrew and his family, the late *Kaniuekutat* and his family, and my friends George and Charlotte Gregoire and their family – who, although they live outside the geographical area covered by the book, gave me some immensely helpful insights. Finally, I want to acknowledge my great debt to two people: the late George Manuel, President of the National Indian Brotherhood of Canada and founder of the World Council of Indigenous People, for his invaluable friendship and guidance; and the Sioux scholar and writer Vine Deloria Jr., both for his writing – which I quote extensively – and for taking the time in very difficult circumstances to read and comment on my manuscript.

Over the years, I have had the good fortune to discuss Native American history with a number of leading professionals in the field, and I would like to thank William Cronon, Francis Jennings, Duane H. King, Neal Salisbury, Bernard Sheehan, Dean Snow and Russell Thornton for helping to deepen my understanding of some of the issues touched on here. I am especially indebted to Alvin M. Josephy Jr. and his wife Betty, both for several hugely helpful conversations and for their generous hospitality. I also want to acknowledge the unstinting assistance and kindness of Dr. Floyd O'Neill, Director Emeritus of the American West Center at the University of Utah, whose companionship and encyclopaedic knowledge have been immeasurably helpful and who heroically agreed to read my text in manuscript form. Needless to say, any remaining errors or omissions are entirely my own responsibility.

I am immensely grateful to Morgan Entrekin, Amy Hundley and their colleagues at Grove/Atlantic Inc. for their unflagging enthusiasm, energy and commitment. Of the other people in North America who have helped me I particularly want to thank Siobhan Oppenheimer-Nicolau, formerly of the Ford Foundation, for her support; Elizabeth Weatherford of the Museum of the American Indian; Anthony Jenkinson; Milley Fraser; and my mother-in-law, Margot Emerick.

On this side of the Atlantic, I am indebted to Jony Mazower, Americas Campaign Officer at Survival International; to Dr. Colin Samson of the University of Essex for his invaluable help in locating sources and references; to Ken Kirby (director of the two-part BBC documentary, *Savagery and the American Indian*) and Sandra Eggleston, my colleagues and companions on several trips to Indian Country; to my niece, Charlotte Wilson for bibliographical first aid; to Jon Riley, who commissioned this book and guided it with exemplary skill through its early stages; to my editors, Christine Kidney and Richard Milner, for their enthusiasm and support; and to Rachel Lockhart, who punctiliously copy-edited the manuscript. I also especially want to thank my agent, Derek Johns of A. P. Watt, for his unwavering encouragement and his excellent editorial advice.

Finally, I must acknowledge the enormous contribution of my family: my mother, for tirelessly reading and rereading and commenting on the text and for a lifetime's encouragement and support; my children, Tom and Kit, for their patience and understanding; and my wife Paula, who diligently went through every draft of every chapter, for her invaluable editorial help, her loyalty, her tolerance, and her company in Indian Country and beyond.

A Note About Terminology

As I discuss in the Epilogue, there are problems with any generic name for the indigenous peoples of North America. For clarity's sake, because there is no simple, widely accepted alternative, I have used both 'Native American' and 'Indian', although I am very aware that there are legitimate objections to both.

Wherever possible, I avoid generic terms altogether and refer to people by 'tribal' names, but this, too, is fraught with difficulty. The names by which most 'tribes' are generally known are usually not those which they use for themselves: often they are derived from the more-or-less disparaging terms their neighbours used to describe them to early European traders and explorers. (For a rough equivalent, imagine visitors from another planet arriving in England, asking who lived across the channel, and being given the answer 'Bloody Frogs'.) Understandably, many groups are now trying to gain recognition for their own names instead, but with a few exceptions – 'Tohono O'odham' rather than 'Papago', for instance – these are still not generally known or accepted. To avoid confusion, I have tended to use the currently most common form, although in some cases – such as *Ani-Yunwiya* for 'Cherokee' and *Hotinonshonni* for 'Iroquois' – I have alternated it with the people's name for themselves.

Finally: the first European explorers, traders and settlers in North America usually referred to the indigenous societies they encountered as 'nations' or 'peoples' rather than 'tribes'. I have generally tried to follow their example in my discussion of the early period, because 'tribe' suggests something more 'primitive' and with less substantial rights than the Euro-American 'state'. Under US law, however, all federally recognized Indian societies are known as 'tribes', and when I talk about a nineteenth- or twentieth-century community as a 'tribe' it is in that restricted sense.

Prologue

In December 1990, three hundred Lakota (Sioux) set out to relive the last journey of Chief Big Foot and his followers a century before. For five days, travelling on horseback and in frail open wagons, sleeping out in temperatures often fifty degrees below freezing, fasting and praying, they battled through the blizzards and vicious arctic winds that sweep across the Great Plains every winter. Their aim was to reach Wounded Knee, South Dakota, a hundred years to the day after Big Foot and most of his band had been killed there by the US Seventh Cavalry, and then, in a special ceremony, to 'wipe away the tears' and free the spirits of the victims.

The ride attracted enormous attention – at least by the standards of Native American stories, which normally have to involve a fatal outbreak of violence or a major scandal over reservation casinos to merit much publicity. Part of the reason, I think, is that, of all the historic sites associated with American Indians, Wounded Knee still has the greatest significance for modern America. As the scene of 'the last engagement of the Indian Wars,' it is the place where Native Americans, in the words of one historian, 'shuffled off the stage of history.' In 1890, it was represented as the final triumph of Progress and Civilization (though with a bittersweet undertow of sadness); over the last century or so – and particularly the last thirty years – shifting attitudes have given it a more rueful and elegiac resonance. This change is graphically symbolized by the historic marker at the site itself, which has been altered to read 'Massacre of Wounded Knee 1890' rather than 'Battle of Wounded Knee 1890.' If you look closely, you can see where a board bearing the new word has been screwed on over the old one.

But though the tone may have changed, Wounded Knee still, ultimately, seems to represent finished business. Dee Brown's *Bury My Heart At Wounded Knee*, which, perhaps more than anything else, helped to promote the more sympathetic view of Indians, ends with this moving quote from Black Elk: 'I did not know then how much was ended. When I look back now from this high hill of my old age, I can still see the butchered women and children lying heaped and scattered all along the crooked gulch as plain as when I saw them with eyes still young. And I can see that something else died there in the bloody mud, and was buried in the blizzard. A people's dream died there. It was a beautiful dream ... the nation's hoop is broken and scattered. There is no centre any longer, and the sacred tree is dead.' Reading it, it is difficult to escape the mood of leaden finality: the sense that the harrowing story of Black Elk's Sioux (and hence of Indian America) is over.

From this perspective, the Wounded Knee Ride looks no more than an epilogue, the coda to some long-closed chapter – and, certainly, much of the press coverage conveyed that impression. Headlines abounded with the word 'ghost' – a reference, in part, to the many followers of the Ghost Dance cult in Big Foot's band, but also, by implication, a description of the riders themselves. And the pictures and television footage tended to emphasize this idea: most of them showed a phalanx of blurry figures reduced to grainy monotone by the snow. Consciously or otherwise, they conjured up powerful archetypal images: the early twentieth-century photographs of Edward S. Curtis (themselves careful recreations of an idealized past) or old films. They created an unmistakable sense that you were watching something not quite *real*, and certainly something that was not really contemporary.

The feeling among the Native American participants was very different. Every evening the riders – known collectively as *Sitanka Wokiksuye* – sat by huge bonfires, discussing, with the pain and emotional intensity of people at a revivalist meeting, their ancestors' experience and its profound meaning for contemporary Lakota. A woman in her thirties, Marie Not Help Him, wept as she recalled how the mothers tried to protect their children by covering them with their bodies. 'I know how brave they were,' she went on. 'I hope that I can be strong like that...' Another speaker, her voice breaking, said simply: 'I've always been looking for something that maybe I could do to help my people, for these people here today and for those people that lost their lives a hundred years ago that were doing something good.'

This depth of feeling about the massacre victims came, in part, from the stories about them, passed down from one generation to the next, which preserve their memory as *individuals*: their characters, their idiosyncrasies, funny or tragic incidents from their lives. (How many Europeans or Americans know even the names of their ancestors a century ago?) But their spirits were also felt as palpable, living beings in the here and now. *Sitanka Wokiksuye* itself was being held in accordance with their instructions, communicated to a young Lakota in a dream five years before. Many of the riders talked of sensing or hearing them on the journey. 'The spirits actually gave me a physical sign of their presence,' said one, 'and that was the sound of their hoofbeats. That I was travelling, actually travelling the same route that they took and they were going along with me.'

This idea was echoed by Birgil Kills Straight, one of the Ride co-ordinators: 'The spirits join us . . . As you fast you come to a point where you know their presence, you see them, you hear them, travel with them, they tell us things towards the future and the past. For us we call it the hoop, the understanding . . . it's all one; it exists within what's called the sacred hoop.'

The belief that we stand at the centre of a reality in which, in some way, past, present and future all converge, is common to many Native American cultures. It means that, in an event such as the Wounded Knee Ride, commemoration of the dead is inextricably mingled with concern for the living and the unborn. The organizers of *Sitanka Wokiksuye* made it very clear that it was not simply a memorial. By ending a hundred years of mourning, they would simultaneously free both the massacre victims and their descendants, allowing *all* the Lakota to start 'mending the sacred hoop.' And this process of national renewal was not only a matter of returning to traditional spiritual practices but – as another co-ordinator, Alex White Plume, explained – taking concrete steps to deal with current problems: coping with social and family breakdown, 'taking care of the environment . . . [and] trying to get away from alcohol and drugs.'

Yet this concern for the present and the future was largely missed by the media. From a Western point of view, the Lakota's talk about the presence of spirits and the sacred hoop only confirmed the impression that they were exotic relics of some more primitive (though not necessarily less attractive) time.

Most onlookers, clearly, were genuinely moved by the Ride and the depth of feeling it generated. But there was an unshakeable sense that the participants were somehow fulfilling the role that was expected of them, the principal role of Indians in US culture throughout the twentieth century: helping America to imagine its own history.

❖   ❖   ❖

Except in a few areas, notably in the Southwest, Native Americans seem eerily absent from most of modern America today. Many Americans have never knowingly seen, let alone met, a 'real' Indian. The landscape of Ohio (apart from a scattering of prehistoric mounds) or Iowa or Kansas tells you virtually nothing about the particularities of the people who lived there before European settlement – how they used the land, what kind of shelters they built, the scale of their societies – or what happened to them. The visible, tangible evidence that they existed at all seems simply to have been obliterated.

But the 'Indian' has not disappeared from American culture. The silence and emptiness left by the people themselves is crowded with surrogates: vivid, simple images which vaguely connote an earlier, more colourful age and which continue to exercise an extraordinary imaginative hold. They appear in films, books and television programmes; in logos (Pontiac cars, Red Man tobacco); in place-names – 'Massachusetts', or the ubiquitous 'Indian Lake' and 'Shawnee Drive'; and in common phrases such as 'Indian giver' (meaning someone who gives you something and then wants it back). Manufacturers use names like 'Apache' and 'Cherokee' to conjure up images of the wild freebooting warrior. (Would you fly an *Aborigine* into battle? Drive a *Swede* across the desert?) In the same vein, there are still sports teams called 'the Braves' and 'the Redskins' – roughly the equivalent, as several Native Americans have pointed out, of calling a team 'the Buck Niggers' or 'the Jewboys'. And visitors to Native communities (as I can personally testify) are still often warned by non-Indians to 'Look out for your scalp!' (This is not, naturally, a genuine warning, like 'Don't go downtown after dark.' It is always delivered with a kind of sullen, uncomfortable jokiness.)

There is now a widespread, uneasy feeling that these images come from 'myths' about the Indian, and over the last thirty years or so a spate of writers and film-makers have promised to reveal, at last, 'the truth behind the myth.' Starting in the 1960s and 1970s, with the powerful and heartfelt *Bury My Heart At Wounded Knee* and films such as *Soldier Blue* and *Little Big Man*, a whole generation of books, films and TV series has tried, often very honourably, to set the record straight by giving a native perspective on the conquest of the West. Advocates of Political Correctness have introduced new terms – *Native American* instead of *Indian* – in the hope of rooting out negative stereotypes. Instead of Hollywood's grunting brute, the Indian is now generally represented as a tragic victim, a gentle, deeply spiritual nature-lover in harmony with a virginal continent. This more sympathetic – and currently more fashionable – view has turned Native Americans into an emblem both of the Green movement (a famous 1970s TV commercial, for instance, under the slogan 'Pollution: It's A Crying Shame', showed a braided Indian in a birch-bark canoe weeping at the mess caused by White people) and of New Age spirituality. Thousands of young Americans and Europeans are now embracing practices like the sweat lodge, the Sun Dance and shamanic drumming in the belief that native cultures embody a timeless ancestral wisdom that Western civilization has lost.

But this romantic version of the Indian, for all its good intentions, is no less mythic than the one it seeks to replace. Analysing the 'romantic colonial vocabulary' used to describe Native Americans – *tribe* rather than *nation*; *medicine man* rather than *doctor, minister, psychiatrist etc.*; *warrior* or *brave* rather than *soldier*, the Cherokee artist Jimmie Durham links it to the eighteenth-century (and even earlier) idea of 'the Noble Savage' and concludes that it 'serves to dehumanize us, and make our affairs and political systems seem not quite as serious or advanced as those of other people.' Ultimately, the 'good Indian' is no more real than the 'bad Indian'.

Why have these ideas about Native Americans – positive and negative – proved so difficult to dislodge? Partly, it is that they have very deep roots, reaching back to the first European attempts to make sense of the 'New World' and its inhabitants in the period immediately following 'discovery'. What unites them is the central belief that 'the Indian' belongs essentially to the past rather than to the present. He (or she) is an exotic relic of some earlier stage that we have already passed through: either – depending on your point of view – a kind of primitive anarchy that we have overcome (in nature, in ourselves) or an innocent Golden Age that we have forfeited through greed and destructiveness.

Over the centuries, this initially innocent notion has been worked and reworked to justify and explain European and American treatment of the Indian. Its key argument is that, because native and non-native inhabit essentially different realities, they cannot be expected to co-exist: by definition, yesterday must always give way to tomorrow. This view reached its apogee with the nineteenth-century idea of the Indian as the *Vanishing American* (note that *vanishing* is a kind of innate quality, as in *vanishing cream*, something you do rather than something that is done to you). While they testify to *our* ability to develop and progress, Native American societies are incapable of change them-selves. As natural and untameable as the wild animals with which they share the wilderness, they cannot adapt when confronted by a more advanced and virile civilization, but are doomed to melt away 'like snow before the sun.' The only hope for the *individual* Indian is to break his or her tribal allegiance and become 'civilized'.

It is easy to see the appeal of this belief. It removes the invasion and conquest of America from the historical arena, where individual human beings make choices and are in some sense morally accountable for their actions, and transforms it into a purely mechanical process. It is sad, to be sure – a kind of operatic tragedy, full of affecting arias like Chief Joseph's surrender speech or Chief Seattle's (heavily rewritten) reflections on Mother Earth – but ultimately it could not have been otherwise. As the reformer Herbert Welsh put it – rather circuitously – as early as 1890: '. . . the belief that the Indian belonged to a doomed race, and that he was incapable of civilization, was so prevalent and so firmly intrenched in the minds of our people as to make them palliate national injustice as the inevitable adjunct of a conclusion that was unavoidable.'

There is a self-fulfilling circularity about this idea, rather like the medieval test for witchcraft in which the suspect was thrown into a pond: if she floated, it proved that she had supernatural powers and should be burnt at the stake; if she drowned, then clearly she wasn't a witch – but she was, of course, dead. Similarly, Native Americans are expected to demonstrate their authenticity by vanishing before the irresistible tide of Progress. If they *fail* to vanish, if they change and adapt instead, then, by definition , they are not really Native Americans. To misquote General Sheridan slightly, the only real Indian is a dead – or, at least, a dying – Indian.

Although the rhetoric of the *Vanishing American* is seldom used today, many of the doctrine's underlying assumptions have never been seriously challenged. Unlike 'native' peoples in Africa and Asia, indigenous Americans have not decolonized, and we have not been forced – or allowed ourselves – to see them in a fundamentally different role. Instead, we have more and more involved variations on the same basic theme which, like layers of calloused skin built up over a raw nerve, still effectively distance America from the fact that it grew to greatness by dispossessing and almost exterminating another people. Refracted through the culture of the most powerful society on earth – and the culture which, more than any other, has moulded the twentieth-century imagination – these stereotypes are now so deeply engrained in our consciousness that they seem almost immovable.

The result, for non-Indians, is profound confusion about who Native Americans are and what has happened to them. For Indians themselves, it is something far more serious. European assumptions about them have, to a great extent, determined their history over the last five centuries and the kind of world they live in today. From their day-to-day dealings with Bureau of Indian Affairs officials on the reservations to the images of themselves they see on television, their experience as peoples and as individuals is shaped largely by *our* misapprehensions.

❀   ❀   ❀

Native Americans have never physically 'vanished' from America. Although their numbers had been so drastically reduced by the end of the nineteenth century that many people thought they were on the point of extinction, in the last hundred years they have increased almost eightfold. Today, there are 554 legally recognized 'Indian tribes' with a combined population of nearly two million, and – according to one recent estimate – a further twenty-five million or more US citizens who have some known Native American ancestry.

But many Native Americans feel, nonetheless, that they are somehow – in the phrase of the Sioux writer Vine Deloria Jr – 'invisible'. There is a revealing story, which I have heard in several tribes and which has become a kind of Indian urban myth, about a visitor to a reservation stopping her car in front of a group of Native American women and asking: 'Where are the Indians?'

Why should native people feel that no one can see them – or, perhaps more accurately, that no one can *recognize* them? Partly it is because, even with their recovery in the twentieth century, they remain a tiny minority – less than one per cent of the US population – and are scattered throughout the country, though with a heavy concentration in the West and Southwest: approximately half of all Indians live in Oklahoma, California, Arizona, New Mexico, Alaska or Washington State. Around 60 per cent of them are now city-dwellers, but – with few exceptions – they tend to be dispersed among other groups rather than congregating in 'Indian areas' where they would be easily identifiable. And most of the remaining tribal lands – which many urban Indians still regard as home – are relatively isolated, so travellers and visitors to major centres are unlikely ever to see them without going out of their way.

But because, as a modern native leader, Suzan Shown Harjo, puts it, 'people always think about Indians in the past tense,' even those who do make the trip to a reservation are often taken aback by what they find. Many native communities now seem less like exotic tribal enclaves than small suburbs, with neat clusters of standardized houses, supermarkets and school buses; others look more like rural slums, with shacks and trailer homes scattered across a landscape strewn with rusting cars, old fridges and all the other squalid detritus of American consumerism. Many of the people you see in a reservation town like Pine Ridge are obese; some are clearly drunk, or have the dazed hangdog look of the problem drinker; almost all of them wear 'modern' clothes (although sometimes with the addition of a piece of traditional jewellery or decoration). Some – as a result of intermarriage with non-Indians – do not even look racially particularly distinct. For someone whose only image of the 'Indian' is still some furred, feathered and beaded figure staring inscrutably out of a nineteenth-century photograph, they seem unsettlingly inauthentic and unclassifiable.

In fact, of course, it is profoundly unrealistic to suppose that *any* people, and especially Native Americans, will look the same as they did a hundred years ago. All cultures evolve: American Indians, in addition, have had to face pressures and enforced changes that are almost unimaginable to most other peoples.

Like the glaciers which gouged out a new landscape at the start of the Ice Age, the European invasion of America over the last four centuries has utterly transformed the world in which native people live. A modern map of 'Indian Country' – the fifty-five million acres or so still under tribal control – bears almost no relation to the pattern of peoples and cultures in 1492. The relentless tide of settlement has uprooted whole nations and deposited them thousands of miles from their homelands. In many areas that were 'thickly peopled' when the first colonists arrived there are now almost no Native Americans, while some of the places with the highest concentrations of Indians today were only relatively sparsely populated in aboriginal times. A few groups have become immensely larger and more powerful: the Navajo, for instance, have grown from a handful of small nomadic bands to the largest tribe in the country, with a population of 250,000, a reservation the size of Belgium, and TV and radio stations broadcasting in their own language. Many others – Massachusetts, Wampanoags, Narragansetts, Natchez and scores more – described as 'great nations' by early explorers – have disappeared altogether, or been reduced to scattered remnants with a few acres of land and little trace of their pre-Columbian culture.

As well as losing most of the land on which their aboriginal way of life depended, generations of Native Americans have been traumatized by a sustained assault on their social, psychological and spiritual world and a breathtakingly ambitious experiment in social engineering. In the period following the end of the 'Indian Wars', native cultural and spiritual practices were outlawed and Indian children were sent in their thousands to boarding schools, where they were kept from their homes sometimes for years at a time and punished – often brutally – for speaking their own languages. The aim was nothing less than to turn them from 'Indians' into 'Americans': to supplant, almost overnight, a whole people's history and sense of identity with someone else's. At the same time, the United States used its immense power over the defeated tribes to reshape the reservations themselves, punishing 'traditionals' who tried to cling to their culture and trying, for much of this century, to destroy tribal status altogether and force Indians to assimilate individually into the American 'melting pot'.

These experiences, not surprisingly, have left Native Americans one of the most troubled minorities in America. Their communities are plagued with social and health problems: poor housing, diabetes, alcoholism, social breakdown, violence, fatal accidents (the second commonest cause of death), homicide and suicide. And, although there are exceptions – such as the tiny Pequot community in Connecticut, which has used its tribal status to create a massively profitable casino and leisure complex – the majority of them are very poor by US standards. According to the Bureau of Labor Statistics, 45 per cent of Indians living on or near reservations are unemployed – as against 8 per cent of Americans as a whole – but even this figure is probably an underestimation, because it excludes several categories of people without jobs. (On many reservations, such as Pine Ridge, unemployment regularly runs at 60 per cent, 70 per cent or even 80 per cent.) Of those who are working, only 25 per cent earn more than $7,000.00 a year.

Looking at these statistics, and the massive upheavals in the Indian world that lie behind them, it is easy to believe that after a hundred years of reservation life the government has succeeded in turning native people into just another group of poor Americans. But beneath the surface, out of sight of a casual visitor, many native communities continue to be profoundly different from the rest of America. On a reservation like Pine Ridge, the houses may look like poor public housing anywhere, but the way they are sited reflects the kinship structures of the bands that settled there more than a century ago. The junk strewn across the landscape may be American, but the way it is arranged, the way it is disposed of and exchanged, still embodies Indian values and experience. As Birgil Kills Straight puts it:

After 100 years and all the attempts to kill us we're still alive, we still have our ... spirituality, our language, we have our own form of economics, we have our own infrastructures. Perhaps you don't see them, but they're still here. A lot of the things that make us distinct and separate from white America, or black America, or yellow America, we shall have it and will continue to have it.

Perhaps this sense of identity survives most strongly in Indian oral tradition. As non-literate societies, pre-contact Native American peoples transmitted every aspect of their culture, from geography and knowledge of plants and animals to history and spiritual beliefs, through word of mouth. Stories, myths and legends therefore occupied an absolutely central place in their lives, embodying a people's deepest sense of themselves and providing, often, the surest and most profound guide to their understanding of the world. Although thousands of these narratives have been lost, many have survived, too powerful, elusive and supple for even the most conscientious missionary to suppress. In scores of tribes, they have kept alive the historical knowledge central to any community – that, despite everything, we are still *us* rather than *them*.

Although many of the oral accounts seem to be very old (some apparently contain references, for instance, to natural events that occurred thousands of years ago), it is difficult to be sure – with very few exceptions – that any of them has come down unaltered from the pre-contact period. Inevitably, the experience of the last five hundred years has seeped in, modifying existing elements so that they offer a more complete explanation of the world. But – like European accounts of the 'discovery' of the 'New World' – these stories still bear the unmistakable imprint of the cultures that produced them. Sometimes they offer a view of some historical episode that differs wildly from 'official' Western history; more often, they reveal fundamentally different values and assumptions. Many tribes, for instance, have mythical accounts of the origin of the various races (echoing the way Europeans mythologized 'the Indian' in terms of Western cosmology) which hold up a surprising distorting mirror to Euro-American culture. A Tohono O'odham (Papago) story describes how, long ago, the hero I'itoi brought the victims of a giant killer-eagle back to life. Those who had been dead the longest and were most decayed and pallid, he turned into white people. Because they had been dead so long that they had forgotten everything they once knew, I'itoi gave them the power of writing to help them record and remember. Clearly, from a Tohono O'odham point of view, literacy is a kind of crutch: far from being an emblem of cultural superiority, it is evidence that Europeans are lost, ignorant and detached from a knowledge of themselves.

It is often difficult to interpret the surviving oral tradition: the written English version of a story not only translates it into another language but also transposes it from the cultural context in which it was originally told. But, even with these limitations, it still tells us unmistakably that we are in touch with a world very different from Euro-America's: a world in which Indians are the central characters, rather than simply bit players; in which the importance of their history lies in its significance for *them* rather than for us; and in which the very concept of history itself is radically at odds with Western assumptions and beliefs.

To begin to understand the experience of Native Americans, we have to try to make the imaginative leap into this universe. At the same time, we have to unpick the threads of the Euro-American culture which has trapped them for so long and see how ideas about 'the Indian' became translated into – and were used to vindicate – the policies used against them and the reality they inhabit today. This means re-examining many of our most basic beliefs about the world, and – ultimately – the very apparatus with which we make sense of it. No single work, obviously, can expect to achieve this at a stroke, but I hope this book can make a contribution. By weaving together 'official' history and archaeology, anthropology, oral tradition and the voices of contemporary Native Americans – drawn both from published writings and from my own many conversations and interviews with Indians over the years – it aims to illuminate, for a non-Indian audience, a history that despite (or perhaps because of) the millions of words devoted to it remains oddly suppressed and hidden.

I want to make it clear, though, that I am not setting out to reveal 'finally – the truth behind the myth!': there is no single 'truth' to reveal, and no single 'myth' concealing it. Nor, as a non-Indian, can I pretend to speak *for* Native Americans by giving 'the Indian side of the story' (something which would, in any case, require hundreds of volumes). Rather, this is my own personal view, evolved over more than twenty years of working with and writing about Native Americans from Alaska to Arizona, of a complex, elusive and hugely misunderstood history.

Part I

ORIGINS

1. This is How It Was:
Two Views of History

Long, long ago, when the world was so new that even the stars were dark, it was very, very flat. Chareya, Old Man Above, could not see through the dark to the new, flat earth. Neither could he step down to it because it was so far below him. With a large stone he bored a hole in the sky. Then through the hole he pushed down masses of ice and snow, until a great pyramid rose from the plain. Old Man Above climbed down through the hole he had made in the sky, stepping from cloud to cloud, until he could put his foot on top of the mass of ice and snow. Then with one long step he reached the earth.

The sun shone through the hole in the sky and began to melt the ice and snow. It made holes in the ice and snow. When it was soft, Chareya bored with his finger into the earth, here and there, and planted the first trees. Streams from the melting snow watered the new trees and made them grow. Then he gathered the leaves which fell from the trees and blew upon them. They became birds. He took a stick and broke it into pieces. Out of the small end he made fishes and placed them in the mountain streams. Of the middle of the stick, he made all the animals except the grizzly bear. From the big end of the stick came the grizzly bear, who was made master of all. Grizzly was large and strong and cunning. When the earth was new he walked upon two feet and carried a large club. So strong was Grizzly that Old Man Above feared the creature he had made. Therefore, so that he might be safe, Chareya hollowed out the pyramid of ice and snow as a tepee. There he lived for thousands of snows. The people knew he lived there because they could see the smoke curling from the smoke-hole of his tepee. When the white man came, Old Man Above went away. There is no longer

any smoke from the smoke-hole. White men call the tepee Mount
Shasta.

Shastika, California

Within most Native American cultures there is no clear distinction
between 'story' and 'history'. Both are part of the oral tradition, the
rich profusion of anecdotes and legends by which each tribe and nation
explains the creation of the world and its own origins and experience.
As a result, from the perspective of most Western scholars, they are
simply 'myths', which – with few exceptions – can tell us almost nothing
worthwhile about 'what really happened.'

But a 'myth' – despite the widespread use of the word to mean
'falsehood' – is not simply a 'lie' or a childish fantasy. As the writer
Ronald Wright puts it:

> Myth is an arrangement of the past, whether real or imagined, in
> patterns that resonate with a culture's deepest values and aspirations.
> Myths create and reinforce archetypes so taken for granted, so
> seemingly axiomatic, that they go unchallenged. Myths are so fraught
> with meaning that we live and die by them. They are the maps by
> which cultures navigate through time.

And the myths of Western culture, even if we have consciously rejected
them, continue to shape and pervade our contemporary view of the
world – including our view of history. Many of the West's most
fundamental assumptions about the universe – the assumptions that
separate us most profoundly from other cultures – are deeply rooted in
our own origin legend. The Book of Genesis is a story of sin, banishment
and loss: it tells us that we are the Lords of Creation, made for a life of
ease and harmony in the Garden of Eden, but that we forfeited
Paradise through our own wickedness. Finding that Eve has taken the
fruit of the tree of the knowledge of good and evil, God first curses the
serpent who 'beguiled' her, and then:

> To the woman he said,
>
> > 'I will greatly multiply your pain in childbearing;
> > in pain you shall bring forth children,

> yet your desire shall be for your husband,
> and he shall rule over you.'

And to Adam he said,

> 'Because you have listened to the voice of your wife,
> and have eaten of the tree of which I commanded you,
> "You shall not eat of it,"
> cursed is the ground because of you;
> in toil you shall eat of it all the days of your life;
> thorns and thistles it shall bring forth to you;
> and you shall eat the plants of the field.
> In the sweat of your face you shall eat bread
> till you return to the ground,
> for out of it you were taken;
> you are dust,
> and to dust you shall return.'

Then, 'lest [man] put forth his hand and take also of the tree of life, and eat, and live for ever . . . the LORD God sent him forth from the garden of Eden, to till the ground from which he was taken. He drove out the man; and at the east of the garden of Eden he placed the cherubim, and a flaming sword which turned every way, to guard the way to the tree of life.'

This primal catastrophe has left us profoundly dislocated: we are exiles in an alien wilderness which we must struggle to subdue. With every generation we move further and further from the gates of Eden, sustained only by dreams of somehow regaining our lost innocence or of creating a new heaven on earth.

Rather than returning us to our original state of grace, the incarnation only deepens our separation from it by enshrining the concept of linear time: by intervening in our destiny at a specific, defined moment, God gives us a fixed point from which our history unravels away from Eden like a ball of string. As the philosopher Alan Watts puts it: '. . . according to St. Augustine of Hippo, the universe is going along in a straight line . . . If time is cyclic, Jesus Christ would have to be crucified again and again. There would not be, therefore, that one perfect and sufficient sacrifice, oblation and satisfaction for the sins of the whole world. Time had to be a straight line from the creation to the consummation to the last judgement.' This concept is one of the fundamental organizing principles by which we try to make sense of reality, underpinning not only the Enlightenment idea of Progress and the theory of Evolution but also our very notion of history itself.

In most Native American cultures, by contrast, there is no fall from grace to begin with. Some traditions have stories about a Creator God or Spirit, but his relationship with his creation is very different from Jehovah's. According to the Lakota, for instance, Inyan (who existed 'at the time of first motion ... before anything had meaning') 'desired that another exist.'

> But there was only Inyan, so no other could be
> unless Inyan created the other from himself,
> as a part of himself, to remain, forever,
> attached to him . . .
>
> He would also have to give
> this creation some of his power
> and a portion of his spirit.
>
> So, Inyan took of himself and shaped a disc,
> this he wrapped over and around himself.
> He named this new being, 'Maka'.
> He desired that Maka be great,
> so he opened his veins and
> allowed his blood to run freely.
>
> At that point, Maka became the earth
> and the liquid of his blood became the water, Mini,
> circling the earth,
> the blue of his blood surrounded Maka
> to become the sky – Marpiya To.
>
> So the other would be, Inyan took of himself, completely,
> now his spirit, power and meaning were reduced.
> He now became inyan – the stone – brittle and hard,
> first of all things, existing from the beginning of motion.

In other words, Inyan is not removed from what he has made, or any part of it: his spirit inhabits the totality, making everything – rocks, water, earth, plants, animals and people – sacred. Again and again, in

Native American stories, human beings are seen as an integral part of a 'natural' order which embraces the whole of creation.

Similarly, although there are numerous myths about wrongdoing and its consequences, there is almost no Native American equivalent to the Judaeo–Christian idea of a kind of communal sin, an inherited curse which isolates us and opposes us to a hostile material world. The created landscape, however forbidding it may seem to an outsider, is as it should be, and 'the people' – like the pre-lapsarian Adam and Eve – are an essential part of it. It is their relationship with the land and its other inhabitants which identifies them as who they are. Their destiny is not to change it or move away from it but to maintain it according to the instructions they received 'long ago' from their Creator or culture hero.

This idea is woven into the life of almost every Native American culture. Small hunting groups express it in rituals like the *Shaking Tent*, which directly reconnect 'the people' with the sacred powers that created them. Many larger societies have elaborate annual ceremonies – the Plains Indian Sun Dance, the Cherokee Green Corn Dance, the Summer and Winter celebrations of the Pueblos – which renew their relationship with the eternal and allow them to relive the drama of their own origins. The sacred realm and sacred time run parallel to ours, and, through ritual, human beings still have access to them. Historic time is therefore less a straight line than a repeating cycle: instead of taking you a step further from your beginning, each year in some sense brings you back to it.

It is, of course, dangerous to generalize: the precise understanding of Time, and the significance attached to it, varied widely from culture to culture. Among some tribes, it was a comparatively hazy notion: when the Kiowa writer and artist Scott Momaday was asked about it, for instance, he replied: '[It] is an interesting concept . . . I don't know that anyone can really explain it . . . I think instead of being something that passes by, it is static, and people walk through time as they might walk through a canyon, and one can pause and stand in time . . . It isn't something that necessarily rushes by, one can take hold of it.' In other groups, it was a central preoccupation: the great agricultural societies of Central America, for example, had sophisticated calendars, which (in the case of the Maya) allowed them to measure time over millions of years with greater accuracy than their European contemporaries. Yet even here it was Time in its cyclical, seasonal aspect that was considered important: the Aztecs, for instance, believed that each cycle lasted fifty-two years and ended with a period of immense uncertainty and danger – an idea which was to have cataclysmic results when the Spanish reached Mexico on the cusp between two cycles.

Inevitably, this concept of Time creates a notion of history very different from the European view. For Native American cultures, an experience gains its significance not from *when it happens* but from *what it means*. If Time is essentially cyclical, there is no simple, straightforward chain of cause and effect: events have to be seen not in chronological relation to each other but in terms of a complex, coherent understanding of the world, rooted in the origin story, in which time, space, spiritual entities and living beings all interact. The function of history is to provide not a linear record, but a blueprint for living, specific to a particular people in a particular place.

Origin accounts vary enormously, consequently, from one culture and region to another. The agricultural societies of the Southwest and the Southeast, for instance, have complex, intricate descriptions of how their ancestors emerged from underground and migrated to their present homes, whereas the Iroquois peoples of the Northeast talk of the first woman falling through a hole in the sky. Many tribes have cycles of stories about a time 'long ago' when animals and humans were essentially the same and could communicate with each other, and there are numerous traditions about how this old order was swept away and the 'first people' were transformed into the creatures we know today by a 'trickster' hero or by a cataclysmic flood or fire.

Yet, for all their range and variety, these stories often have a similar feel to them. When you set them alongside the biblical Genesis, the common features suddenly appear in sharp relief: they seem to glow with the newness and immediacy of creation, offering vivid explanations for the behaviour of an animal, the shape of a rock or a mountain, which you can still encounter in the here and now. Many tribes and nations call themselves, in their own languages, 'the first people', 'the original people' or 'the real people', and their stories locate them firmly in a place of special power and significance. A Tohono O'odham in Arizona can see, through the heat-shimmer of the desert, the sacred peak of Baboquivari which stands at the centre of the universe; traditional Pikuni (Blackfeet) still make pilgrimages to Badger-Two Medicine in Montana, part of the 'Backbone of the World'. Far from telling them that they are locked out of Eden, the Indians' myths confirm that (unless they have been displaced by European contact and settlement) they still live in the place for which they were made: either the site of their own emergence or creation, or a 'Promised Land' which they have attained after a long migration.

Native Americans were unconcerned if their neighbours' myths differed from their own: their neighbours, after all, were created to be part of a different landscape, and would naturally understand their origins through stories that made sense of their own unique experience. As the modern Sioux writer Vine Deloria Jr. explains:

> People believed that each tribe had its own special relationship to the superior spiritual forces which governed the universe and that the job of each set of tribal beliefs was to fulfil its own tasks without worrying about what others were doing. Tribal knowledge was therefore not fragmented and was valid within the historical and geographical scope of the people's experience. Black Elk [a prominent Lakota spiritual leader], talking to John Neihardt, explained the methodology well: 'This they tell, and whether it happened so or not, I do not know; but if you think about it, you can see that it is true.'

But this approach has always jarred with the Western, Judaeo–Christian tradition. Exiles from Eden are not *part* of a particular place, with a unique connection to *particular* rocks and mountains, rivers and trees: they are separate from the inanimate 'natural' world to which they have been banished and can manipulate and exploit it at will. They see this material universe as the work of a conscious, rational and all-powerful Creator which must, therefore, be governed by rational, discoverable rules that operate consistently at all times and in all places for all beings. And they believe that they have received, through God's Word, a unique revelation of His true nature which gives them a global, literal account of reality and allows them to dismiss other people's beliefs as factually wrong.

Almost since the time of Columbus, the Native American ability to syncretize two realities – to accept that different people have different truths or to believe that two apparently contradictory statements can be true in different ways – has baffled and frustrated Europeans brought up with the idea of a single, monolithic truth. The accounts of missionaries, from the seventeenth-century Jesuit *Relations* on, bubble with impotent rage at the Indians' refusal to accept that because European beliefs are *right* their own beliefs must be *wrong*. Father Paul Le Jeune, a French missionary who spent the winter of 1634 with three Innu (Montagnais) families on the shore of the St. Lawrence, reported, for instance, that:

> The Savages do not throw to the dogs the bones of female Beavers and Porcupines, – at least, certain specified bones; in short, they are very careful that the dogs do not eat any bones of birds and of other animals which are taken in the net, otherwise they will take no more except with incomparable difficulties ... It is remarkable how they gather and collect these bones, and preserve them with so much care, that you would say their game would be lost if they violated their superstitions. As I was laughing at them, and telling them that Beavers do not know what is done with their bones, they answered me, 'Thou dost not know how to take Beavers, and thou wishest to talk about it.' ... I told them that the Hiroquois ... threw the bones of the Beaver to the dogs, and yet they took them very often: and that our Frenchmen captured more game than they did (without comparison), and yet our dogs ate these bones. 'Thou hast no sense,' they replied, 'dost thou not see that you and the Hiroquois cultivate the soil and gather its fruits, and not we, and that therefore it is not the same thing?' I began to laugh when I heard this irrelevant answer. The trouble is, I only stutter, I take one word for another, I pronounce badly; and so everything usually passes off in laughter.

Unsurprisingly, the modern scientific tradition still shares many assumptions with the missionary culture from which, in part, it developed. In language much like Father Le Jeune's, twentieth-century scholars have confidently dismissed Native American beliefs about their history as 'superstition' and then gone on to provide their own version, based on empirical evidence and 'common sense', of 'what really happened.' The hundreds of Indian origin myths, for example, are uniformly rejected – except insofar as they may contain a few nuggets of 'fact' about a migration or a natural event – in favour of the 'proven' scientific account. A highly regarded textbook, Carl Waldman's *Atlas of the North American Indian*, gives the generally accepted view:

> After decades of guesswork and unfounded theories of lost European tribes and lost continents, it is now held as conclusive that mankind first arrived in North America from Asia during the Pleistocene age via the Bering Strait land bridge, also known as Beringia. There were four glaciations in the million-year Pleistocene, with ice caps spreading down from the north; these were separated by interglacial periods. The Wisconsin glaciation (corresponding to the Wurm glaciation in Europe) lasted from about 90,000 or 75,000 to 8,000 BC. It is theorized that at various times during the Wisconsin, enough of the planet's water was locked up in ice to significantly lower the oceans and expose now-submerged land. Where there is now 56 miles of water 180 feet deep in the Bering Strait, there would have been a stretch of tundra possibly as much as 1,000 miles wide, bridging the two continents. The islands of today would have been towering mountains. The big game of the Ice Age could have migrated across the land bridge. And the foremost predator among them – spear-wielding man – could have followed them. These Paleo-Siberians were the first Indians, the real discoverers of the New World.

In fact, as the Sioux writer Vine Deloria Jr. shows, in his recent book *Red Earth, White Lies*, the evidence for the land bridge theory is very far from 'conclusive'. Even within its own scientific terms, it is riddled with gaps and ambiguities: some apparently human artefacts and remains in Mexico, for example, have been dated to more than 200,000 years old, an age which would challenge not only the contention that the first people arrived in America via the Bering strait but also current ideas about human evolution. Nonetheless, it is, in many ways, an awe-inspiring achievement: using only a few fragments of data, scholars have managed to create a compelling narrative which has been almost universally accepted as fact. It is a tribute both to the vigour of Western science and to the enormous confidence that we place in it.

But whereas archaeologists see their account *replacing* origin legends as a description of American prehistory, some Native Americans –

accustomed to co-existing with other peoples whose stories differ from their own – seem able to accommodate it without abandoning their own beliefs. Alfonso Ortiz, who grew up in a Tewa village and then went to an American university to train as a social scientist, strikingly exemplifies the capacity for this kind of double vision:

My world is the Tewa world. It is different from your world ... Archaeologists will tell you that we came at least 12,000 years ago from Asia, crossing the Bering land bridge, then spreading over the two American continents. These archaeologists have dug countless holes in the earth looking for spearpoints, bones, traces of fires; they have subjected these objects to sophisticated dating analysis – seeking to prove or disprove a hypothesis or date. I know of their work. I too have been to Soviet Asia and seen cave art and an old ceremonial costume remarkably similar to some found in America. But a Tewa is not so interested in the work of archaeologists.

A Tewa is interested in our own story of our origins, for it holds all that we need to know about our people, and how one should live as a human. The story defines our society. It tells me who I am, where I came from, the boundaries of my world, what kind of order exists within it; how suffering, evil and death came into this world; and what is likely to happen to me when I die ...

Our ancestors came from the north. Theirs was not a journey to be measured in centuries, for it was as much a journey of the spirit as it was a migration of a people. The Tewa know not when the journey southward began or when it ended, but we do know where it begins, how it proceeded, and where it ended. We are unconcerned about time in its historical dimensions, but we will recall in endless detail the features of the 12 places our ancestors stopped.

We point to these places to show that the journey did indeed take place. This is the only proof a Tewa requires. And each time a Tewa recalls a place where they paused, for whatever length of time, every feature of the earth and sky comes vividly to life, and the journey itself lives again.

But increasingly, in a kind of mirror image of our own intolerance, Native Americans are rejecting the scientific account altogether and insisting – like some Christian fundamentalists – that their own explanation of their origins is literally and exclusively true. In some communities, the issue has become emotive and contentious, turning acceptance of the origin legend into a talisman of cultural pride and identity. To understand this, you have to see it in the context of the Indians' recent historical experience: generations in which native beliefs, languages and practices have been ridiculed and often brutally suppressed.

But the debate also has an important legal and political dimension. If, as archaeology suggests, Native Americans arrived in America at a specific date and then moved around more or less incessantly, nudging and modifying and displacing each other as they went, then their claim to an absolute relationship with a particular landscape is undermined. They are reduced, more or less, to the same immigrant status as other North Americans: the European invasion which dispossessed them was just the most recent of the series of migrations that brought them to America in the first place. As well as seeming to weaken the overall legitimacy of Indian land claims, archaeology and ethnography has been used against tribes in specific cases: opponents of the Sioux' campaign to regain the Black Hills, for instance, produced evidence which, they said, demonstrated that the Sioux had only moved into the area within the last three centuries and that other tribes had lived there before them.

But the implications of the controversy over origins go even deeper. The scientific view is deeply rooted in our culture and our understanding of the world. It has clear parallels with the Genesis story, telling us that Native Americans, like all of us, are wanderers on the face of the earth, exiles from the African Eden where human beings first lived. (When scientists first suggested that we are all descended from a single female ancestor, they dubbed her 'Eve'.) Like the biblical account, it describes an epic trek through a hostile wilderness with immense imaginative power, conjuring images of a few heroic fur-clad figures battling through a blizzard to conquer a new continent and then, over generations, evolving into the myriad societies of aboriginal America. And, like all good myths, it reinforces our basic perception of reality. It confirms that history is a linear process whose meaning comes from change: as we move further and further from our own beginnings we also move upwards, progressively conquering both an alien world and our own ignorance and irrationality. In the process, we leave behind other, less 'developed' peoples: 'barbarous tribes' – in the words of the English historian Hugh Trevor-Roper – 'whose chief function in history . . . is to show the present an image of the past from which, by history, it has escaped.'

This idea gives us a sort of ruler by which we can measure the relative level of 'advancement' of other societies. Our culture – the culture of scientific enlightenment, rooted in Christian civilization – stands at the top of the ladder, the undisputed summit (so far) of evolution: beneath us stretch the inferior levels through which our ancestors passed in their relentless struggle to improve. These stages are objectively definable – hunter-gatherer, farmer, band, tribe, chief-dom, state – and all human populations belong to them at some moment in their history. As 'the founder of modern anthropology,' Edward Tylor, put it in 1871:

> [My] standard of reckoning progress and decline is not that of ideal good and evil, but of movement along a measured line from grade to grade of actual savagery, barbarism, and civilization. The thesis which I venture to sustain, within limits, is simply this, that the savage state in some measure represents an early condition of mankind, out of which the higher culture has gradually been developed or evolved, by processes still in regular operation as of old, the result showing that, on the whole, progress has far prevailed over relapse.

This intellectual framework, in one form or another, still informs most scholarly writing about American Indians. In some books, like Peter Farb's *Man's Rise to Civilization*, it provides an explicit structure for analysing and comparing different cultures. In others, it simply underlies the entire argument in an unconsidered, perhaps unconscious way, so that Harold Driver, for instance, in his standard textbook *Indians of North America*, can write: 'A comparison of rates of cultural evolution in the New World with those in the Old World shows that American Indian cultures developed faster from their first appearance until about 7000 BC . . . By the time the Indians began to farm . . . they were only about two thousand years behind the earliest farming in the Old World . . . From this time on, however, the Indians fell behind . . .'

If you accept this idea of a kind of pre-ordained pattern of development measured by an evolutionary clock, then peoples like the

American Indians are, in a sense, living in our past. Our response to them is profoundly ambivalent: we pity (and perhaps despise) them for their backwardness, while at the same time seeing them wistfully, even longingly, as vestiges of our own lost innocence. We study them for clues to our own history; we debate whether their primitiveness is the result of circumstances or innate inferiority; we try to help them fulfil their destiny by making them more like us; we pilfer their cultures for fragments of the ancestral wisdom that we feel we forfeited through Original Sin or the rise of capitalism or the development of Patriarchy. What we cannot do is accept that they live with us in a contemporary reality.

It would be quite wrong to hold modern science solely responsible for this view: the belief that Europeans and Native Americans are at different stages of development has underpinned European attitudes since the time of Columbus. Through the centuries, it has validated the certainty that some force greater than ourselves (God, History, Evolution) destines Europeans and Euro-Americans – for better or worse – to subdue the wilderness and supplant the 'Indian'. And of course it validates our conviction that our view of the world, our perception of time, history and the origins of people, is destined to supplant theirs. From our Olympian perspective at the pinnacle of creation, there can be no permanent co-existence, no equality, between the 'objective' reality we see and the legends of more 'primitive' people.

If we are to begin to understand the experience of Native Americans, we have to challenge the tyranny which this view has established in our minds.

2. Contact: In the Balance

The arrival of Columbus in the West Indies has a unique place in our history. Writers and historians talk about it as a moment of enormous, almost sacred, significance. It is hard to imagine any other event inspiring the kind of breathless portentousness that you find in, for example, Samuel Eliot Morison's account of the last hours before the *Pinta*, the *Santa Maria* and the *Niña* finally made landfall:

> On rush the ships, pitching, rolling, throwing spray – white waves at their bows and white wakes reflecting the moon ... With the sixth glass of the night watch, the last sands are running out of an era that began with the dawn of history. A few minutes now and destiny will turn up a glass the flow of whose sands we are still watching. Not since the birth of Christ has there been a night so full of meaning for the human race.

Since the 1940s, when Morison was writing, revisionists have increasingly challenged this view of Columbus, claiming that his importance has been over-estimated (he died believing he had reached Asia, and someone else would have reached the Americas if he hadn't), or that he was a calculating villain rather than a visionary hero. But the myth of the 'discovery' of the New World has not been easy to shift. In 1994, for example, the headmaster of a prominent New England private school took it as the central *motif* for a stirring essay on the aims of education:

> On the night before Columbus landed ... what did the Indians dream about? ... On that night before the Old World and the New converged, there were dreams on shore and in the *Pinta* and the *Niña*. And, on the morrow, the core of things would change forever ... Our mission is to prepare our students to see sails on the horizon where once there had been only canoes.

Why does this one historical instant continue to exercise such a potent grip on our imaginations? Partly, perhaps, it is because it seems to represent the collision between two quite disparate and incompatible realities. On the one side is Europe, quarrelsome, messy, dynamic, seething with energy and the spirit of discovery; on the other, an unknown continent, a vast Shangri-La, which for tens of thousands of years had lain in a kind of suspended animation, outside history, outside the mainstream of human experience. What gives the situation its poignancy and its drama is that neither side can anticipate, or even conceive of, what we know: that one of them is doomed to subdue and supplant the other. Inevitably, whether they want it to or not, their meeting will simultaneously end the strange, beautiful, timeless sleep of Indian America and create a new, unimaginable American dream.

This vision of pre-contact America – the vision of a timeless, passive 'virgin land' on which a tiny native population had barely made an impact – has haunted and tantalized us for centuries, making the transition from myth to – until recently – accepted scientific fact. Only twenty-five years ago, for instance, the modern ecologist and philosopher John Stewart Collis could confidently declare that when European settlement started

> ... the whole of the North American continent was six thousand years behind European civilization. It was only inhabited by Red Indians, and not more than a million of them, while long stretches of wild meadow and primeval forest, extending like years into the distance, had no human dwellers at all. A wildly beautiful land, enormously fertile, carrying but a million Indians – it is difficult to conceive now.

Collis goes on to describe the noble simplicity of the Indians' life, exhorting us to:

> ... remember ... the things they did not want, the clothes they did not wear, the houses they did not build, the roads they did not need, the laws they did not make, the goods they did not sell ... how they could see in the dark, how they could run swifter than wild horses, how they could wrestle with the eagle on equal terms, how they could hear over immense distances, how they could run naked in the

snow and frost without feeling cold; how they lived with nature from
sunrise to sunset . . .

It is easy to see the appeal of this image: like, say, a Native American
origin legend, it satisfies a profound psychological need in the culture
which produced it. The feelings it evokes – bittersweet wistfulness
about a lost world of innocence and harmony, mingled with pride in
our own achievements – fit perfectly with our contradictory attitude
towards the past. And by stressing the differences between Old World
and New, by presenting their meeting as part of some grand historical
process which could only have one outcome, it affirms the importance
of our ancestors while at the same time removing from them any real
personal responsibility for what happened.

It is a tribute to the enormous power of this idea that it has persisted
in the face of overwhelming evidence that – even in the limited terms
of Europe's own world view – it is extravagantly wrong.

❖   ❖   ❖

Collis's picture of a pristine North America depends, crucially, on the
belief that it was 'only' inhabited by 'not more than a million' Indians.
He derived this figure, probably, from the work of the anthropologist
James Mooney, who in 1910 made the first serious academic attempt
to establish the size of the Native American population at the time of
contact. Basing his estimate on the accounts of early European
travellers in different parts of the continent, Mooney came up with a
total of 1.148 million for the whole of North America north of Mexico.

This conclusion was almost immediately challenged by other scholars. Mooney's dependence on European writers made his findings
highly questionable: there was no way of telling how accurate their
observation was, or even whether or not they were deliberately lying.
Mooney seems to have shared some of these misgivings himself,
because in calculating his total he systematically reduced – in some
cases by fifty per cent or more – many of the figures given by his
sources. Because his estimate was based on the population of Indian
groups *at the point when Europeans first encountered them*, moreover,
it took no account of the impact of European diseases, which often

raced ahead of the frontier, decimating or exterminating tribes years before contact was made. The archaeologist H. J. Spinden, writing in 1924, argued that the evidence from Indian burial mounds in the eastern woodlands suggested a population for that area *alone* of 'several millions.'

Despite these obvious weaknesses, Mooney's figure was endorsed by several leading experts in the field, including, crucially, the pioneering American anthropologist A. L. Kroeber. For many writers and academics in the first part of this century – among them, presumably, John Stewart Collis – it attained the status of accepted fact.

There is no question that estimating the Indian population of America in 1492 is quite exceptionally hard: the evidence is maddeningly sparse, incomplete and open to wildly differing interpretations. Serious scholars from several disciplines have approached the subject in good faith and managed to produce staggeringly inconsistent results, often hundreds or even thousands of per cent apart from each other. But it is worth asking why Mooney's figure, by far the lowest 'respectable' estimate, should have seemed so overwhelmingly the most authoritative.

Part of the answer is suggested by one of the foremost modern researchers in the field, Henry F. Dobyns. 'The idea that social scientists hold of the size of the aboriginal population of the Americas,' he writes, 'directly affects their interpretation of New World civilizations and cultures.' This statement – as the historian Francis Jennings points out – also holds true if you reverse it. Traditionally, we have tended to associate dense populations with 'advanced civilizations' and small, sparse populations with 'primitive cultures'; so, the lower your opinion of Native American cultural achievement, the smaller your estimate of their numbers is likely to be. Collis's contention that there were 'no more than a million' Indians is intimately bound up with his belief that they were 'six thousand years behind European civilization.'

As with the question of Indian origins, there is a strong (though often unacknowledged) political edge to this debate. Liberals often seem more willing – or even eager – to accept that European settlement cost many millions of Native American lives, while conservatives tend to cling to the view that there was only a small, 'backward', pre-

Columbian population – an idea that not only seems to reduce the scale of the human tragedy, but also makes the triumph of European culture appear more inevitable and, finally, more desirable. It is no accident that, in the century since the final military conquest of the Indians – and particularly during the last thirty-five years – a growing questioning of American history has been accompanied both by increasing respect for Native American cultures and by an upward revision of population estimates.

Modern scholars have not only critically reassessed Mooney's calculations, they have also brought new approaches to the problem. One method involves estimating how many people a particular area could support with the technology available to the Indians at the time; another takes the nadir population at the end of the nineteenth century as a base and uses information about the impact of European settlement elsewhere as a guide to the likely rate of decline in North America, trying to project backwards to find a pre-contact figure.

There is still no consensus, but most contemporary researchers would agree that the population must have been many times greater than Mooney's one million or so. In particular, scholars now believe that epidemics of European diseases were far more devastating to native people than had previously been imagined. Recent academic estimates for the pre-Columbian population range between just over 2 million and 18 million, but the nearest to a generally accepted figure is probably Russell Thornton's suggested total of 7 million or more. Added to the far higher numbers for Mexico, Central and South America, where the large agricultural civilizations supported much greater population densities, this gives a figure for the western hemisphere as a whole of 75 to 100 million (compared with around 70 million for Europe) and suggests that perhaps one human being in five in 1492 was a native of the Americas. Clearly, this is a very different world from Collis's virgin wilderness.

*   *   *

Trying to recreate America in 1492 is extremely difficult. No Native Americans north of Mexico had written records, and many of their cultures – including most of those that bore the brunt of the first contacts along the Atlantic coast – are now extinct. But using a mixture of ethnographic and archaeological evidence, European accounts and tiny fragments of Indian oral history, it is possible to build up at least a tentative general picture which both academics and native people themselves would accept as broadly accurate.

Perhaps the most striking feature of it is the enormous cultural and social *variety* of Native America. At the end of the fifteenth century there were probably more than six hundred autonomous societies in what is now the United States and Canada, each following its own way of life. Some gauge of this diversity is provided by language: in contrast, say, to Europe, where most languages can be traced back to a single Indo-European source, scientists believe that in North America north of Mexico there were, perhaps, twelve quite distinct and apparently unrelated linguistic groups, in some cases more dissimilar than English and Chinese.

The wide range of cultures reflects, to a great extent, the huge geographic and climatic variations of North America. If you had a satellite picture of the continent in 1492 you would see, across the top of Alaska and Canada, a narrow rim of arctic tundra occupied by Inuit (Eskimo), who lived by fishing and hunting sea mammals; further south, covering most of Canada east of the Rockies and pushing down into northern New England, was a vast coniferous forest, too cold for agriculture, where nomadic hunting peoples like the Innu, the Cree and the Dene followed the seasonal migrations of caribou, moose, elk and other game. Further south again, in the prairies of southern Canada and in a great wedge through the middle of the United States, was a huge area of windswept plains and grasslands where herds of bison – perhaps totalling sixty million or more animals – roamed. Here, too, the aridity of the land and the extreme cold of the winters were unconducive to farming and most people continued to live by hunting, although in the eastern part of the area some groups had begun to cultivate maize and other crops, only venturing on to the plains for part of the year.

These central and northern regions are the parts of aboriginal America that most closely approximate to Collis's (and many other people's) view of it: large tracts of land sparsely populated by small bands of hunters who had made little permanent impact on the landscape. Even here, though, there was considerable diversity, with each group developing a way of life finely adapted to its own local environment and producing its own distinctive artefacts, crafts, songs, stories and dances.

Elsewhere, however, the picture changes dramatically. Across the Rockies, in California and most of Oregon, the lusher landscape and more temperate climate supported a much denser population, who lived primarily by gathering a profusion of wild plants. Further north, stretching along the Pacific seaboard from Washington State to Alaska, were peoples such as the Nootka, the Haida and the Kwakiutl, whose life centred on harvesting the enormous quantities of salmon that swarmed up their rivers every spring to spawn. So abundant were the natural resources of the area that the Northwest coast Indians were able to live in permanent villages and to evolve complex, hierarchical societies with a rich ceremonial life. They built substantial plank houses (some as large as sixty feet long), wove blankets, clothes and baskets out of shredded cedar bark, and developed an extraordinary, quite distinctive style of woodcarving: their intricate, brightly coloured wooden masks, boxes, house fronts and 'totem poles', decorated with the figures of animals and supernatural beings like the thunderbird, are perhaps the best-known and most recognizable images in North American Indian art.

On the other side of the continent, extending in a broad band up the East coast from the Gulf of Mexico to southern New England, was a humid region of mountains, valleys and coastal plains densely covered in deciduous and coniferous woodland. Although hunting and – particularly along the north shore of the Gulf – fishing remained important, most of the peoples of this region were predominantly farmers, living in permanent towns and villages and tending gardens of maize, beans, squash and other crops. Social life was highly organized, revolving around a series of seasonal ceremonies and rituals like the 'Green Corn Dance', and with a strong emphasis on sports such as lacrosse or the 'stick game'. In some areas, several different tribes or communities formed themselves into larger confederacies – such as the League of Five (later Six) Nations in the north, or the Powhatans and Creeks further south – each of which might number 60,000 or more people.

Finally, in the hot, dry hills and lowlands of Arizona and New

Mexico, several different cultures co-existed: semi-nomadic peoples such as the Navajos and Apaches; desert farmers and food-gatherers like the Tohono O'odham and the Pima; and the Tewa, Zuñi and other Pueblos, who built compact, well-protected towns of adobe houses and lived by an ingenious form of agriculture which allowed them to develop the highest population density north of Mexico. The desert tribes produced spectacular, brilliantly patterned basketry and pottery, and the Pueblos, in particular, (like the agricultural tribes further east) followed an annual cycle of ceremonies, in which the drama of their origins was re-enacted by magnificently dressed dancers.

This highly selective account can only hint at the range of aboriginal American societies: in all, anthropologists have identified eleven or so distinct 'culture areas', each containing hundreds of local variations. But, for all their differences, most Native American groups do seem to have shared some common characteristics which sharply distinguished them from European cultures and which powerfully affected their experience after contact.

To begin with, although some peoples – particularly in the south, where there was strong Mexican influence – used gold, silver and copper for decoration, only a tiny minority had metal (predominantly copper) tools or weapons. Stone, bone, wood and obsidian were worked into spearpoints, arrowheads, knives and scrapers, but they were not durable enough to make the same kind of impact on the landscape as iron and steel. To modify their environment, therefore, Native Americans relied heavily on fire, which they used to clear forest, drive prey towards kill-sites and – in some areas – create large, parklike spaces (much commented on by early European observers) to attract deer and other game.

A second, related factor was the absence of large domestic animals in North America, which meant that instead of the 'intensive', ploughing-and-manuring agriculture practised in Europe, Native American farmers used 'extensive' techniques, cultivating an area for a few years and then moving on to let the soil recover. Most groups – hunters and plant-gatherers as well as agriculturists – viewed land as a common resource rather than a commodity that could be *owned*. Tribes and families had the right to hunt, fish or grow crops in defined places, but the concept of a fenced-off parcel of land being the exclusive property of an individual would have been utterly alien to most, if not all, Native Americans.

The Indian attitude towards land was part of a broader, more fundamental understanding of reality which underpinned the whole of native life. Although, again, there were enormous local variations in mythology and ritual, some of the essentials of this world-view were shared by many, if not most, cultures. Perhaps the most basic element was the belief in *sacred power*: the idea that everything in the universe was interconnected and possessed a spiritual force or energy that could affect the lives of 'the people' and of all other living things. Gaining power and the aid of powerful beings was absolutely vital: for success in hunting, plentiful crops, good health, thriving children and victory in battle. But power was also dangerous. By wrongdoing or negligence you could all too easily offend one of the spirits and see your food supply dwindle, your family sicken or your community defeated. And there was always a possibility that enemies would turn power against you, making you ill or appearing in the form of a wolf or a bear to harass and attack you.

In societies where the culture is transmitted orally, experience and understanding are embodied in stories and legends that often offer the profoundest guide to how a people perceive reality. Almost every Native American group has scores of tales about a trickster – usually a coyote – which gives an immediate sense of a world poised endlessly on the brink of miracle and disaster. Like the clown in other cultures, the trickster is often lazy, lecherous, cowardly and deceitful, making people laugh by flouting authority and breaking taboos that they would not dare to transgress themselves. But he is also, in many tribes, a hero or a creator, responsible for shaping the reality in which 'the people' live. Changing his form in order to dupe an unsuspecting innocent or sleep with someone else's wife, devising ingenious plans to outwit an opponent and then – sometimes – being too clever by half and ending up outwitted himself, the Trickster vividly expresses the spontaneity and unpredictability of a universe in constant flux.

We tend to classify this world-view as 'animistic' and 'primitive', but in many respects it is comparable to the beliefs of religious traditions that we normally think of as 'advanced', particularly those of China and India. Buddhism, for instance, according to the writer John Snelling, stresses 'the dynamic nature of existence ... We are forever trying to break the dynamic world-dance, which is a unity, into separate "things", which we then freeze in the ice of thought. But the world-dance doggedly refuses to remain fragmented and frozen. It swirls on, changing from moment to moment, laughing at all our pitiful attempts to organize and control it.'

Native Americans negotiated this uncertain but marvellous universe by the help of ritual and ceremony. Ritual was usually the gift of a benign deity who had brought it to 'the people' 'in the beginning', or it was acquired by a culture hero on a journey to some other dimension or level of reality. (Many cultures believed that an upper and a lower world existed in parallel to this one and that they could be visited by someone with the necessary power.) By following the prescribed instructions, 'the people' were able to secure the favour and assistance of powerful spiritual forces. But there was far more at stake here than simply gratifying immediate physical needs. Because everything in the universe was interrelated, and because 'the people' were at the centre of it, their rituals not only regulated their own relationship with the sacred and with other living beings but also ensured that the whole natural order was properly maintained.

One of the central concepts, found among peoples all the way down the East coast and, in various forms, in many other parts of the continent as well, was the animals' spiritual 'masters' (or 'keepers' or 'owners') who controlled the game on which hunters depended for food. Killing a deer or a partridge did not in itself reduce the stock of game, because – as the anthropologist Ruth Underhill says – the animals 'did not really die. They simply sloughed off furs or feathers and went back to their original home.' But if game was killed *in the wrong way* or without the proper ritual, if the meat was treated disrespectfully, wasted or not shared generously among the whole group, then the animal masters would become angry and withhold food in the future. As an elderly Innu hunter in Labrador, whose family still lives largely by hunting, explains:

When a kill is made, the hunter gives away what he has killed. Then the same type of animal will be killed again ... I have been a hunter all my life, and I have always taken care of what I killed. I have always shared what I killed. It has to be that way – the animal masters want it. It is how *Karipuru kassi kueu* [the Master of all the animals] wants it.

For groups like the Innu and their neighbours the Cree, who depended entirely on hunting, pleasing the masters through rituals like *mukushan* (a sacred meal made from the bone marrow and fat of game animals) and securing their aid through dreams and visions was absolutely crucial to survival. And even among peoples like the Cherokee and the Iroquois, who lived primarily by farming, preserving a proper connection with the animal world was considered essential not only for food but for the spiritual well-being of the community.

Agriculture also, of course, had its own rituals. Where hunting was generally the domain of men, cultivation was usually the realm of women, who in many cases controlled the land as well as doing most of the work. Native American agriculturists – like peoples in many different parts of the world – saw a strong association between female fecundity and the fruitfulness of the earth. (The concept of the earth as a mother was, in fact, common to many different tribes, including some non-farmers.) Blue Corn Woman and White Corn Woman, the Tewa (and the other Pueblo) culture heroes who first brought maize to the people and are commemorated in a host of different rituals and dances, are mirrored in the mythologies of many other farming tribes. The Cherokee Corn Woman, Selu, for instance, who could scrape corn from her armpits and loins, was killed by her sons as a witch. But before she died, she promised to stay with them in the form of corn, as long as they honoured her with the Green Corn Dance and other ceremonies.

In many societies, particularly among the agricultural tribes, the worlds of men and women were kept strictly separate: mingling them, especially when a woman was menstruating, could sap or pollute their respective powers. There were other boundaries, too, which could only be crossed by ritual: the rites of passage – birth, puberty, marriage and death – and the transition between peace and war, when men became warriors and gained access to the sources of power. In a world without fixed borders, where identity was conferred by culture rather than by race or national frontiers, ritual could also be used to transform outsiders into members of the group. Many societies formally adopted captives, particularly women and children, into their own communities, sometimes giving them the names and roles of individual tribespeople who had died.

At the heart of this ritual universe was the idea of interdependence and equilibrium. People took from the animal world, but reciprocated with gestures of respect and, ultimately, returned their bodies to the ground to help sustain new generations of living things. Social life, and particularly dealings between different groups, revolved around the carefully calculated exchange of gifts, which symbolized mutual accept-ance and goodwill but also subtly expressed the relative power of both sides. The same preoccupation with balance seems, generally, to have governed warfare, which was seldom undertaken either to exter-minate or to dispossess an enemy. According to a contemporary Native American historian, Nanepashemet:

> When two native communities went to war against each other there were certain limitations upon what they were going to do. One might be conceived to be an injured party that was seeking to balance their relationship . . . with a neighbour they were at odds with. They were careful about proportions: they would not injure the enemy any more than necessary. It was more of a point of honour, not necessarily even to kill any of the enemy but to drive them from the field, or to discourage them or to at least embarrass them . . . so that they would be left alone.

Preserving all the elements of this complex order in proper relation to each other demanded constant effort and attention. Almost every group had specialists – shamans or priests – who through experience or training had acquired the ability to see deeply into the heart of reality, to prescribe new, more effective means for attaining power and to diagnose the cause when things went wrong. Frequently, problems such as disease, famine or defeat in war were directly attributed to a failure to carry out the necessary rituals, and spiritual leaders would demand that the whole community should return to the original instructions it had received 'in the beginning.'

Anthropologists point to the many similarities of belief, mythology and ceremony among different peoples as proof that, far from being becalmed in a kind of changeless, timeless prehistory, Native American societies were open, vital and dynamic, pragmatically accepting new cultural practices from each other. This appears to be borne out by the evidence of extensive trade networks, linking areas as far apart as present-day Mexico and Canada, which carried, presumably, not only materials and artefacts but people and ideas back and forth across the continent.

The peoples of the western hemisphere in 1492 shared one final, crucially important characteristic: They had almost no resistance to a whole range of diseases, from the common cold and measles to smallpox and bubonic plague, which had developed independently in the Old World.

❖   ❖   ❖

Reconstructing Europe at the time of Columbus is, of course, a great deal easier for us than trying to recreate native America. We still have written records dating from that period, and we are connected to the people who wrote them by an unbroken cultural tradition which makes their motives and behaviour at least partially familiar and comprehensible. But seeing the world through their eyes still requires a huge effort of the imagination. A globe with no western hemisphere is curiously lopsided; a diet without tomatoes, potatoes and maize and a history without the United States is almost inconceivable. The last five hundred years has created many of our most basic assumptions: inevitably, it is very difficult even to identify many of them, let alone unmake their effect on our thinking.

By modern standards, Europe in 1492 would have seemed sparsely populated – the British Isles, for instance, probably had a population of about five million, less than a tenth of the total today. With an overwhelmingly rural way of life and relatively poor communications, most people probably spent their lives close to where they were born and identified themselves as much by region or community as by country. Nonetheless, despite widespread differences of custom and tradition, Europe was far more homogeneous than aboriginal America. Across the continent, people lived predominantly by agriculture, and for the vast majority of the population day-to-day existence revolved around broadly similar activities – ploughing, sowing, tilling, harvesting, raising and slaughtering livestock – using a common technology based on draught animals and iron implements. The social structure and political institutions of most of the major powers were moulded by the same basic concepts of kingship and feudal obligation. And, over the whole of Western Europe, the Catholic Church still exercised enormous centripetal force, drawing together different peoples into a genuine continental culture with a shared religious understanding of the world and a lingua franca which allowed the administrative class to communicate across national boundaries from Scandinavia to the Mediterranean.

The power of the Church was rooted in a common historical experience. Most Western Europeans were living in the ruins of the Roman Empire, descendants either of subject peoples or of the 'barbarian' tribes that had finally breached the imperial defences a thousand years before. The Church, seeing itself as the direct heir of Constantine's empire, preserved the ascendancy of Rome in European life and made an explicit connection between Christendom and Roman civilization. This profoundly affected the way in which the élite, at least, defined itself in relation to non-European – and, specifically, non-Christian – societies.

The most important non-Christian culture for Europeans was, of course, Islam. In the seventh and eighth centuries, Arab invaders had swept up through the Iberian peninsula and over the Pyrenees, only finally being halted at the Battle of Poitiers by Charles Martell in a victory which became one of the enduring legends of the Christian world. Although they were expelled from France, the Muslims remained in much of Spain, where an Islamic state was established in 756.

In many ways, Islam and medieval Christianity were very similar. Both were militant religions with their roots in the Judaic traditions of the Middle East (the Muslims, generally more tolerant of Christians than Christians were of them, acknowledged this connection, recognizing Christ as a prophet and accepting that Jews and Christians, like themselves, were 'people of the book'); both believed that they possessed a universal and exclusive truth, revealed by God, which it was their duty to convey to the whole of humanity; both were warrior faiths, obsessed with martyrdom. The long drawn-out struggle between them, which heightened these tendencies on both sides, powerfully shaped Europeans' perceptions of the world beyond their own borders and how they should deal with it.

In the struggle to free Spain of Muslim domination, Christian military commanders from Aragon, Castile and Leon formed bands of tough, highly trained soldiers who quickly became the most formidable fighting force in Europe. Their unyielding religious fanaticism mirrored the Muslims' own concept of a 'Holy War', and when, in 1071, the Ottoman Turks attacked Byzantium, seized Armenia and moved down the eastern Mediterranean to capture Palestine and Jerusalem, it was the Spanish example that inspired the other Christian powers to try to free the Holy Land from Turkish rule.

The Crusades were, ultimately, a chastening experience for the Europeans: despite temporary successes, they lacked the manpower, the logistical ability and the wealth to dislodge a powerful and confident Islamic empire which felt itself to be at the centre of the civilized world. The Ottomans continued to consolidate and extend their power until finally, in 1453, they were able to take Constantinople itself, opening large parts of eastern Europe to Muslim domination.

The impact of the Crusades was paradoxical: on the one side, they heightened Christendom's sense of physical and metaphysical insecurity, inducing an attitude towards Islam (and, by extension, other cultures) that now seems feverishly paranoid; on the other, they expanded Europe's horizons, stimulating trade and introducing a whole range of new goods – lemons, sugar, rice, spices and silk – as well as developing an awareness of Arab science and medicine.

The campaign against the Muslims in Spain, meanwhile, was proving more successful. By the end of the thirteenth century, Castile had conquered Islamic Andalucia and was using the coastal port of Seville, long a major link with North Africa, as a base for trade and exploration as well for launching expeditions against the Arab heartlands across the Mediterranean. In 1469, the marriage of Ferdinand and Isabella united Castile and Aragon, and their combined forces were finally able to complete the conquest of the Moors. In January 1492 – witnessed, among others, by Christopher Columbus – the last Moorish king of Granada submitted to the Spaniards and watched helplessly as they raised their banners and a giant silver cross above his city.

With the expulsion of the Arabs (and, shortly afterwards, the Jews), Spaniards had finally attained what they had been fighting for for more than seven centuries. During that time they had developed a formidably brutal and efficient military culture that suddenly found itself redundant. Now, with enormous self-confidence and religious triumphalism, but with a dark undertow of fear and paranoia, they looked around for other lands to conquer. As Francisco López de Gómara wrote in 1523, 'the conquest of the Indies began when that of the Moors was over.'

Already, in 1490, Spaniards had started to colonize the Canary Islands, hoping that the native Guanche people would provide them with a cheap and plentiful workforce. Instead, the Guanche rapidly died out from diseases against which they had no resistance.

Two years later, Columbus persuaded Ferdinand and Isabella to finance his expedition in search of new islands, new commercial opportunities, new sources of wealth and labour.

✲ ✲ ✲

Although the experience of the struggle against Islam was crucially important, particularly in Spain, it was only one factor in forming attitudes and responses to the New World. The European imagination, especially in countries whose last armed confrontation with Muslim civilization had been during the crusades, was also crowded with other concepts and images which created very different expectations.

One of the most potent was the widespread belief in the existence of an 'earthly Paradise', a land of miraculous beauty, ease and plenty, free from the woes and troubles of the world. There was no absolute agreement about where this 'Paradise terrestre' was to be found, but many people identified it with the biblical Eden and located it somewhere in 'the extreme east of the earth.' According to one well-known medieval account it lay beyond the land of Prester John (a mythic Christian king, variously believed to live in Asia and North Africa) and was the source of the four great rivers of the world, one of which fed 'the well of youth, for they that drinke thereof seme to be yong alway, and live without great sicknesse . . . for it is so vertuous . . .'

The earthly Paradise itself was 'the highest lande in all the worlde, and it is so high that it toucheth nere to the cycle of the Mone, for it is so high y^t Noes floude might not come thereto which covered all the earth about.'

This idea must have been enormously vivid for medieval Europeans. After the Easter story, Genesis was perhaps the best-known Christian myth, and its haunting account of how our ancestors were expelled from a garden of endless delight was kept constantly in the minds of the predominantly illiterate population, not only by church services but also by the brilliant images decorating the painted walls and stained-glass windows of church buildings themselves and by annual events such as the cycles of mystery plays held in many towns and cities. The belief in the Judaeo–Christian Eden seemed to be buttressed, or at least echoed, by the second major strand of European thought, the Graeco–Roman, with its poems and myths about a Golden Age of peace and plenty at the dawn of history from which Mankind had progressively fallen away.

During the Middle Ages a number of 'travellers' tales', purporting to give 'true accounts' of journeys to distant parts of the world, fed the yearning for an earthly paradise and for a host of other marvels and wonders. *The Voiage of Sir John Maundeville*, for instance, which first appeared in French around the middle of the fourteenth century and was subsequently translated into several other languages, including Latin and English, offered a detailed description not only of the 'Paradise terrestre', but also of giants, monsters, anthropophagi (people who ate their own young), human beings with faces in their chests and creatures which were part man, part beast. Unlike many of the heroes and tricksters in American Indian mythology, whose combination of human and animal was key to their power and understanding, these bestial creatures were usually presented as depraved and terrifying, the dark antithesis of the near-angelic beings who were thought to inhabit the earthly paradise. These two opposing ideas – the angelic and the brutish – created the twin categories into which strange and exotic peoples could be placed.

The author of Mandeville's *Voiage* (probably a Frenchman who took material from a number of existing sources, including Pliny, and presented them as the adventures of 'Sir John'), modestly admitted that he had not seen the earthly paradise himself, but he offered several 'first-hand' accounts of peoples who seemed to be living close to Man's original condition. The inhabitants of Sumatra, for instance:

> ... go al naked and they scorne all them that are clade for they say that God made Adam & Eve all naked ... and there is no woman we-ded, but women are all common there, and they forsake no man. And they say God commaunded to Adam & Eve ... Encrease & multiply and fyll the earth, and no man may say there, This is my wife, & no woman may say, this is my husbande. And when they have any children they give them to whom they will of men that haue medled with them. Also the lande is all common, for every man taketh what he will, for that one man hath in one yere now, an other man hath another yeare. Also all the goods, as corne, beastes and all maner thing of that country are all in common. For there is nothing under locke, as riche is one man as another ...

In retrospect, of course, there is something laughable about the idea of the Sumatrans – or anybody else – fitting themselves so accommodatingly to the requirements of someone else's myths. But given the beliefs of the time – that everyone was descended from the same pair of ancestors and must have some sort of relationship with the same God – it was a reasonable enough assumption. What is striking, though, is the *ambiguity* of the picture that 'Mandeville' paints. On the one side, it clearly suggests innocence and natural virtue, a society free of the selfishness, competitiveness and artifice that plague our world. On the other, in its almost salacious description of sexual freedom and common ownership, it hints at something else entirely: a people who, because they live without the conventions of 'civil society' – marriage, property, law – that distinguish the fallen man from beasts and allow him to keep his own baser nature in check, are themselves little better than animals. Between these two poles, these two conflicting versions of our own past, the idea of the 'savage' was to chart its unsteady course.

The 'discovery' of America coincided with – and encouraged – a heightening of Europe's jumbled attitude towards strange people. A series of related changes – the Black Death of the fourteenth century, which had killed perhaps a third of the population; dynastic conflicts like the Wars of the Roses in England; and the shift towards a money-based economy – marked the gradual, painful transition from a Europe of fluid feudal monarchies to one of clearly demarcated – and ferociously competitive – nation states. It was a process that left millions of people traumatized and insecure, heightening both their yearning for a Golden Age and their terror of a lapse back into bestial chaos. At the same time, growing frictions within the Church, which within fifty years of Columbus's first voyage had led to the Reformation in England, were creating an atmosphere of mounting religious intolerance. Armed with this strange arsenal of ideas, cravings and fears, Europe set out for its encounter with Native America.

                                    ✿   ✿   ✿

Columbus's first impressions of the New World and its inhabitants convinced him that he had indeed stumbled on a Golden Age. He wrote to his royal patrons:

> So tractable, so peaceable are these people, that I swear to your Majesties there is no better nation on earth. They love their neighbours as themselves, and their discourse is ever sweet and gentle, and accompanied with a smile, and though it is true that they are naked, yet their manners are decorous and praiseworthy.

Keenly aware that he carried Ferdinand and Isabella's commercial hopes with him, Columbus was quick to point out that 'the Indians' had economic potential as well as charm. Too trusting to resist capture, and too docile to rebel once caught, they would clearly make excellent slaves. 'From here,' he enthused, 'in the name of the Blessed Trinity, we can send all the slaves that can be sold.'

He was disappointed. No one knows how many native people lived on Hispaniola (the modern island of Haiti, where the Spaniards first established themselves) in 1492, but contemporary observers put the population at between two and four million, and a recent estimate suggests it might have been as high as eight million. By 1520, it had fallen to just 20,000. Like the Guanches of the Canaries before them, the Caribbean natives were virtually exterminated by the extreme brutality of the colonists and the impact of diseases against which they had no resistance: the first smallpox epidemic on Hispaniola in 1507, for instance, was said to have wiped out entire communities. The catastrophic collapse of the island population forced the Spaniards to travel further afield in search of slaves, leading to the first major explorations of the American mainland.

If the Caribbean natives suggested the Golden Age, the urban societies of Central America and Mexico must have seemed like a nightmare version of Islam, rekindling and intensifying all the Spaniards' old feelings of hate and insecurity when confronted by a powerful infidel civilization. Mexico City was larger than any city in Europe at the time, a vast expanse of canals, plazas, markets, temples and brightly painted houses, shops and schools. An army of a thousand men kept the streets clean; waste was removed by barge to be processed as fertilizer, and the élite, like Moorish nobles, bathed every day. (When meeting Spaniards, they often held flowers to their noses to disguise the stench.) But in a world where the Islamic faith was routinely described as diabolical, the Aztec religion, with its cult of human sacrifice, seemed inexpressibly appalling.

It is extremely difficult now to grasp the beliefs and motives of the Conquistadores as they cheated, tortured, burnt, maimed, murdered and massacred their way through South and Meso-America, causing such ferocious destruction that their compatriot Pedro de Ciéza de Léon complained that 'wherever Christians have passed, conquering and discovering, it seems as though a fire has gone, consuming everything.' The easiest explanation is that they were simply cynical desperadoes who – as Cortés told the Mexicans, in a grim and perhaps unconscious irony – 'have a certayne disease of the harte, and golde healpeth us.' But there must have been more to it than that. Although their own exploits surely provided far more vivid spectacles of undeserved suffering, Cortés and his men were obviously profoundly shocked at the sight of ritual sacrifice victims, and their shuddering response had an impact on European perceptions that still affects us today. (Seeing human sacrifice as the defining feature of Mexican civilization is rather like seeing hanging, drawing and quartering as the defining feature of Shakespeare's England.) Before torturing and killing Montezuma and seizing Mexico City in 1521, Cortés made repeated attempts to convert him to Christianity, as if this one act could justify the unimaginable devastation of conquest. Clearly, there must be a perspective from which this view of reality – an apparently insoluble compound of greed, cruelty, deceit, opportunism and piety – makes some sort of sense.

You can get a fleeting insight into it from the 'Requirement' which the Pope imposed on the Spaniards when he 'gave' them most of South America in 1493. Before proceeding to the use of physical force, the Conquistadores were instructed first to recite a document to the Indians, demanding that they should

> ... recognize the Church as your Mistress and as Governess of the World and Universe, and the High Priest, called the Pope, in Her name, and His Majesty in Her place, as Ruler and Lord King ...
>
> And if you do not do this ... with the help of God I shall come mightily against you, and I shall make war on you everywhere and in every way that I can, and I shall subject you to the yoke and obedience of the Church and His Majesty, and I shall seize your women and children, and I shall make them slaves, to sell and dispose of as His Majesty commands, and I shall do all the evil and damage to you that I am able. And I insist that the deaths and destruction that result from this will be your fault.

The idea that reading this document could genuinely absolve the Spanish from all responsibility for their actions now seems completely mad – and, indeed, it had its critics at the time, notably the great humanitarian churchman Bartolomé de las Casas, who said it made him wonder whether 'to laugh or cry.' But at some level, if only the level of wishful thinking, it clearly satisfied some urgent need for the Conquistadores: in a world of manic legalism, where only adherence to the outward forms of the true faith was ultimately important and where everything could be forgiven by following a church-sanctioned mechanism, it was able to assure them of the justice of their cause and the salvation of their souls.

During the sixteenth century, the same mix of curiosity, avarice and religious fervour carried successive waves of Spaniards from their bases in the Caribbean and Central America into what is now the southern United States, establishing a widening pattern of antagonism and conflict between European and native. But, further north, contact between Europeans and native Americans had barely begun. Reports

of the Spaniards' discoveries created a ferment of excitement and
activity in the rest of western Europe, but, with the partial exception of
Portugal, the other powers were simply not prepared for the daunting
task of large-scale conquest and colonization. The most they could do
was to despatch token fleets in the frantic hope that by putting in an
appearance before anyone else they could establish sovereignty over
vast territories which they had no immediate prospect of being able to
possess physically. King Henry VII was quickest off the mark: in 1497
he financed a voyage along the Atlantic seaboard by John Cabot, who
promptly claimed a vast area – including Newfoundland – for the
English crown. Portugal and France quickly followed with expeditions
of their own, but although they made a few tentative attempts at
settlement – French Huguenot colonies in South Carolina and Florida
in the 1560s and England's ill-fated Roanoke colony twenty years later
– none of Spain's European rivals had the confidence and resources
needed to establish a permanent presence on the North American
mainland before the seventeenth century.

But while the explorers were making their state-chartered
expeditions to project national power (if only symbolically) or look for
mythic cities, contacts were also going on at a very different level. Soon
after Columbus and Cabot's 'discoveries' (and possibly even before
them), Basque and English seamen had started to make the perilous
voyage across the Atlantic to work the teeming waters off Newfoundland. The stories they brought back of vast, virtually untapped shoals of
cod and enormous schools of sea mammals quickly attracted fishing
and whaling fleets from all over maritime western Europe, generating
an enormously profitable business. By 1580, according to the historian
Donald P. Quinn, the Newfoundland fishery involved five hundred
vessels a year, making it 'amongst the largest European enterprises.'

The first consistent contact with native people seems to have
developed when the fishing and whaling crews started coming ashore
to dry or process their catches. Local Indians, curious about men who
looked so strikingly different and fascinated by their strange boats,
clothing and implements, would sometimes cautiously approach them
(often carrying gifts) to get a better look. The sailors soon began
exchanging European cloth, trinkets, iron tools and utensils for fresh
meat, maize, berries and other foodstuffs (a diet based largely on dried

and salted foods must have been extremely monotonous) and for beaver pelts and other furs which were scarce and highly prized in Europe and which could be re-sold at a profit when they got home. This tentative barter system soon grew into a thriving informal trade: it was already well established when Cartier ascended the St. Lawrence in 1534 and found Native Americans (probably Micmacs) who were apparently well versed in the ways of Europeans and eager to do business with him.

The trading relationship tended to reinforce the idea that the Indians were living in a Golden Age. Unlike the farming nations encountered by the Spanish, the coastal peoples of eastern Canada and northern New England were predominantly hunters, without permanent settlements and with very little property, who appeared to move freely over an unbounded landscape just as the inhabitants of the earthly paradise were supposed to do. They lived by gathering the bounty of nature and seemed unstintingly generous with their few possessions: Cartier reported that the Micmacs ended up with 'nothing but their naked bodies, for they gave us al whatsoever they had,' and Lescarbot, writing at the start of the next century, declared: '. . . the savages have that noble quality, that they give liberally, casting at the feet of him whom they will honour the present that they give him.' Simple, free, open-handed and untainted by art, calculation or avarice: these, surely, were exactly the kind of Noble Savages that Mandeville and others had led Europeans to expect that they would find in especially favoured corners of the world.

It is much more difficult to look at the encounter from the other side, and try to glimpse how Native Americans perceived Europeans. Whole cultures have simply disappeared, or been transformed out of recognition by the last four centuries. On the basis of the limited information that we do have, it seems likely that the encounter with Europeans along the East coast in the sixteenth century looked almost unimaginably different to Native Americans at the time. To quote Nanepashemet again:

The native world view was a lot different from the European world view, because native people did not believe there was finite knowledge. Knowledge was infinite. Any person could acquire new knowledge and introduce it to his community and it would be accepted if it was useful. So the idea of the Europeans and their material culture and their beliefs was alien to people, but their cultural make-up allowed them to accept new information . . . They were able to accept European goods, although they used many things according to their own cultural dictates, like using brass kettles for producing arrowheads and spoons and ornaments, as well as using them for cooking. And using European cloth in native tailoring. Those things . . . were just adapted to their own cultural needs.

The trade with Europeans was, from the Native American point of view, a form of ceremonial gift exchange which allowed them to bind the newcomers into their world of mutual obligation. Their 'generosity' was not naïveté, as many Europeans thought, but neither was it cynical opportunism. As Lescarbot (an unusually sympathetic and perceptive observer) pointed out: '. . . it is with hope to receive some reciprocal kindness, which is a kind of contract, which we call, without name: "I give thee, to the end that thou shouldst give me."' This, for the Indians, was how the universe worked.

For over a century – more than three generations – informal trade remained the key relationship between Native Americans and Europeans in northeast North America, shaping the expectations that each side had of the other. It certainly had its negative aspects: European disease devastated several groups and some encounters, particularly those involving Englishmen, seem to have been depressingly predictable, with an unprovoked (and probably, from the Indian viewpoint, incomprehensible) display of European arrogance or aggression causing a sudden slide into conflict. But others appear to have been harmonious and to have led to a practical, uncomplicated co-operation that – to begin with, at least – seemed to bring mutual benefits. The fragments of surviving evidence show that these contacts were often more than commercial transactions: in some of them you get a surprising, touching hint of human warmth which suggests that both Europeans and Indians were able to transcend their own myths and build strong personal relationships across the cultural divide. They were not yet trapped by our gloomy determinism, by the sense that they were part of some fateful historical collision between two inimical worlds.

Perhaps because they had no imperial ambitions, the Basques appear to have developed the closest relationship with native people. As early as the 1530s there are descriptions of Innu being invited aboard Basque ships not only to trade but to socialize: the sailors entertained them with cheese, almonds, raisins and other European foods, and marvelled at their ability to pick up the Basque language. These accounts are tinged with unaffected admiration: a Basque from Fuentebarrabia, Clemente de Odeliza, for instance, described the Innu as 'extraordinarily capable and ingenious', and the historian Lope de Isasti wrote of them as 'real allies and friends.' By the start of the seventeenth century, the worlds of 'Christian' Basque and 'heathen savage' were so intermingled that – according to the members of at least one English expedition – the distinction between them had become confusingly blurred. In May 1602, the crew of Bartholomew Gosnold's ship the *Concord* noticed a well-equipped Basque 'shallop' approaching them off the coast of Maine and naturally assumed that the six people on board must be 'distressed Christians', but as the boat drew near they were startled to see that the occupants were in fact men 'of a black, swart complexion', one wearing black serge breeches and a waistcoat, another blue breeches, and the rest naked. The Indians confidently boarded the English ship, speaking 'divers Christian words', and 'seemed to understand much more than we, for want of Language could comprehend.'

There is no question that the cultures of Europe and America were, in some ways, tragically predisposed to conflict and mutual misunderstanding. But in episodes like the Innu encounter with the Basques, you can sometimes catch tantalizing glimpses of another relationship, a kind of ghost of what might have happened if the cards had been shuffled slightly differently. What finally destroyed it was the European decision to move from trade to occupation of the land.

Part II

INVASION

3. Northeast: One

Why should you take by force that from us which you can have by love? Why should you destroy us, who have provided you with food? What can you get by war? We can hide our provisions, and fly into the woods; and then you must consequently famish by wronging your friends. What is the cause of your jealousy? You see us unarmed, and willing to supply your wants, if you will come in a friendly manner, and not with swords and guns, as to invade an enemy.

Wahunsonacock, *Powhatan*, 1609

Perhaps more than anywhere else in North America, the coastal rim of the Northeastern United States seems to deny its Indian past. Cities such as Baltimore, Providence and Boston have some of the evolved, organic feel of European towns, and their historic centres – handsome classical public buildings, Georgian terraces, even the occasional half-timbered house – are clearly deeply rooted in English culture. Much of the countryside, particularly in New England, is even more Old World (and Olde Worlde), with a mellow patchwork of farms, villages, woods and neat little colonial towns undisturbed by any evidence of a different human reality. The Indians seem to survive merely as part of New England's love affair with autumn melancholy: bittersweet figments living on rather wispily in the annual Thanksgiving celebration and the litany of melodic Algonquian placenames that still haunt the landscape.

This minor-key wistfulness is nothing new. In 1787, the poet Philip Freneau was nostalgically evoking an already lost past in his poem 'occasioned by a visit to an old Indian burying ground':

By midnight moons, o'er moistening dews;
In habit for the chase arrayed,

> The hunter still the deer pursues,
> The hunter and the deer, a shade!
>
> And long shall timorous fancy see
> The painted chief, and pointed spear,
> And Reason's self shall bow the knee
> To shadows and delusions here.

The transformation of most of the coastal Indians, in less than two centuries, from living people into 'shadows and delusions' creates enormous difficulties in trying to understand their world and what happened to it. Although there are a few tiny native communities left in the area from southern New England to Virginia, their languages and much of their oral tradition are extinct. Our view of East coast Indian cultures and ways of life therefore depends almost entirely on the writings of seventeenth- and eighteenth-century Europeans – missionaries, explorers, traders, colonists – who generally had a strong conscious or unconscious interest in presenting native people in a particular way and who sometimes, it seems, straightforwardly lied. Even those who were most sympathetic and/or tried most scrupulously to be honest were understandably entrenched in their own culture and probably misinterpreted much of what they saw.

The long absence of the Indians themselves has also allowed an unusually rich profusion of ideas about them and the reasons for their disappearance to take root and flourish. By the mid-nineteenth century, the wistful tendency represented by Freneau had evolved into a heartfelt yearning for the vanished world of native New England. In 1845, for instance, Ralph Waldo Emerson plaintively confided to his journal:

> We in Massachusetts see the Indians only as a picturesque antiquity. Massachusetts, Shawmut, Samoset, Squantum, Nantasket, Narraganset, Assabet, Musketaquid. But where are the men?

Underlying this catalogue of defunct peoples is an unmistakable feeling of loss, a pang at the decline of modern New England from a more natural and innocent state. Emerson's friend Henry D. Thoreau made the point explicitly eleven years later when, listing the animals that had become extinct since the start of European settlement, he complained: '... I cannot but feel as if I lived in a tamed, and, as it were, emasculated country. Is it not a maimed and imperfect nature that I am conversant with?' The implication here is plain: like the late-lamented 'cougar, panther, lynx, wolverene, wolf, bear, moose' and other animals, Native Americans were *part* of nature, a people who, after thousands of years, had made no discernible impact on the 'perfect', 'untamed' and 'unmaimed' wilderness of North America. Europeans, on the other hand, had debauched the virgin landscape in a little more than two centuries, destroying the pristine habitat on which Indians – like other wild creatures – depended, and so driving them to extinction.

But a second, apparently contradictory strand of thought saw the New England natives as their own worst enemies. 'The Indians melted away, not because civilization destroyed them,' growled the historian Francis Parkman in 1867, 'but because their own ferocity and intractable indolence made it impossible that they should exist in its presence.' This view echoed the opinion of the early nineteenth-century politician and self-proclaimed authority on Indians Lewis Cass, who believed that some 'strong exciting' racial characteristic impelled native people to 'Their own ceaseless hostilities [which] have, more than any other cause, led to the melancholy depopulation . . .'

It is precisely because untangling these ideas about the East coast Indians is so difficult that it is also so important. The English colonies in the seventeenth century were a crucible, creating a precedent for the invasion and conquest of the rest of America and, at the same time, a template for justifying and understanding it. And, despite the lack of certain kinds of evidence, the work of archaeologists, anthropologists and historians over the last thirty years has created a fragile but rich historical mosaic (much of it gleaned from the contradictions, omissions and interstices of contemporary accounts) which both challenges and explains the apparently conflicting simplicities of Emerson and Parkman.

❉   ❉   ❉

Scholars classify the native peoples of New England and the mid-Atlantic states as part of the larger Northeast Woodlands culture area, a vast region extending from Maine to the Carolinas and sprawling inland as far as the Great Lakes and the Mississippi drainage. The 400 years since the start of European settlement represents only a tiny fraction of the human history of this part of North America: according to archaeologists, the first 'palaeo-Indians' entered it 12,000 years ago or more, starting a process of continuous occupation, experiment and cultural development which led ultimately to the distinctive way of life found at the time of contact.

The first inhabitants of the Northeast were probably nomadic Ice Age hunters who lived by hunting mammoth, musk ox, giant beaver and other large mammals. As temperatures rose, however, this way of life became impossible: the big game animals died out or moved north, and the retreating glaciers gave way first to treeless tundra, then to spruce and birch forest and finally to the present mixture of deciduous and coniferous woodland. The palaeo-Indians responded by hunting smaller species and gradually diversifying into fishing and – eventually – food-gathering.

A limited form of agriculture began to appear about 3,500 years ago, and as it spread to other areas, generating a larger and more settled population, it fuelled the development of bigger, more complex societies. The most influential were the 'mound-building' Adena and Hopewell cultures, which built massive earthworks and burial mounds in geometric, plant and animal forms (the effigy of a snake near Locust Grove in Ohio, for example, is more than two hundred yards long) and developed an extensive trade network across and beyond the region. After about AD 700, a new civilization in the Mississippi Valley brought several innovations to the Northeast – notably maize – which gradually mingled with the existing cultures of the area to form the pattern of societies and ways of life encountered by Europeans.

By the time the first French and English explorers tentatively probed the Atlantic seaboard in the sixteenth century, the Northeast was home to scores of different peoples. Members of North America's largest linguistic stock, the Algonquians, occupied most of the region, but a wedge of Iroquoian-speaking nations drove up through what is now upper New York State and along the St. Lawrence, and along the southern and western fringes of the area were a scattering of other Iroquoians and Siouans. Scholars speculate that the northern Iroquoians may have been relatively recent migrants from further south, whose more intensive maize-based agriculture allowed them to displace or absorb existing Algonquian groups.

If you try to grasp this picture by looking at a map, it can at first glance seem confusing. There are none of the simple straight lines we expect from political divisions: the names – particularly along the Atlantic seaboard, which bore the first brunt of contact – are a wild jumble, all squashed together or tilted at odd angles to fit. South of the St. Lawrence, in what is now Maine and Nova Scotia, you find Micmacs, Malecites, Passamaquoddies, Penobscots and Abenakis; below them, along the southern New England coast, are Massachusetts, Narragansett, Wampanoag and a scattering of smaller tribes, with, just to the west, Nipmucs, Pequots and Mohegans; south again, between Long Island and Chesapeake Bay, are Montauks, Wappingers, Lenni Lenape (or Delawares) and Powhatans. To make sense of it, you have to realize that what you are seeing is a snapshot of one moment in a constantly changing situation: these are not nation states, but groups of culturally – and often physically – related peoples who move within frontiers shaped by custom and mutual understanding rather than legal definition. But the impression of chaos – one of the key European perceptions of the eastern Indian – is illusory: although they managed their relationship with the land and with each other in a profoundly different way, their world was at least as orderly as contemporary Europe's.

The more fluid approach starts with subsistence. Except in what is now Maine, where the northern Algonquians remained almost exclusively dependent on hunting, eastern Native Americans generally practised a mixed economy based on an annual cycle of activities closely adapted to the resources of their own area. During most of the year, they lived in permanent towns or villages of birch-bark covered 'longhouses' or wigwams – often surrounded by a tall defensive palisade of logs – and cultivated maize, beans and squash in nearby fields or 'gardens'. At different seasons, however, some or all of the people would spread out from this base community to harvest a rich variety of other foods – deer, fish, wildfowl, clams, nuts, berries and more – from woods, rivers, lakes and ocean.

Although men often cleared the fields, most of the farming was done by women, who followed a distinctive pattern that puzzled many

European observers. After centuries of selective cultivation in Meso-America to increase its nutritional value, maize had become – in the words of the Dutch traveller Isaack de Rasieres – 'a grain to which much labour must be given, with weeding and earthing-up, or it does not thrive.' The Algonquians painstakingly planted it, five or six grains at a time, in 'heaps like molehills', and then, as it started to grow, piled on more earth to protect the roots from birds. Beans, squash, pumpkins and tobacco were planted around the maize (which created a natural beanpole, often growing to five or six feet), and women would then tend the crops, meticulously keeping the weeds down with clamshell hoes, until, by the end of the summer, the fields had become a dense carpet of intertwined foodplants. When, after eight or ten years, the soil began to become exhausted, the Indians simply left it to regenerate and cleared new fields.

Some nineteenth- and twentieth-century scholars have viewed this system not as real farming at all but simply as a kind of part-time horticulture. The anthropologist A. L. Kroeber, for instance, claimed that the Native American 'was not a farmer in our sense of the word' at all, and that 'Agriculture ... was not basic to life in the East; it was an auxiliary, in a sense a luxury ... excess planting was not practised, nor would it have led to anything in the way of economic or social benefit nor of increase of numbers. Ninety-nine per cent or more of what might have been developed remained virgin ... '

It is worth looking a moment at this contention because it seems to confirm the central idea of both the Thoreau and Parkman traditions: that North America at the time of contact was more or less an untouched wilderness. As with the related subject of Native American population figures, this is more than simply an academic issue. Behind it lurks the ever-present question of how far Indians really 'used' the land and how justified or inevitable, therefore – in European eyes – was their removal. The eighteenth-century theorist of international law, Emerich Vattel, succinctly expressed what – to the conventional Western view – is at stake:

> While the conquest of the civilized Empires of Peru and Mexico was a notorious usurpation ... colonies upon the continent of North America might, if done within just limits, have been entirely lawful.

The people of those vast tracts of land *rather roamed over them than inhabited them*. [My italics]

Although the idea that American Indians 'roamed' remained a basic tenet for advocates of – and apologists for – European colonization, the recorded experience of early travellers and settlers give a very different picture of native life. As early as 1585, Thomas Hariot, describing the Algonquians of the Carolinas, commented on their 'ingenious' agriculture, including the use of 'a graine of marveilous great increase; of a thousand, fifteene hundred and some two thousand fold'; a generation later, one Jamestown colonist estimated that a single Indian group, the Kecoughtans, had 3,000 acres of cornfields under cultivation. More conclusive proof of the extent of native agriculture comes from the simple fact that the first English colonies were only able to survive their first years because the surrounding Native Americans supported them with a ceaseless supply of maize and other produce. Clearly, this would have been impossible if Indian farming had not generated regular surpluses.

❖ ❖ ❖

While women's lives revolved largely around the rhythm of sowing, hoeing and harvesting, men's work was still to a great extent dictated by the older, more irregular pattern of hunting and fishing, in which bursts of intense activity (and sometimes danger) away from home alternated with periods of relative idleness. In spring they erected fishing weirs on the rivers, hunted migratory birds and burnt the undergrowth from large areas of forest to create grassy 'parks' that attracted game and were easy to move through; later in the year, they might travel into the woods to hunt or build canoes, or make fishing trips to the coast; in autumn, after the harvest, there was often a second cycle of brush-clearance.

In October, villages generally broke up into family units to hunt, meeting a couple of months later and then remaining together for the rest of the winter. Often, continuous use and occupation had deforested a large area around their main settlements, and they would spend the coldest part of the year at a different site – perhaps a well-wooded valley – with plenty of fuel. One colonist, seeing the importance the Indians attached to warm fires, commented: 'Their Fire is instead of our bed-cloaths.'

The mobility of Algonquian societies was one factor in making Europeans underestimate the importance of farming in their economy. Another, almost certainly, was the division of labour, which English colonists found constantly surprising. 'The men bestowe their times in fishing, hunting, wars and such manlike exercises,' wrote John Smith of the Indians of Virginia, 'scorning to be seene in any woman like exercise, which is the cause that the women be verie painefull and the men often idle. The women and children do the rest of the worke. They make mats, baskets, pots, morters, pound their corne, make their bread, prepare their victuals, plant their corne, gather their corne, beare all kind of burdens and such like.' Further north, in New England, Christopher Levett stated even more bluntly: 'Their wives are their slaves, and do all the work; the men will do nothing but kill beasts, fish, etc.' What made this even more remarkable was the women's apparently uncomplaining acceptance of their role, which, according to Lescarbot, they were 'neither forced nor tormented' to perform. (Colonists recorded that the Indians, for their part, retorted – as John Clayton put it – by calling 'the Inglish men fools in working themselves and keeping their wives idle.') While it may be that Indian men really worked less than their wives, it is also true that a visitor to a native community would have seen very little of what they *did* contribute, since most male pursuits took them away from home. Unlike Native Americans, moreover, Europeans tended to see the male preserves of hunting and fishing as leisure rather than subsistence activities. This heightened the impression of male indolence and further undermined the Indians' – to European eyes – already tenuous claim to 'use' the land. During the course of the seventeenth century, these initially innocent misapprehensions were transmuted into arguments to justify dispossessing native people, leaving – long after it had outlived its political usefulness – a powerful legacy of ideas about the 'virgin wilderness' supposedly discovered by the first settlers.

Other aspects of Native American life offered further rich opportunities for European misunderstanding and exploitation. East coast Algonquian society could not be understood in the simple binary terms of a nation state (you're either English or not English): it was woven together from several distinct strands which created a complex web of allegiances and obligations and gave each individual a set of complementary identities. As Nanepashemet explains: '... people had different ways of identifying themselves. There was personal self identification. There was being a member of a lineage, which might extend into many other communities. There was the community identification, and identification with people who spoke the same language.' Which one of these complementary identities was paramount at any given moment depended on circumstances: the time of year, what you were doing, where you were.

Probably the most fundamental element was the 'clan' or 'lineage', a group of blood relatives tracing their descent from a common – usually female – ancestor. This form of kinship often bound together not just a few families but hundreds of individuals, because, as a seventeenth-century Dutch observer reported, the Indians 'reckon consanguinity to the eighth degree.'

But the Algonquians also belonged to extended families, bands and villages which cut across the ties of blood relationship. Because they were exogamous (i.e., you could not marry within your own lineage), any marriage not only united the very different worlds of men and women but also created a bond between two kin groups. Each level of society, from the single household up, inevitably connected the individual to a network of people outside the clan and created another focus for loyalty. Social scientists tend to view this sort of arrangement simply as a mechanism for extending mutual obligations: as Edward B. Tylor breezily put it in 1888, 'Among tribes of low culture there is but one means known of keeping up permanent alliance, and that means is intermarriage.' We get a more intuitive – if still only dim – sense of what it meant to the Algonquians themselves by thinking about our own overlapping feelings for our families, our in-laws, our neighbourhood, our workplace, our country.

The 'nations' encountered by Europeans were, in effect, alliances of two or more interrelated lineages. What gave them, to a great extent, their collective identity and power was the quality of the leaders – generally known as *werowances* in Virginia and *sachems* or *sagamores* in New England – who represented and acted for the whole group in

Invasion

areas of common interest such as the allocation of hunting territories or diplomacy with other peoples. A *werowance* or *sachem* normally inherited his office, but the degree of real authority he was able to exercise depended largely on his personal attributes: family connections, wealth, charisma, political skill and – sometimes – military or religious prowess. To retain power he had to attract and keep the support of his people, and if – in the colonist William Wood's blunt phrase – his 'fair carriage bear him not out the better, they will soon unscepter him.'

The Algonquian form of leadership confronted Europeans with an apparent conundrum: as Roger Williams, who lived close to the Narragansett for years and was one of the few English Puritans to develop a real (though perhaps rather limited) insight into Native American society, put it: 'The Sachims, although they have an absolute Monarchie over the people; yet they will not conclude of ought that concernes all, either Lawes or Subsidies, or warres, unto which the people are averse, and by gentle perswasion cannot be brought.' In other words, they were despots who – because they lacked any institutional means of enforcing their authority – depended ultimately on consensus.

This was not, in fact, unlike the position of many pre-medieval monarchs in Europe (the word *king* is related to *kin* and originally meant 'chief of a tribe'), but to the subjects of an emerging nation state it seemed paradoxical. Its weakness, from their point of view (and they were not slow to exploit it) was that it left Algonquian societies subject to fragmentation and secession. If you did not like where you were living, you could leave and join relatives somewhere else; whole communities might break away and form their own tribe, or attach themselves to another leader. By the same token, a successful *sachem* or *werowance* could extend his (or, occasionally, her) influence by attracting or conquering a number of smaller groups and forging them into a larger alliance capable of concerted action. The Powhatan leader Wahunsonacock, for instance, after struggling for years 'to make his name and famely great,' eventually held sway over a 'confederation' of about thirty other tribes with a combined population of 12,000 or more. But even here, political cohesion depended ultimately on the allegiance that the 'Great Emperour' could command from his 'sub-kings' and the support that they, in turn, received from their peoples, making it vulnerable to the same disintegrative forces as other levels of society.

The common thread running through every level of East-coast society and every aspect of Indian life was the ubiquitous belief in 'power'. Although – with a few exceptions, particularly in the north of the area – *werowances*, *sachems* and *sagamores* were not themselves shamans, they shared the vision of a world shaped and interpenetrated by potent numinous forces. Here, as in so many other areas, there were none of the rigid, hard-and-fast distinctions of European culture: in a universe where every human act has spiritual ramifications and can affect the well-being of 'the people', there is no clear-cut boundary between 'sacred' and 'secular'. Shamans – or *pow-wows* – used their abilities not only to ensure successful hunts and harvests and to heal the sick, but also to act as political, diplomatic and military advisers. (They were often, in fact, thought to be invulnerable in war.) In some societies, people with exceptional spiritual powers formed a formal élite council to help the *sachems* or *werowances*.

Perhaps the best way to understand the coastal Algonquian world is as a series of bilateral, reciprocal relationships: between men and women; between families, lineages and tribes; between humans and the realm of spirits. Contacts and movements between these different spheres had to be mediated through rituals and gift exchanges which acknowledged the respective positions of the two sides and committed them to fulfilling their mutual obligations. A concrete – and still contemporary – model is provided by the Innu hunter's relationship with the Animal Masters, with its expectation that ritual expressions of respect and an open-handed sharing among the different members of the group will bring a reciprocal gift of food from the 'bosses'.

These themes were reflected (as far as we can tell) in the whole cycle of celebrations marking the Algonquian year. Roger Williams noted how, for instance, at the *Keesaqúnnamun* harvest festival, a group of men danced before the singing villagers and then gave their wealth to a poor member of the community. At another celebration, the *Nickòmmo*, the host or hostess donated goods 'according to and sometimes beyond their estate' to other people. (Anthropologists see this kind of behaviour as a way of reducing the potential for friction by redistributing wealth, but from an Algonquian perspective it must have seemed to embody a much profounder truth about the world: that to give is to receive. As a Canadian Shuswap Indian friend once put it: 'The more you give, the richer you are.')

The ceremonies regulating extra-tribal relations followed a similar pattern. Diplomats opened trade or peace negotiations with presents that tacitly expressed both what they hoped to receive in return and their understanding of the relative power of the two groups. Subordinate tribes offered tribute of food, animal skins or *wampum* – highly valued beads, made out of marine shells, which could be used as a kind of money – to the dominant *sachem* in a confederacy, secure in the knowledge that, if it was accepted, they could expect to be protected.

The same principle of reciprocity and balance applied in areas of conflict. Murder, for instance, was not a crime against an abstract and impersonal state but an injury to the victim's kin group which obliged his or her relatives to seek retribution. In most tribes, however, the forfeit of the murderer's life could be commuted into a payment of goods to the dead person's family, which simultaneously re-established equilibrium between the two clans and stopped the dispute unravelling into an endless blood feud. Similar arrangements sometimes seem to have prevented or ended wars between tribes: in 1615, for instance, according to Champlain, the Hurons and their Algonquian neighbours settled a dispute with a payment of *wampum*. The thinking behind this kind of behaviour rested on shared and probably largely unspoken assumptions, but we get some insight into it from what a Lenape Indian told a seventeenth-century Pennsylvanian (presumably because he felt that a European needed to have the rules spelt out):

We are minded to live at Peace: If we intend at any time to make War upon you, we will let you know of it, and the Reasons why we make War with you; and if you make us satisfaction for the Injury done us, for which the War is intended, then we will not make War on you. And if you intend at any time to make War on us, we would have you let us know of it, and the Reasons for which you make War on us, and then if we do not make satisfaction for the Injury done unto you, then you may make War on us, otherwise you ought not to do it.

There were, of course, conflicts and divisions that could not be contained. Communities would sometimes split irrevocably along the

fault-lines of lineage, and in the atmosphere of tension and competition
generated by the jostling for position between different *sachems* or
werowances and kin groups, fighting seems to have been fairly common,
with war parties (usually of young men) setting out to punish an
infringement of territory, seize captives or establish dominance over
another tribe. But even these aims were largely shaped by ritual. The
purpose was rarely to dispossess or exterminate an enemy (women
and children were seldom killed, although they were often captured
and adopted), and after inflicting limited damage, the victors usually
withdrew, perhaps carrying a tribute of food or other goods to
symbolize their new relationship with the losers.

The eastern Algonquians' supposed 'savagery' and 'ferocity' in war is
– like their 'primitive' agriculture – a central tenet of the case made
against them by Parkman and his followers. Kroeber, for instance,
claims that they were locked into a life of 'insane, unending, continuously attritional' warfare, and that this pattern was 'so integrated into
the whole fabric of Eastern culture, so dominantly emphasized within
it, that escape from it was well-nigh impossible . . . The group that tried
to shift its values from war to peace was almost certainly doomed to
early extinction.' Harold E. Driver claims that 'The most distinctive
feature of the warfare pattern in the East, as compared with other
areas . . . was the emphasis on the torture of prisoners,' and confidently
asserts that 'no young man ever thought of getting married or of being
accepted as an adult citizen until he had slain an enemy and brought
back a scalp to prove it.'

This view seems peculiar for two reasons. First, a moment's reflection suggests that the way of life it describes would have been
unsustainable: there would have been no time for subsistence activities,
no security in which to pursue them and – as Francis Jennings points
out – the universal requirement to kill an enemy before getting married
would have led 'inexorably, year after year, not just to a low level of
population, but to total extinction.'

Second, it is flatly contradicted by several early accounts of the
Indians, both positive and negative. When Roger Williams witnessed a
war between the Pequots and the Narragansetts, for instance, he
considered it 'farre lesse bloudy and devouring than the cruell Warres
of Europe.' The English soldier Captain John Underhill reported,

slightly patronizingly, that his Indian allies 'greatly admired the manner of Englishmen's fight' but considered that 'it is too furious, and slays too many men;' while another colonist, Captain John Mason, was undisguisedly contemptuous of Indian warfare: describing one battle he wrote, '. . . they run and met them and fell on pell mell striking and cutting with Bows, Hatchets, Knives, &c, after their feeble Manner: Indeed it did hardly deserve the Name of *Fighting*.' While it is generally accepted that the Iroquoian tribes further west did sometimes torture prisoners in the pre-contact period, the Frenchman Marc Lescarbot – one of the earliest and most reliable observers of the eastern Algonquians – maintained that 'I have not read or heard tell that any other savage tribe behaves thus to its enemies.' In fact, he stated categorically that 'our sea-coast Indians' did not practise torture.

The description of Native American life offered by Kroeber and Parkman seems so preposterous and self-serving that it can easily drive one into embracing the pastoral idealism of Thoreau and Emerson at the other extreme. In fact, both these apparent opposites have the same root: a tendency, conscious or unconscious, to abstract Indians from the human reality that *we* inhabit, thereby removing their experience from the arena of morality and history in which our relations with other people are normally considered. The awkward truth is that the Algonquian world was neither a depraved nightmare nor an idyll. Like any society, it was an irreducible mixture of conflict, harmony, brutality, nobility, hardship and joy. As the Virginia colonist William Strachey reported apparently with some surprise: among Native Americans, as 'amongst Christians', some were 'great people . . . some very little . . ., some speaking likewise, more articulate and plaine, and some more inward and hollow . . ., some curteous and more civill, others cruell and bloudy.'

The crucial point about the East-coast world is that it *worked*. Over thousands of years, the Algonquians had developed a prosperous and ingenious way of life that made intelligent use of their resources and kept them in some sort of harmony with the rest of creation. Although it looked superficially disorganized to Europeans, it had a kind of bicycle-riding equilibrium – an ability to keep upright by perpetual motion and balance – which made it, fundamentally, at least as stable as the more leaden cultures of the Old World. What drove it ultimately out of control was a lethal combination of alien diseases and an encounter with people who – inconceivably – did not live in a reciprocal universe.

*   *   *

One of the ironies of the 'discovery' of America is that it rapidly increased rather than reduced the differences between Native Americans and Europeans. In 1492, although the western hemisphere was larger, richer and more populous than Europe, both were largely self-sufficient and economically dependent primarily on a combination of agriculture and internal trade. Almost immediately, however, the balance between the two sides tipped in Europe's favour, and the disparities then grew at an exponential rate. The draining of wealth, ideas and products from the New World to the old fuelled an enormous extension of European global power and contributed to a rapid and continuing rise in population, prosperity and cultural vitality. Native America, on the other hand, experienced an almost unimaginably catastrophic collapse as a result of conquest and disease. At the same time, the diffusion of maize from America to the rest of the world caused a population explosion in Africa, ultimately allowing Europeans to replace their dying Native American labour force with black slaves.

As European strength and self-confidence in the New World grew, the map of Europe itself was being transformed by a sharpening of national and religious boundaries. In the aftermath of the Reformation, the old patchwork of feudal kingdoms and principalities linked (theoretically, at least) by a common acceptance of papal authority was giving way to a collection of quarrelling nation states whose only allegiance was to their own political and commercial self-interest.

By the last third of the sixteenth century, the effects of their rivalry were being felt along the entire Atlantic seaboard of North America. In 1565, after ousting France from the area, Spain established St. Augustine in Florida (the first permanent European settlement in what is now the United States) and began sending successive waves of slavers, missionaries and – as an unintended stowaway – epidemic disease up the East coast in search of more conquests. Further north, the casual exchange of trinkets and animal skins had developed into an immensely profitable international trade, fed largely by a seemingly insatiable European appetite for beaver hats. Companies of French, English and Dutch merchants were all feverishly seeking new supplies – and trying to secure government monopolies to exploit them – with little regard to which country officially 'owned' the areas they were exploring. It was becoming clear to all Spain's major competitors that if they wanted a share of America's apparently unlimited riches they could not rely simply on an assertion of sovereignty 'by right of discovery': to be a contender, you needed to occupy the land you claimed.

France moved first, founding – after several false starts – Port Royal in what is now Nova Scotia in 1605, with the simultaneous aims of protecting and extending its commercial activities and containing Spanish expansion from Florida. The Netherlands followed: in 1612 it established a trading post on Manhattan Island, and over the next few years a thin ribbon of Dutch settlement started to spread up the Hudson River until, by 1617, it had reached Fort Orange (the present-day Albany, New York).

For all their apparent fragility, these tiny colonies had an enormous impact, changing the nature of native–European relations in the Northeast and transforming the lives of thousands of Indians who had never met – and would never meet – a Frenchman or a Dutchman. Their power came from the fur trade, which had already begun to push its tentacles deep into the continent, undermining the Indians' self-sufficiency and drawing them, in increasing numbers, into an economic system controlled from London, Paris and Amsterdam. As the century progressed, this process intensified and accelerated.

How did a barter system with such apparently innocent beginnings end up ensnaring – and, in some cases, destroying – the native population of most of North America? Part of the explanation is that its effects, like the diseases that often travelled with it, were contagious. Metal tools and weapons did not simply alter the lives of the tribe who acquired them: they also affected enemies and neighbours, who suddenly found themselves at an enormous disadvantage and were forced to seek their own sources of European goods in order to feed and defend their people. This in turn had an effect on *their* neighbours, destabilizing yet another set of finely calculated, ritually maintained inter-tribal relationships and plunging still more groups into a desperate quest for trade.

Once Indians were enmeshed in the system, it radically altered their life in ways that made it almost impossible for them to go back. Hunting for furs interrupted the normal cycle of subsistence activities and led to an erosion of the skills needed to make artefacts – such as cooking pots – for which the trade offered a ready European alternative. From being self-sufficient farmers or hunter-gatherers in a genuine – if precarious – equilibrium with their world, Indians quickly became specialist producers in a global economy that could only exist by taking more from them than it gave back. The immense profits of the trade simply lay in the difference between what a merchant paid for furs in America and what he received for them in Europe; although most Native Americans almost certainly never saw it in these terms, every transaction ultimately undermined their own position, channelling, in effect, still more wealth and power from the New World to the Old.

Many individual traders, particularly among the French *coureurs du bois* who travelled far into the interior in search of new sources of furs, developed close personal relationships with their suppliers, frequently marrying native women and starting 'Indian' families. But the large companies which dominated the fur trade seem to have viewed the Native American purely as a commercial resource. To begin with, they were forced to go along with the Indian understanding of trade as a form of ceremonial exchange between peoples, but as the balance of power shifted in their favour they increasingly abandoned any pretence of reciprocity. In its advanced stages, the fur trade became a kind of drug peddling, with merchants gaining control over Indians by creating and feeding an addiction which they knew would ultimately prove fatal. A letter from a Hudson's Bay Company agent in western Canada, written two hundred years after the first settlements in New England, gives a glimpse of how, throughout the colonial period, the fur trade monopolies rationalized this approach as good business practice:

I have made it my study to examine the nature and character of Indians and however repugnant it may be to our feelings, I am convinced they must be ruled with a rod of Iron to bring and keep them in a proper state of subordination, and the most certain way to effect this is by letting them feel their dependence upon us ... In the woods and northern barren grounds this measure ought to be pursued rigidly next year if they do not improve, and no credit, not so much as a load of ammunition, given them until they exhibit an inclination to renew their habits of industry. In the plains, however, this system will not do, as they can live independent of us, and by withholding ammunition, tobacco and spirits, the Staple articles of Trade, for one year, they will recover the use of their Bows and spears, and lose sight of their smoking and drinking habits; it will therefore be necessary to bring those Tribes round by mild and cautious measure ...

The establishment of permanent colonies, which were expected to pay their own way as quickly as possible and then to show a profit for their investors, fanned the demand for furs. Tribes living near the trading posts soon exhausted the supply of beaver and other fur-bearing animals in their own areas, and were forced to invade their neighbours' hunting territories or to establish control over peoples living further afield in order to acquire the skins they needed to trade. At the same time, the greater European presence increased Native American exposure to the deadly effects of Old World diseases and alcohol. Both colonists and Indians saw the association between contact and a decline in the native population, even if they did not identify biological infection as the cause: in 1610, Membertou, *sagamore* of France's trading partners, the Micmac, told Marc Lescarbot that in his youth his people had been 'as thickly planted there as the hairs upon his head,' but that since the arrival of the French their numbers had diminished dramatically. But the urgent need for trade goods forced them, again and again, to run the risk of further disaster.

The colonies also introduced a new factor in the situation. New France, New Netherlands and – eventually – New England were not simply trading posts: as their names suggested, they were – from a European perspective – extensions of the Old World powers that had established them. When the Micmacs made a trading agreement with the French king's representative Pierre de Monts at Port Royal, they were effectively allying themselves with the Crown itself.

It is clear that the two sides viewed this arrangement differently. For

France, like the other colonial nations, heathen savages could only enter into a formal relationship with a Christian monarch as subjects or – at most – clients. The Indians, on the other hand, much to the amusement and exasperation of European observers, continued to see their dealings with the French in traditional terms, as a ritual exchange between equals. The Jesuit missionary Father Pierre Biard reported:

> . . . they set themselves up as brothers of the King, and it is not to be expected that they will withdraw in the least from the whole farce. Gifts must be presented and speeches made to them, before they condescend to trade; this done they must have the Tabagie, in other words, the banquet. Then they will dance, make speeches and sing *Adesquidex, Adesquidex*. That is, that they are good friends, allies, associates, confederates, comrades of the King and of the French.

From both perspectives, however, the new relationship had profound implications, with each side becoming drawn into the other's affairs and stumbling, in the process, on the dynamics of a different world. When France backed her trading partners in (usually trade-motivated) forays against other peoples, she was – as she saw it – protecting vital political and commercial interests. In Indian terms, however, she was fulfilling the obligations of an alliance that had been cemented through the exchange of gifts. This was not lost on either her friends or their enemies, and often had far-reaching consequences for French policy. In both 1609 and 1610, for instance, Frenchmen armed with muskets proved the decisive factor in enabling war parties of Hurons, Algonquins and Innu to defeat the Iroquoian Mohawks. This earned France the enmity of the most powerful confederacy in the Northeast, the Iroquois League of Five Nations, driving it into the arms first of the Dutch and then of the English and ultimately giving England a crucial advantage in the battle for North America.

From the Native American side, the results were even more momentous. Colonial expansion was a lottery which gave tribes limited control over whom they did business with and little opportunity to assess the likely long-term consequences of what they were doing. Most of them can only have had a hazy sense that, when they made trading agreements, they were binding themselves not just to the few individuals they saw in front of them and to an unseen 'King' but to something infinitely more powerful on the other side of the Atlantic. As colonial rivalry intensified, thousands of Indians found that they had unwittingly signed up as auxiliaries or even front-line troops in a series of increasingly vicious European wars. In the short term, the question of whether you turned out to be on the winning or the losing side must have seemed both crucially important and terrifyingly capricious. In the long term, as with the fur trade itself, there were no Native American winners.

❖   ❖   ❖

While France and the Netherlands were frantically establishing and expanding their trade networks, England was becoming more obsessed with the idea of settlement. A sharp rise in the population (between 1550 and 1650 it nearly doubled) and a complex of social and economic changes – the abolition of the monasteries, price inflation caused by the influx of American bullion, agricultural enclosures – had together caused an enormous increase in unemployment, landlessness and beggary. In the jittery mood of the post-Reformation period, when dissenters at home and enemies overseas seemed to pose a constant threat to the security and legitimacy of the state, these problems appeared particularly menacing, and – not for the last time – a number of influential figures hit on the idea of exporting them. As Sir Humphrey Gilbert put it in his *Discourse*:

> We might inhabit some part of those countries [America] and settle there such needy people of our country, which now trouble the commonwealth, and through want are enforced to commit outrageous offences, whereby they are daily consumed by the gallows.

But men like Gilbert and his half-brother Sir Walter Ralegh did not see colonization simply as a convenient way to get rid of undesirables: it also seemed to offer an almost mystical gateway to both personal wealth and national greatness. Fired by accounts of the Spanish conquest of Mexico and Peru and convinced that England's own earthly paradise awaited her somewhere in the New World, they fantasized about finding a source of fabulous wealth and a large native labour force to exploit it for them. At the same time, the Protestant English could demonstrate their credentials as a major Christian power by 'reducing the savages to civilitie' and garnering a harvest of souls for the true faith.

The Elizabethan adventurer's inner world seems almost as unfathomable as the Spanish Conquistador's, and it is hard to judge how far men like Ralegh saw religious conversion as a genuine motive and how far it was simply a flimsy gauze draped decorously over their self-interest. Certainly there was an element of calculation about it: when Richard Hakluyt the elder (at Ralegh's prompting) put the cause for colonization to the Queen, he gave as the principal aim the salvation 'of millions of those wretched people, the reducinge of them from darkness to lighte, from falsehoodde to truthe, from dombe idolls to the lyvinge God, from the depe pitt of hell to the highest heavens.' This kind of rhetorical appeal proved, throughout the sixteenth and seventeenth centuries, one of the most reliable means of securing royal approval and popular support for colonial ventures. But its very efficacy (the New England colonies a little later discovered that a request for money for missionary work was the surest way to get ordinary people to open their purses) suggests that it gratified a real and understandable psychological need. It is difficult to resist a request for help which, by definition, asserts your own cultural and religious superiority over everybody else.

Unquestionably, consciously or otherwise, much of the propaganda for colonies presented a picture of people straight out of the Golden Age who needed and would appreciate an English presence. When the first English edition of Cartier's travels was published in 1580, the dedication (probably by Hakluyt the younger) contained a strong plea for plantations to civilize 'this savage nation,' who were, 'though simple and rude in manners, and destitute of the knowledge of God or any good lawes, yet of nature gentle and tractable, and most apt to receive the Christian Religion, and to subject themselves to some good government.' This rosy vision continued to entrance would-be colonists and investors for more than a generation, prompting the belief that they could expect an amicable, paternalistic relationship with grateful natives.

But many of the professional soldiers and adventurers who were most active in promoting colonization had very different ideas, shaped

both by Spain's experience in the New World and by England's own
conquest of the Irish in the 1560s and 1570s. As the historian Nicholas
Canny points out, the 'years in Ireland were years of apprenticeship,'
which saw the development of many of the policies towards 'savage
people' that were later used in North America. Sir Humphrey Gilbert,
for instance, one of the first men to receive a royal patent to colonize
in America, was a veteran of the Irish campaign, in which he had
terrorized the population by ordering that:

> The heddes of all those (of what sort soever thei were) which were
> killed in the daie, should be cutte off from their bodies and brought
> to the place where he incamped at night, and should there bee laied
> on the ground by eche side of the waie ledying into his owne tente
> so that none could come into his tente for any cause but commonly
> he muste passe through a lane of heddes which he used *ad terrorem*
> ... [It brought] greate terrour to the people when thei sawe the
> heddes of their dedde fathers, brothers, children, kinsfolke, and
> freinds ...

Significantly, the justification for this indiscriminate brutality was
that the Irish were 'savage heathen': their Catholicism was really a form
of 'paganism', and their practice of transhumance – i.e., moving herds
of animals from one area to another during the course of the year to
graze – made them nomads and hence barbarians who could be treated
like wild beasts.

The contradictory elements in English thinking about the 'plantations' are neatly summarized in Hakluyt's list of 'Inducements to the
liking of the voyage intended towards Virginia', drawn up in 1585. 'The
ends of this voyage,' he wrote, 'are these: 1, to plant Christian religion;
2, To trafficke; 3, To conquer; Or, to doe all three.' When the colonial
enterprise finally got under way in the same year, this characteristic
mixture of bullish arrogance, ruthless pragmatism and unrealistic
expectations came close to destroying it.

❖   ❖   ❖

The first 'plantation' was Ralegh's Roanoke colony, founded on an
island off the North Carolina coast. Instead of trying to grow crops, the

settlers seem to have spent most of their time looking for non-existent gold mines, while the Governor, Ralph Lane, led a series of unprovoked attacks against the local Indians on whom they depended for food. Unsurprisingly, with only fitful and inadequate support from England, the settlement disappeared within a year.

The Jamestown colony in Virginia, established in 1607, was afflicted with similar problems. After almost a century of European marauding along the coast the local Native American confederacy, the Powhatans, were understandably suspicious of the newcomers. To make matters worse, the settlers arrived in the middle of a tribal conflict between the Powhatans and the Chesapeakes, and apparently became caught in the crossfire. (According to one story, Powhatan shamans had told Wahunsonacock that he should surprise and defeat the Chesapeakes before they destroyed him. He did so, only to be told that another power would arise in the area to conquer his confederacy.) In the first few weeks, the settlers were attacked several times by Indian war parties, until Wahunsonacock managed to hold his men to an uneasy peace. Although he remained full of misgivings, he clearly thought that a more peaceful relationship might give him access to trade goods and – possibly – valuable military assistance against his enemies.

During the first summer alone, half the original colonists died from disease. The survivors, like their predecessors at Roanoke, made little attempt (beyond looking for gold-mines) to support themselves: by 'wasting their old Provisions, and neglecting to gather others,' as the colony's historian Robert Beverly put it in 1705, they were soon in such desperate straits that 1609 and 1610 became known as 'the starving time.' Their only hope – again like the Roanoke settlers – lay in the willingness of Native Americans to feed them. As George Percy frankly admitted, it was Indian 'Bread, Corne, Fish, and Flesh in great plentie which was the setting up of our feeble men, otherwise we had all perished.'

The Virginia Company had anticipated that native supplies would be needed for the first year. It instructed the colonists to 'have Great care not to Offend the naturals' and to buy 'Corn and all Other lasting Victuals ... before that they perceive you mean to plant among them ...' (Firm evidence that the colony's hard-headed masters, at least, were under no illusion about the natives' willingness simply to 'subject themselves' to English rule.) But there was a clear expectation that Jamestown would soon be self-sufficient.

In fact, apart from one short interlude, the colonists were 'constrained yerely to buy Corne of the Indians' for nearly two decades. This dependence quickly came to dominate the relationship between the two sides, creating huge practical and psychological problems and exposing the deep inconsistencies in English attitudes towards the native. The supremacy of Christian civilization was the central justification for the plantations, yet here were civilized Christians relying on the goodwill and agricultural skill of savages who, by definition, did not know how to use the land. A sense of how painfully humiliating the authorities found this runs through many of their communications to the colonists. In 1621, for instance, the London Council instructed Jamestown to break its dependence on 'the Salvages . . . whom long ere this should have beene fed and relived by the English, not the English by them . . .' Two years later, the Governor declared:

> Nothing can be more dishonorable to O[r] nation then to stand in need of supplies of O[r] most necessarie food from these base Salvages nor more dangerous, then to have O[r] lives, and the life of the colony it self, to depend uppon the uncertaine hope of trade wth them.

In other ways, too, the Indians failed to fulfil expectations. They were supposed to live 'without any law or government', but Wahunsonacock was 'a great emperour', and he and his sub-kings clearly exercised real authority over a large population: according to Alexander Whitaker, the Powhatans 'both honour and obey their Kings, Parents and Governours', and even the critical John Smith wrote that 'Although the Country people be very barbarous, yet have they amongst them such government, as that their Magistrates for good commanding, and their people for due subiection and obeying, excell many places that would be counted very civill.' Savages were meant to be feckless and improvident, but Wahunsonacock had an enormous storehouse crammed with the surplus produce that he traded to the settlers. While they were expected to see the self-evident advantages of Western civilization and willingly subject themselves to 'civility', moreover, with very few exceptions (most notably Wahunsonacock's daughter, Pocahontas), they turned out to be 'in noe sort willinge to sell or by fayer meanes to part with their children' to be converted to Christianity and educated in an English school. In fact, most disturbingly of all, the traffic was largely in the other direction: scores of settlers appeared to prefer 'savage' to 'civilized' life and, in spite of the threat of severe punishment, deserted Jamestown to live in Native American communities where they could enjoy an ample diet and relative freedom.

Logically, of course, the English should have seen the divergences between what they expected and what they encountered as evidence that the Powhatans were not really 'savage'. In fact, all too comprehensibly and predictably, they quickly transformed all the reasons for admiring native society into reasons for reviling it. If the Indians were not helpless and biddable, they were something worse: if they had the power to threaten English security and self-esteem, the only possible explanation was that it came from Satan himself. John Smith – like almost every other observer – was quite explicit on this point in his description of Powhatan religion:

> All things that were able to do them hurt beyond their prevention, they adore with their kinde of diuine worship; as the fire, water, lightening, thunder, our ordinance, peeces, horses, &c. But their cheife God they worship is the Diuell. Him they call Oke & serue him more of feare then loue.

By the same token, Wahunsonacock was a bloodthirsty tyrant who ruled by terror (unlike the English, whose systematic use of beating, torture and executions was sanctioned by God and civil society), and the settlers who went to live with the Indians were surrendering to the lustful savage in themselves.

As the reality of dependence sank in, both the perception and the treatment of native people rapidly worsened. Although the Indians were often happy enough to trade, the colonists' ceaseless demand for food was a constant source of friction. Under the leadership of Captain John Smith, the English developed a system of compulsory purchase: if the Indians refused to sell corn, they took it by force, leaving a few trinkets as token payment. By this method, wrote Smith, 'I durst undertake to have corne enough from the Salvages for 300 men, for a few trifles. And if they should be untoward (as it is most certaine they are) thirty or forty good men will be sufficient to bring them all in subiection . . .' In times of desperate hunger, the English often abandoned even this scanty pretence of fair-dealing and simply stole what they wanted, threatening or killing anyone who tried to stop them. As a result, the Native Americans frequently went hungry themselves or did not have enough seed to plant for the following year. 'Our people starved,' wrote Robert Johnson candidly in 1612, 'and the poor Indians by wrongs and injuries were made our enemies . . .'

Occasionally, despite Wahunsonacock's best efforts, Native American resentment and anger against this kind of treatment erupted in violence: George Percy reported how a party of colonists searching for supplies were found 'slayne wth them mowthes stopped full of Breade beinge down as it seamethe in Contempte and skorne thatt others mighte expecte the Lyke when they shold come to seeke for breade and reliefe amongste them.' Incidents like this, which in Indian terms conveyed a carefully calculated warning, reinforced the English belief that Native Americans were irredeemably savage and that the only way to deal with them was by terrorizing them into submission.

To ease the tension, the Native Americans offered to teach the colonists how to grow maize and construct fishing weirs, but the settlers concentrated on producing tobacco for export to England and continued to rely on their ability to wheedle or bully food out of the Native Americans or – increasingly – simply to take it by force. The Virginia Bay Company continued to instruct the colonists that 'all just, kind and charitable courses shall be holden with such of them, as shall conforme themselves to any good and sociable traffique,' and some settlers did make a heroic effort to live peacefully and deal equitably with the Indians. But Smith believed this was dangerous sentimentality. He wrote later:

> The Salvages being acquainted, that by command from *England* we durst not hurt them, were much imboldned; that famine and their insolencies did force me to breake our Commission and instructions; cause *Powhatan* fly his Countrey, and take the King of *Pamaunki* Prisoner; and also to keepe the King of *Paspahegh* in shackels, and put his men to double taskes in chaines, till nine and thirty of their Kings paied us contribution, and the offending Salvages sent to *James* towne to punish at our owne discretions: in the last two yeares I staied there, I had not a man slaine.

The Powhatans did not simply passively accept the growing power of the English: within their own terms, they tried to contain it and turn it to their advantage. Like Smith, Wahunsonacock (known to the settlers as Powhatan) was a wily, forceful, intelligent and sometimes ruthless man with a remarkable political grasp. When, for instance, the English tried to acquire suzerainty over the whole Powhatan confederacy by inviting Wahunsonacock to 'come to his Father' at Jamestown to receive gifts and be crowned as a subject king of James I, Wahunsonacock clearly understood the significance of accepting presents from a 'father'. Being, in Smith's grudgingly admiring words, a 'subtile Salvage', he replied: 'If your king have sent me presents, I also am a king, and this my land; 8 daies I will stay to receave them. Your father is to come to me, not I to him, nor yet to your fort, neither will I bite at such a baite.' The ceremony was held instead in the Powhatan capital, and when it was over Wahunsonacock symbolically 'gave his old shoes and his mantle' to the Englishman who had conducted it. In the same year, the English offered an alliance against the Powhatans' enemies the Monacans. Wahunsonacock at first accepted but then suddenly changed his mind, fearing that the English might switch sides. It was an inspired intuition: in 1609 the colonists were instructed to make an alliance with the Monacans as a check to Powhatan.

But nothing had prepared the Indians for the brutal asymmetry created by English settlement. Instead of an equilibrium maintained by symbolic exchanges and displays of strength and status, they suddenly found themselves in a world where, whatever they did, however carefully they calibrated their gestures and responses, the balance of power kept tipping away from them. The chief of the Paspahegh gave Smith an extraordinarily clear-sighted assessment of the situation from the native point of view, in which you can still see a desperate hope that the old reciprocal universe will reassert itself:

> We perceive & well know you intend to destroy us, that are here to intreat and desire your friendship, and to enjoy our houses and plant our fields, of whose fruit you shall participate, otherwise you will have the worst by our absence, for we can plant anywhere, though with more labour, and we know you cannot live if you want our harvest, and that reliefe wee bring you; if you promise us peace we

will beleeve you, if you proceed in revenge, we will abandon the countrie.

But the peace never came. Instead, Indian numbers started to collapse through repeated epidemics and the English population, despite appalling mortality rates, seemed to be constantly replenished and increased from an unseen source. As more immigrants arrived, they started to spill out of the small area where Wahunsonacock had tried to contain them, filling the vacuum left by Indian depopulation and encroaching on fields that were still being used. At the same time, the depleted Powhatans found that they were expected to feed the ever-growing stream of colonists, who – as English self-confidence grew – became more and more aggressive, unpredictable and hostile. In 1621, George Thorpe (one of the few Englishmen who consistently tried to deal fairly with the Indians) described the mood of the settlers:

> There is scarce any man amongst us that doth soe much as afforde them a good thought in his hart and most men wth theire mouthes give them nothinge but maledictions and bitter execrations beinge thereunto falslye caried wth a violent misp[er]swation . . . that these poore people have done unto us all the wronge and iniurie that the malice of the Devill or man cann affoord . . .

By 1618, when Wahunsonacock died, Powhatan culture was in crisis. In a pattern that was to become familiar in tribes all across the continent, the Indians' bewilderment, despair and hunger for salvation found expression in a charismatic prophet, the Pamunkey war chief Nemattanew. A spectacular figure who appeared in a feathered cloak evoking the Powhatan deity Okee (which earned him the name Jack of the Feathers from the colonists), Nemattanew promised a return to the tranquillity of the old, pre-English world through a renewal of sacred power. He became close to the new Powhatan leader, Wahunsonacock's brother Opechancanough, urging him to take a stand against the expanding colony. What finally precipitated the counter-attack was the murder of Nemattanew himself in 1622.

With exemplary generalship, Opechancanough co-ordinated a surprise assault on the English in which 347 settlers (more than three times the original population of the colony in 1607) were killed. The casualties would have been far higher but for a warning to Jamestown from a converted Indian. As it was, the main settlement and about three-quarters of the colonists survived.

The 'Powhatan Uprising' completed the transformation of the Virginia Indians, in English eyes, into subhuman beasts. Smith described them as 'perfidious and inhumane people', Edward Waterhouse thought they had 'put not off onely all humanity, but put on a worse and more than unnaturall bruitishnesse.' The colonists were relieved of all obligation to behave with restraint: the Powhatans and their allies were to be brought to 'ruine or subiection' with 'horses, and blood-Hounds to draw after them, the Mastives to seaze them, which take this naked, tanned, deformed Savage, for no other then wild beasts . . .' The aim was to root the Native Americans 'out for being longer a people on the face of the Earth.' In one incident alone, 200 Indians died when the English concluded a treaty with the rebellious Chiskiacks and then gave them poisoned sack to toast the two peoples' 'eternal friendship.'

The Indians' attack on the colony was also seen as a licence to take their land. 'We, who hitherto have had possession of no more ground than their waste, and our purchase,' wrote Edward Waterhouse exultantly, '. . . may now by right of Warre, and law of Nations, invade the Country, and destroy them who sought to destroy us: whereby wee shall enjoy their cultivated places . . . Now their cleared grounds in all their villages (which are situate in the fruitfullest places of the land) shall be inhabited by us . . .' Bizarrely, but significantly, as this argument was developed during the 1620s into a coherent ideology of conquest, the Virginia Indians, on whose farming the colonists had so long depended, were reinvented in the old image of the non-agricultural nomad. According to the influential Samuel Purchas, the seizure of Indian land was justified because God had intended it to be cultivated rather than left as an 'unmanned wild Countrey, which they range rather than inhabite.'

Looking at the history of Jamestown is rather like seeing an ultrasound picture of an embryo, in which all the features are discernible but not yet fully formed. In New England, the image is clearer: almost every element in it is more extreme, throwing the whole relationship between Native Americans and Europeans into sharper relief and showing the unmistakable shape of things to come.

4. Northeast: Two

'A new found Golgotha'

Mitark, the last hereditary chief, called people together on Indian Hill at sunset and told them that he was going to die and while he was talking a white whale arose from the water of Witch Pond and Mitark said thats a sign that another new people the colour of the whale [will come] but don't let them have all the land because if you do the Indians will disappear. Then he died and shortly after the white people appeared.

Recorded by Gladys Tantaquidgeon among
the Gay Head Wampanoag, 1928

The name 'New England' was coined by Captain John Smith, who explored the coast in 1614 for a company of merchant venturers and claimed it, typically, as his 'discovery'. In fact, of course, the area had been known to Europeans for almost a century or more: certainly since Verrazano's voyage in 1524, and probably (since Verrazano encountered natives who already seemed to have had some experience of traders) for even longer. During the second half of the sixteenth century, Basque and French entrepreneurs had established a thriving fur trade with the coastal tribes, and, by the time of Smith's voyage, the authorities in New France were attempting to extend formal French control over the area. Dutch merchants, meanwhile, were starting to push up from their base on Manhattan Island.

Like other early observers, Smith was hugely impressed by the landscape of southern New England. The Indian custom of removing trees and burning undergrowth had created vast open spaces – one account suggested that the Narragansett country had been completely cleared for a distance of eight to ten miles from the coast, while Verrazano reported seeing areas that could be easily crossed 'even by a large army' – and the whole coastline was thickly dotted with Indian towns, villages and farms. Given a country 'so planted with Gardens and Corne fields,' Smith enthused, 'and so well inhabited with a goodly, strong and well proportioned people . . ., who can but approve this a most excellent place, both for health and fertility?' He concluded (with a self-contradiction that mirrors the Virginians' capacity to consume the produce of Indian farming while denying that they were farmers) by saying that: '. . . of all the foure parts of the world that I have yet seene *not inhabited*, could I have but meanes to transport a Colonie, I would rather live there then any where [My italics].'

Smith's scheme for a New England colony won strong support from Sir Ferdinando Gorges, a professional soldier with a deep interest in 'plantations' who had been involved in several of the earlier, aborted attempts at colonization. Together, the two men devised a plan, whereby Smith (now dignified with the grandiloquent title 'Admiral of New England') would take two shiploads of colonists to the area. The project ended in fiasco when the 'Admiral' was captured and imprisoned for several months by the French, but Gorges persisted in his ambition. In 1619 he sent an expedition to the area under Captain Thomas Dermer, accompanied by a Wampanoag Indian called Squanto, who (with nineteen others) had been captured five years before by members of Smith's crew. Unlike earlier kidnap victims, Squanto amply fulfilled Gorges' expectations by acting as an emissary for the would-be colonists.

In the summer of 1620, however, everything he and Dermer had achieved was undone when another crew invited some Wampanoags on board their ship and shot them without provocation, fuelling a new upsurge of Indian anger and resentment. On Martha's Vineyard, the Wampanoag *sachem* Epenow, still deeply embittered after being kidnapped and held captive himself, led an attack against the expedition in which most of the crew were killed outright and Dermer was fatally wounded.

But despite this debacle, Gorges was not disheartened. Before his death, Dermer had reported a major change in the situation in New England which had radically altered the balance of power between native and English. Since Smith's visit six years before, an epidemic – or a series of epidemics – of 'the plague' (perhaps smallpox or chickenpox) had swept through the coastal tribes, killing ninety per cent or more of the population in some villages (Squanto's own community,

Patuxet, for example, had been completely wiped out) and making the whole area, in the words of the historian Neal Salisbury, 'a vast disaster zone, comparable to those left by modern wars and other large-scale catastrophes.' Clearly, thought Gorges, the aftermath to such a cataclysm would be the ideal moment to establish a 'plantation': however hostile they were to the English, the shocked and bewildered survivors would be in no state to mount effective opposition. He therefore developed a new, more ambitious plan for large-scale colonization, and sought a royal patent for the whole territory between Virginia in the south and New France in the north, including a considerable area claimed by Virginia itself. The charter was sealed on 3 November 1620, and eight days later the *Mayflower*, with a hundred or so prospective colonists on board, landed at Cape Cod. Their leaders carried a copy of Dermer's last letter, which recommended Squanto's depopulated village of Patuxet – renamed 'Plymouth' by Captain John Smith – as a possible site for a settlement.

*   *   *

. . . an Indian *in those parts . . . [told] us of his dreame many yeers since . . . Before many witnesses . . . hee said 'That about two yeers before the* English *came over into those parts there was a great mortality among the* Indians, *and one night he could not sleep above half the night, after which hee fell into a dream, in which he did think he saw a great many men come to those parts in cloths, just as the* English *now are apparelled, and among them there arose up a man all in black, with a thing in his hand which hee now sees was all one* English *mans book; this black man he said stood upon a higher place then all the rest, and on the one side of him were the* English, *on the other a great number of* Indians: *this man told all the* Indians *that God was* moosquantum *or angry with them, and that he would kill them for their sinnes . . .*

From: *The Clear Sun-Shine of the Gospel Breaking Forth upon the Indians in New England*, by Thomas Shepard, 1648

The experience of the coastal tribes in southern New England between 1616 and 1620 was all too typical. According to Henry Dobyns, there were almost a hundred epidemics and pandemics of European diseases among Native Americans between the first contact and the beginning of the twentieth century: in other words, a 'serious contagious disease causing significant mortality invaded Native American peoples at intervals of four years and two and a half months, on the average, from 1520 to 1900.' The rapidity and virulence of the outbreaks meant that the same community could be struck several times within the space of only a generation or two, giving it no time to recover. 'Without doubt,' writes the Cherokee historical demographer Russell Thornton, 'the single most important factor in American Indian population decline was an increased death rate due to diseases introduced from the Eastern Hemisphere.'

The impact of this disaster on Indian life is hard to imagine. The death rate far exceeded anything that modern Western nations have experienced: the First World War, for instance, which is often seen as the apotheosis of mass destruction, killed around 2 per cent of the British population over a four-year period. Many Native American communities lost 75 per cent or more of their members within just a few weeks, the kind of losses predicted for a nuclear holocaust, and certainly greater than those suffered at Hiroshima. The survivors, inevitably, were shocked, grief-stricken and bewildered. 'Those that are left, have their courage much abated,' wrote Robert Cushman of the Indians round Plymouth, 'and their countenance is dejected, and they seem as a people affrighted.'

Governor Bradford of Plymouth, writing in the 1630s, gave a vivid account of the 'plague':

> ... they [the Indians] fall into a lamentable condition as they lie on their hard mats, the pox breaking and mattering and running one into another, their skin cleaving by reason thereof to the mats they lie on. When they turn them, a whole side will flay off at once as it were, and they will be all of a gore blood, most fearful to behold. And then being very sore, what with cold and other distempers, they die like rotten sheep.

The survivors faced other problems. The epidemics often meant that they missed crucial phases of the annual subsistence cycle – planting, harvesting, hunting – and were quickly brought to the edge of starvation. At the same time, the intricate pattern of reciprocal relationships between and within groups was thrown into disarray. The virtual elimination of whole lineages – including, often, *sachems* and other high-ranking individuals – disrupted the complex web of kinship and authority that held communities together and drastically altered the relative positions of different nations. Powerful confederacies could suddenly find themselves reduced to a handful of families and forced to put themselves under the protection of former opponents or tributaries: following the outbreak of 1616–20, for instance, the leader of the once-populous Wampanoag, Massasoit, had to humble himself before his people's traditional enemies, the Narragansett, who had largely escaped the epidemic.

Perhaps most vitally of all, European disease undermined the Native Americans' confidence in themselves and their view of the world. The failure of the shamans to contain and cure smallpox and bubonic plague was the failure of an entire system of belief: the rituals, ceremonies, checks and balances were no longer working, and the whole universe seemed to be spinning terrifyingly out of control. In a reaction that was to be echoed again and again as the same catastrophe befell other native peoples, some New England Indians sought an explanation of what had happened in terms of their own spiritual shortcomings, such as abandoning – in the face of the epidemics – the usual burial customs and interring the victims in mass graves instead. (The survival of the Narragansett in 1616–20 was taken as evidence for this idea: the supreme deity, *Cautantowwit*, had spared them because they had continued to bury their dead in the proper way.) Others interpreted the epidemics as proof of the Europeans' greater spiritual power. In 1616, for instance, when they succumbed to the plague, some of the Massachusett saw it as the fulfilment of a prophecy delivered the year before by a French captive, who had told them that his God could destroy them. This belief in the newcomers' religious potency – reinforced by the fact that so few Europeans seemed to be affected by the epidemics – led to a number of deathbed conversions to Christianity. 'Divers of them,' wrote John Winthrop in 1633, 'in their sickness, confessed that the Englishmen's God was a good God; and that, if they recovered, they would serve him.'

The Pilgrims themselves looked for a religious meaning in the epidemics. 'Thus farre hath the good hand of God favoured our beginnings...' they reported when they reached the depopulated Patuxet. 'In sweeping away great multitudes of the natives ..., a little more before we went thither, that he might make room for us there.' This was more than an expression of conventional piety: it was a recognition that, without the effects of disease, English colonies might never have been successfully established in New England. Native Americans such as the people of Patuxet prepared the way for the colonists, using their knowledge and experience to select and clear the best sites for villages and then, with the onset of the plague, suddenly leaving them unoccupied and ready for the newcomers. (They left, though, grisly reminders of 'the good hand of God': as late as 1622, the 'bones and skulls' of the dead at Plymouth 'made such a spectacle...' according to Thomas Morton, that 'it seemed to me a new found Golgatha.')

More than fifty of the first settlements were built on the remains of Indian communities, a pattern that was to be repeated as the frontier moved west. As the historian Francis Jennings eloquently puts it: 'The American land was more like a widow than a virgin. Europeans did not find a wilderness here; rather, however involuntarily, they made one. Jamestown, Plymouth, Salem, Boston, Providence, New Amsterdam, Philadelphia – all grew upon sites previously occupied by Indian communities ... The so-called settlement of America was a *re*settlement, a reoccupation of a land made waste by the diseases and demoralization introduced by the newcomers.'

❖　❖　❖

Although they arrived in the New World thirteen years after the first Jamestown settlers, the 'Pilgrim Fathers' are generally seen as the true spiritual founders of America. There is something disreputable about the gentlemen adventurers and desperate indentured labourers who went to Virginia looking for a quick profit and then, in the space of a few generations, evolved into a slave-owning aristocracy. The Pilgrims, by contrast – people of the 'middling' or 'industrious sort' who moved with their families to the New World in the hope of finding a permanent home where they could practise their religion unmolested and govern their own affairs – became a heartening symbol for generations of immigrants seeking a fresh start in America. Since the time of the American Revolution, when they were claimed as antecedents by the rebellious colonists, they have been seen as embodying America's highest ideals: independence, self-reliance and a simple, unshakeable sense of right and wrong. Their dealings with the Indians are often held up as a model of scrupulous fairness, showing how America could – and, at its best, did – treat its native people. It is Thanksgiving, when Native Americans and colonists solemnly shared the bounties of nature, rather than Smith's armed assaults on the storehouses of Powhatan, that seem to represent the real beginnings of the American nation. It is therefore important to examine the Pilgrims and their behaviour in some detail.

The 'Pilgrims' were members of a small Protestant sect which believed that the Church of England was corrupt and that they must obey the injunction in the Second Book of Corinthians: 'Come out from among them and be ye separate, saith the Lord.' They had tried living for some years in the more tolerant atmosphere of the Netherlands, but felt that even here their distinct identity – and their Englishness – was under threat. A group of them had therefore returned to England, planning to settle in America.

Only about a third of the Plymouth colonists were actually 'Pilgrims' – the remainder were 'Strangers', whose motives for the voyage were primarily economic rather than religious – but it was the 'Pilgrims' who provided the leadership and wrote the '*Mayflower* Compact', by which the settlers agreed to 'Covenant and Combine ourselves together into a Civil Body Politic.' While it was of paramount importance to establish a community where the Separatists' religious identity and beliefs could be safeguarded against Anglicanism and other 'infections', they were also concerned to generate a good return on the capital that they, and their merchant venturer backers in London, had invested in the project. These aims were not seen as in any way contradictory: as one of the colony's leaders, Edward Winslow, neatly expressed it, New England was for those in whom 'religion and profit jump together.'

The Pilgrims' preoccupation with 'separation' profoundly affected their attitude towards other communities, including Native Americans. Their Indian policy took shape during their brief stay on Cape Cod, where they tried to avoid all contact with the local tribes, merely sending out the colony's military commander, Miles Standish, from time to time to 'find' (i.e., pilfer) stocks of food. 'It was God's good providence that we found [some of the Indians'] corn...' wrote Bradford, 'for we knew not how we should find or meet with any Indians, except it be to do us a mischief.' For four months after their arrival at Patuxet, they adopted a similar approach, but it soon became clear that short foraging expeditions could not feed a hundred people or more indefinitely. As winter set in, the settlers' situation became increasingly desperate, and by the spring of 1621, about half their number had died of disease and starvation.

It was the neighbouring Wampanoags who moved first to make contact. Although, understandably, they had been aggrieved by the colonists' behaviour, they saw possible benefits for both sides in a better relationship. The settlers, clearly, urgently required food and instruction in how to survive in New England; the Wampanoags, for their part, were desperately looking for some way to re-establish the equilibrium of a world that was already, as a result of the arrival of Europeans, falling into disarray. Their numbers had been drastically depleted by the recent epidemic, and they now found themselves at a severe disadvantage in their dealings with other tribes, especially the Narragansett – who, having avoided the plague, were asserting their superior strength by high-handedly demanding large amounts of tribute – and the Micmac, who, armed with French weapons, were regularly raiding the coast in search of corn and other produce to help them sustain their own increasingly precarious position in the fur trade. Encouraged by Squanto, who had been living with the Wampanoag since Dermer's death, and Samoset, a Maine Indian who had also been taken captive by the English, the Wampanoag *sachem*, Massasoit, gradually came to see an alliance with Plymouth as a means to restore some of his lost power. After a three-day gathering, probably to purge the Indians ritually of their former hostility towards the English (Bradford, typically, saw it as a form of witchcraft, writing that they had met 'to curse and execrate them [the English] with their conjurations'), he sent Squanto and Samoset to arrange a meeting, which resulted in a formal treaty.

Some historians have argued that, whatever went wrong subsequently in the colonization of America, this first agreement between natives and settlers was fair and even-handed, showing the good faith and good intentions of both sides. In fact, it contains many of the seeds of later misunderstanding and conflict. The treaty provided that each side would help the other in the event of an attack by a third party, but many of the other clauses clearly favoured the English. Massasoit, for instance, had to use his authority to ensure that his 'neighbour confederates' also observed the treaty and that any Indian guilty of an offence against the English should be handed over to the colony for trial, but here was no reciprocal requirement that an English offender against the Wampanoags should be delivered to them for justice. The Pilgrims also seem not to have been above a little deception: the original agreement provided that both sides would disarm when they met, but in practice the colonists often carried weapons, and in the official account written by Nathaniel Morton (and Bradford's private history) the passage relating to English disarmament is omitted.

Perhaps most fundamental of all, the treaty agrees that 'King James would esteem of him [Massasoit] as his friend and ally,' a phrase which the Wampanoag almost certainly interpreted as meaning that they were entering a more or less equal partnership. According to Morton, however, it signified that Massasoit 'acknowledged himself content to become the Subject of our Soveraign lord the King aforesaid, His Heirs and Successors; and gave unto them all the Lands adjacent, to them and their Heirs forever.' As Neal Salisbury points out, 'these discrepancies ... indicate that among themselves the English regarded the treaty as one not of alliance and friendship between equals but of submission by one party to the domination of the other.' Many of the basic concepts in the English view, moreover, such as the ideas of sovereignty and the transfer of title to land, would have been profoundly alien to Algonquian culture.

Some of these cultural differences quickly became apparent. From the Native American perspective, the significance of the treaty lay not in the document itself but in the exchange of gifts and speeches accompanying it, which ritually ended the enmity between the two peoples and redrew the boundaries separating them. Their new relationship was not merely a political alliance, but a spiritual realignment that brought the two peoples into a shared social network where they were bound together by mutual obligation. Shortly after the treaty was signed, passing Wampanoags started calling in at Plymouth, expecting their new friends to offer them food and accommodation. For the Pilgrims, so fearful of pollution even by their own compatriots that they had been forced to emigrate, these casual visits by 'Savages' seemed to transgress all the physical, cultural and religious barriers on which their sense of identity and purpose in the New World depended. They hastily dispatched Edward Winslow and Stephen Hopkins to Massasoit to explain that they saw the relationship as a formal arrangement between leaders, and that henceforth Plymouth would only receive the *sachem* himself or one of his representatives.

Winslow's report of the trip gives a vivid, if unconsciously humorous, sense of the Pilgrims' moral panic at the blurring of the distinctions between their world and the Indians'. All the way to Massasoit's village the two Englishmen were invited to eat and drink with every group of Wampanoags they met, and when they arrived, they were invited to spend the night, sharing a plank bed with Massasoit himself, his wife and two other men. The following day, they were begged to stay longer, but they refused. 'We desired to keep the Sabbath at home, and feared we should either be light-headed for want of sleep, for what with bad lodging, the savages' barbarous singing (for they use to sing themselves asleep), lice and fleas within doors, and mosquitoes without, we could hardly sleep all the time of our being there; we much fearing that if we should stay any longer, we should not be able to recover home for want of strength.'

After the rigidly authoritarian and legalistic society they had left behind in England, the Pilgrims also found the fluidity and dynamism of the Indian world deeply unsettling. Having believed they could control all the local tribes through Massasoit, they were unnerved to discover that, far from being an absolute monarch, he had only limited power over his own people and even less over his 'neighbour confederates'. As rivalries and jealousies among different Indian leaders (including, at one point, between Massasoit and his own brother) continued to erupt, often intensified by the behaviour of the colonists themselves, the Pilgrims were understandably uneasy about their own security. Their response was to conclude a series of separate, bilateral agreements with the different groups, making them all – as the English saw it – 'Loyal Subjects of King James'. (Again, there is some evidence that they were less than scrupulous in these arrangements: on at least one occasion, for instance, they seem to have added a *sachem*'s name to a treaty retrospectively so that they could justify attacking him on the grounds that he had violated its terms.) Through this expanding system of alliances, the Pilgrims began to realize one of their – and their backers' – prime commercial ambitions, the development of a trade in furs.

But both their religious purity and their hegemony over their Native American neighbours was soon under threat from other quarters, as new English colonies started to appear along the coast. The Pilgrims quickly took action to suppress the little settlement of Wessagusset, so incensing the local Massachusetts Indians by murdering four of their leaders that it was no longer safe for the colonists to remain, and then turned their attention to Ma-re Mount, a new 'plantation' founded by the non-Separatist, Thomas Morton. Morton managed to threaten, simultaneously, the religious, social and cultural underpinnings of the Separatist way of life by making his indentured servants partners in the colony and maintaining cordial and relaxed relations with his Massachu-sett neighbours, whose company he clearly preferred to most of his compatriots'. ('The more Salvages the better quarter, the more Christians the worser quarter,' he wrote.) His worst offence was to erect a maypole – with the help of Indians who had come 'of purpose to see the manner of our Revels' – and to allow the 'savages' to join in the celebrations. Complaining that Morton had become 'Lord of Misrule, and maintained (as it were) a School of Atheism,' Bradford had him deported in 1628.

But the tide of settlement was becoming increasingly difficult to resist. In 1629, the Massachusetts Bay Company received a royal charter to settle the area between the Merrimack and Charles Rivers and to establish, in effect, a self-governing Puritan commonwealth there. Unlike Plymouth, Massachusetts Bay had vast resources (its well-connected backers invested £200,000 in the project, while the Pilgrims had been able to raise a mere £7,000), and its leaders promoted the new colony vigorously.

There was no shortage of potential colonists. At the end of the 1620s and beginning of the 1630s, thousands of the – largely Puritan –

'middling sort' in England found their economic security undermined by a deep recession and their religious beliefs threatened by a growing official hostility to Calvinism. At the same time, glowing accounts of New England described a land of infinite abundance, sparsely populated by friendly natives, that seemed to be there for the taking. So exaggerated were some of these reports that Captain Christopher Levett, writing in 1628, was moved to try to set the record straight: 'Neither must men think that corn doth grow naturally, (or on trees,) nor will the deer come when they are called, or stand still and look on a man until he shoot him . . .; nor the fish leap into the kettle . . ., which is no truer than that the fowls will present themselves to you with spits through them.' Massachusetts Bay cleverly exploited this idea: the company seal, showing a smiling Indian standing between two trees and saying: 'Come over and help us,' conveyed the message that, by emigrating, colonists would be fulfilling their Christian duty as well as creating a new, more prosperous life for themselves and their families.

Between 1630 and 1633, the 'Great Migration' brought some 3,000 English settlers to Massachusetts Bay. Even before their arrival, the epidemics and conflicts of the previous two decades had begun to make New England more like the propagandists' fanciful descriptions of it. Large areas that had been cleared and settled by Native Americans were reverting to forest: William Wood, for example, described places 'where the Indians died of the plague some fourteen years ago' that were now covered with 'much underwood . . . because it hath not been burned.' Where the Pilgrims had felt themselves to be surrounded by – as Bradford put it – 'a hideous and desolate wilderness, full of wild beasts and wild men,' Massachusetts Bay was planted in an area that had already been largely cleared of Native Americans. John Winthrop Sr., the new colony's main architect and – from 1630 – its Governor, was confident that the Indians would pose little threat to its settlers, writing: 'there are not so many of them in 20: miles compasse as wilbe of us.'

Unlike the founders of either Jamestown or Plymouth, Winthrop was a trained lawyer who devoted considerable thought and ingenuity to establishing a legal basis for colonization. Like other Europeans at the time, he assumed that a Christian prince could assert sovereignty over a 'heathen' people and their territory, and he believed that Charles

I had effectively delegated this authority in New England to the Massachusetts Bay Company. He also invoked the widely accepted theory of *vacuum domicilium*: that land which had not been 'subdued' (i.e., brought under European-style cultivation) could legitimately be taken and 'improved'. Since most of the territory used by Native Americans was, by this definition, 'unsubdued', and since, as 'savages', they had no 'civil government' which could be said to exercise its own sovereignty, it followed that they had neither a 'natural' nor a 'civil' right to the land (although it was accepted that they had a 'moral right' to their fields and gardens, which suggested occupation on the European pattern).

There were English critics of Winthrop's policy, most notably the extreme Separatist Roger Williams, who argued that native people did possess sovereignty and that, as a result, the colonists could not merely rely on the royal patent but must buy title direct from the *sachems*. Williams remained an influential figure (his views continued to affect debate over land rights in New England until well into the eighteenth century), but he was quickly marginalized by the leaders of Massachusetts Bay. He became – literally, from the English point of view – a lone voice in the wilderness, living with the Narragansett, from whom, in 1636, he bought enough land to found the dissident colony of Providence Plantation (later Rhode Island).

Although it rejected Williams' argument, the Massachusetts Bay Company recognized that, in practice, Indians might 'pretend right of inheritance' to areas that were required for settlement, and the colonists were instructed to make 'reasonable composition' with them in order 'that wee may avoyde the least scruple of intrusion.' But in agreeing a 'composition', the Indians were not – from the colonists' perspective – simply consenting to the sale of property; they were also surrendering it, and themselves, to English jurisdiction. There was no question of retaining tribal independence within the colony's boundaries, or of reasserting tribal control over an area once it had passed into English hands: the transfer of land and authority was strictly a one-way traffic.

For most Native Americans, of course, the transaction almost certainly looked very different. The nearest equivalent to a 'composition' in their political system was either an alliance between two distinct groups or the symbolic transfer of allegiance from one *sachem* to another. This process might have involved conceding the new leader certain rights within their territory and agreeing to pay him tribute in exchange for support and protection, but it would not have meant either vacating the area completely and irreversibly or dissolving their identity as an autonomous society. The contract in July 1636 between the fur trader William Pynchon and the village of Agawam gives a revealing glimpse of the Native American viewpoint. A total of thirteen Indians signed the document, in which they agreed to sell a tract of four or five miles along the Connecticut River, but retained the right to 'have and enjoy all that cottinackeesh, or ground that is now planted; And have liberty to take Fish and Deer, ground nuts, walnuts akornes and sasachiminesh or a kind of pease' within it. As the colonists grew more assertive and their aims became clearer to the Indians, the profound difference between the views of the two sides began to spark serious conflict.

To begin with, however, as Winthrop had foreseen, there was little friction. The local Massachuset and Pawtucket, reduced to a combined population of only about two hundred, welcomed Massachusetts Bay – as Massasoit had welcomed Plymouth – largely for the protection it seemed to offer against more powerful enemies and rivals. As well as allowing the English to settle on land depopulated by the epidemics, they were so enfeebled that they appear to have accepted the colony's assumption of legal jurisdiction over them, which made them – in the words of Neal Salisbury – no more than 'domesticated subjects'. There are numerous records from the early history of Massachusetts Bay of court cases between settlers and their Native American neighbours. Many of them – in an ironic commentary on English claims that they were stable farmers while the Indians were rootless nomads – revolved around disputes over the colonists' roaming livestock, which often damaged native crops and were then killed in revenge by the Indians.

But despite this partial incorporation of Indians into its own legal framework, Massachusetts Bay shared Plymouth's unease about developing too close a social relationship with them. Following the Pilgrims' example, the company instructed its colonists that 'for the avoyding of the hurt that may follow through over much familaritie with the Indians, wee conceive it fitt that they bee not permitted to come to your plantation but at certain tymes and places to be appointed them'.

When – in a striking demonstration of just how far their economic independence had been undermined – growing numbers of Native Americans started working as servants to settlers, the colony's Court of Assistants became alarmed and hastily ruled that, in future, no one could employ an Indian without its express approval. The same urge to maintain barriers between English and 'savage' led Massachusetts Bay to ban the cultivation or use of tobacco by settlers and – once building materials had arrived from England – to prohibit them from constructing wigwams rather than houses.

By 1633, the expanding colony had absorbed all the 'surplus' land and were starting to encroach on areas still used by the surviving bands, who – according to Edward Johnson – had begun to 'quarrell with them about their bounds of Land.' In the same year, both Indians and settlers were seriously affected by a prolonged drought, which only ended when – as both sides seem to have agreed – the English God responded to the Puritans' prayers by sending rain. Shortly afterwards, another devastating outbreak of smallpox swept through the region, leaving the colonists virtually untouched but killing most of the remaining Indians around Massachusetts Bay and spreading south and west to ravage two powerful groups that, up to now, had largely escaped: the Narragansetts and their neighbours the Pequots. The inference for the demoralized remnants of the Massachusett and the Pawtucket was clear: the English God had punished them for daring to challenge the colony. Governor Winthrop drew a similar conclusion when he wrote: 'God hath hereby cleared our title to this place.'

But Massachusetts Bay's demand for new lands was growing more quickly than its 'title' to them could be 'cleared' by disease. As early as 1633, religious differences and discontent over the running of the colony had begun to drive some groups of settlers to look further afield for somewhere to establish their settlements. Their decision to move into the fertile Connecticut Valley led to one of the defining incidents of colonial history, the 'Pequot War', which not only resolved many of the issues dividing the Puritan community but finally settled the question of how English and Native Americans were to live together.

❖   ❖   ❖

At the start of the 1630s, the Pequots were one of the most powerful groups in New England, controlling a large area in what is now eastern Connecticut and dominating a number of tributary tribes. One early account says that they, and their close relatives the Mohegans, were relatively recent arrivals in the area, possibly a splinter-group of the Hudson Valley Mahicans who had moved east and terrorized several local peoples into submission. (According to this version, the name *Pequot* means 'destroyers'.)

In the immediate aftermath of the first settlements, the Pequots, a little inland from the coastal tribes and insulated from the first waves of disease and land-seizure, were able to turn the new situation to their advantage. In the 1620s, they used their powerful position to establish a commercial monopoly with the Dutch, controlling the trade in furs and amassing vast quantities of the highly prized *wampum*, which, as Indians were drawn into the European economic system, was used more and more as a kind of currency throughout New England, even – for a short period – being formally recognized as legal tender by Massachusetts Bay. The power and arrogance of the Pequots created resentment among many of their tributaries, who were denied direct access to European goods and required to pay large amounts of tribute and who, as a result, initially welcomed the English.

Beginning in 1633, the Pequots were struck by a rapid succession of disasters which quickly threw them into crisis. When they discovered that the Dutch had begun dealing with other Indians in the area, they angrily killed some of their rivals at the House of Good Hope trading post, and the Dutch replied by kidnapping and murdering their *sachem*, Wopigwooit, and suspending trade with them. The Pequots' response was to make two fateful and fatal decisions: they chose Wopigwooit's son Sassacus to succeed him, in preference to the Mohegan *sachem* Wonkus, a violent, jealous and vindictive man who from now on became implacably hostile to his Pequot relatives; and they sent emissaries to Boston inviting the English to trade with them in place of the Dutch.

Almost simultaneously, the Pequots were hit by another catastrophe: the new outbreak of smallpox, which now, finally, ravaged them as earlier infections had devastated the coastal tribes. As well as killing a large part of their population, the epidemic further loosened the

Pequots' grip on many of their tributary tribes, just at the moment when large-scale English settlement was beginning to upset the finely balanced system of tribal relationships in the Connecticut Valley. When the Pequots tried to reassert their position, either by harrying settlers themselves, or by supporting and protecting subject tribes that had attempted to prevent incursions on to their territory, they provoked a quite disproportionate – and to the Indians completely unaccountable – English response. In 1636, following the deaths of two English traders, the Massachusetts Bay colony ordered Captain John Endecott to sail to Block Island and kill every Indian male he found there. Ninety Indians were murdered, most of them Narragansetts who were uncon-nected with the Pequots, and Endecott then set out to attack the Pequots themselves, burning two of their villages but, in the event, only killing one man. The Pequots responded by trying to form an alliance with the Narragansett *sachem* Canonicus, warning that, if he failed to join them in containing the settlers, the English would defeat Sassacus first and then turn against the Narragansett themselves at a later date. Canonicus wavered, but finally decided – apparently as the result of an intervention by Roger Williams – to ally himself with Massachusetts Bay.

Undaunted, Sassacus unilaterally launched a series of very limited attacks on Fort Saybrook in the Connecticut Valley, clearly expecting – or at least hoping – that this carefully calculated signal would be enough to restore the honour of his people and deter further English aggression. In keeping with Indian custom, his men at one point called a truce and asked the English Lieutenant Gardiner if he had 'fought enough'? When Gardiner showed no inclination to make peace they enquired, clearly anxious to discover what kind of warfare they should expect, 'if we did use to kill women and children?' to which Gardiner replied 'that they should see that hereafter.' The Pequots replied with a typical show of bravado, saying: 'We are Pequits, and have killed Englishmen, and can kill them as mosquetoes, and we will go to Connectecott and kill men, women, and children, and we will take away the horses, cows, and hogs.'

The Pequots carried out their threat in April 1637. The *sachem* of one of their former tributary tribes had asked for their help against the settlers of Wethersfield, who had dispossessed him. Sassacus responded by sending a war party, which killed nine settlers, twenty cattle and a horse and took two women captive. Even this, when set against Endecott's massacre on Block Island, seems (and was almost certainly intended to be) a fairly measured reprisal, but it provoked intense fear and anger amongst the colonists. Their panic was fuelled by the defeated Wonkus – known to the English as Uncas – who voraciously seized the opportunity to undermine Sassacus's position by suggesting that 'out of desperate madnesse' he planned an all-out war against the settlers.

Massachusetts Bay had expressly forbidden the Connecticut settlers to attack the Pequots, but Wonkus's urgings gave them the justification they needed. When the Connecticut General Court declared an 'offensive warr' against Sassacus on 1 May 1637, Thomas Hooker wrote to John Winthrop Sr. explaining that 'The Indians here our frends were so importunate with us to make warr presently that unlesse we had attempted some thing we had delivered our persons unto contempt of base feare and cowardise, and caused them to turne enemyes against us: Agaynst our mynds, being constrayned by necessity, we have sent out a company...' There were, however – as Winthrop must have known – other motives for the decision. The Connecticut settlers were determined to establish their independence from Massachusetts Bay, which still asserted jurisdiction over them, and realized that their case would be enormously strengthened if they could take action first and defeat the Pequots single-handedly. As well as demonstrating the fledgling colony's military power, victory would give it a potent claim, by 'right of conquest', to both the Pequots' land and their control of the lucrative traffic in *wampum* beads and furs. There is some evidence that the timing of the war was determined by this inter-colonial rivalry, and that the supposed offences of the Pequots (some of which had occurred years before and had not, in fact, been committed by Pequots) were little more than a pretext.

Connecticut raised a war party of ninety English soldiers, under the command of Captain John Mason, a professional soldier who had fought in the Dutch Wars in Europe, and seventy Mohegans and 'River Indians' led by Wonkus, who quickly demonstrated that he was 'faithfull to the English' by murdering seven Pequots they encountered *en route*. According to Mason, who left a graphic and detailed account of the

war, the expedition's 'commission' was to go directly to the Pequots'
territory and launch a punitive raid against them, but he felt they
should adopt another strategy. Although he is unwontedly coy about this
plan, it is clear that it aroused considerable opposition from two of his
lieutenants, Lion Gardiner and John Underhill, who were only persuaded to agree to it after the chaplain, Mr. Stone, had sat up all night
'commend[ing] our situation to the Lord ... to direct how in what
manner we should demean our selves ...' We cannot now be certain,
but from subsequent events it seems likely that God was being asked
to decide whether the English, His Chosen People, could legitimately
assist Him in 'clearing their title' to America by, for the first time,
deliberately exterminating an entire nation. Stone's conclusion – that
he was 'fully satisfied' with Mason's proposal – was to have enormous
implications not merely for the Pequots but for all Native Americans.

Following his new plan, Mason sailed to Narragansett Bay, where he
told Canonicus 'that we were now come, God assisting, to Avenge our
selves upon them [the Pequots].' Canonicus – perhaps concerned to
win favour with the English by proving himself as good a friend as
Wonkus – sent his war leader Miantonomo and 200 warriors to join the
expedition.

Wonkus told Mason that there were two well-fortified Pequot
settlements: one, close at hand, at Mystic, and the other – where
Sassacus and most of his men were – a few miles further on. Keen to
kill the *sachem* himself, Wonkus urged that the expedition should
launch simultaneous attacks against both communities, but Mason
decided to destroy Mystic first and move against Sassacus later. As
rumours of this plan spread among the soldiers' Indian allies, the
Narragansett began to melt away, 'manifesting great Fear,' according
to Mason. Since Mystic was militarily the easier target, however,
cowardice seems an unlikely explanation; a more probable explanation,
borne out by later events, is that the Narragansett were appalled at
Mason's – in Indian terms – unjustifiable ruthlessness. Mason asked
Wonkus 'what he thought the Indians would do?' and Wonkus replied
that 'The NARRAGANSETTS would all leave us, but as for HIMSELF
He would never leave us: and so it proved ...'

Approaching the Pequot fort at Mystic late at night, the English
'heard the Enemy Singing ... with great Insulting and Rejoycing,'

apparently because 'seeing our Pinnaces sail by them some Days before, [they] concluded we were affraid of them and durst not come near them . . .'

The soldiers attacked at dawn. A sentinel saw them and cried out 'Owamux! Owamux!' ('English! English!') but most of 'the Enemy' were still, as Mason put it, 'in a dead indeed their last Sleep.' Mason and his men broke in, wildly firing and hacking at the terrified Pequots – mostly old men, women and children with few weapons – until:

The Captain . . . said, WE MUST BURN THEM; and immediately . . . brought out a Fire Brand, and putting it into the Matts with which they were covered, set the Wigwams on Fire . . . the Indians ran as men most dreadfully Amazed.

And indeed such a dreadful Terror did the ALMIGHTY let fall upon their Spirits, that they would fly from us and run into the very Flames, where many of them perished.

. . . And thus in little more than one Hour's space was their impregnable Fort with themselves utterly Destroyed, to the Number of Six or Seven Hundred . . . There were only Seven taken Captive & about Seven escaped.

. . . *Thus was God seen in the Mount, Crushing his proud Enemies and the Enemies of his People . . . burning them up in the Fire of his Wrath, and dunging the Ground with their Flesh: It was the LORD's Doings, and it is marvellous in our Eyes!*

The ruthlessness of the attack appalled most of the colonists' Indian allies: this, clearly, was warfare of a kind they had never seen or imagined before. You can sense their horror even in Captain Underhill's triumphalist account of the aftermath:

Our Indians came to us, and much rejoiced at our victories, and greatly admired the manner of Englishmen's fight, but cried Mach it, mach it; that is, It is naught, it is naught [wicked], because it is too furious, and slays too many men.

As the English withdrew, they were attacked by a war party of 300 Pequots from the other town, who showered them with arrows before hurrying on to Mystic. Enraged by what they found there, the warriors immediately set off again in pursuit of the killers, but the English –

armed with muskets and artillery pieces against the Indians' bows and
arrows – managed to beat off the attack and reach the four ships
waiting for them. On one 'shallop', Mason found Captain Patrick and a
contingent of forty men sent by Governor Winthrop 'to Rescue us,
supposing we were pursued, though there did not appear any the least
sign of such a Thing.' This belated attempt by Massachusetts Bay to
ensure that it had a stake in the victory (and its spoils) clearly irritated
Mason, who 'plainly told' Patrick that 'in truth we did not desire or
delight in his Company.'

But the Bay Colony, determined not to relinquish its claims over
Pequot territory, decided that it must shoulder the main responsibility
for continuing the war against Sassacus. Within a few weeks, a new
force of 120 men under Israel Stoughton had joined Patrick to seek out
and destroy the surviving Pequots, and over the next few months the
remaining 'enemies of God's people' were harried almost to extinction.

The virtual extermination of the Pequots stunned the other Indians
of southern New England. If the English had the power – and were
willing – utterly to destroy the strongest and most feared confederacy
in the region, then no tribe had the means to defend itself militarily.
For many groups, the best hope for survival now seemed to lie not in
outright defiance, but in accepting the colonists' predominant position
and using negotiation, diplomacy and ingratiation to win their favour –
or at least avoid rousing their anger. Within a few weeks, several tribes
– including the *wampum* producers of eastern Long Island – had
shown that they recognized this new reality by voluntarily submitting
themselves to the 'protection' of the English.

There also seem to have been colonists with misgivings about what
had happened. Captain Underhill was clearly replying to criticism when
he wrote: 'It may be demanded, Why should you be so furious? (as
some have said). Should not Christians have more mercy and compassion?' He echoes Mason by taking his defence from the Old Testament,
presenting the English – typically – as the put-upon underdog in a
crusade against Evil:

> . . . I would refer you to David's war. When a people is grown to such
> a height of blood and sin against God and man . . . Sometimes the
> Scripture declareth women and children must perish with their

parents ... We had sufficient light from the Word of God for our proceedings.

Although it has a peculiarly ugly and insincere ring for a modern reader, it is important to remember that this kind of theological reasoning was central to the Puritan understanding of history. Every incident, however trivial, was scrutinized for evidence of divine providence: a group of settlers in 1630, for instance, recorded that when they were approached by 'some hundreds' of natives, God, instead of allowing the Indians to attack, 'caused ... [them] to help us with fish at very cheap rates.' This kind of view of the world, heavily imbued with the Calvinist doctrine of pre-destination, allows people no independent motivation – or even, in a sense, morality: they are merely puppets manipulated by God or the Devil in the working out of some great cosmic drama. In such a context, it is difficult to interpret an event as momentous as the massacre at Mystic as anything but divinely ordained. The Pequot War helped, therefore, to choke off other possible approaches to the native-English relations, and to tip the debate over the rights of the colonists decisively in favour of the most rabidly anti-Indian faction. From now on, there would be powerful proof that the killing and displacement of Indians who resisted the English enjoyed God's sanction.

*   *   *

Puritanism also contributed in other ways to the progressive unravelling of the Native American world. For years, the Bay Colony had been raising funds in England to fulfil the 'principall Ende' of its charter, to 'wynn and incite the Natives ... to the Knowledg and Obedience of the onlie true God and Savior of Mankinde, and the Christian Fayth,' but by 1642, according to Thomas Lechford, 'there hath not been sent forth by any Church to learn the Natives language, or to instruct them in the Religion.'

The attitude of the Puritans towards proselytization had always been ambivalent – if, as most Calvinists believed, only a minority even of God's Chosen People, the English, were saved, what chance was there of discovering members of the Elect among 'savages'? – but this lapse clearly created a damaging impression in England. When Massachusetts applied for a royal patent to expand into Narragansett Bay, the English authorities turned the request down, clearly unconvinced by the colonists' promise to take the gospel 'to the Natives, that now sit there in darkness'. To make matters worse, Roger Williams, who had consistently vilified the Puritans for their high-handedness towards Native Americans and their lack of true religion, was successful in obtaining a charter for *his* settlements in the area. Clearly, something had to be done.

Massachusetts shouldered its missionary responsibilities in a typically legalistic and calculating way, developing a strategy that quietly but effectively advanced its worldly aims while appearing to fulfil a religious duty. Like the massacre at Mystic, this policy – based on the same assumption that European and Native American societies could not co-exist – established an approach to 'the Indian problem' which was to be followed by generations of Europeans and Euro-Americans. Just as the Puritans' destruction of the Pequots created a precedent for later genocidal wars, so their 'conveying of the Gospell to the Natives' effectively created the reservation system.

The key feature of this policy was that Indians living within the colonies' borders should be segregated in 'praying towns', where, under the *political* control of the English authorities, they could be offered religious instruction and 'reduced to civilitie'. In March 1644, five *sachems* in the Bay Colony's chartered limits signed a 'covenant of voluntary subjection,' in which they formalized their subject status by surrendering themselves, their people and their land to be governed by Massachusetts' 'just lawes and orders, so farr as wee shalbee made capable of understanding them,' and then committed themselves 'from time to time to bee instructed in the knowledg and worship of God.' Two years later, after a further outcry in England over the Puritans' spiritual inactivity, John Eliot, the 'Apostle to the Indians', started preaching. Over the next quarter of a century, he established more than a dozen 'praying towns', where the converts – equipped with English tools – learnt European skills such as spinning and made themselves useful to the colonists by manufacturing brooms, baskets and eelpots, and selling fish, venison and berries.

Although, undoubtedly, some Native Americans did genuinely convert to Christianity (sometimes in the belief that it would give them access to the source of the Europeans' superior power and protect them against disease), Eliot himself, towards the end of his career, admitted that his results had been disappointing. His associate, Daniel Gookin, conceded in 1674 that of 1,100 'praying Indians', only 119 were baptized or in full communion. The effect of the missions, however, went far beyond this tiny minority. In most tribes, the social, political and spiritual realms were inextricably intertwined, and by decreeing that 'no Indian shall at any time pawwaw, or performe outward worship to their false gods' and that anyone 'deniing the true God ... shalbe put to death', the colonists were subverting the authority of the *sachems* and destroying both the ritual life of the community and the network of kinship obligations that held the group together and gave the individual his or her sense of identity. As Neal Salisbury puts it: 'In requiring the potential convert to reside in a praying town, Puritan missionaries demanded nothing less than a complete repudiation of not only his culture but his community.'

There is, inevitably, little direct testimony from Native Americans themselves about how they saw the missionary effort, but the evidence that we do have strongly suggests that many, if not all of them, recognized its destructive effects. The Narragansett *sachems* showed their usual clear understanding of the threats to their continued integrity and autonomy as a people when they asked Roger Williams in 1653 'to present their petition to the high Sachems of England, that they might not be forced from their religion, and, for not changing their religion, be invaded by war.' And the Wampanoag *sachem* Metacom, son of Massasoit, told a group of Rhode Island Quakers (who 'knew it to be true') that his people 'had a great Fear to have any of their Indians should be called or forced to be Christian Indians' because 'such were in everything more mischievous ... and ... the English made them not subject to their Kings ...'

It is, in a way, bleakly fitting that Metacom (known to the English as King Philip), should have been at the centre of the final desperate attempt by the southern New England tribes to avert their own destruction. In the half-century since his father had welcomed the Pilgrims, the tiny Plymouth settlement had relentlessly eroded the Wampanoag land-base, despite repeated assurances that the encroachment would stop, and when, in 1671, Metacom protested he was forced to sign a humiliating treaty of capitulation. He reputedly told an English friend: 'But little remains of my ancestor's domain, I am resolved not to see the day when I have no country.'

Most accounts of 'King Philip's War' suggest that it started when Metacom, bitterly aggrieved at his treatment, secretly travelled to the other tribes in the Northeast to foment a general uprising against the English. But there is some evidence that this supposed 'conspiracy', like the 'warr' of the Pequots, was deliberately fabricated – or at least exaggerated – by the Puritans, to give them a pretext for resuming the armed conquest of the Indians. As Roger Williams drily observed: 'All men of conscience or prudence ply to windward, to maintain their wars to be defensive.'

When a group of Quakers tried to mediate, the Governor of Plymouth 'refused to have ther quarrell desided; and in a weckes time after we had bine with the Indians the war thus begun.' Not only did the Puritans apparently make the first move, moreover, but Massachusetts and Connecticut seem to have seized, with indecent haste, the opportunity finally to settle accounts with the Narragansett, even though – as Williams said – the *sachems* held 'no agreement with Philip, in this his rising against the English,' and at least one leader advised against 'stirring up' another enemy when the colonies had 'difficulty ynough with . . . one.' The result, ultimately, was a massacre which dwarfed even the assault on Mystic: according to one source, two thousand Narragansett men, women and children perished in a single incident, most of them burnt to death. Increase Mather gleefully reported that when the survivors 'came to see the ashes of their friends, mingled with the ashes of their fort . . . where the English had been doing a good day's work, they Howl'd, they Roar'd, they Stamp'd, they tore their hair; . . . and were the pictures of so many *Devils* in Desperation.'

The war was fought with great ferocity by both sides. Metacom won some notable victories, and for some months kept the Puritans on the defensive, but eventually he was fatally weakened when, under direction from the Governor of the newly created New York colony, his forces were attacked and defeated by Mohawks. Helped by some of the 'praying Indians' and by the Mohegans (Wonkus was by now too alcoholic, obese and pox-ridden to fight himself, but he sent a contingent to support the English), the colonists managed to turn the tide. Metacom's wife and child were captured – 'It must have been as bitter as death to him ...' wrote Mather, 'for the Indians are marvellously fond and affectionate toward their children' – and 'King Philip' himself was finally killed. His head was placed on a spike above the entrance to Plymouth, and his family and hundreds of other Indians – including many who had surrendered under promise of protection – were sold into slavery in Bermuda. With this cataclysmic defeat, Indian resistance in southern New England was effectively broken.

The grim symmetry of the Wampanoags' fate – Massasoit helps the newcomers to establish themselves in a new continent, and two generations later they expel his descendants in chains to another world – is not the only irony. While thousands of Native Americans were burnt or hacked to death as 'diabolical savages', Wonkus, whose drunkenness, cruelty and treachery epitomized the European idea of 'the savage' (having murdered the Narragansett *sachem* Miantonomo on English instructions, he reportedly ate part of the body with the words: 'It is the sweetest meat I ever ate. It makes my heart strong.') and who refused to accept the Christian religion, was remembered as the 'great Friend' of God's chosen people. As wistful yearning came to replace racial and religious hatred as the dominant attitude towards New England's native people, James Fenimore Cooper completed the transformation of Wonkus by using his anglicized name for the gentle Uncas, his fictional Vanishing American, so turning the first of the Mohegans into *The Last of the Mohicans*. By 1789, the surviving Mohegans themselves had caught the prevailing melancholy mood. Complaining that 'all our Fishing, Hunting and Fowling is entirely gone,' they petitioned the State of Connecticut for help:

> The times are Exceedingly Alter'd, Yea the times have turn'd everything upside down, or rather we have Chang'd the good Times, Chiefly by the help of the White People, for in Times past, our Fore-Fathers lived in Peace, Love, and great harmony, and had everything in Great plenty ... But alas, it is not so now ...

5. New York and the 'Ohio Country'

'We shall not be like father and son, but like brothers'

Unlike most of southern New England, upper New York State still has a palpable Native American presence. After four centuries in which most of their neighbours were swept away by successive tides of disease, settlement and warfare, a scattering of Iroquois communities still dots the map, from Akwesasne on the Canadian frontier – where you can buy tax-free cigarettes at the Eastern Door Convenience Store or the Wolf Clan Truck Stop – to the Allegheny reservation on the Pennsylvania border.

Although they are relatively small – the largest is just over 30,000 acres, the smallest a mere 32 acres – and surrounded and interpenetrated by the noise and muddle of modern America, these enclaves still have some of the distinctive feel of independent societies. Whereas many of the present-day Indian settlements in New England originated as 'praying towns' under tight colonial control, the six Iroquois peoples – the Mohawk, Onondaga, Seneca, Oneida, Cayuga and Tuscarora – have never surrendered the right to define themselves or to run their own lives. While the relentless pressure to assimilate has undoubtedly eroded their culture and created enormous tensions and divisions within their communities, they have stubbornly clung on to their languages, their religious beliefs, their social structure and, crucially, the conviction that they remain sovereign nations. On the outskirts of Syracuse, New York, for instance, is the 7,000 acre 'Onondaga Nation Territory', where – unlike most other Native American reservations, which are now generally run by councils elected on the Western model – the government still consists of traditional chiefs appointed by clan mothers.

The key to this extraordinary genius for endurance and renewal is the Iroquois' unique religious and political confederation, the *Hotinon-*

shonni or League of Five (later Six) Nations, which, as well as giving them a deep sense of their separate identity and destiny, enabled them to play a crucial role in the history of colonial America which still has repercussions today. It was the *Hotinonshonni*, more than any other native group, that shaped the experience of Native Americans on the colonial frontier in the century between King Philip's War and the American Revolution. Its influence was not confined to its military and diplomatic power, which compelled the Europeans, and particularly the British, to forge a different kind of relationship with it; its organization and working also attracted (albeit sometimes grudging) admiration from many of the colonists, helping to create new attitudes towards 'the Savage' and contributing to the development of European and Euro-American political thought until well into the nineteenth century.

Because of its fame and importance, generations of Europeans and Euro-Americans have written about the League, leaving a mass of historical and ethnographic material. Much more unusually, its survival into the present means that there is also an alternative, *Iroquois* version of the origins of the *Hotinonshonni* and its relations with the Europeans which reaches back in an unbroken line to the seventeenth century. Although some of this oral tradition has been lost and much of it, like all histories, has been modified over the centuries, it gives us a remarkable insight into the Native American world and an indigenous understanding of events for which there are no other authentic Indian sources.

THE IROQUOIS CREATION ACCOUNT

In the distant past, all the earth was covered by deep water, and the only living things there were water animals. There was no sun, moon, or stars, and the watery earth was in darkness. People lived above the great sky dome. A great ever-blossoming tree grew there in the cloud world, where it shaded the councils of the supernaturals. One day the Great Chief became ill, and he dreamed that if the tree were uprooted he would be cured. He further commanded that his pregnant daughter, Sky Woman, look down at the watery darkness. He told her to follow the roots of the tree, and to bring light and land to the world below. The fire dragon that floated in the hole gave her maize, a mortar, a pot, and firebrands for cooking. Then the Great Ruler wrapped her in the light of the fire dragon and dropped her through the hole.

The animals of the cloud sea were stirred into action by the descending light. Waterfowl rose to cushion Sky Woman's descent with their wings. Beaver dove to find earth to make dry land for Sky Woman. But Beaver drowned and floated lifelessly to the surface. Loon, Duck, and others all tried and failed as well. Finally Muskrat tried, and came back with a paw-full of earth that would spread and grow. 'Who will bear it?' he asked. Turtle rose to bear the growing earth, and the waterfowl gently guided the falling Sky Woman to the new land. Turtle, the Earth Bearer, is still restless from time to time, and when he stirs there are earthquakes and high seas.

Time passed and Sky Woman gave birth to a daughter. The daughter grew rapidly, and when she reached maturity she was visited by a man. He placed two arrows within her, one tipped with chert and the other not. The daughter in turn bore twins. The handsome good twin was born first the usual way, and he was called 'Teharoniawako' (Holder of the Heavens). The ugly evil twin forced himself out through his mother's armpit, killing her in the process. He was called 'Sawiskera' (Mischievous One). In grief, Teharoniawako created the sun from his mother's face. The Evil Twin made darkness to drive the sun west. Teharoniawako drew the moon and the stars from his mother's breast, and created great mountains and straight rivers to grace the land. Sawiskera jumbled the mountains and made the rivers crooked. Teharoniawako set forests on the hills and fruit trees in the valleys, but Sawiskera gnarled the forests and hurled storms against the land. Teharoniawako created human beings, and planted maize, tobacco and other useful plants. Sawiskera created monsters, and made weeds and vermin to attack the plants made by Teharoniawako. Teharoniawako built a fire, which made Sawiskera's legs flake. Teharoniawako then threw more wood on the fire and soon Sawiskera's entire body began to flake, and he ran away. Eventually Teharoniawako defeated his brother, striking him with deer

antlers, and banished him to an underground cave. Yet Sawiskera
can still send out wicked spirits, and their persistence ensures that
there is both good and bad in all things.

The *Hotinonshonni*'s Algonquian enemies called them the 'killer
people', which Basque fishermen translated as *Hilokoa* and French
missionaries eventually wrote down as *Hiroquois*. Thus, like many other
Native American peoples, they came to be known to Europeans not by
their own name but by their neighbours' – generally unflattering –
descriptions of them. More recently, scholars have applied the word
Iroquoia to the Five Nations' homeland, and *Iroquoian* not only to the
Hotinonshonni themselves but to a whole group of culturally and
linguistically related peoples – rather as *Germanic* refers to other
northern Europeans as well as Germans.

At the time of contact, there were Iroquoians scattered over various
parts of eastern North America, but the biggest concentration was a
large wedge lying across the present-day US–Canadian border. The
Hotinonshonni themselves straddled most of New York State and
neighbouring parts of Pennsylvania, Ontario and Quebec; further west,
around the eastern Great Lakes, stretched a string of similar societies:
the Huron, Petun (or Tobacco), Neutral and Erie confederacies. Both
the Iroquois' own accounts and Euro-American scholars suggest that
these peoples were relatively recent arrivals: according to the currently
most widely accepted academic theory, based on archaeological and
linguistic research, they moved to the area from Appalachia around AD
900. By this point, they already had a number of distinctive cultural
traits which allowed them, social scientists believe, to displace and/or
absorb the existing Algonquian-speaking population. Unlike their
Algonquian neighbours at the time, they had already learnt to cultivate
maize as well as beans and squash, which allowed them to develop a
higher population density. Moreover, their 'matrilocal' social structure
– in which married couples live with the wife's mother's family –
followed a pattern that, according to anthropologists, gives an advantage
to expanding tribal peoples. As Dean Snow puts it: '... matrilocal
residence ... breaks up groups of fraternal males, which in turn
suppresses both feuding and internal warfare. At the same time, it
facilitates the organization of external warfare, allowing the intrusive

society to deal effectively with violent resistance from the people being displaced.'

The Iroquois themselves, of course, did not – and do not – view their own society in these abstract and utilitarian terms. For them, as their origin myth makes clear, the significance of maize comes not from the power it gives them to dominate other people but from its status as one of the sacred gifts on which their life depends. (Another version of the story expresses this idea in a different way: when Sky Woman's daughter is buried, maize and other plants spring from her grave, and the Good Twin calls the earth 'Our Mother' because 'their mother had become one with the earth.') The most basic responsibility of the *Hotinonshonni* is to celebrate and sustain this relationship with the sacred through the annual ceremonial cycle, which starts with the Midwinter Ceremony – 'the time when all things are new again' – and moves through a series of ten more seasonal dances and rituals. The aim of the cycle is not directly to solicit spiritual help – the Iroquois, unlike many other peoples, believe it is wrong to *ask* the Creator for anything – but to 'express our appreciation for all life.' As the oral tradition records: 'All these ceremonies will bring us closer to our Creator to remind us of our purpose in this life: to be grateful for all the things we have.'

Similarly, the Iroquois actually *experienced* their 'matrilocal residence pattern' as the 'Longhouse', the focus of their social and emotional life and the central motif of their culture (*Hotinonshonni* means, literally, 'People who build Longhouses'). The Longhouse was a single-storey, birch-bark covered building with a barrel-shaped roof which housed an entire lineage: the – usually elderly – 'clan mother', all her female descendants and their husbands and children. Above the door was carved the clan totem, and inside, flanking a wide central corridor, were separate compartments for each nuclear family, equipped with sleeping platforms, storage areas and a hearth, which was generally shared with the neighbour opposite. As the population of a building grew – in some cases, it could reach as many as a hundred people – extra compartments were added to accommodate the new families. Some longhouses, as a result, could be quite enormous: the remains of one, dated to at least one hundred years before Columbus, are 334 feet long.

According to several *Hotinonshonni* sources, the League was founded around 1450, although some scholars date it to the following century. The oral tradition, which is full of vivid references to the pervasive fear and instability of the Iroquois world at the time, records that Deganawida, 'the Peacemaker', was the son of a young Huron virgin who dreamt that her child 'will be a messenger of the Creator and will bring peace and harmony to the people on earth.' When he grew up, the young man told his mother and grandmother: 'I shall now build my canoe from this white stone, for the time has come for me to start my mission in this world. I know I must travel afar on lakes and rivers to seek out the council smoke of Nations beyond this lake, holding my course toward the sunrise. It is now time for me to go and stop the shedding of blood among human beings.'

Moving from west to east through the territory of the Five Nations, Deganawida encountered a group of hunters who were fleeing from the bloodshed in their own village. He instructed them: 'Go back to your people and tell them that good news of peace, power and righteousness has come to your nation.' Continuing on his journey, he met an evil woman who lured hunters inside with the promise of a meal and then poisoned them. He told her that she must 'stop this wicked practice and accept the good message that I bring from my father ... people shall love one another and live together in peace.' The woman accepted the message, vowing never to harm anyone again, and Deganawida said: 'Since you are the first to accept the Law of Peace, I will declare that it shall be the women who shall possess the title of Chieftanship. They shall name the Chiefs.'

In perhaps the best-known version of the story Deganawida's next convert was a vicious cannibal, Ayonhwathah (later to be anglicized and fictionalized by Longfellow as *Hiawatha*), who also repented when the Peacemaker gave him 'a new mind.' Deganawida sent Ayonhwathah to carry the message of peace to Thadodaho, a particularly malevolent Onondaga shaman with snakes in his hair, while he himself took it to the Mohawk Nation. After demonstrating his spiritual power, Deganawida succeeded in converting the Mohawks, who became the founders of the League.

But Thadodaho, meanwhile, had rejected Ayonhwathah's approaches and, in a fit of fury, killed his three daughters. Devastated, Ayonhwathah started towards the Mohawk country. As he reached a lake, a flock of ducks carried the water away so that he could cross dry-shod. The bottom was strewn with shell beads, which Ayonhwathah collected and put in a buckskin bag. Some of them he threaded on strings as a symbol of his grief.

Deganawida found Ayonhwathah wandering aimlessly in the forest. Taking the beads, he made more strings and then, laying them out one at a time, he spoke, for the first time, the words of the 'Requickening Address', the ceremony of condolence. This cleared Ayonhwathah's mind of grief, and together he and Deganawida went on to convert the other four nations of the League. Finally, they returned to Thadodaho and, backed by the full authority of the Five Nations, were at last able to 'make his mind straight.' Thadodaho was then invited to become Speaker of the League, an office which conferred on him the status of first among equals, and at his village Ayonhwathah planted the 'Great Tree of Peace,' under whose shade 'we have prepared seats for you and your cousin *Sachems* to keep and watch the Confederate Council Fire.'

The *Kaianerekowa* (Great Law) established by Deganawida is immensely complex and intricate. At its heart is the fifty-strong Council of League Chiefs, to which all the Five Nations contribute delegates (or *royaneh*). The selection process varies from nation to nation, but in every case the chiefs are male and the decision to appoint – and, if necessary, remove – them is made by clan mothers, thus ensuring a balance both between the sexes and between the different clans. A man of outstanding ability who does not qualify for one of the hereditary *sachemships* controlled by the clans may nonetheless still join the Council by becoming a 'Pine Tree Chief'. The League in its totality is conceived as a giant Longhouse, with the Senecas guarding the western door, the Mohawks the eastern door and the Onondagas keeping the fire in the middle. Each chief is a tree or a support pole, helping to strengthen the structure as a whole.

The Five Nations are not all equally represented on the Council – there are fourteen Onondaga *royaneh*, for example, but only eight Senecas – but this does not mean that power is unevenly distributed, because decisions are reached through consensus rather than majority voting. To increase the chances of agreement, issues are sometimes discussed first in a caucus (a word thought to derive from the Algonquian *cawaassough*, meaning an adviser). Particularly when there are strong differences, the older chiefs may also wait until everyone else has spoken and then try to find some common ground between them. If, after exhaustive discussion, there is no consensus, each nation – or even each faction within a nation – is free to go its own way as long as it does not harm any other member of the League. The danger that disagreement will degenerate into open conflict is reduced by the network of clan affiliations, which extends across national boundaries: a Cayuga belonging to the Wolf Clan, for instance, will regard an Oneida Wolf Clan member as his clan brother, which means he is strictly prohibited from making war against him. League decisions, as well as treaties, important historical events and the provisions of the Great Law itself, are symbolized in intricately patterned 'wampum belts' and passed down orally through 'Wampum Keepers', who are specially selected and trained to remember them word for word.

The League, with its blending of male and female, hereditary and elected, and its remarkable success in ending the endemic warring between the *Hotinonshonni* without the use of force or a strong executive, has fascinated and inspired generations of European and Euro-American thinkers, many of whom have seen in it a possible answer to some of the enduring political questions of their own culture. Lewis Henry Morgan, a nineteenth-century lawyer whose book, *The League of the Iroquois*, is often cited as the foundation of modern ethnology, proclaimed that: 'Their whole civil policy was averse to the concentration of power in the hands of any single individual, but inclined to the opposite principle of division among a number of equals . . .

The government sat lightly upon the people, who, in effect, were governed but little. It secured to each that individual independence, which the . . . [Iroquois] knew how to prize as well as the Saxon race . . .' Using Morgan's work as a source, Friedrich Engels saw the *Hotinonshonni* as a perfect example of the Marxist idea of 'Primitive Communism': under their 'wonderful constitution,' he wrote in *The Origin of the Family, Private Property and the State*, there are 'No soldiers, no gendarmes or police, no nobles, king, regents, prefects, or judges, no prisons, no lawsuits . . . There cannot be any poor or needy . . . All are equal and free – the women included.' The theme of women's rights was taken up by members of the suffrage movement: as Harriet Maxwell Converse put it, rather flowerily:

> As the woman of today stands advocate and petitioner of her own cause, should she not offer an oblation of gratitude to the memory of the Iroquois Indian who called the earth his 'mighty mother' and who, through a sense of justice, rendered to the mothers of his people the rights maternal, political, social, civil, religious and of land!

But to interpret the League in terms of the preoccupations of Western culture is to – at least partially – misunderstand it. Although personal autonomy was (and is) very important to the Iroquois and other native peoples, the Great Law was not founded on the kind of abstract concept of individual human rights developed in Europe during the Enlightenment. Unlike the monarchies of the Old World, the *Hotinonshonni* had no fixed social or political hierarchy from which a citizen might need legal protection: indeed, the very *idea* of an individual as an unchanging entity with inalienable rights would have been largely meaningless in a society in which, through ritual, a captive could be given the identity of someone who had died. Deganawida's vision, deeply rooted in the Iroquois origin story, was very different: it saw the universe as a compound of good and evil in which the harmony of Teharoniawako's world was constantly being warped and unbalanced by the activities of his wicked twin. The Peacemaker's mission, as the many accounts of the League's formation make clear, was to re-establish the natural equilibrium on which the well-being of individuals, societies and the whole of creation depended. He achieved this not by *destroying* witches and wrongdoers but by *healing* them, 'making their minds straight' so that they could rediscover the fundamental goodness in themselves – an idea movingly expressed in the redemption of cannibals and sorcerers such as Thadodaho. Deganawida's role, therefore, was essentially shamanic: to correct the imbalance which caused both personal and collective ill-health. He himself was quite explicit about this: 'Health means Peace, for that is what comes when minds are sane and bodies cared for.'

The story of Deganawida still permeates the working and symbolism of the League. When a man becomes a *royaneh*, he inherits the name and function of one of the fifty chiefs who sat on the first Council. Meetings still begin with the elaborate Condolence Ceremony, which dispels the 'insanity of grief' in those who have lost relatives since the last council and 'raises up' dead chiefs by ritually installing the new holders of their office. And Wampum Keepers continue to recite, in every detail, the terms of the Great Law and the experiences that shaped the history of the *Hotinonshonni*.

THE ORIGIN OF MAN

When Teharonhiawako created all the waters, plants, trees and animals of the world, he decided that he should create a being in his likeness from the natural world.

He wanted this being to have a superior mind so it would have the responsibility of looking after his creations. Then he decided it would be better if he created more than one being and give to each similar instructions and see if over a period of time, they would carry them through.

The first being Teharonhiawako made was from the bark of a tree; the second from the foam of the great salt water; the third from the black soil, and the last from the red earth.

All this he did in one day. He started in the early morning as the sun greeted the new day by picking certain types of bark from the tree [of] life and created a human form, reflected against the sky the form gave a yellowish appearance. Teharonhiawako decided that this would be one type of human that would exist on this world. After Teharonhiawako finished his first human, he then went to the great salt waters and took from the sea some white foam, together with other elements of the natural world he created another being. This being appeared pale in contrast to the natural surroundings, but he was satisfied that he has [sic] created another special kind of human being. Next Teharonhiawako travelled to the thickest part of a large forest and brought out some black soil, again with other elements of the natural world he created another human being. This being was very dark in colour and he was pleased that he had created still another type of being for the world.

Now Teharonhiawako thought to himself, it is getting towards

the end of the day and I have created three beings, since every-
thing on this world exists in cycles of four, I will create one more
being. Thus he again looked for something different within the
natural world and this time he found some reddish-brown earth.
With this he again combined other elements from the land and
created a human form. When he finished he observed that this
form blended very well with the natural surroundings, especially
against the setting sun, which gave the form a reddish colour.

Teharonhiawako now gathered the four human forms into one
area and said to himself, 'I have been very careful in providing
certain characteristics into each form that will reflect their own
unique and strong qualities. I will now give life to each form and
see if they benefit from their gifts.'

As the beings came to life he observed just how evident their
uniqueness became. The white being was the first one to move
about, he was also the most curious, observing closely all his
surroundings. Next, the black and yellow slowly started to move
about. When the black being picked a brightly coloured object
that he was attracted to, the white being pounced on him and
pushed him to the ground, taking over the object. At that same
instant, the yellow being stood up for the black and soon, a fight
broke out between the three.

Teharonhiawako noticed that the fourth being was still sitting
on the ground, camouflaged by his surroundings. Now it became
clear to Teharonhiawako that there was no way these four could
exist in the same environment and survive.

Teharonhiawako stopped their quarrelling and brought them
back to one place and told them, 'There is a reason why you were
not created in the same manner, just as there are birds and
animals who look alike, they are different in their ways, so are
you. They have their own language, their own songs but have
learned to share their world. It is for this reason that I have
created you, that in time you will all learn to respect and
appreciate your differences. It is very evident that I can not put
you together to watch over my creations, for you would probably
destroy it as well as yourselves. You need to learn how to get along
with each other, as well as with other living things. I will help you

do this, but first I will have to keep you apart. You will come back together after a time when I have sent a messenger to visit each of you and give you a way to be thankful for the good things, as well as respect for other living creatures.'

Teharonhiawako then took the white, black and yellow beings across the salt waters and placed them far from each other. The red being he kept at his place of origin. Teharonhiawako told him, 'You will be called Onkwehonwe (original being). You will call me Sonkwaiatison (The Creator), I have given you the gift of life. You were created from the earth of this Island. I now realize that you would not survive very long among the others, for you are too much a part of nature, which is good, but you will need time before you come in contact with the other beings. You will also be given a sacred way by a messenger who will visit you and your descendants.'

Now Teharonhiawako thought to himself, 'They will all have a chance to learn of the reason for their existence and of a good way to live.'

Jacques Cartier bartered with Iroquoian-speaking relatives of the Five Nations during his explorations of the St. Lawrence between 1534 and 1542, and there is archaeological evidence that, by around 1550, European trade goods had started to reach the *Hotinonshonni* themselves. Much of this traffic, however, probably came either through casual contacts or via other Indians. The Iroquois' traditional Algonquian enemies stood between them and the St. Lawrence, making regular trade with the French almost impossible. The *Hotinonshonni* became all too aware of how vulnerable this made them when, in 1609, Samuel de Champlain and a party of his Huron and Algonquian allies broke with the traditions of Indian warfare and used firearms against an army of Mohawks. Although the Iroquois intermittently signed peace treaties and traded with the French over the next 150 years, this attack – which is still commemorated in a wampum 'Record Belt' – created a bitter hostility which France was never able entirely to overcome.

In 1614 the Dutch established Fort Nassau (later to be rebuilt as Fort Orange) close to present-day Albany, New York. With direct

access to European goods, the Iroquois were able to build on the
military and political strength of the League to become the dominant
Native American power in the region. But in 1634, this growth was
abruptly halted when, for the first time, an epidemic of smallpox swept
through the *Hotinonshonni* and neighbouring peoples, killing at least
half the population in little more than three months. Mortality was
particularly high among the elderly and the very young, simultaneously
devastating both the accumulated knowledge of the culture and its
hopes for the future.

For a society which saw such a close association between physical
health and the well-being of the universe, the impact of the disease
must have been particularly terrible. One response – demonstrating
the Iroquois' extraordinary resilience and gift for self-renewal in the
face of disaster – was probably an increase in the numbers and activities
of the shamanic organizations which traditionally dealt (and still deal)
with sickness. These so-called 'Medicine Societies', which are among
the most complex in any Native American culture, harness a range of
spiritual forces to diagnose and cure illnesses: for the Husk Faces, for
instance, the tutelaries are agricultural spirits, while the Company of
Mystic Animals – as the name suggests – uses bear, otter and other
potent 'animal masters'. The exact form of a curing ritual is often
selected in response to one of the patient's dreams, which the
Hotinonshonni – rather like Freud – see as expressions of suppressed
desire that must be acknowledged and fulfilled.

As evidence that they were profoundly changed by European
contact, anthropologists point out that one of the Medicine Societies'
most distinctive features – the 'false face' masks with hideously
distorted eyes, noses and mouths which some members wear during
ceremonies and which have become probably the best-known images
in Iroquois culture – do not seem to have occurred before the
seventeenth century. The *Hotinonshonni* themselves, however, explain
the masks through stories which emphasize their *meaning* rather than
their chronological origin. According to oral tradition, when the Creator
was finishing his work he met the headman of the Faces, who claimed
that it was *he* who had made the world. They decided to settle the
question by seeing who could make a distant mountain come to him.
The Creator was successful, and when the headman spun round to see

what had happened his face smashed into the rock. Although he had lost, the Creator realized that the headman had significant power, so he asked him to help hunters and cure the sick. The headman agreed, on condition that the people made portrait masks of him and gave him offerings of tobacco and corn mush.

The decades following the first outbreak of smallpox brought further turmoil to the Iroquoian world. Starting in 1641, the *Hotinonshonni* launched a series of attacks on their relatives around the Great Lakes which resulted, by 1657, in the virtual destruction of the Eries, Neutrals and Hurons. Some historians have seen these conflicts – often called 'Beaver Wars' – primarily as attempts by the Iroquois to secure new sources of pelts after over-hunting their own stocks of fur-bearing animals. It is likely, however, that they were at least in part an extreme form of the traditional 'mourning wars', held to avenge and replace the dead, which the massive losses caused by European disease had driven out of control. Certainly, although the Five Nations are sometimes accused of having 'exterminated' the other Iroquoians, their aim does not seem to have been genocidal. As the *Hotinonshonni* scholar Te-ha-ne-torens puts it: 'To read the history . . . written by non-Indians one is led to believe that all of the Hurons were massacred by the Five Nations, that none were given any quarter, that all died at the stake, etc.' In fact, he points out, 'After the Hurons were conquered by the Five Nations in 1650 many were taken in by the Iroquois. Whole villages were adopted by the Senecas and Mohawks.' Evidence for this process of wholesale absorption comes not only from the Five Nations' own traditions – there is still a surviving 'Huron Alliance Belt' from the time – but also from documentary sources. French records, for instance, show that in 1657 a party of Five Nations chiefs went to Quebec to persuade nearly 600 Huron refugees to settle among the Mohawks, and a decade later Jesuits reported that almost two-thirds of one Iroquois community were adopted Hurons and Algonquians.

Te-ha-ne-torens and other historians have suggested that the French – and particularly the Jesuits – deliberately exaggerated the Iroquois' brutality for their own purposes. The Hurons were France's major Indian allies in the area and many of them had already accepted Jesuit missions and converted to Catholicism, so the French clearly had compelling motives for backing them. In an attempt to defeat the Five

Nations and extend its influence into their territory, New France tried repeatedly to divide the *Hotinonshonni* against themselves and to incite their Native American neighbours to attack them, and it may have sought to justify this strategy by painting the League – as the Connecticut Puritans painted the Pequots – as uniquely cruel and vicious. But it is also possible that at least some Europeans, trying – naturally enough – to make sense of what they saw in terms of their own culture, simply misunderstood what the Iroquois were doing. Even before it had been disrupted by contact, the fluid world of the Iroquoians – with its constant shifts of population, allegiance and even identity – must have been immensely difficult for someone brought up with the rigid certainties of the nation state to interpret. In the sudden vortex created by trade, disease, warfare, settlement and missionary activity it was thrown into what looked like chaos. Not only did the Five Nations absorb refugee Hurons and Neutrals, but many *Hotinonshonni* themselves converted to Catholicism and moved to French missions in Canada. (By 1700, it has been estimated, around two-thirds of all Mohawks were living in Quebec.) Through all these changes, the Iroquois population continued relentlessly to decline, reaching, by 1700, less than a quarter of its level in 1630.

The colonial map, meanwhile, was also being dramatically redrawn, with profound consequences for the Iroquois – and, ultimately, for Indians throughout North America. In 1664, England seized New Netherland from the Dutch, renaming it New York, and ten years later the Duke of York (later James II) appointed Edmund Andros to be the new colony's Governor. Unlike the founders of New England, who wanted to found a 'city on a hill' free from the religious and political restrictions of the Old World and uncorrupted by the savagery of the New, Andros was a pragmatic royalist whose main aim was to extend and consolidate the power of the English empire. For him – as for the French in Canada – Indians were less a physical and spiritual threat than a potential asset in the intensifying struggle between France, Spain and England for mastery of North America. His radically different approach was to set the tone for much of Britain's dealings with Native Americans over the next century.

Andros came to office almost as King Philip's War erupted in New England, and, fearful that the conflict might develop into a general uprising against the English, he incited the Mohawks to launch the fatal attack which finally broke Metacom. Immediately afterwards, however, he let it be known 'that all Indyans, who will come in and submitt, shall be received to live under the protection of the Government...' Refugees from the war flooded into New York, and Andros firmly prohibited the New England colonies from either pursuing them or paying the Mohawks to capture them. He even refused to return the seven 'principle Indians' held to have instigated the war.

Andros justified his stance by claiming that unless the Indians were confident of his protection they would be driven into the arms of the French, thereby increasing the threat to all the English settlements in America. It seems clear, however, that he was also trying to enhance the power of New York – and hence the Crown – at the expense of the more independent-minded Puritan colonies. In 1677 he called a conference at Albany, at which the Mohawks undertook not to carry out raids in New England and the Puritans agreed, in return, that only New York should treat directly with the Iroquois. This limit on their autonomy, which effectively made them subsidiary to New York, evidently displeased Massachusetts Bay and Connecticut, but there was not a great deal they could do about it: unlike independent Rhode Island, the new colony was a royal possession and could not be challenged or ignored with impunity.

Andros made the Iroquois the cornerstone of his Native American policy, because, with the collapse of the Mahicans and other Algonquians, they had become – as his successor Thomas Dongan put it in 1687 – 'the awe and dread of all the Indians in these parts of America, and ... a better defence to us than if they were so many Christians.' He signed a treaty with the Five Nations, acknowledging their pre-eminent position and allowing them to draw other tribes – their 'children' – into an alliance with the English. Anyone joining this 'Chain of Covenant,' he explained, 'shall be protected from any outrage or force and I shall not suffer them to bee disturbed or harmed, but shall looke upon any violence offered that way, as done to my selfe.' He seems to have been as good as his word: the Schagticokes, for instance, gratefully renewing their membership of the alliance in 1700, recalled that 'wee were allmost dead when wee left New England and were first received into this government.'

The strategy behind the Covenant Chain was simple. It was eloquently expressed by Governor George Thomas of Pennsylvania when
he addressed representatives of some of the older colonies in 1744:

> These Indians by their situation are a Frontier to some of [the
> English colonies], and from thence, if Friends, are Capable of
> Defending their Settlements; If Enemies, of making Cruel Ravages
> upon them; If Neuters, they may deny the French a Passage through
> their Country, and give us timely Notice of their Designs. These are
> but some of the Motives for cultivating a good Understanding with
> them ... This has been the Method of Newyork and Pennsylvania,
> and will not put you to so much Expence in Twenty Years as the
> carrying on a War against them will do in One.

But, from the start, the two sides clearly saw the Covenant Chain
very differently. For the Iroquois, it was an extension of the same
principles that underlay the League: an association of essentially
autonomous peoples who combined for mutual defence. Deganawida
had already foreseen that other groups might want to take refuge with
the *Hotinonshonni*: the Wing or Dust Fan of the Confederate Nations
– perhaps the best-known of the wampum belts – explicitly provides
that 'If any man or any nation outside of the Five Nations shall obey
the Laws of The Great Peace and make known their disposition to the
Chiefs of the Confederacy, they may trace the Roots to the Tree and if
their minds are clean and they are obedient and promise to obey the
wishes of the Confederate Council, they shall be welcome to take
shelter beneath The Tree Of The Long Leaves.' According to Te-ha-
ne-torens, the *Hotinonshonni* have records of at least thirty-nine other
Native American groups that were taken in by the League. As he puts
it: 'Iroquois territory, especially after the white man came, became the
great asylum of many Indian peoples. It became a great "melting pot"
of dispossessed Indian peoples.'

While, unquestionably, the dependent nations were junior partners,
they were not *subjects*, and could not be legally compelled to accept
decisions of the League (although, of course, their relative weakness
might make it very difficult for them to refuse). As so often in Native
American societies, the relationship was seen in terms of reciprocity
and kinship: just as, within the League, the Mohawks, Onondagas and

Senecas were 'older brothers' and the Cayugas and Oneidas 'younger brothers', the non-Iroquois members of the alliance were frequently known as 'nephews' and would respond by addressing the *Hotinon-shonni* as 'uncles'.

The English, however, chose to view the Chain as a kind of pyramid, with New York at the top, the Iroquois (and, to some extent, the New England colonies) in the middle, and the various dependent Native American nations at the bottom. Authority over all these peoples and their lands flowed down the hierarchy from its ultimate source in the English Crown. This fitted with the still essentially feudal notions of seventeenth- and early eighteenth-century Europe and, at a stroke, gave England a defensive buffer for her settlements and – in her terms – sovereignty over any group that sought protection from the League. The Iroquois were encouraged to extend their influence far beyond the existing colonies into the interior, thereby acquiring English 'title' to vast tracts of North America – particularly the fertile 'Ohio Country' – that other European powers were also trying to acquire. In an attempt to bolster this dubious claim, writers such as Cadwallader Colden, whose first volume of a history of the Five Nations appeared in 1727, represented the League as an imperial power subjecting other peoples 'by right of conquest.' As Francis Jennings puts it: 'Lacking a reasonable alternative until the French could be forced off the continent, the British donated an empire to the Iroquois in order to claim it for themselves.'

The *Hotinonshonni*, for their part, were well aware of the threat posed to their own independence by their relationship with England and resisted it with consummate diplomatic skill. According to their oral tradition, the 'Two Row Wampum,' for instance, which shows two parallel lines of dark beads, 'symbolizes the agreement and conditions under which the Iroquois welcomed the white peoples to this land.'

'You say that you are our Father and I am your son.' We say, 'We will not be like Father and Son, but like Brothers.' This . . . belt confirms our words. These two rows will symbolize two paths or two vessels, travelling down the same river together. One, a birch bark canoe, will be for the Indian People, their laws, their customs and their ways. The other, a ship, will be for the white people and their laws, their

customs and their ways. We shall each travel the river together, side
by side, but in our own boat. Neither of us will make compulsory
laws or interfere in the internal affairs of the other. Neither of us will
try to steer the other's vessel.'

England was still far too reliant on the Iroquois' protection and
goodwill to risk a direct challenge to their independence. As the
eighteenth century progressed, the European competition for American
colonies was becoming even more feverish. French traders, moving
down the Mississippi, had already pushed far into the interior, and in
1701 France consolidated her presence in the area by appointing the
first Governor. By 1718, when New Orleans was founded as the capital
of the new province, the Spanish were at work on the Alamo and had
already moved north and east into the Plains region, establishing a
chain of mission stations which at one point passed only fifteen miles
from the nearest French settlement. Both countries sent out
expeditions to explore further and seek the friendship of the Plains
tribes. The English, meanwhile, were pushing south and west from
their seaboard colonies to make trading agreements with the Cherokees, Chickasaws, Choctaws, Creeks and neighbouring tribes, bringing
them dangerously close both to French Louisiana and to Spanish
Florida. These constantly shifting frontiers provided almost limitless
opportunities for conflict, with the European powers ruthlessly manip-
ulating settlers and traders for their own ends, or – increasingly –
finding that a local friction between colonists had dragged them into a
wider confrontation which, try as they might, they could not avoid or
contain.

For thirty-eight of the seventy-four years between 1689 and 1763
England (and, after the Act of Union in 1707, Britain) was at war with
one or both of her colonial rivals in North America, who also spent
much of the time fighting between themselves. In almost every one of
these conflicts, Native Americans played a crucial part, often contributing the bulk of the troops for colonial war parties – which sometimes
contained no more than a handful of Europeans – and almost invariably
suffering the heaviest losses. Even people who were generally unsympathetic to Native Americans acknowledged the importance of their
contribution: when General Braddock (having arrogantly ignored

Indian advice) led the British to defeat at Fort Duquesne in 1755, for instance, George Washington wrote of the Indians: 'They are much more serviceable than twice their number of white men. If they return to their nation, no words can tell how much they will be missed.'

Throughout this period – despite disputes between members of the League and lapses into neutrality – the *Hotinonshonni* remained Britain's most powerful and consistent allies in North America, and the need to maintain good relations with them forced the colonial authorities to follow France's example and accommodate more to the demands of Indian culture. The very image of the 'Chain of Covenant' owed more to the rich metaphorical language of the *Hotinonshonni* – the Longhouse, the Great Tree of Peace – than to the literalistic legalism of Europe. Soldiers and administrators quickly learnt that, in order to secure Iroquois agreement and co-operation, they had to adopt the Native American style of diplomacy, in which meetings were primarily rituals of reciprocity, held to renew the foundations of the alliance itself. Only after days of feasting, speeches and exchange of gifts could they begin to transact specific business, and even then – given the consensual nature of Iroquois culture – a definite decision might take weeks of discussion, or never be reached at all. William Bull describes one conference at Albany

> There were about 130 men from the Six Nations, their wives and children made up above 300. They made huts for themselves on the hills ... Here they had fresh meat, bread and beer served to them every day, the cost each day amounting to £85 our currency ...
>
> On the 4th of July ... they condoled with His Excellency on the death of the Prince of Wales, and His Excellency returned the condolence on the loss of several of the warriors and sachems [for] they never proceed upon business till the ceremony of condolence is performed ...
>
> On the 6th, the Governor [sat] in a chair in the street, before his house, and the council of this province, and the commissioners from South Carolina, Boston and Connecticut being seated on either side of him, and the Indian Secretary seated at a table before him, and the Six Nations seated on logs placed in the street ... He then cautioned them against the artifices of the French, and proposed to them to destroy the French Fort at Niagara on their land ...

On the 8th of July they answered the Governor, paragraph by paragraph.

The British relationship with their allies, and particularly with the Iroquois, partly reflected and partly contributed to a generally more favourable European view of Native Americans during much of the eighteenth century. The horrifyingly cruel and destructive wars between Catholics and Protestants in the previous century – and, in England, the Civil War – had left many people, particularly among the élite, deeply wary of the kind of religious extremism that had driven the Puritans to New England and sanctioned their treatment of the Indians there. Christian dogma was under attack both from Enlightenment philosophers such as Voltaire and Hume, who had begun to question the very roots of its claim to an exclusive, revealed truth, and from science – especially the work of Sir Isaac Newton – which seemed to confirm the Deist view of the universe as a giant machine set in motion by an impersonal prime mover rather than the Theists' belief that it was the creation of a personal, interventionist God. Although History was still understood as a linear process, its dominant force was increasingly seen as the scientific principle of inevitable Progress rather than divine intervention. This encouraged the idea that there might be a systematic relationship between different cultures and societies: that they might, in fact, represent different stages of development.

Revulsion from the bigotry, intolerance and 'superstition' of seventeenth-century Christianity was accompanied by a new enthusiasm for the other major strand of European civilization: the legacy of the 'pagan' ancient world. Painters, poets, composers and architects strove for the classical ideals of order, harmony and the supremacy of human Reason, using forms and *motifs* drawn directly from Graeco–Roman culture. One of the most popular themes, a kind of shadow side to the belief in Progress, was the Golden Age, the period at the dawn of history when, it was thought, humanity lived free of modern venality and tyranny. The new art of landscape design turned parks and gardens into images of Arcadia where nymphs and swains could frolic in pastoral bliss, and in a few cases – such as Marie-Antoinette's hamlet in the grounds of Versailles, where she and her ladies played at being shepherdesses – people actually tried to act out the fantasy of lost innocence.

This climate created an intense interest in indigenous Americans. In his famous essay *On the Cannibals*, the sixteenth-century French philosopher, Michel de Montaigne, had already written in Arcadian terms about three Brazilian Indians he had met in Paris.

> Those peoples . . . seem to me to be barbarous only in that they have been hardly fashioned by the mind of man, still remaining close neighbours to their original state of nature . . . it seems to me that what experience has taught us about . . . [them] surpasses . . . all the descriptions with which poetry has beautifully painted the Age of Gold.

In the most famous passage, Montaigne recorded that the 'natives, unaware of what price in peace and happiness they would have to pay to buy a knowledge of our corruptions,' were taken on a tour of the city, where they were shocked to see men 'fully bloated with all sorts of comforts while . . . [others] were begging at their doors, emaciated with poverty and hunger: they found it odd that those destitute . . . [men] should put up with such injustice . . .'

Other writers, particularly the Jesuits working among the Hurons and other peoples in Canada, stressed many of the same themes. Paul Le Jeune, who lived with a group of Innu (Montagnais) in 1634, mingles contempt for their 'wretchedness' and disapproval of their religion with a kind of wistful admiration for their 'naturalness' and open-handedness:

> . . . if it is a great blessing to be free from a great evil, our Savages are happy; for the two tyrants who provide hell and torture for many of our Europeans, do not reign here in their great forests, – I mean ambition and avarice . . .
>
> I almost believed, heretofore, that the Pictures of the Roman Emperors represented the ideal of the painters rather than men who had ever existed, so strong and powerful are their heads; but I see here upon the shoulders of these people the heads of Julius Caesar, of Pompey, of Augustus . . .
>
> . . . if it is a great blessing to be free from a great evil, our Savages are happy; for the two tyrants who provide hell and torture for many of our Europeans, do not reign here in their great forests – I mean ambition and avarice . . .
>
> . . .

The absence of ceremony spares these simple people many words. It seems to me in the golden age they must have done like this . . .

Some of the enthusiasm for the 'Noble Savage' was simply fashion. Gangs of youths in Paris, for example, cut their hair Iroquois-style and called themselves Mohawks, while English aristocrats vied with each other to entertain the *Hotinonshonni* leader Theyanoguin (known to the Europeans as Hendrick) when he was brought to London to meet Queen Anne in 1710. There was, however, a less frivolous side to it. The Baron de Lahontan, who stayed with the Hurons between 1683 and 1694, wrote a series of influential books about his experiences which again emphasized the sharp difference – as he saw it – between the liberty of Native Americans and the tyranny suffered by Europeans. One of his Huron informants told him:

> We are born free and united brothers, each as much a great lord as the other, while you are all the slaves of one sole man. I am the master of my body, I dispose of myself, I do what I wish, I am the first and the last of my Nation . . . subject only to the great Spirit . . .

Lahontan's ideas – he coined the word 'anarchy' to describe the Hurons' political system – were widely disseminated not only through his own work but through a series of plays and operas. Perhaps the best known was Delisle de la Drevetière's *Arlequin Sauvage*, the story of a French woman fleeing to live in freedom with her Native American paramour, which became hugely popular and made an enormous impression on – among others – the young Jean-Jacques Rousseau. In England, even the Tory Anglican Samuel Johnson, as well as inveighing against the iniquities of slavery, wrote an affecting account of an 'Indian chief' unjustly deprived of his land and liberty. You can get a sense of how far this cultural shift had gone from comparing the devil-infested descriptions of Indian culture given by the Virginians and the Puritans – or even the Jesuits – with Jean-Bernard Bossu's account of his visit to Fort Toulouse in 1759. Along the way, he and his party met throngs of Indians who plied them with bread, turkeys, venison, pancakes, eggs and tongues, and when he arrived he heard a chief declaiming:

> Young men and warriors! Do not disregard the MASTER OF LIFE. The sky is blue – the sun is without spots – the weather is fair – the

ground is white – everything is quiet on the face of the earth, and the blood of men ought not to be spilt on it. We must beg the MASTER OF LIFE to preserve it pure and spotless among the nations that surround us.

To a certain extent, this outpouring of enthusiasm for Native America was only the most extreme example of a pattern that has recurred again and again over the last five hundred years: while settlers on the frontier continue to see the 'savage' as a demon fit only to be killed and dispossessed, their compatriots living in large towns or imperial capitals have become romantically infatuated with the 'poor Indian'. In the eighteenth century, however, this process was accompanied by a real intellectual excitement and curiosity. As Europeans tried hesitantly to identify principles for a new, less despotic political system, and their descendants in the New World groped towards self-government and independence, there was a genuine feeling that Native Americans – and, particularly, the egalitarian and non-coercive League of the Iroquois – might offer a possible model. The Onondaga *sachem* Canasatego clearly struck a chord with some of his listeners when, frustrated by the squabbling of the English colonies, he told the Commissioners of Pennsylvania, Virginia and Maryland in 1744:

> We heartily recommend Union and a good agreement between you, our brethren . . .
>
> Our wise forefathers established union and amity between the Five Nations; this has made us formidable; this has given us great weight and authority with our neighbouring nations.
>
> We are a powerful Confederacy; and, by your observing the same methods our wise forefathers have taken, you will acquire fresh strength and power.

Among Canastego's audience was Benjamin Franklin, who took notes on his speech and used several elements from the *Hotinonshonni* constitution in his own plan for a confederation of the colonies ten years later. 'It would be a very strange thing,' he argued, 'if Six Nations of ignorant savages should be capable of forming a scheme for such a union, and be able to execute in such a manner as that it has subsisted ages, and appears indissoluble; and yet that a like union should be impracticable for ten or a dozen English Colonies.' Thomas Paine, the radical Quaker who first used the phrase 'United States of America', was also deeply preoccupied with the Iroquois, and wrote, in 1794, that 'the condition of millions, in every country in Europe, is far worse than if they had been born before civilization began, or had been born among the Indians of North-America . . .' Although the extent to which the American Founding Fathers were *directly* influenced by the *Hotinonshonni* is open to question – over the last few years it has been the subject of a heated academic debate – it is quite clear that the intellectual atmosphere in which they worked had been profoundly shaped by the *idea* of the League and the close identification of Native Americans with liberty.

But, however genuine, this greater sympathy and admiration for Native Americans did not halt the process of their destruction. Tribes continued to be devastated by disease; settlers continued to pour into Indian lands, sometimes resorting to massacre or forcible removal if they encountered resistance, despite occasional – and generally very feeble – attempts by the governors to stop them; and many imperial officials and generals, untouched by the more liberal attitude at home, continued to view Native Americans, even as they exploited them, with a hatred and bigotry rivalling Captain John Mason's. The French governor of Louisiana, for instance, reported after one imperially inspired conflict: 'The Choctaws . . . have raised about four hundred scalps, and made one hundred prisoners . . . [This] is a most important advantage which we have obtained, the more so, that it has not cost one drop of French blood, through the care I took of opposing those barbarians to one another. Their self-destruction operated in this manner is the sole efficacious way of insuring tranquillity in the colony.' And the English soldier Lord Jeffrey Amherst thought Indians 'a vile and fickle crew,' whom, when he no longer needed their military support, he was 'fully resolved . . . to extirpate . . . root and branch.'

The Iroquois were not immune from this hostility or from the erosion of their own land and power, but with immense diplomatic skill they managed to maintain a key role for themselves. By continuing to take in tribes displaced from other areas – including, in 1722, their own relatives the Tuscaroras, who had been driven out of North Carolina and were formally adopted as the Sixth Nation of the League – they were able to maintain their population and their formidable military strength. At the same time, they cleverly reminded Britain that they held the balance of power, playing on English insecurities by subtly suggesting that they might be compelled to transfer their allegiance to the French. In 1753, for instance, on the eve of the conflict that led to the Seven Years War, Theyanoguin complained to New York about the steady advance of settlers on their land and their exposure to French attack while 'you sit in peace and quietness here.' He then let slip that the French had sent *wampum* to the Iroquois with an invitation to talk, adding drily that their intention was probably to lure the Mohawks to a feast and murder them. When the Governor of New York Admiral George Clinton ignored the hint and refused to offer adequate redress, Theyanoguin was furious: 'The covenant chain is broken ... You are not to expect to hear of me any more, and Brother we desire to hear no more of you.'

The Lords of Trade in London were horrified at Clinton's failure to mollify the *Hotinonshonni*. 'When we consider of how great consequence the friendship and alliance of the Six Nations is to all His Majesty's colonies and plantations in America in general as well as to New York in particular,' they wrote to him, 'we cannot but be greatly concerned ... Fatal consequences ... must inevitably follow from a neglect of them.' In an attempt to mend fences, they sent William Johnson, a Briton who had been living among the Mohawks for more than a decade, to woo Theyanoguin with promises and presents.

Johnson was a man of considerable political importance (though possibly not as considerable as he would have liked us to believe), whose relationship with the *Hotinonshonni* epitomizes Britain's ambiguous attitude towards her Native American allies in the late colonial period. After emigrating to New York in 1738, he set up a trading house in the Mohawk Valley and became immensely wealthy, acquiring a huge estate and building a Georgian mansion where he lived in feudal splendour, regularly entertaining his Iroquois neighbours, suppliers and clients. As well as learning their language and enthusiastically joining in their feasts and dances, he married (by Iroquois custom) a Mohawk woman, Molly Brant, who bore him eight children. It was the kind of life which, one imagines, Thomas Morton might eventually have led at Ma-re Mount if the colony had not been closed down by the Puritans.

Johnson's closeness to the Mohawks made him a natural intermediary between the *Hotinonshonni* and the British, and in 1746 New York appointed him 'colonel of the Iroquois.' Yet, for all his understanding of their culture and his evident affection for Mohawk friends and (through his wife) relatives, Johnson never – as later generations of imperial administrators put it – 'went native.' His role, based on the accumulation of a vast personal fortune and the exercise of patronage, was far closer to that of a powerful, if enlightened, English lord (he was, in fact, given a baronetcy by a grateful government) than to the position of a *Hotinonshonni* leader. He worked diligently to protect the Iroquois against mistreatment – he arranged, for example, for the construction of a fort to protect one community in 1753, and on another occasion demanding the removal of illegal settlers from Mohawk land – but only so long as their survival served (or, at least, did not threaten) the long-term aims of the British empire. When, in the Seven Years War, a clear divergence appeared between the interests of the Crown and the *Hotinonshonni*, he unquestioningly supported the Crown.

The flashpoint for the conflict was the intensifying Anglo-French competition in Ohio. Over the preceding century, this area, to the west of English Pennsylvania and sandwiched between French Canada and Louisiana, had absorbed a whole plethora of tribes and fragments of tribes displaced by European settlement and internecine warfare. The largest and most powerful groups were Delawares, Shawnees and Mingos (the name given to the Iroquois living in Ohio), but Abenakis, Ottawas and members of scores of other tribes had also fled there. This cosmopolitanism gave Ohio cultural and political connections to areas as far away as present-day Georgia and Atlantic Canada, making it – as it had been in the pre-contact period – a vital crossroads for Indian trade, diplomacy and information.

Most of the Ohio Indians, in the view of both the English and the *Hotinonshonni*, were subsidiaries of the Iroquois through the Covenant Chain. When France claimed the area, however, and Britain started building forts to deter her, the Six Nations – already under mounting pressure in their own heartland – found their authority over their western 'nephews' beginning to wane. At the same time, the westward thrust of the colonies carried still more dispossessed Indians and a stream of Anglo-American settlers into the area, threatening the hunting grounds not only of the 'dependent' peoples but also of the most westerly of the Six Nations themselves, the Seneca. By the 1740s, a few native leaders in Ohio had begun trying to organize a concerted Indian resistance movement to halt the frontier, further weakening the Iroquois' grip on their 'dependants'.

When hostilities between France and England broke out in 1754, the Six Nations remained effectively neutral, although – despite Theyanoguin's threats – the Mohawks continued to be generally pro-English, while the Senecas, understandably, tended to favour the French. An Iroquois war party helped the British at Pittsburgh in 1755, but the arrogance and incompetence of General Edward Braddock left the Indians still more alienated. 'It is now well known . . . how unhappily we have been defeated by the French . . .' complained the Oneida chief Scarouady. 'We must let you know that it was the pride and ignorance of that great general that came from England . . . He looked upon us as dogs and would never hear anything that was said to him . . . Those that come from over the great seas . . . are unfit to fight in the woods.' The British responded by creating a new Department of Indian Affairs and, in 1756, making Johnson the Superintendent of its northern division. The Mohawks, at least, clearly approved the decision: 'We love him, and he us,' said Theyanoguin's brother approvingly.

Johnson's mission was to overcome the Iroquois' growing anger and frustration and, by reactivating the Covenant Chain, to cement them into a firm anti-French alliance. He appeared to have succeeded – and certainly claimed to have succeeded – in 1759, when a party of Seneca and English troops captured the French Fort Niagara. It now seems clear, however, that the Seneca themselves suggested the attack for their own reasons, which precisely mirror the strategies of the Europeans. Having got rid of the French, with English help, they now intended to expel the English as well. By 1761, they had persuaded the other League Chiefs at Onondaga to plan a general uprising against Britain.

From the Seneca point of view, this plan probably seemed the last chance to reassert the Iroquois' authority over the western tribes and to preserve their independence. The relative strength of the *Hotinon-shonni* had depended on their position as a third force between France and Britain, and it was clear that, whichever side now won, they would lose this crucial bargaining counter. Stories were rife that, with the defeat of the French, Britain planned to subdue not only France's Indian allies but her own. These suspicions were fuelled by Lord Jeffrey Amherst, who, against Johnson's advice, simply abandoned his Native American troops, many of whom were starving as a result of the destruction of their villages and cornfields, when he no longer needed them.

The swirl of rumour, anxiety and discontent found a focus in a Delaware visionary, Neolin, the Enlightened, who, in 1761, began to attract a large following among the Ohio tribes. Like Nemattanew in Virginia, and hundreds of other prophets before and after, he believed that Native Americans had brought disaster to themselves by neglecting the traditional sources of their spiritual power and adopting the ways of the Europeans. In 1762 Neolin made a spiritual journey to the land of the Master of Life, who told him:

> The land on which you are, I have made for you, not for others: wherefore do you suffer the whites to dwell upon your lands? Can you not do without them? ... Before those whom you call your brothers [i.e., Europeans] had arrived, did not your bow and arrow maintain you? You needed neither gun, powder, nor any other object. The flesh of animals was your food, their skins your raiment. But when I saw you inclined to evil, I removed the animals into the depths of the forests ...
>
> Drive from your lands those dogs in red clothing [the British]; they are only an injury to you. When you want anything, apply to me ... Become good and you shall want for nothing.

Neolin's message spread rapidly through the 'Ohio Country' and beyond, galvanizing the supporters of armed resistance into action, and in May 1763 thousands of Senecas, Ottawas, Delawares, Chippewas and others rose against the British. Johnson had no doubt where his loyalty lay: after working for years to link the Iroquois and the western tribes through the Covenant Chain, he now tried frantically to turn them against one another. In a letter to General Gage, he described 'the great pains I have been constantly at in dividing them and preventing their unanimity ... rendering an union impracticable which cannot be too much guarded against.'

'Pontiac's War' – typically, the English assumed the uprising must be the work of one man, and named it after an Ottawa war chief who was, in fact, only one leader among many – was fought with great ferocity by both sides. The insurgents killed more than two thousand settlers, most of them illegal squatters on Indian land, and took nine British-held forts. In response, Amherst resolved to 'punish the delinquents with entire destruction,' instructing that 'no prisoners' should be taken and initiating a primitive kind of germ warfare with the order 'to send the small pox among the disaffected tribes . . .' His attempt to enlist the Native Americans' deadliest enemy for the British war effort worked: the commander of Fort Pitt invited some of the besieging Delawares to a parley, and gave them smallpox-infected blankets from the fort hospital as a token of esteem. As the ensuing epidemic raged, it progressively undermined the Indians' ability to fight, and the tide of war quickly turned against them. Some of the hostile chiefs were forced to make peace in September 1764, when, in the Treaty of Detroit, they acknowledged British sovereignty by accepting that King George was their *father* rather than their *brother*. Two years later, Pontiac and the other remaining insurgents surrendered at the Treaty of Oswego.

Johnson, meanwhile, had already persuaded the five eastern Iroquois nations that their best interests lay in a British victory, and by the end of 1763 the Seneca had been quietly readmitted to the Covenant Chain with little more than a stern admonition from the other League chiefs. Many backwoods settlers were angered at this leniency towards hostile tribes, which they compared with – as they saw it – their own shabby treatment by the government. As the historian Bernard Knollenberg puts it, 'it was perfectly clear that the British army had dismally failed not only to protect the colonial frontiers but even to punish the Indians promptly.'

Settler dissatisfaction was further fuelled by the Royal Proclamation of 1763, which attempted to fix a firm frontier along the spine of the Appalachians between the English colonies and 'Indian Country' and stipulated that further territory could be acquired only by the Crown and with the full consent of the tribes concerned. The ostensible aim was to maintain the peace, allowing Native Americans to feel secure in their homelands and reducing the chances of illegal settlement or fraudulent land deals sparking another conflict. Some historians, however, have seen it as little more than a pretext for maintaining a large military presence in North America to intimidate, and if necessary suppress, the increasingly discontented colonists. Others share the cynical view of George Washington, who – while planning to extend his estate beyond the border – wrote to a friend: 'I can never look upon that proclamation in any other light (but I say this between ourselves) than as a temporary expedient to quiet the minds of the Indians.'

Whatever its ultimate motive or motives, there was an outcry in the colonies against the Royal Proclamation. From the colonists' point of view, it was just one more imperial shackle, an intolerable violation of their 'inherent right to circumscribe their own boundaries,' and the efforts by the royal governors to deter or remove illegal settlers provoked outrage, offering yet more proof – if proof were needed – of the Crown's tyranny and disregard for its own subjects. In the fervour of the American Revolution, this first and last attempt by Britain to halt, or at least control, the frontier was swept aside with all the other paraphernalia of royal 'despotism'. The Proclamation's main lasting significance is that the procedure it laid down for acquiring Indian land has remained an important legal precedent in both the United States and Canada.

The War of Independence, when it came, was the final blow to the Iroquois' military power and territorial integrity. Realizing their extreme danger, many of the League Chiefs, particularly among the western nations, counselled neutrality, but the intense pressures to take sides proved too strong. Sir William Johnson, foreseeing the conflict with the colonies, had worked assiduously to bind the Six Nations still closer to the Crown, arranging for his talented protégé – and brother-in-law – Thayendanegea to receive an English education and grooming him for leadership as a Pine Tree Chief. Johnson himself had died in 1774, but at the outbreak of hostilities Thayendanegea was invited to London to renew – yet again – his people's relationship with Britain, and he seized the opportunity to exploit, for the last time, the Iroquois' position as the third force in a war between Europeans. He complained vociferously about continuing land violations, and bluntly told the king that *Hotinonshonni* support was conditional on these grievances being 'settled to our satisfaction whenever the troubles in America end.'

The Tuscaroras and Oneidas, meanwhile, were being wooed to the

American cause by Samuel Kirkland, a New England missionary who had worked among them for some years. In an attempt to heal the growing rift, the League Chiefs met at Onondaga, but the divisions between the Nations proved too deep and they failed to reach a consensus. The crisis worsened in 1777, when Onondaga was struck by an epidemic of smallpox which killed three *sachems*. The survivors took the extreme measure of extinguishing the fire at the centre of the Longhouse, thus symbolically suspending the work of the League. A delegation gave the British the 'melancholy news' that 'there is no longer a council fire at the capital of the Six Nations.'

The Mohawks quickly suffered a series of devastating American attacks which forced many of them to flee to Canada. Despite repeated provocations from the rebels, the western *Hotinonshonni* were able to remain largely neutral until 1779, when George Washington ordered that the Iroquois' territory should not 'merely be overrun but destroyed.' General John Sullivan promptly invaded western New York, cutting down the Indians' orchards and crops, burning their villages and destroying more than a million bushels of corn, while Colonel Daniel Brodhead, in what became known as the 'squaw campaign', massacred hundreds of *Hotinonshonni* women and children.

As always, the justification for this brutality was the supposed 'savagery' of the Indians. The Americans reviled the British, as the British had reviled the French, for their willingness to use Native American forces against 'civilized' Europeans, and the Indians' supposed atrocities were a major theme of rebel propaganda. Perhaps because of his close association with the British, his undoubted military skill, or the fact that, with his patina of English culture, he raised worrying questions about the distinction between 'savagery' and 'civilization', Thayendanegea (known to the colonists as Joseph Brant) was particularly vilified: one nineteenth-century writer memorably described him as 'the most ferocious being ever produced by human nature.'

In fact, Thayendanegea forbade torture and, whenever he could, freed civilians, believing that 'it is a shame to destroy those who are defenceless.' On one occasion he returned a captive child with a brief note: 'Sir, I send you by one of our runners the child which we will deliver, that you may know whatever others do, I do not make war on women and children.' Perhaps in a reference to the Loyalists fighting alongside him, he added: 'I am sorry to say that I have those engaged with me in the service, who are more savage than the savages themselves.'

Thayendanegea's harrying of the rebels was so successful that, by 1781, the new American governor of New York (another George Clinton) was forced to admit: 'We are now ... deprived of a great portion of our most valuable and well inhabited territory ... We are not in a condition to raise troops for the defence of our Frontier.' The following year, however, Britain suddenly abandoned the campaign to retain her American colonies, leaving the Indians, as Joseph Brant wrote, 'as it were between two Hells.' With the British defeat, Thayendanegea and many of his followers were forced to leave for Canada with the United Empire Loyalists, but most of the Crown's other Native American allies were denied even this way out. To the horror of the Indians and the outrage of many of the officials who had dealt with them, the Treaty of Paris in 1783 contained no provision for the protection of the Indians who had fought so hard and died in such numbers – it is estimated, for instance, that half the Iroquois had perished in the War of Independence – for the Crown. One Englishman lamented that a clause honouring existing treaty obligations 'might have been easily reserved and inserted ... which would have saved the Honor of Government ...'

By the 1790s, the *Hotinonshonni* were scattered and divided and the great Longhouse of the League seemed in ruins. Most of the Iroquois were in Canada; those who remained in New York faced an almost continuous assault on the few pockets of land left to them. Demoralized, and deprived of most of their traditional subsistence activities, they seemed to be slithering into the morass of problems that have afflicted so many defeated Native Americans: drunkenness, violence and social breakdown. Without the condolence ceremony and the other rituals that bound them together, their communities were plagued by growing fears and suspicions of witchcraft.

But out of this chaos and despair, with their extraordinary gift for revival, the *Hotinonshonni* produced yet another visionary leader who led them away from the brink of cultural extinction. Skanyadariyoh (Skanientariio), or Handsome Lake, was a Seneca who, in 1799, collapsed and appeared to die after a long illness induced by alcoholism.

In his coma, he had the first of a series of encounters with the Creator, in which he was told that he must give up drinking or die, and subsequent visions revealed further instructions which the *Hotinonshonni* must follow to ensure their own well-being and the survival of the world. The result was a new code, the *Gai'wiio* or Good Message, which allowed the Iroquois to adopt some aspects of European culture, such as domestic animals and individual-family houses, but also demanded that they should retain and revitalize the sacred ceremonial cycle and other aspects of their traditional life.

Like Deganawida before him, Skanyadariyoh gave the *Hotinonshonni* a new direction and a new purpose at a time when they seemed close to destruction. As they were crowded on to smaller and smaller reservations during the nineteenth century, his message allowed them to adapt, in some measure, to the new society which was rapidly establishing itself around them and, at the same time, to maintain their own identity. After two centuries of almost unimaginable change, in which the *Hotinonshonni* have been plagued by internal divisions and unrelenting external pressures, his vision, and the long tradition of Iroquois culture which it embodies, have still not been extinguished.

6. Southeast

'Get a little further: you are too near me'

When we lived beyond the great waters there were twelve clans belonging to the Cherokee tribe ... back in the old country in which we lived[,] the country was subject to great floods.

So in the course of time we held a council and decided to build a store reaching to heaven. The Cherokees said that when the house was built and the floods came the tribe would just leave the earth and go to heaven ... we commenced to build the great structure and when it was towering into one of the highest heavens[,] the great powers destroyed the apex, cutting it down to about half of its height. But as the tribe was fully determined to build to heaven for safety[,] they were not discouraged but commenced to repair the damage done by the gods. Finally they completed the lofty structure and considered themselves safe from the floods ... after it was completed[,] the gods destroyed the high part again ... Then the tribe held another council and concluded to move out of the floody [sic] country and hunt one more dry and suitable to their liking. So[,] they journeyed for many days and years and finally came to a country that had a good climate and [was] suitable for raising corn and other plenty upon which the tribe subsisted. Other red tribes or clans to the Cherokee tribe began to come also from the old country. The emigration continued for many years, never knowing that they crossed the great waters. In the course of time the old pathway which had been travelled by the clans was cut by the submergence of a portion of the land into the deep sea. This path can be traced to this day by the broken boulders.

Long years after they had settled in their new homes in the new country[,] they began to hunt for the clans of the Cherokee tribe

... after a fruitless search for the others [they] finally gave it up and established a new system of seven sacred clans to the tribe. From that day to this[,] they have been searching for the five lost clans of the Cherokee.

From: A *Cherokee Vision of Eloh'*

Perhaps more than any other part of the United States, the Southeast belies the idea that Native American societies are static and incapable of development. From the wooded mountains and lush valleys of the Atlantic coast to the flat grasslands of Texas on the Gulf of Mexico, the area has been shaped and reshaped by Indian civilizations trying to embrace and adapt to new conditions. The wreckage of their experiments is strewn across the landscape, and their cultural legacy still affects the lives of hundreds of thousands of modern Americans, both Native and non-Native.

This dynamic tradition was already well established long before Columbus. As early as 2500 BC, the hunter-gatherer peoples of the area had started to adopt pottery and other traits from the growing agricultural civilizations of Meso-america, and by around a thousand years later the first of a succession of highly organized farming cultures had appeared. From about 1000 BC on, the current of cultural change shifted, with new developments coming not from Meso-america but from the Adena-Hopewell 'mound-building' tradition that dominated much of the Northeast. Around AD 700, however, a new culture appeared in the Mississippi Valley which seems, once again, to have been heavily influenced by Meso-america. Based on the cultivation of new and more productive strains of maize developed in Mexico, it allowed more intensive agriculture, a greater population density and the emergence of highly stratified, theocratic societies.

The similarities with Meso-american civilization are instantly apparent if you look at 'Mississippian' artefacts – pottery, masks, sculpture and copper sheets marked with stylized skulls, bones, weeping eyes or feathered serpents – or at the layout of their towns. Communities were heavily fortified and built around large, flat-topped pyramids surmounted by the houses of leading men or temples containing the 'eternal flame' which lay at the heart of the community's religious life.

They could be enormous: at its zenith in the twelfth century, the largest, Cahokia – close to the present-day St. Louis – extended six miles along the Illinois River. With a central pyramid covering sixteen acres and reaching a height of 100 feet, 85 smaller temples and burial mounds, and a population estimated at between 10,000 and 75,000, Cahokia was the largest city north of Mexico and comparable in size to European capitals such as London and Paris during the same period. (Significantly, however, scholars still sometimes refer to it as a *village*, while many smaller Old World communities, such as medieval Bristol, are invariably described as *cities*.)

Within a few centuries, the new culture seems to have spread over much of eastern and central North America. Some scholars believe that this expansion was too rapid and intense to be explained simply by the normal process of cultural dissemination, but must have been the result of invasion and conquest. One theory is that the first Mississippians were ancestors of the Natchez, a group encountered by the earliest European explorers in the 'core area' of the culture, who had migrated into the region from Mexico, subjugated some of the indigenous population and then extended their influence through trade and warfare.

There is, certainly, compelling circumstantial evidence for this idea, borne out by the Natchez' own oral tradition, which recounts how they migrated to the Mississippi from the Southwest. Early French accounts describe their society as being strongly hierarchical, strikingly different from their neighbours but with powerful echoes of Meso-america. At its head was the 'Great Sun', a supreme ruler venerated as a direct descendant of the sun god. When a Great Sun died, his wife and close followers were strangled so that they could accompany him into the afterlife, and his sisters – the 'Women Suns' – nominated his successor. Below the 'royal family' were nobles, 'honoured men', and commoners, known as 'stinkards'. Under the complex caste system, all members of the nobility had to marry stinkards, with only the children of female aristocrats preserving their noble rank.

Whatever the ultimate source of the Mississippian Culture, by the time of European contact it had transformed the lives of scores of different Native American peoples in the Southeast. The accounts of the Spanish de Soto expedition to the area between 1539 and 1543 gives us our only – and often tantalizingly uninformative – glimpse of what their world was like.

De Soto landed at Tampa, in Florida, with 550 soldiers, a group of black and Mexican slaves, some workmen (including smiths to make collars and chains for captives), 200 horses, war dogs and a herd of pigs, which not only provided food but destroyed Indian crops and flushed out ambushes. Driven by the perennial quest for gold, they started north through a landscape of woods and intensively cultivated river valleys that reminded them of Peru and Middle America, with vast fields of maize – sometimes stretching for miles at a time alongside the road – and large towns governed by rulers who travelled on litters and wore tunics of cotton and feather-mosaic. The Indians signalled de Soto's approach with a relay of beacon-fires, but they were unable to stop the expedition, which left a trail of desecrated temples, plundered storehouses and razed towns in its wake.

After spending the winter near Tallahassee, the Spaniards moved into what is now Georgia in the spring of 1540. Crossing the Savannah River, they entered a state called Cofitachiqui, where the people (almost certainly Creeks) were 'very clean and polite,' and 'more civilized than any ... seen in all the territories of Florida, wearing clothes and shoes.' The ruler was a young woman, adorned with furs and pearls, who came to greet the expedition accompanied by a fleet of canoes full of presents. According to de Soto's secretary, 'Indians of rank bore [her] on their shoulders with much respect, in a litter covered with delicate white linen. And she crossed in the canoes and spoke to the Governor quite gracefully and at her ease. She was a young girl of fine bearing; and she took off a string of pearls which she wore on her neck, and put it on the Governor as a necklace to show her favour ...'

De Soto kidnapped the young woman and forced her to guide him into the Appalachians, where he was convinced he would find gold. At a place called Xualla (perhaps the modern Qualla, North Carolina) they made what was probably the first European contact with the Cherokee: the 'Tsalagi' greeted them with the usual hospitality, plying them with gifts and providing bearers for their journey. Shortly after they left, the Creek 'princess' escaped, taking with her, to de Soto's chagrin, the box of pearls that he had intended to demand as the price for her release. After stumbling across the mountains, the hungry and exhausted

Spaniards finally reached a great terraced Cherokee town, where they were given 300 dogs to eat.

Failing to find gold, de Soto turned Southwest towards the territory of the Creeks again. At Coosa, he was greeted by men playing flutes and a ruler dressed in a robe of marten skins. The soldiers seized the chief and several of his people as slaves and moved on towards Choctaw country, where they were welcomed by Tuskaloosa, 'the suzerain of many territories, and of a numerous people.' De Soto made the usual demand for women and bearers and the chief promised to gather them at a town called Mabila, but when the Spaniards arrived they discovered that the Choctaws had strengthened their defences and prepared for war. In the ensuing battle, the Spanish suffered heavy casualties, but they finally rallied and fired the town, burning most of the inhabitants to death. The following spring, de Soto provoked a similar incident in the Chickasaw town where the expedition had spent the winter, resulting in the loss of eleven of his men and most of his horses.

The same pattern was repeated again and again as the Spaniards moved north and west through present-day Alabama, Mississippi, Louisiana, and Arkansas. As they were preparing to cross the Mississippi, 200 warriors (probably Quapaws), wearing 'great bunches of white and other plumes of many colours,' appeared in an armada of canoes laden with skins, buffalo furs, dried fruit and fish. The Indians put their presents ashore, but then withdrew in fear, and the Spaniards fired after them, killing several men. In Arkansas, the people abandoned their large, densely populated towns as the expedition approached, but the Spaniards still managed to capture a number of men and women, as well, of course, as systematically pillaging their stocks of food.

After another winter, de Soto started his return journey. Reaching the Mississippi again, he fell ill, but still sent a message to a town on the other bank, demanding carriers and provisions and claiming – with a chilling cynicism which suggests he had gained at least a minimal understanding of native culture – that he was the 'Child of the Sun' and that 'whence he came all obeyed him, rendering their tribute.' The chief, clearly not easily intimidated, replied laconically that the Child of the Sun should be able to dry up the river. By now too weak to cross over and punish him, de Soto ordered his men to destroy another town nearby as an example. The unsuspecting inhabitants were taken completely by surprise, and the Spanish chronicler reported that 'The cries of the women and children were such as to deafen those who pursued them.' Shortly afterwards, de Soto died, and his men, claiming that he had 'ascended to the Sun,' buried him secretly in the Mississippi, fearing an Indian attack if his body were discovered.

De Soto was, apparently, the victim of an Old World 'fever' brought to the New World in Spanish ships. Even before his death, the same – or similar – pathogens had begun their lethal advance through the native population, and for the next century or so European disease continued the process of destruction in the Southeast almost unaided by Europeans themselves.

* * *

After thus living for ages in peace and prosperity[,] the Cherokee tribe increased greatly in population. They built the cahtiyis *[town houses] throughout the seven clanned nation[,] organized on the broad principle of universal brotherhood, which included the whole world except the five lost clans.*

Then it happened, while the Cherokee tribe thus lived in their new country, that strange white canoes appeared on the broad expanse of great waters. The clans gathered on the shore in wonder and astonishment at the arrival in their waters of these strange vessels. These white canoes hovered in sight for several days as though not confident that they would be received with welcome by the tribe. The clans[,] thinking they were beings from heaven[,] began to beckon them to come to the shore. The clans also prepared corn in which was cooked sweet nuts, venison and other prepared food to be presented to these white beings in their canoes. White being an emblem of purity with the Cherokees, they looked upon these white beings as a pure race from the upper world. The white beings of the white canoes were soon convinced that no harm was to be expected and they landed. The strangers were received with welcome by the tribe and food was brought in and given them.

Tobacco which had been purified and called the chola [tsola or

*native tobacco] of peace was also brought, together with pipes,
and the strangers were asked to smoke with the clans.*

From: *A Cherokee Vision of Eloh'*

By around the middle of the seventeenth century, when the English
and French first reached the interior of the Southeast, Mississippian
Culture had collapsed. Probably as a result of epidemics, perhaps
compounded by other cultural or political problems, most of the large
metropolitan centres such as Cahokia had been abandoned, and the
surviving population had dispersed to smaller farms and villages.

In the far west of the area, bordering the southern Plains, lived the
Caddoan-speaking Caddos; further east were the Natchez, and then,
stretching in a broad 'U'-shape, a string of Muskogean-speaking
peoples: Chickasaws and Choctaws in Mississippi and Louisiana; a
powerful Creek Confederacy in what is now Alabama and Georgia; and
Yamasees on the Georgia–South Carolina border. Further north in
South Carolina were the Catawbas – remotely related to the Sioux –
and the Iroquoian-speaking Tuscaroras. Scores of smaller groups, from
Calusas in Florida to Tonkawas in Texas, were scattered across the
region.

The largest nation, with a 40,000 square-mile territory centred on
the mountains of western North Carolina and eastern Tennessee and
including parts of five other present-day states, were the 20,000 or so
Cherokee. Occupying the area to the south of their relatives, the
Iroquois – you can trace the family connection in their name for
themselves, *Ani-Yunwiya*, or 'Principal People', which distantly echoes
the Iroquois' *Onkwehonwe*, 'Original People' – they were frequently at
war with one or more of the Five Nations, who vied with them for
domination of Kentucky and West Virginia. Seven of their sixty-four or
so communities – the 'mother towns' of the seven clans – were
considered especially important, but, unlike the League of the *Hotinonshonni*, the *Ani-Yunwiya* had no real central authority. Each town was
governed by a council of 'Beloved Men', usually warriors or orators of
outstanding ability. Women enjoyed a higher status than among many
other peoples, and sometimes became political leaders. (One 'Beloved
Man' pointedly remarked to a British governor: 'It is customary among
[us] to admit women to our councils ... [Since] the white people, as

well as the red, are born of women, is not that the custom among them, also?')

Except in southern Florida and along the rim of the Gulf of Mexico, where groups such as the Calusas lived primarily by gathering shellfish, most of the peoples of the Southeast followed a broadly similar way of life based on the cultivation of maize, beans, melons, tobacco, sunflowers and other crops. Like their neighbours to the north, they supplemented these staples with a wide variety of wild foods, which – thanks to the mild climate and high rainfall – were particularly plentiful. The rivers of the area teemed with fish, while the lush valleys and forests of oak, pine and hickory yielded bear, deer, turkey, wildfowl and other game as well as nuts and berries. Even when a harvest failed or was destroyed by enemies, this natural abundance was generally enough to prevent starvation.

If you had visited a Southeastern community in the late seventeenth or early eighteenth century, you would have come first to the 'town fields', where, at certain times of year, the whole population, men and women, worked together. Produce from the fields was generally kept in a storehouse and used by the chief to entertain visitors, provide for the poor and, in times of hardship, feed the entire community. Entering the town itself, you would have passed through a stockade (in the 1670s, an English trader described a Cherokee town as being enclosed by a wall two feet thick and twelve feet tall) and into a network of streets lined with individual dwellings. Creek homes sometimes consisted of as many as four separate buildings – kitchen, store room, winter and summer dwellings – grouped around a small square; the Cherokees, before the advent of European axes made the use of logs more common, generally lived in rectangular, one- two- or three-room wattle-and-daub houses with a fireplace and sleeping platforms at one end. One observer vividly recorded that: 'They lash in-and-out canes, and plaster them over with white clay mixed with small pieces of talc, which in a sun-shiny day gives to these houses ... a splendour of unpolished silver.'

The heart of the community was generally a square of hard-packed earth, sometimes set on a terrace, surrounded by four shed-like buildings where members of the council gathered for meetings. This was the focal point for important rituals and festivals, with a sacred communal fire in the centre, and was kept meticulously clean. Nearby would be a sunken area, used for informal dancing and for games like *chenco* (or 'chunkey'), played with throwing sticks or rolling stones, or the 'stick game', an aggressive version of lacrosse known as 'the little brother of war'. In some communities, there might also be a conical 'hothouse', where people could congregate in bad weather.

For the Southeastern peoples, like Native Americans elsewhere, the year revolved around a series of sacred ceremonies. The most important, through most of the region, was the Green Corn Dance or 'Busk' (from the Creek *boskita*, 'to fast'), held in the late summer to celebrate the harvest and initiate a new annual cycle. The town was scrupulously brushed and cleaned, the participants ritually purified themselves – the Cherokee by 'going to water', or bathing; the Creek by drinking the 'black drink', a powerful purgative – and fires throughout the community were extinguished. Old clothing, tools and household goods were destroyed and replaced, and a fresh moral and spiritual start was made with the pardoning of wrongdoers – except for murderers – and the healing of rifts between individuals and clans. The process of renewal ended, after four (or sometimes eight) days of fasting, feasting, ceremony and dance, with the rekindling of fires from the relit sacred flame.

The roots of the Green Corn Dance – which some scholars, pointing out the importance of the 'eternal fire' and other similar elements in Meso-american culture, believe to be a survival from the Mississippian tradition – go to the heart of the Southeastern peoples' understanding of the world. Although the details vary from culture to culture, it invariably commemorates the gift of maize by an ancestral 'Corn Woman' whose blood has the power to bring forth crops. (Selu, the Cherokee goddess, was killed as a witch by her sons, and in one version the corn sprang from the spot where her blood fell. In other accounts, the Woman asks to be killed, and tells her relatives to drag her body around a field which is later found to be full of corn.) Even after death, the goddess continues to feed the people in the form of maize, but only so long as they continue to celebrate the Green Corn Ceremony. According to one source, she reminded the Cherokee that 'elsewhere you will find no milk whose source is inexhaustible like mine' and warned that there would be famine if they neglected her. 'If you forget to think of me . . . but make use of me without remembering my words, I will fling among you The Desolator!'

The strong association between women's blood and fertility made it a powerful – and hence potentially dangerous – force and reinforced the need for a strict separation between the worlds of male and female. As in many societies, girls and women had to seclude themselves during menstruation, and during the *boskita* and other ceremonies couples were expected to practise abstinence. Men also refrained from sexual activity when they were preparing for, and taking part in, war. James Adair, an eighteenth-century Irish trader who lived with the Cherokees for almost forty years, wrote that: 'Tradition, or the divine impression on human nature, dictates to them that man was not born in a state of war; and as they reckon they are become impure by shedding human blood, they hasten to observe the fast of three days.' Transforming themselves from peaceful members of their own community into warriors required them to undergo ritual purification and then to summon the assistance of underworld beings (often a giant snake) that were fundamentally inimical to the power of women.

The taboo against mingling the worlds of warfare and women prompted many early European observers to comment on the Native Americans' sexual restraint. 'Generally,' as the eighteenth-century French traveller, J.C.B., put it, 'savages have scruples about molesting a woman prisoner, and look upon it as a crime, even when she gives her consent.'

The world below was only one level in the Southeastern Indians' complex map of the universe. There was also a sky world – home of the 'Master of Life' or 'Master of Breath' and the ultimate source of all the people's blessings – which, while normally separate, could also be visited by visionaries and shamans capable of making the ritual transition back and forth. In addition, each of the four cardinal points had its own spiritual significance, represented by a symbolic colour. Writing at the turn of the century, the ethnologist James Mooney noted that among the Cherokee for instance: 'East = red = success; triumph; North = blue = defeat; trouble; West = black = death; South = white = peace; happiness.' The Creeks actually incorporated the symbolism into their social and political structure, dividing their fifty communities between 'Red Towns', which had overall responsibility for defence and warfare, and 'White Towns', which provided most of the confederacy's civil chiefs and governed during peacetime.

Although there was considerable variety in the colour symbolism of different peoples, Mooney notes that 'for obvious reasons black was generally taken as the symbol of death, while white and red signified, respectively, peace and war.' Cherokee oral tradition records that, as a result, the Indians were 'confused in the invasion of the white people, for their colour represented "purity and spirituality".'

✿   ✿   ✿

Then the white strangers which were supposed to be visitors from heaven ... on account of their white skins ... asked that they be allowed a small piece of ground upon which to camp, cook and sleep; it was charitably granted. These strangers were entertained by the Cherokee clans very charitably and food and other articles of comfort were freely given to them. Then these strangers made known their desire and willingness to remain with the native Cherokee clans[,] if they were allowed to purchase a small piece of ground upon which to camp and sleep. They made known to the tribe that they only needed a small piece of land about the size of a bull hide. This modest request was freely granted to the strangers and sold to them for a trifling consideration. The supposed heavenly strangers then cut one of the ox hides which they had brought with them into a small string which they stretched around a square enclosing several hundred square yards. This they claimed to be in accordance with the purchase agreement to which the tribe finally agreed, saying at the same time that they had been deceived. Other purchases of land were made for which a consideration was always given by the white heavenly strangers, after the cession of which the tribe always acknowledged that they had been deceived.

Then the tribe finally came to the conclusion that this white stranger was from the opposite pole of the heavens and put on his white skin for the purpose of deceiving. Then the Cherokee tribe began to destroy the white invader ... But the white invader begin to use firearms against them and the Cherokee tribe was driven back farther and farther.

From: *A Cherokee Vision of Eloh'*

The first known encounter between the *Ani-Yunwiya* and the British came in 1654, when an 'invading' party of Cherokees defeated a combined colonial–Indian force in Virginia, but there seems to have been no regular contact until after the establishment of a permanent English settlement in South Carolina in 1670. In 1684 the new colony signed a treaty with eight *Ani-Yunwiya* towns, and in 1690 the Irish trader Cornelius Dougherty became the first of many British traders to settle permanently with the Cherokee. By the following year, another familiar pattern had evidently been established: South Carolina ordered an inquiry into a report that colonists had, 'without any proclamation of war, fallen upon and murdered' several Cherokees.

Although conflicts continued intermittently – the Cherokee complained bitterly about the capture of some of their people as slaves, and in 1715 joined a general Indian uprising against the South Carolinans – the *Ani-Yunwiya* and the colonists managed to maintain an uneasy peace for most of the early colonial period. To begin with, both sides benefited from a thriving commercial relationship. As early as 1700, the Cherokee had acquired guns and were contributing to a burgeoning 'Indian trade' in hides and other native produce: in the first fifteen years of the eighteenth century alone, South Carolina was able to export a million deerskins.

In 1721, in an attempt to systematize dealings with the *Ani-Yunwiya*, the governor of South Carolina signed a treaty with the chiefs of thirty-seven of their towns and appointed a 'supreme head of the Nation' to deal with the colony. Nine years later, concerned about growing French influence, Sir Alexander Cuming visited the Cherokee to reinforce the relationship by offering the *Ani-Yunwiya* a trade and defence pact with the Crown. A new 'emperor', *Moytoy* of Tellico, was selected, and 'with great Solemnity Sir Alexander was placed in a Chair ... Moytoy and the Conjurers standing about him, while the Warriors stroak'd him with thirteen Eagles Tails, and their Singers sung from Morning 'till Night ... After this Solemnity of stroaking was over, Sir Alexander ...

required Moytoy and all the head Warriors to acknowledge themselves dutiful Subjects and Sons to King George.'

It is doubtful whether the Cherokees understood the agreement in the same way, but after some prevarication seven chiefs accepted an invitation to travel to England to cement the alliance with the king in person. Among the delegation was a young man called *Attakullakulla*, known to the English as 'the Little Carpenter', who subsequently became one of the outstanding *Ani-Yunwiya* leaders of the eighteenth century. He and the other ambassadors were startled to discover that the vogue for 'savages' had made them celebrities in Europe. 'They are welcome to look upon me as a strange creature,' *Attakullakulla* caustically observed of the crowds that gathered to see him. 'They see but one, and in return they give me an opportunity to look upon thousands.' The Cherokees gave the king 'the Crown of the Cherokee Nation,' five eagles' tails and 'four scalps of Indian enemies, all of which His Majesty was graciously pleased to accept.' They told the Lords Commissioners:

> The crown of our Nation is different from that which the great King George wears ... but to us it is all one; and the chain of friendship shall be carried to our people ... Though we are red, and you are white, yet our hands and hearts are joined together. When we shall have acquainted our people with what we have seen, our children from generation to generation will always remember it. In war we shall always be as one with you; the great King George's enemies shall be our enemies; his people and ours shall be always one, and shall die together.

In fact, the by now familiar ingredients of colonial encounter – disease, imperial rivalry and unrelenting pressure on land – kept the alliance with England under almost continuous stress. Less than ten years after *Attakullakulla*'s visit to London, the Cherokee succumbed to a smallpox epidemic, brought to South Carolina on slave ships, which killed almost half their population in a matter of months. James Adair vividly described the victims' despair at seeing their own disfigurement: 'Some shot themselves, others cut their throats, some stabbed themselves ... many threw themselves with sullen madness into the fire and there slowly expired ...' Religious leaders 'broke their old consecrated physic-pots, and threw away all the other pretended holy things . . . imagining they had lost their divine power' and believing, like the shamans of New England, that the disease was retribution for the abandonment of traditional spiritual practices.

France saw this catastrophe as an opportunity to extend her own influence. In the frantic competition for power, she had already forged an alliance with the Choctaws, enlisting their help in 1729 in a genocidal war against the Natchez (like Connecticut's Narragansett allies against the Pequots, the Choctaws were shocked at the scale of the destruction) and inciting them to attack the English-inclined Chickasaws. French, Spanish and English, meanwhile, had all been trying to woo the powerful Creeks, and James Oglethorpe, who founded Georgia in 1733, had succeeded in extracting a partial concession when, to secure English trade, the confederacy agreed that it would 'give no encouragement to any other white people . . . to settle amongst us, and that we will not have any correspondence with the Spaniards or French.' Now, in an attempt to weaken South Carolina's hold on the *Ani-Yunwiya*, a French agent visited Chota, the 'capital' of the Cherokee 'Emperor' recognized by Britain, and persuaded the war leader, *Oconostota*, that the English had introduced the epidemic deliberately.

The British were thoroughly alarmed. Although – as Lord Amherst's behaviour after Pontiac's Rebellion would amply demonstrate – they were not above using germ warfare, good relations with the Cherokee were, for the moment, an essential element of colonial policy. 'It is absolutely necessary for us to be in friendship with [them],' wrote the Governor of South Carolina a few years later. 'While we call them friends we may consider them a bulwark at our backs.' The Frenchman was promptly arrested and imprisoned, but for most of the 1740s and early 1750s the *Ani-Yunwiya*'s loyalty to Britain wavered, strained by the colonists' incessant encroachment on their land. In 1752, *Moytoy*'s successor, *Caneecatee* (known to the colonists as Old Hop because he walked with a limp), complained: 'When I was a little boy the white people began to settle thick in the country, and all the ground from that [Charleston] to this was ours . . . but now I find we are disbarred from it . . . The Lower Towns people received some presents or consideration for it, but neither I nor my people living in the Mother Town of all [Chota] ever got anything . . .'

As the Seven Years War approached, however, the *Ani-Yunwiya* reaffirmed their commitment to the British cause. *Attakullakulla* had spent much of the previous decade in Canada, ostensibly as a prisoner of the Ottawas, and his contacts with the French authorities seem to have led him to believe that Britain was likely to win the impending struggle for European domination of North America. In June 1755, the *Ani-Yunwiya* agreed that, if Britain would build forts to protect their towns from the French, they would send men to help the English war effort.

Britain built the forts as promised and the Cherokee sent a large contingent to fight on the Virginia frontier, helping to turn the tide of war in England's favour, but relations between the two sides quickly deteriorated. In 1758, the commander and some of the soldiers from Fort Prince George, who were supposedly protecting the Cherokee community of Keowee, took part in a drunken rape of *Ani-Yunwiya* women. Some of the younger Cherokee warriors, already incensed at the murder of a party of friendly *Ani-Yunwiya* two years before, took revenge by attacking frontiersmen, and within weeks a war had broken out. Amherst, no longer dependent on Cherokee military support, launched a brutal campaign against the *Ani-Yunwiya*, and in 1761, close to starvation and reeling from a fresh outbreak of smallpox, they were forced to make peace.

The following year, three Cherokees visited London, and came back shocked by what they had seen: 'The number of warriors and people all of one colour which we saw in England,' said *Ostenaco*, the 'Mankiller', 'far exceeded what we thought possibly could be.' Convinced that further armed resistance against so powerful an opponent was futile, the Cherokee leadership took a conciliatory tone in the years following the end of the Seven Years War. As thousands of settlers, no longer constrained by fear of the French or the need to cultivate Native American allies, breached the limits laid down in the Royal Proclamation of 1763 and flooded west into *Ani-Yunwiya* territory, *Attakullakulla* and the other chiefs were forced to surrender tract after tract of land, relying on nothing more than increasingly desperate appeals to the colonists' better nature to protect them from further encroachment. After one agreement, in 1768, the elderly *Oconostota* said:

The land is now divided for the use of the red and the white people, and I hope the white people on the frontier will pay attention to the line marked and agreed upon. I recommend to them to use kindly such of their red brothers, the Cherokees, as chance to come down into the settlements. We have now given the white men enough land to live upon, and hope in return to be well used by them.

Within a year, he was writing to the Crown agent:

The white people pay no attention to the talks we have had. They are in bodies hunting in the middle of our hunting grounds ... The whole nation is filling with hunters, and the guns rattling every way on the path, both up and down the river. They have settled the land a great way this side of the line.

The growing tension between settlers and royal officials in the years leading up to the American Revolution was complicated, in the Southeast, by the fact that many of the representatives of the Crown had family ties to the 'savages' they were trying to protect. Captain John Stuart, who in 1763 became Superintendent for the southern tribes – the counterpart to Sir William Johnson's position with the Iroquois – followed the tradition established by Irish traders in the late seventeenth century and married a Cherokee woman. Stuart's appointees as royal agents to the *Ani-Yunwiya*, Alexander Cameron and John McDonald, also took Cherokee wives and settled permanently with the tribe. Their sympathies, naturally, were far more with their adopted peoples than with the often bigotedly anti-Indian settlers invading their land. Cameron made his views plain when he wrote of the backwoodsmen: 'No nation was ever infested with such a set of villains and horse thieves.' The families of British traders and officials – often literate, prosperous English-speakers at ease in the non-Indian world but profoundly committed to their own tribes – formed a dynastic 'mixed-blood' élite among the Cherokee (and to some extent the Creek) that was to have a profound impact on the history of the Southeast Indians long after the American Revolution.

On 17 March 1775, *Attakullakulla*, *Oconostota* and several other chiefs were forced to sign the 'Henderson Purchase', in which, for £10,000-worth of trade goods, they surrendered much of present-day Kentucky and Tennessee – almost half the *Ani-Yunwiya*'s remaining territory – to Daniel Boone and a land-speculator called Richard Henderson. For some of the younger Cherokee, this cession was the last straw. *Attakullakulla*'s own son, *Ciu Canacina* (Dragging Canoe), refused to agree to it, angrily (and presciently) declaring:

> Where are now our grandfathers, the Delawares? We had hoped that the white men would not be willing to travel beyond the mountains. Now that hope is gone. They have passed the mountains, and have settled upon Cherokee land. They wish to have that usurpation sanctioned by treaty. When that is gained, the same encroaching spirit will lead them upon other land of the Cherokees. New cessions will be asked. Finally the whole country, which the Cherokees and their fathers have so long occupied, will be demanded, and the remnant of Ani-Yunwiya, 'The Real People,' once so great and formidable, will be compelled to seek refuge in some distant wilderness. There they will be permitted to stay only a short while, until they again behold the advancing banners of the same greedy host. Not being able to point out any further retreat for the miserable Cherokees, the extinction of the whole race will be proclaimed. Should we not therefore run all risks, and incur all consequences, rather than submit to further laceration of our country? Such treaties may be all right for men who are too old to hunt or fight. As for me, I have my young warriors about me. We will have our lands.

When he had finished, *Ciu Canacina* turned to one of the speculators: 'You have bought a fair land, but there is a black cloud hanging over it. You will find its settlement dark and bloody.'

From the point of view of the other elderly chiefs, Dragging Canoe's determination to halt the frontier by force was unrealistic and profoundly dangerous: if the *Ani-Yunwiya*, however intolerably abused, took up arms against Anglo-America, they would only provoke their own destruction by an invincible enemy. His analysis, however, reflected a growing understanding of Native American history and destiny which had been gathering pace among the frontier tribes since the uprising of the early 1760s. The 'nativists', as they are sometimes called, looked at the predicament of their own peoples within a wider context, pointing to the fate of scores of groups in New England and Virginia as evidence of what might happen to them. A few years later, their most famous proponent, the Shawnee Tecumseh, was to ask:

> Where today are the Pequots? Where the Narragansetts, the Mohawks, the Pocanets and many other once powerful tribes of our people? They have vanished before the avarice and oppression of the white man . . .

The Delaware shaman Neolin, who inspired Pontiac and many of his followers, was only one of many 'prophets' who believed that Indians had brought this disaster on themselves by embracing aspects of European culture and neglecting the spiritual roots of their own power. Only by rejecting alcohol, Christianity and other impurities introduced by the 'whites', and returning to their own rituals and ceremonies, could Native Americans find the strength needed to repel the invader.

Although it promoted a revival of 'traditional values', nativism in fact represented a new development in the Native American world. It created a diplomatic network, far more durable and extensive than the aboriginal system of *ad hoc* alliances, which at its height stretched from the Great Lakes to the Gulf of Mexico and drew together scores of peoples – many of them traditional enemies – in a common cause. The Shawnee, who were often the prime movers, maintained more or less permanent embassies among other nations to negotiate and co-ordinate action. Underpinning the whole movement was a new *racial* consciousness: nativists identified themselves as members not merely of specific tribes but of a 'red race' which was in fundamental opposition to the invading 'white race'. (Even here, however, the distinction was generally more cultural than biological: nativist groups continued to adopt and assimilate European captives.)

The belief that the Native American and 'white' worlds were essentially irreconcilable clearly represents a radical departure for cultures that had to begin with, almost invariably, welcomed the newcomers and the technical innovations they had brought. It reflects, partly, a growing awareness that the dependency on trade goods had undermined the Indians' autonomy and reduced them to an increasingly desperate competition in which, prompted by Europeans, they were now in danger of exterminating each other. Even more basically, it mirrors the European – and particularly the English – view that 'savage' and 'civilized' societies could not co-exist. Time and again, Native Americans had agreed new, more restricted boundaries which they hoped would finally allow them to live permanently alongside Europeans, only to find that, within a few years, they had to concede more. This history of broken promises and repeated removals profoundly shaped nativist beliefs: it can be clearly seen, for instance, in the story of an unnamed Shawnee shaman who died and travelled to the sky world, where his 'grandfather' gave him a dire warning: 'Beware of the religion of the white man: . . . every Indian who embraces it is obliged to take the road to the white man's heaven; and yet no red man is permitted to enter there, but will have to wander about forever without a resting place.'

Many nativists saw the outbreak of the American Revolution as the opportunity they had been waiting for, and early in 1776, a party of Mohawks, Shawnees, Delawares and others visited the Cherokee to invite them to join a pan-Indian alliance against the colonists. The delegates reported that their journey had taken them seventy days, far longer than they had expected, because, when they had tried to pass through an area 'which but very lately used to be Shawnee and Delaware hunting grounds,' they had found it 'thickly inhabited [by whites] and the people all in arms,' and had been 'obliged to go down a great way on the other side of the Ohio and to take a round of near 300 miles to avoid being discovered.' Unrolling a nine foot long war belt, 'strewed over with vermilion . . . paint,' a Shawnee declared: 'It is plain that they intend to extirpate us, and I think it better to die like men than to diminish away by inches . . . Our cause is just, and I hope the Great Being who governs everything will favour [it].'

Dragging Canoe enthusiastically accepted the war belt, but *Attakullakulla* and the other elderly Cherokee leaders, convinced that the rebels might win and full of foreboding, sat 'dejected and silent'. Their fears were quickly justified. Nancy Ward, a 'Beloved Woman' who was married to a colonist and opposed war, blunted the force of Dragging Canoe's campaign by warning the settlers, and the colonies promptly retaliated by sending an army of more than six thousand troops to invade Cherokee territory. Even though only a minority of the *Ani-Yunwiya* had taken up arms, the Americans made no distinction between 'hostile' and 'friendly' Indians and indiscriminately destroyed fifty of the Nation's towns. By May 1777, with hundreds of their people dead, hundreds more held as prisoners or sold as slaves, and the remainder reduced to the edge of starvation, the old chiefs were forced to sue for an end to a war they had not started or fought. The price, as usual, was further land cessions. In an acute assessment of Euro-American behaviour, *Onitositah* (Corn Tassel) complained:

> When we enter ... into treaties with our brothers, the whites, their whole cry is *more land!* Indeed, formerly it seemed to be a matter of formality with them to demand what they know we durst not refuse ...
>
> Let us examine the facts of your present irruption into our country ... What did you do? You marched into our territories with a superior force ... your numbers far exceeded us, and we fled to the stronghold of our extensive woods, there to secure our women and children ... You killed a few scattered and defenceless individuals, spread fire and desolation wherever you pleased, and returned again to your own habitations ...
>
> Your laws extend not into our country, nor ever did. You talk of the law of nature and the law of nations, and they are both against you.
>
> Indeed, much has been advanced on the want of what you term civilization among the Indians; and many proposals have been made to us to adopt your laws, your religion, your manners and your customs. But, we confess that we do not yet see the propriety, or practicability, of such a reformation, and should be better pleased with beholding the good effect of these doctrines in your own practices than with hearing you talk about them ...
>
> You say: Why do not the Indians till the ground and live as we do? May we not, with equal propriety, ask: Why do not the white people hunt and live as we do?

Ciu Canacina refused to accept the peace terms. He and hundreds of his followers moved down the Tennessee River to Chickimauga (near the present-day Chattanooga), where they were closer to British supplies and less vulnerable to attack, and continued an unremitting guerrilla war against the rebels and – with the end of the American Revolution in 1783 – the newly formed United States.

The colonists' victory removed any lingering ambiguity about the ultimate intentions of Anglo-America. No longer constrained by the frontier established by the Royal Proclamation, the new republic could extend westwards as far as the Pacific. The provincial English gentlemen who had made the Revolution, however, were determined to achieve 'expansion with honour', undertaking to deal with Native Americans 'in utmost good faith' and to continue the British practice of making formal treaties to ensure the orderly purchase and settlement of land. Ultimately, they thought, this process of national growth would benefit Euro- and Native Americans alike. As products of the Enlightenment, they believed – in the words of Jefferson's friend, Benjamin Rush – that 'Human nature is the same in all Ages and Countries,' and that there was therefore no reason why, with the proper education and equipment, the 'savage hunter' could not become a 'civilized farmer.' 'While they are learning to do better on less land,' wrote Jefferson himself, 'our increasing numbers will be calling for more land, and thus a coincidence of interests will be produced between those who have lands to spare, and want other necessaries, and those who have such necessaries to spare, and want lands.'

This idea was part of a long 'humanitarian' tradition, rooted in the 'praying towns' of colonial New England and prefiguring Indian policy in the second part of the nineteenth century. Although presented as an alternative to extermination, it did not envisage a long-term future for Native Americans either as distinct societies or as an identifiable ethnic group. Jefferson – like many later politicians – believed that the dwindling Indian population would simply be absorbed by the swelling tide of Euro-Americans. 'You will mix with us by marriage,' he told a delegation of Delawares in 1808. 'Your blood will run in our veins and will spread with us over this great island.' To encourage this process, one state, Virginia, even offered a bounty in 1784 to the 'white' partner in Indian/Euro-American marriages.

But few frontiersmen saw intermarriage as a solution to 'the Indian Problem'. Even before the American Revolution, the English traveller John D. F. Smith had found 'the most rancorous antipathy' to Native Americans among the colonists, who 'talk of extirpating them totally from the face of the earth, men, women, and children.' The war – in which most Indians had sided with the British – had deepened this hostility still further. (As usual, even Indians who had remained neutral or fought alongside the Americans were indiscriminately lumped together, in the popular imagination, with the 'enemy' majority.) One of the charges made against George III in the Declaration of Independence was that he had 'endeavoured to bring on the inhabitants of our frontiers, the merciless Indian savages, whose known rule of warfare is an undistinguished destruction of all ages, sexes and conditions,' and the congressional committee which subsequently shaped Native American policy spoke of the Indians as 'aggressors in the war, without even a pretence of provocation.'

This deep-seated animosity towards Indians, mixed with the exhilarating sense of freedom after a hard-fought struggle, created a heady new atmosphere in which settlers were even less willing to accept restraint from the United States than they had been from Britain. As early as 1789, the Secretary of War was complaining about flagrant treaty violations: 'If so direct and manifest contempt of the authority of the United States be suffered with impunity, it will be in vain to attempt to extend the arm of government to the frontiers.' Like the British, the federal government sometimes tried to expel illegal squatters, but generally ended up accepting their presence and forcing the Indians to accommodate them by surrendering more land. Then – within, sometimes, only a few months – the whole process would begin again as yet more settlers breached the new boundaries.

In the decades following independence, economic problems, rampant speculation and disputes over title drove more and more settlers west in search of their own land, keeping the United States in almost permanent conflict with Native Americans. In the 'Old Northwest', the area south of the Great Lakes which had seen the most intense nativist activity, Indians continued their struggle long after their former British allies had made peace: according to one estimate, between 1783 and 1790 they killed 1,500 settlers in raids on isolated communities. The Northwest Ordinance of 1787, designed to encourage American settlement and development of the region, sparked a more organized resistance. Although it provided that the Indians' 'lands and property shall never be taken from them without their consent' and that they 'shall never be invaded or disturbed, unless in just and lawful wars authorized by Congress,' the Ordinance was, in practice, no more successful than earlier proclamations in protecting Native Americans against invasion, murder, rape and theft, and by 1790 hundreds of aggrieved warriors were up in arms. A coalition of Shawnee, Potawatomis, Ottawas, Ojibways, Delawares and others, led by the able Miami chief Little Turtle, destroyed two expeditions sent by President Washington to 'pacify' the area, and was only finally defeated by an overwhelmingly superior force at the Battle of Fallen Timbers in 1794. The survivors fled to Fort Miami, still held by a British garrison that had encouraged and supplied them, but the commander, fearful of being drawn into open war with the United States, refused to open the gates, and hundreds of Indians were killed by pursuing Americans.

Little Turtle and many of his followers, finally convinced that they could not win militarily, adopted a more 'accommodationist' approach, accepting annuities from the US government in exchange for land and allowing Quaker missionaries to set up 'demonstration farms' to show them Euro-American agricultural techniques. Their attitude encouraged American hopes that Washington's 'civilization' policy could work, and at the same time provoked strong opposition from nativist factions among their own peoples. Following the Treaty of Greenville in 1795, in which the tribes of the Old Northwest ceded virtually all of present-day Ohio and much of Indiana, the rising Shawnee leader Tecumseh developed the thesis that no Native American tribe or individual had the right to sell land. As he was to tell William Henry Harrison some years later: 'Sell a country! Why not sell the air, the clouds and the great sea, as well as the earth? Did not the Great Spirit make them all for the use of his children?'

During the first decade of the nineteenth century, Tecumseh and his brother Tenskwatawa, 'the Prophet', became the focus for a revitalized nativist movement. Like the Iroquois Handsome Lake, Tenskwatawa had led a dissolute life before seeing a vision of the Native American creator, who revealed to him that Anglo-Americans 'grew from the scum of the great water, when it was troubled by an evil spirit and the froth was driven into the woods by a strong east wind. They are numerous, but I hate them. They are unjust; they have taken away your lands, which were not made for them.' In 1808, the two brothers founded the 'Prophet's Town' in Indiana, where people from different tribes could live together, insulated from the corrupting influence of 'white' America. Here they developed the concept of a permanent Indian state, co-existing with the United States but separated from it by a fixed boundary.

To begin with, Tecumseh hoped that by demonstrating their unity and the strength of their own culture, Native Americans could persuade the 'whites' to accept this idea. It became increasingly clear, however, that Anglo-America was not prepared for such a radical change of heart. In 1809, Governor Harrison gathered a group of unrepresentative chiefs at Fort Wayne, plied them with drink and duped them into 'selling' three million acres of Indiana for $7,600. Tecumseh was outraged, and began to make preparations to halt the frontier by force. Travelling from Canada to Georgia, he urged scores of tribes to join a huge pan-Indian coalition which, by remaining resolutely united and only striking when the time was right, would finally succeed where Metacom and Pontiac had failed.

Although his brother made a disastrous pre-emptive attack on the Americans in 1811, Tecumseh managed to restrain most of his followers until 1812, when the outbreak of a new conflict between Britain and the United States gave him the opportunity he had been waiting for. 'Here is a chance . . .' he told a meeting of Native American leaders, 'such as will never occur again – for us Indians of North America to form ourselves into one great combination.'

The British, recognizing Tecumseh's military gifts, appointed him a brigadier general, and he scored a string of spectacular successes in the Great Lakes area, but by now American settlement had already pushed far enough west to rupture the Indians' diplomatic network, splitting the southern and northern tribes and making it almost impossible for them to co-ordinate action effectively. When Tecumseh's friend Sir Isaac Brock, the British commander, was killed and replaced by the incompetent Colonel Henry Proctor, the tide of war turned against the Indians. In October 1813, Proctor – despite being begged by the Indians to stand his ground – fled before an advancing American army, and Tecumseh died covering his retreat.

But, in the Southeast, his message was still making converts. Most of the Cherokees – apart from the Chickimaugans – and the Choctaws, aware of their own vulnerability, had resisted the call to arms, and some, anxious to prove their loyalty to the United States, had even contributed men to the American forces. A growing minority of Creeks, however, proved more receptive. Since the American Revolution, a series of gifted civil leaders – often, like many of the Cherokee élite, the children or grandchildren of Scottish traders who had a deep understanding of Euro-American culture – had managed to keep the confederacy united and at peace with the United States, but the unrelenting encroachment on *Muskogee* territory had increasingly undermined their authority. By 1808, when Tecumseh first visited the Creeks, they had already lost millions of acres in fraudulent land 'purchases', and, possibly under his influence, the council decided that any chief who agreed to an unauthorized cession should face the death penalty. Tecumseh left a relative, Seekaboo, to teach his brother's nativist religion, and in 1813 hundreds of 'Red Sticks' – so-called because of their vermilion-painted war clubs – were ready to obey the Prophet's instructions: 'War now. War forever. War upon the living. War upon the dead; dig up their corpses from the grave; our country must give no rest to a white man's bones.'

The Red Sticks' campaign finally destroyed the unity of the Creeks. Under enormous US pressure, the 'White Sticks' from the 'Peace Towns' arrested and executed eight 'hostiles' who had killed settlers, thereby provoking a spiralling civil war between nativist and pro-American factions. Divisions deepened when the Red Sticks clashed with state militia and attacked Fort Mims, bringing the United States directly into the war. When General Andrew Jackson invaded the nativists' heartland with an army of 3,500, burning towns, killing men and forcibly relocating women and children, he was accompanied not only by Cherokee, Choctaw and Chickasaw regiments but also by contingents from the Creeks' own 'White Stick' majority. Massively outnumbered and outgunned, the Red Sticks were finally surrounded at their stronghold at Horseshoe Bend on the Tallapoosa River in March 1814. In a ferocious day-long battle – during which Jackson's life was saved by a Cherokee – 750 of the 1,000 or so Red Stick defenders were killed. Some of the handful of survivors fled to the comparative safety of Spanish-held Florida, where growing numbers of displaced Creeks – known as 'Seminoles', probably from the Spanish *cimarrón*, 'wild people' – had established settlements. Here, they continued a war against the invaders for more than a generation, finally forcing the United States army to withdraw without achieving a decisive victory.

The Creek confederacy emerged from the conflict critically weakened. Perhaps half the Red Sticks' fighting men had been killed in only nine months, and most of their communities had been destroyed. The White Sticks' casualties had been lighter, but they still had to pay a substantial price for a war in which, in many cases, they had fought for the United States. All but one of the chiefs who signed the notorious Treaty of Horseshoe Bend, in which the confederacy was forced to surrender twenty-three million acres as 'compensation' for the war, had been allies of the Americans.

The lesson of this catastrophe was not lost on the *Muskogee* or their neighbours. It suggested that the fundamental principles which, from the Native American point of view, governed relations between societies had broken down. In a reciprocal universe, a policy of political submission and voluntary land cessions should have brought protection from the United States, while low levels of warfare should have deterred further aggression. In fact, both accommodation and resistance had seemed only to accelerate the influx of settlers and the loss of Indian land. Even nativism, while finally recognizing that Europeans would never, in the long term, agree to live reciprocally with Native Americans, had failed to reconnect Indians with the sacred power they needed to expel them.

✿   ✿   ✿

Brothers! I have listened to many talks from our great father. When he first came over the wide waters, he was but a little man . . . very little. His legs were cramped by sitting long in his big boat, and he begged for a little land to light his fire on . . . But when the white man had warmed himself before the Indians' fire and filled himself with their hominy, he became very large. With a step he bestrode the mountains, and his feet covered the plains and the valleys. His hand grasped the eastern and the western sea, and his head rested on the moon. Then he became our Great Father. He loved his red children, and he said, 'Get a little further, lest I tread on thee . . .'

*Brothers I have listened to a great many talks from our father.
But they always began and ended in this – 'Get a little further;
you are too near me.'*

Speckled Snake, Creek

Even before the Red Sticks War, a number of Southeastern Indians
had pondered this problem and begun to evolve a different policy
which, they hoped, could ensure their survival. Predominantly prosperous, 'white', educated Cherokees from the influential 'mixed-blood'
dynasties, their privileged – but often uncomfortable – vantage-point
on the border between two worlds gave them a kind of cultural double
vision, enabling them to see and understand Euro-American motives
almost from the inside. They concluded that Anglo-America's refusal
to co-exist with Native Americans stemmed from the perception that
they were 'savages' and the belief that – as Benjamin Lincoln put it in
1792 – 'Civilized and uncivilized people cannot live in the same
territory, or even in the same neighbourhood.' To be allowed to remain
in their homelands, therefore, Indians must overcome 'white' hostility
by becoming 'civilized'.

But, while it was culturally accommodationist, the new strategy
shared the nativists' absolute commitment to retaining tribal territory.
When the Cherokee Nation in Georgia formally became a republic in
1820, with an elected bicameral legislature, a European-style judicial
system and a police force of 'light horse', it made the unauthorized sale
of land an act of treason, punishable by death. Four years later,
members of the National Council declared that, having already surrendered most of their original territory to Britain and the United States,
they were left with only just enough to provide for themselves and their
children, and it was now 'the fixed and unalterable determination of
this nation never again to cede one foot more of land.'

In 1821 the Cherokee genius Sequoyah succeeded, after years of work,
in producing a written form of the language. Obsessed by the idea of
'catching and taming a wild animal,' he painstakingly isolated the
eighty-six syllables of spoken Cherokee and then assigned a symbol to
each one. This made learning to read and write exceptionally easy – all
it required was memorizing the characters – with the result that, almost
overnight, virtually all the *Ani-Yunwiya* became literate. In 1827, the

Nation adopted a written constitution, modelled on the United States', and in 1828 a Cherokee newspaper, the *Phoenix*, began publication.

At the same time, thousands of Cherokee were adopting other aspects of Euro-American culture. The old stockaded towns and communal fields were increasingly abandoned in favour of small American-style farmsteads, where individual families cultivated wheat, apples, peaches, tobacco and cotton and raised livestock. Missionaries were invited to open schools and churches. A census of the nation in 1825 found that it already contained 7,600 houses, 18 schools, 10 sawmills, 31 grist mills, nearly 3,000 ploughs, 46,000 pigs and 22,000 cattle. Some of the more assimilated élite had become successful entrepreneurs, amassing large personal fortunes and living much like their rich 'white' neighbours. Lewis Ross, for example, owned stores, a mill, three ferry boats and more than forty black slaves: according to visitors from New England, his 'elegant white house' was 'as neatly furnished as almost any in Litchfield County,' and there were 'Negroes enough to wait on us.'

For many *Ani-Yunwiya* these changes were deeply troubling. To replace maize with wheat, to transform farming with ploughs and other heavy implements, and to make domestic animals the principal source of meat and skins was to do more than substitute one set of practical skills for another: it was to strike at the very heart of the culture. The symmetrical association between women and maize on the one hand and men and animals on the other was central to the Cherokees' vision of reality. It underlay not only the annual subsistence cycle and the ritual calendar, but also the *Ani-Yunwiya*'s relationship with each other and with the fundamental forces of the universe. To disrupt it was to invite social and cosmic disaster.

Throughout the early nineteenth century, 'conservative' elements opposed the process of 'modernization'. In 1805, a group of 'traditional-ists' separated themselves and moved west into Arkansas, where – for the time being – they could follow the old way of life. In 1811, as the tide of nativism was rising once again, a Cherokee prophet called *Tsali* told the *Ani-Yunwiya* that they must:

> Go and ... plant Indian corn and gather it according to the ways of your ancestors, and do away with the mills. The Mother of the Nation

[the maize goddess, *Selu*] has abandoned you, because the grinding breaks her bones. She wants to come back to you, if you will get the white men out of the country and go back to your former ways.

... You may keep good neighbourly relations with [the 'whites'] ... just see to it that you get back from them your old Beloved Towns.

In the late 1820s, a conservative leader (ironically called White Path) led a revolt against the 'mixed-blood' élite's plans to undermine the customary powers of the clans. But the 'progressive' movement proved too strong to resist. As more Cherokee converted to Christianity and sent their children to school, a growing minority of the nation came to see themselves and their culture through the prism of Anglo-American beliefs and assumptions. This process, which over the next century was to become familiar to most native groups, made the clash between 'savagery' and 'civilization' an internal conflict, dividing not only communities but individuals against themselves. Encouraged to believe that their families were 'dirty heathens', their shamans fraudulent 'conjurers' and their myths and rituals false, Native American children grew up deeply confused and, often, seething with self-hatred. Success, it seemed, lay in acknowledging the inferiority, if not the wickedness, of everything to which they were emotionally most closely tied and ruthlessly trying to suppress it in themselves.

This shift is vividly shown in the *Address to the Whites*, written in 1826 by Elias Boudinot, the brilliant young Cherokee who, two years later, at the age of twenty-four, was to become the first editor of the *Phoenix*. Despite being only one-sixteenth 'white', Boudinot adopted a European name, dressed like a southern gentleman, and spoke in flawless English. Like *Ciu Canacina* and *Onitositah* before him, he was an outstanding orator in the grand Cherokee tradition, but where their speeches had bristled with cultural self-confidence, there is no mistaking the tone of apology and the acceptance of Euro-American values in his. Although his analysis of Native American decline echoes Tecumseh's, the conclusion he draws is very different. He demands that the United States should respect the nation's borders not because – as Corn Tassel had argued – the *Ani-Yunwiya* are *culturally different* and can not be expected to live like 'whites', but for precisely the opposite reason: they are potentially the same, and allowing them to 'progress' in peace will be the most effective way of ensuring that they 'catch up' with their 'civilized' neighbours:

> What is an Indian? Is he not formed of the same materials with yourself? For 'of one blood God created all the nations that dwell on the face of the earth.' Though it be true that he is ignorant, that he is a heathen, that he is a savage; yet he is no more than all others have been under similar circumstances. Eighteen centuries ago what were the inhabitants of Great Britain?
>
> You here behold an *Indian*, my kindred are *Indians*, and my fathers sleeping in the wilderness grave – they too were *Indians*. But I am not as my fathers were ... I have had greater advantages than most of my race; and I now stand before you delegated by my native country to seek her interest ... and by my public efforts to assist in raising her to an equal standing with other nations of the earth ...
>
> It needs not the power of argument on the nature of man, to silence forever the remark that 'it is the purpose of the Almighty that the Indians should be exterminated.' It needs only that the world should know what we have done in the last few years ...
>
> Yes, methinks I can view my native country, rising from the ashes of her degradation, wearing her purified and beautiful garment, and taking her seat with the nations of the earth ...
>
> There is, in Indian history, something very melancholy ... We have seen everywhere the poor aborigines melt away before the white population. I merely speak of the fact, without at all referring to the cause. We have seen, I say, one family after another, one tribe after another, nation after nation, pass away; until only a few solitary creatures are left to tell the sad story of extinction.
>
> Shall this precedent be followed? I ask you, shall red men live, or shall they be swept from the earth? With you and this public at large, the decision chiefly rests.

Support for the 'progressives' was not confined, however, to the assimilated élite and the growing minority of Christianized and school-educated Cherokee. Many of the most conservative traditionalists also backed 'modernization', convinced by men like *Kooweskoowee* (John Ross), the exceptional 'mixed-blood' leader who became Principal Chief in 1828, that it was the only way to retain the sacred landscape which gave them their sense of meaning and identity. The same logic

persuaded the Chickasaws, Choctaws and – eventually – the Creeks to
follow the Cherokee example and adopt 'civilized' institutions, although,
in every case, the process was accompanied by painful internal conflicts.

But, for all the political skill of the 'progressives', and their ability to
argue their case in terms of Anglo-American moral and legal assumptions, events were moving against them. In 1803, with the acquisition
of Louisiana from France, the size of the United States had doubled at
a stroke, giving an enormous impetus to the young republic's westward
expansion and sharpening its sense of destiny and identity. The new
mood, heightened by fears that immigration from other parts of Europe
would 'swamp' the predominantly 'Anglo-Saxon' character of the
United States, was, in a sense, a retreat from Enlightenment humanism
and a return to the Puritans' belief in themselves as God's Chosen
People. Where seventeenth-century New Englanders had seen the
'clearing' of Indians by disease as evidence that God intended the
English to possess their land, so early nineteenth-century Americans
saw the sudden opening of the area beyond the Mississippi as confir-
mation that some divine or historic providence had ordained them to
occupy the whole continent. Americans represented not merely a
superior culture, but a distinct *race* with a unique destiny in the New
World.

Time and again, as the American frontier advanced, it reached areas
previously held by the French and Spanish – and occasionally, as in the
Southeast, even by the British – where these hard-and-fast racial
distinctions had been blurred by generations of intermarriage, economic interdependence and cultural exchange. The French and Spanish
authorities had used sometimes brutal methods to make Native Americans accept certain aspects of 'civilization', particularly Catholicism, but
had not generally established firm physical or social boundaries
between colonists and natives. In some areas, this symbiosis had created
a 'middle ground', where people of mixed ancestry had evolved their
own distinct culture and a crucial role as brokers and intermediaries
between Native American and European.

The expanding United States tended to sweep away, or at least
marginalize, these pockets of ambiguity. As James Mooney put it: '...
it never occurred to the man of Teutonic blood that he could have for
a neighbour anyone not of his own stock and colour. While the English

colonists recognized the native proprietorship so far as to make treaties with the Indians, it was chiefly for the purpose of fixing limits beyond which the Indian should never come after he had once parted with his title ... The Indian was regarded as an incumbrance to be cleared off, like the trees and the wolves, before white men could live in the country.' This view simplified the complex drama of the frontier into an elemental struggle not only between 'savagery' and 'civilization' but also, increasingly, between two essentially incompatible 'races'. 'No State can achieve proper culture, civilization and progress ...' wrote Martin Van Buren in 1837, 'as long as Indians are permitted to remain.'

Less than forty years after independence, eleven new states had joined the union and several territories were preparing for statehood. The swelling tide of new representatives shifted the balance of power in the republic and, increasingly, entrenched frontier prejudices in Washington itself. Already, in 1802, in exchange for surrendering their claims to western territory beyond their existing borders, the states had insisted that the federal government should 'extinguish' all remaining Native American title *within* their boundaries. The following year, Jefferson, disappointed that the Shawnee and other tribes were con- tinuing their vigorous resistance to American expansion, and increas- ingly worried that the presence of non-European peoples would undermine the vitality of the United States (a concern which also prompted him to suggest repatriating freed slaves to Africa), proposed a new solution to the 'Indian Problem' which would satisfy the states' demands. Tribes could be persuaded to surrender their land in the east and then given equivalent tracts west of the Mississippi, on territory which the United States had acquired from France but did not yet require for settlement.

By the mid-1820s, 'removal' had become official US policy. Like the earlier 'plan for civilization', it was justified on humanitarian grounds. Its advocates argued that, wherever Anglo-Americans had settled in close proximity to indigenous communities, the Indians had quickly become depleted by disease, alcohol and the unequal contest with 'civilization'. Removal to the west, where missionaries and government officials could protect them from unscrupulous drink-peddlers and other undesirable elements and at the same time teach them the skills required to live alongside 'whites', must, surely, be in their best

interests: indeed, it was the only viable alternative to complete extermination. Outlining the scheme to Congress in 1825, President Monroe
suggested that its advantages would be obvious enough to Native
Americans to 'surmount all their prejudices in favour of the soil of their
nativity, however strong they may be.' He went on:

> Their elders have sufficient intelligence to discern the certain
> progress of events in the present train, and sufficient virtue, by
> yielding to momentary sacrifices, to protect their families and poster-
> ity from inevitable destruction. They will also perceive that they may
> thus attain an elevation to which as communities they could not
> otherwise aspire . . .

The Southeastern Indians were particularly vulnerable. The traffic
in deerskins, in which they had been intimately involved, had increasingly been replaced by a thriving cotton trade – spurred on by the
invention of the cotton gin in 1790 – in which they were at best
marginal producers and at worst obstacles to land-hungry whites. Much
of their remaining territory was rich farmland, and the more they
'improved' it in the hope of turning themselves into acceptable
neighbours, the more desirable they made it to would-be plantation-
owners. A popular song at the time went:

> All I ask in this creation
> Is a pretty little wife and a big plantation
> Way up yonder in the Cherokee Nation.

In the years after 1803, the states tried repeatedly to persuade the
'Five Civilized Tribes' to accept removal, but, although some more
traditional people did drift west, the vast majority stood firm behind
the increasingly determined 'progressive' leadership. Having previously
complained about the 'savagery' of the Indians, Southeastern Anglo-
Americans now blamed the government for having 'instructed [them]
in the arts of civilized life and . . . thereby imbued them with a desire
to acquire property.' As Native American resistance hardened, the
states demanded more and more insistently that the federal government should honour its commitment to extinguish Indian title, even if
this meant unilaterally abrogating treaty obligations to tribes who were
unwilling to move. Indian treaties, they maintained – in the words of

Governor Gilmer of Georgia – were merely 'expedients by which ignorant, intractable, and savage people were induced without blood-shed to yield up what civilized people had the right to possess by virtue of that command of the Creator delivered to man upon his formation – be fruitful, multiply, and replenish the earth, and subdue it.'

In 1828, Andrew Jackson was elected President. Some modern historians have disputed James Mooney's economical description of him as 'a frontiersman and Indian hater,' pointing out that he raised an adopted Creek boy as his son and claiming that he genuinely believed Removal would benefit Native Americans, but, whatever his motives, there is no question that he was deeply sympathetic to the demands of 'whites' in the Southeast. Although Indian Affairs was supposedly a federal responsibility, he quickly tipped the wink to the southern states that, if they chose to take matters into their own hands, he would not stand in their way. 'Build a fire under them [the Indians],' he reputedly told Georgia's congressmen. 'When it gets hot enough, they'll move.'

Georgia did not hesitate to take the hint. The clamour for Indian land had intensified still further with the discovery of gold in Cherokee territory earlier that year, and, even before Jackson's inauguration, the state legislature voted to extend its jurisdiction over the Native Americans living within its own borders. The Cherokee Nation was to be surveyed and divided into 'land lots' and 'gold lots', which were then to be distributed among Georgia's citizens by a public lottery. Each Cherokee family was, in theory, entitled to one 160-acre holding, but no title deeds were given, and Indians resisting the seizure of their property were subject to summary imprisonment. At the same time, the state made it illegal for an Indian to testify against a 'white' in court, thereby effectively inviting its citizens to plunder the Native Americans at will. The National Council was forbidden to meet – except for the purpose of making land cessions – and 'white' people living within the Nation's boundaries were required to swear an oath of allegiance to the state or face a four year jail sentence.

Mississippi and Alabama quickly followed Georgia's lead (although Alabama was slightly less punitive), and in May 1830, at Jackson's instigation, Congress passed the Indian Removal Act, providing for the compulsory resettlement of the Southeastern tribes in 'Indian Territory' (roughly present-day Oklahoma). The Choctaws were the first to submit, agreeing to exchange their ancestral lands in Mississippi for a new homeland where they would be 'forever secure' against incorporation 'in any Territory or State.' About a third of the tribe chose the alternative of taking an individual allotment and becoming a citizen of the state, but the federal agent refused to register their selections and, with a few exceptions, they were forced to join the exodus west. The following year, Alexis de Tocqueville watched a 'numerous band' of the emigrants reaching the Mississippi in the depths of an 'exceptionally severe' winter:

> ... there were among them the wounded, the sick, newborn babies, and old men on the point of death. They had neither tents nor wagons, but only some provisions and weapons. I saw them embark to cross the great river, and the sight will never fade from my memory. Neither sob nor complaint rose from that silent assembly. Their afflictions were of long standing, and they felt them to be irremediable.

The Creeks, who had already lost all their land in Georgia, voted to remain in Alabama and submit to state law, but they were told this was impossible. They finally accepted removal, but before they could emigrate they were overrun by 'white' land-grabbers who drove them from their homes, seized their crops and livestock and used fraud, bribery and intimidation to 'buy' individual holdings. In despair, some of the Creeks attacked settlers in retaliation, sparking yet another war with the Americans and 'accommodationist' elements among their own people, and most of the survivors – the men in irons – were driven west by the army. Oral traditions recorded over a century later give a vivid sense of the horror of the experience. According to one account, an old woman carrying 'a small bundle of her belongings ... began a sad song which was later taken up by the others ... "I have no more land. I am driven away from home, driven up the red waters, let us all go, let us all die together ..."' Another source describes how:

> Many fell by the wayside, too faint with hunger or too weak to keep up with the rest ... A crude bed was quickly prepared for these sick and weary people. Only a bowl of water was left within the [sic] reach, thus they were left to suffer and die alone. The little children piteously cried day after day ... They were once happy children ...

There were several men carrying reeds with eagle feathers attached to the end. These men continually circled around the wagon trains or during the night around the camps ... Their purpose was to encourage the Indians not to be heavy hearted nor to think of the homes that had been left.

By the end of the removal process, it was estimated that the Creeks had lost 45 per cent of their population.

The Cherokee, however, stubbornly refused to emigrate. In a visit to Washington, Ross met delegates from the Iroquois League and, in a speech echoing Dragging Canoe's impassioned warning two generations before, told them that after having been made 'to drink of the bitter cup of humiliation; treated like dogs ... our country and the graves of our fathers torn from us,' Native Americans now found themselves 'fugitives, vagrants and strangers in our own country.' Although the other 'Civilized Tribes' had abandoned their homeland, the bulk of the Cherokee 'still remain firmly upon our ancient domain,' where 'our position ... may be compared to a solitary tree in an open space, where all the forest trees around have been prostrated by a furious tornado.'

The Cherokee contested Georgia's right to assert jurisdiction over them in the courts, and in 1832 Chief Justice John Marshall found in their favour, concluding that 'The Cherokee Nation ... is a distinct community, occupying its own territory, ... which the citizens of Georgia have no right to enter, but with the assent of the Cherokees themselves, or in conformity with treaties and with the acts of Congress.'

The Cherokee were overjoyed: Elias Boudinot wrote that it was 'glorious news' which created 'a new era on the Indian question.' Their euphoria was short-lived, however. Jackson – reputedly with the words 'John Marshall has made his decision; now let him enforce it' – rejected the ruling and encouraged Georgia to continue its harassment of the Indians. In the following months, the state went ahead with its lottery, and the 'winners' swarmed through the Nation, evicting thousands of Cherokees and seizing their livestock. For all their money and connections, the mixed-blood élite were not immune: John Ross and his family were driven from their plantation and forced to retreat to a one-room cabin across the border in Tennessee.

The persecution of the Cherokee contributed to a growing revulsion among Europeans at what they saw as American hypocrisy. 'You will see them one hour lecturing their mob on the indefeasible rights of man,' wrote the English traveller Frances Trollope, 'and the next driving from their homes the children of the soil, whom they have bound themselves to protect by the most solemn treaties.' But many Americans – particularly New Englanders, who had become progressively more sympathetic to native people since their own 'Indian Problem' had been decisively resolved more than a century before – were equally outraged at Georgia's behaviour. A number of missionaries in Cherokee country, including Samuel Worcester, whose case had precipitated John Marshall's Supreme Court decision, suffered abuse, expulsion and, on occasion, imprisonment for refusing to acknowledge the jurisdiction of the state. Anglo-American well-wishers mounted perhaps the most extensive and well-orchestrated pro-Indian campaign in American history, organizing public meetings and contributing funds to sustain the Cherokees' legal struggle after Jackson, claiming that the Nation had been abolished and therefore did not exist, had cut off its treaty annuities from the United States.

But Jackson was immovable. He continued to encourage Georgia as it flouted the laws of his own government, and by 1834 a number of influential Cherokee – including Elias Boudinot, his uncle The Ridge (known to 'whites' as 'Major Ridge' for his part in the Red Sticks War) and The Ridge's son John – had at last reached the conclusion that there was no alternative to emigration. At least 80 per cent of the population still supported John Ross and his 'National Party', but the pro-removal 'Treaty Party' entered secret negotiations with the state, and in December 1835, in the infamous 'Treaty of New Echota', Boudinot and others signed away the last remnants of their country for $5 million and a new homeland in Indian Territory. Although there is some evidence that they may have been bribed (certainly their property was withdrawn from the lottery wheel), they seem to have been motivated primarily by the conviction that this was the best course of action for the Nation. They undoubtedly knew, in view of the Cherokee constitution's penalty for unauthorized land cessions, that they had taken an enormous, and probably fatal, risk. The Ridge commented: 'I have signed my death warrant,' and Boudinot said: 'We can die but the great Cherokee Nation will be saved . . . Oh, what is a man worth who will not dare to die for his people?'

Neither John Ross nor any other officer of the Cherokee Nation had signed the treaty, and when it came before Congress it was described by John Quincy Adams as an 'eternal disgrace upon the country.' Nonetheless, despite intense opposition, Jackson secured its passage by one vote. When Ross tried to go to Washington to protest, a party of Georgia Guard crossed the state line into Tennessee and arrested him. *Junaluska*, the Cherokee who had saved Jackson's life at Horseshoe Bend, travelled to the capital himself to appeal to the President in person, but Jackson abruptly told him: 'Sir your audience is ended, there is nothing I can do for you.'

The Cherokee were given two years to make their preparations and leave. Several bands, including many of the 'Treaty Party', set off at once, but the vast majority were still resolute that they wanted to stay in their homeland. 'We the great mass of the people think only of the love we have to our land,' three of them wrote to Ross. 'To let it go will be like throwing away . . . [our] mother that gave . . . [us] birth.'

The government sent a contingent of troops to enforce Cherokee adherence, but its commander, General Wool, found that the Indians denied having made a treaty and were 'almost universally opposed' to it. Thousands, worried that by accepting rations they might compromise themselves, 'preferred living upon the roots and sap of trees,' and 'Many have said they will die before they will leave the country.' 'The whole scene,' he confided in a letter, was 'heart-rending,' with 'white men . . . like vultures . . . watching, ready to pounce upon their prey and strip them of everything they have or expect from the government of the United States.'

Even the Treaty Party was shocked by the rapacity of the settlers. Less than two months after the treaty had been approved by Congress, Major Ridge was appealing to Jackson for protection against 'the white people . . . [who] have got our lands and now . . . are preparing to fleece us of the money accruing from the treaty. We found our plantations taken either in whole or in part by the Georgians – suits instituted against us for back rents for our own farms.' The scenes of pillage described by The Ridge on the eve of his people's expulsion from their homeland curiously echo their first encounter with Europeans during the de Soto expedition nearly three centuries before: 'The lowest classes of the white people are flogging the Cherokees with cowhides, hickories, and clubs. We are not safe in our houses ... This barbarous treatment is not confined to men, but the women are stripped also and whipped without law or mercy ...'

Despite their continual harassment, most of the Cherokee continued to stand firm behind Ross, who repeatedly pressed the United States to nullify the treaty. By the end of the two years given for removal, less than an eighth of the Nation had emigrated, and – despite pleas for an extension – General Winfield Scott and 7,000 troops were sent to remove the remainder by force. A few hundred Cherokee avoided capture or managed to escape – sometimes thanks to help from 'white' friends or sympathizers – and hid in the mountains of North Carolina, where their descendants still live today. The vast majority were rounded up at bayonet-point and held in stockades, where hundreds died from hunger and disease, before being moved to Indian Territory. Watching them leave, a missionary wrote:

> It is mournful to see how reluctantly these people go away, even the stoutest hearts melt into tears when they turn their faces towards the setting sun – & I am sure that this land will be bedewed with a Nation's tears – if not with their blood.

His words were prophetic. A Georgia volunteer who subsequently became a Confederate colonel wrote towards the end of his life: 'I fought through the civil war and have seen men shot to pieces and slaughtered by thousands, but the Cherokee removal was the cruellest work I ever knew.' The Indians were heartbroken, poorly supplied with food and clothing and often forced to travel at the most dangerous time of year, and sickness, brutality, cold and despair took such a toll that the journey west became known as *Nunna daul Tsunyi* (literally, 'the trail where we cried'). At least 4,000, and perhaps as many as 8,000, are thought to have died on the 'Trail of Tears', reducing the population – which, after centuries of decline, had begun to recover in the decades before removal – by between 20 per cent and 40 per cent. The survivors, struggling to re-establish themselves in Indian Territory, remained bitterly divided over the fraudulent treaty that had sent them there. In the summer of 1839, assassins carried out the threatened death penalty on Boudinot and the two Ridges, and only outstanding statesmanship by Ross prevented the Nation erupting into all-out civil war.

The tragedy of the 'Five Civilized Tribes' has always seemed especially poignant to American historians. Their experiment – a kind of auto-social engineering – was the antithesis of the recalcitrant 'savagery' expected from Native Americans. Instead of rejecting the values on which the United States was built, the Southeastern tribes seemed eagerly to embrace many of them, tacitly acknowledging the superiority of 'civilization' and signalling their willingness to be, in some sense, 'American'. Their expulsion seemed to close off the prospect of a different version of US history, in which even Indians could be seen as having benefited from the arrival of Europeans and participating in the blessings of the American dream.

It is, understandably, easy to sympathize with and admire people whose behaviour affirms rather than challenges one's own fundamental beliefs in this way, and the literature is full of paeans to the Indians' remarkable 'progress' and anger at their treatment. Grace Steele Woodward, for example, in her classic history *The Cherokees*, writes:

> This image of any primitive tribe or nation from dark savagery into the sunlight of civilization is a significant event. But in the case of the Cherokee, the event is both significant and phenomenal. Between 1540 and 1906, the Cherokee tribe of Indians reached a higher peak of civilization than any other North American tribe.

For Woodward and other historians, it is the 'advancement' of the 'Civilized Tribes' towards the American ideal, their acceptance of Western political principles and their appeal to US law, that makes their betrayal by the government such an egregious national dishonour. In fact, however, it was their very success in Euro-American terms that made the pressures against them irresistible. Their economic prosperity made non-Indians still more covetous of their land and hastened the move towards a racial rather than cultural definition of 'savagery': if Indians could not be dispossessed because they had failed to cultivate the soil, then they had to be removed because they were biologically inferior. The nations unwittingly weakened their own position by incorporating this kind of racial classification in their own Western-style constitutions: the Cherokee, for instance, ruled that neither black slaves nor white men living in the Nation could vote.

Alvin M. Josephy echoes many other scholars when he calls the removal of the Southeastern tribes 'one of the blackest chapters in American history.' It was, unquestionably, an appalling episode. But what was about to happen to scores of native peoples further west, including the 'Five Civilized Tribes' in their new home in Indian Territory, was in many ways far worse.

7. Southwest

Return of the white brother

Now Montezuma [a Tohono O'odham culture hero] called all the tribes together and said, 'I am greater than anything that has ever been, greater than anything which exists now, and greater than anything that will ever be. Now, you people shall build me a tall house, floor upon floor upon floor, a house rising into the sky, rising far above this earth into the heavens, where I shall rule as Chief of all the Universe.'

The Great Mystery Power descended from the sky to reason with Montezuma, telling him to stop challenging that which cannot be challenged, but Montezuma would not listen. He said: 'I am almighty. Let no power stand in my way. I am the Great Rebel. I shall turn this world upside down to my own liking.'

Then good changed to evil. Men began to hunt and kill animals. Disregarding the eternal laws by which humans had lived, they began to fight among themselves. The Great Mystery Power tried to warn Montezuma and the people by pushing the sun farther away from the earth and placing it where it is now. Winter, snow, ice, and hail appeared, but no one heeded this warning.

In the meantime Montezuma made the people labour to put up his many-storied house, whose rooms were of coral and jet, turquoise and mother-of-pearl. It rose higher and higher, but just as it began to soar above the clouds far into the sky, the Great Mystery Power made the earth tremble. Montezuma's many-storied house of precious stones collapsed into a heap of rubble.

When that happened, the people discovered that they could no longer understand the language of the animals, and the different tribes, even though they were all human beings, could no longer understand each other. Then Montezuma shook his fists toward the sky and called: 'Great Mystery Power, I defy you. I shall fight

*you. I shall tell the people not to pray or make sacrifices of corn
and fruit to the Creator. I, Montezuma, am taking your place!'*

*The Great Mystery Power sighed, and even wept, because the
one he had chosen to lead mankind had rebelled against him. Then
the Great Mystery resolved to vanquish those who rose against
him. He sent the locust flying far across the eastern waters, to
summon a people in an unknown land, people whose faces and
bodies were full of hair, who rode astride strange beasts, who
were encased in iron, wielding iron weapons, who had magic
hollow sticks spitting fire, thunder, and destruction. The Great
Mystery Power allowed these bearded, pitiless people to come in
ships across the great waters out of the east – permitted them to
come to Montezuma's country, taking away Montezuma's power
and destroying him utterly.*

From *Montezuma and the Great Flood*

The Southwestern United States, a hot, arid area of desert, mountains
and pine-covered hills, is the polar opposite of the Northeast not only
geographically and climatically but also culturally and historically.

Where pre-Columbian New England was inhabited by a number of
essentially similar, linguistically related Indian societies, the Southwest
was a bewildering mosaic of different cultures living in sometimes
uneasy symbiosis with each other. And while, in the Northeast, this
Indian reality seems to have been all but obliterated centuries ago, in
large areas of Arizona and New Mexico, the Anglo-American presence
still feels often only skin-deep. Even today, in the low desert south of
Phoenix, you can find scores of tiny Tohono O'odham villages where
the women sit in the shade of *ramadas* (open-walled, grass-roofed
shelters) weaving intricately patterned traditional baskets from yucca,
beargrass and devil's claw. Travelling north to the vast Navajo reservation, you can drive for hours through a dreamlike landscape of bluffs,
eroded grassland and weird red-rock formations (Monument Valley is
on the reservation), broken only occasionally by a house, a traditional
hogan or hut, or a little flock of sheep reduced to insect-scale by the
immensity of the desert. When you reach a town, the gas station looks
American enough, but going inside to pay you may notice that the

commentary on the televised basketball game is in Navajo rather than English. And further east, at Acoma Pueblo in New Mexico, you can glimpse what the first Spaniards must have seen when they first reached the area in the middle of the sixteenth century: a dense huddle of adobe houses – perhaps the oldest continuously inhabited community in the country – crowded on to the top of a sheer-sided *mesa* rising dramatically out of the heat shimmer, where the people still follow the same annual cycle of ceremonies and festivals that their ancestors practised hundreds of years before Columbus.

This remarkable diversity and endurance stems from a history which has consistently pulled the Southwest away from the rest of North America towards Meso-america. If you look at the 'Southwest culture area' on a map, you find that it straddles the present international boundary, stretching from the edge of the Great Basin in Nevada to the states of Chihuahua and Sonora in Northwestern Mexico. Its proximity to the great civilizations of Middle America not only gave the region a distinct cultural identity long before European contact, but also ensured that the encounter, when it did come, was with Spain rather than with Britain or France. When the Southwest was finally acquired by the United States in the middle of the nineteenth century, it had already been shaped by three centuries of co-existence between Europeans and Indians who had evolved very different solutions to the problems of living together.

Perhaps the simplest way to understand the complex pattern of peoples and cultures in the Southwest is through the area's 'prehistory'. (Since there were no written records before the arrival of Europeans, 'prehistory' effectively means everything that happened prior to contact, thereby reinforcing the assumption that the 'history' of North America only began with its 'discovery'.) Because many of the native societies have been – comparatively – so little disrupted, it is relatively easy to trace their development from earlier communities. Not only are many of their own oral traditions still unusually complete, but the hot dry climate has preserved an abundance of archaeological material.

Like 'Palaeo-Indians' elsewhere, the first Southwesterners seem to have been big game hunters who arrived in the area at least 25,000 years ago – and possibly much earlier – and then, over generations, gradually evolved more specialized cultures adapted to the climate and resources of the area. As many large mammal species retreated or died out at the end of the Ice Age and lakes and waterways dried up, people over much of the region increasingly adopted a 'desert foraging' way of life, based on hunting small game, snakes and insects and gathering edible plants such as yucca, juniper, prickly pear and piñon.

Then, around 3500 BC, some groups seem also to have started growing maize – the earliest known instance of cultivation north of Mexico – and during the next three millennia or so, wherever climatic conditions permitted, agriculture became an increasingly important part of the economy. The first true farming civilization, the Mogollon, appeared around 500 BC in mountains on the present-day Arizona–New Mexico border. Here, on the banks of streams and along easily defended ridges, communities started building larger, more permanent villages of wood-framed, semi-subterranean 'pit houses' and using digging sticks to cultivate plots of corn, squash, tobacco and cotton. Over the next few centuries – perhaps as a result of Mogollon influence – a similar way of life was adopted by peoples in several different parts of the region, eventually reaching the ancestors of the modern Yuman-speaking tribes on the Colorado River – the Mojave, Yavapai, Yuma, Havasupai, Maricopa and others – who continued to practise it into 'historic' times. The Mogollons' own culture seems to have died out as a separate tradition after around AD 1200, but it is thought that the Mogollon *people* survived and evolved into the modern Zuñi.

Meanwhile, a second farming culture, the Hohokam (from a Piman word meaning 'Vanished Ones'), had begun to develop in the arid valleys of the Salt and Gila Rivers to the west. Although in its earliest stages it seems to have been very like the Mogollon, around AD 600 it was suddenly transformed by a series of new innovations. Hohokam communities became larger, with ball courts, earthworks and, in some instances, platform mounds, and, instead of relying simply on flood-water, the people started to dig extensive systems of ditches – one network eventually covered 150 miles – to irrigate their crops. These changes suggest a strong Meso-american influence, which – like the Mississippian culture of the Southeast – may have been introduced by migrants from Mexico.

Unlike the Mississippians, however, Hohokam society seems to have remained fairly peaceful and egalitarian – at least until its final stages, when there is some evidence that it may have started to develop a more stratified social system under a priest-ruler. The main settlement, Snaketown, contained about one hundred pit houses and extended, at its height, over more than 300 acres. Although we cannot recreate its life in detail, the fragments of evidence we have hint at a world of brilliant colour and enormous cultural vitality. The Hohokam produced magnificent textiles, pottery and jewellery, and were perhaps the first people in the world to master etching, using fermented saguaro cactus juice to burn images into shells which they had acquired through trade with the California coast.

After about AD 1100, a series of migrations from the north brought new influences to the area. Although the Hohokam often seem to have co-existed peacefully with the newcomers, sometimes even living alongside them for several generations in the same village, their distinctive culture gradually ebbed away. They lost many of their skills, including the art of etching, and started to build adobe houses like their neighbours to the north. Finally, around AD 1500, they seem suddenly to have left Snaketown and other major centres and scattered to smaller communities in the desert. The present-day Piman peoples, who still live in isolated settlements and practise desert farming, are thought to be descended from them.

One of the most spectacular late Hohokam sites is at Casa Grande, south of Phoenix, where a huge, partially ruined five-storey adobe building rises starkly from the desert, dominating the landscape for miles around. Its scale and isolation make it seem oddly disconnected from its surroundings, as if it was left behind by some alien civilization that has long since returned to its own galaxy. This eerie impression is deepened by the official guidebook, which tells you that nobody knows who lived here or why, like other Hohokam settlements, it was abandoned.

The Pimas on the nearby Gila River reservation, however, still have a vivid oral tradition about Casa Grande. Far from being an unsolved mystery, the fate of the house and its inhabitants is part of a continuous history that connects the tribe with its own remote past. According to one elderly woman:

The story that was told to me by my maternal grandfather was that these people, the Hohokam, who lived there, had a chief, his name was Sivan. And a group of people, some other tribe from the east, from the direction of the rising sun, we say, came in and lived with them, and some time during that period they had a disagreement, and the Hohokam were chased out of that big house. So they came and built a house nearby and they [the newcomers] would come and drive them out, chase them from their home, their village, and to this day you can see these mounds [where they built new settlements], clear into Phoenix. But we have no years: we don't know how many years they lived at each. But it was an ongoing battle, off and on, from these people that came from the east.

Her account also explained some features of the building that have puzzled archaeologists:

When they were building that house, logs were floating down the Gila River, so they went and dragged the logs over to use in the house. I read something about it one time: some white scholars were wondering where the logs came from. They said: 'Might it have been a tropical climate back then? Might there have been trees growing there?' But it's only common sense that there were logs floating down the river and they were used in the house.

And there was a wall built around, so there was protection from the enemies of other tribes. And there's a hole high up in the wall of the house, and they say now that it was used to tell the seasons [an observatory]. But in the story, it was a lookout, so they could see the enemies coming and call out to the people working in the fields so that they could go into that big house. And that's the story that was handed down to me by my grandfather.

At the time of European contact, the Pimas themselves, centred on the Gila and Salt River region, still retained many recognizably Hohokam cultural traits, including a distinctive style of pottery and the use of irrigation to water their plots of beans, squash and pumpkins. They lived in permanent communities of round, earth-covered houses thatched with grass, and were socially and politically highly organized: the men worked co-operatively in the fields, and a single leader, elected by the village headmen, provided the kind of central authority that would, presumably, have been needed to co-ordinate the kind of major works carried out by the Hohokams.

The Pimas' close relatives, the Tohono O'odham ('Desert People'), by contrast, living to the south in a huge expanse of desert with few rivers or permanent streams, had reverted – if they were, indeed, originally Hohokams – to a less settled way of life. Most O'odham communities in the east of the area moved regularly between summer villages in the valleys, where seasonal flash floods irrigated their crops and filled reservoirs with water for drinking and washing and where the women could harvest a range of wild foods, and winter hunting camps in the mountains. Further west, where water was even scarcer, the people lived a semi-nomadic existence based on hunting, fishing, gathering and trade. Although members of different communities recognized their kinship with each other, there was little formal 'tribal' organization: most villages were autonomous, governed by a headman and a council made up of all the adult males.

One factor in the decline of the Hohokam was almost certainly the rise of the third great Southwestern agricultural tradition, the Anasazi (from a Navajo word meaning 'Ancient Ones'), which began to emerge around 100 BC. Its heartland was an arid area of high *mesas* and deep canyons in the 'Four Corners' region, where the present-day states of Utah, Arizona, Colorado and New Mexico meet. During its first stage – known as the 'Basket Maker', because of the high quality of the basketry found at sites dating from that period – the Anasazi were clearly still in transition from a 'foraging' way of life. They built distinctive domed houses of logs and mud over shallow depressions in the ground, and only cultivated maize and squash to supplement a diet that still consisted predominantly of game and wild plants. By around AD 400, however, farming had become more central to their culture, and – probably as a result of Mogollon influence – they were beginning to live in larger, more permanent villages of stone-lined pit houses roofed with wood. Over the next three centuries, the Anasazi domesticated the turkey, acquired a range of additional crops, including cotton, beans and new, more efficient varieties of maize, and adopted several technological innovations, including bows and arrows and stone axes.

After about AD 700, Anasazi communities began to assume the distinctive 'Pueblo' pattern that can still be seen in towns like Acoma today. Tight clusters of flat-roofed stone-and-mud or wood-and-mud houses replaced the old underground dwellings, which were retained only as ceremonial centres known as *kivas*. By the use of ingenious techniques such as terracing and reservoir-canal irrigation, they transformed large areas of dry plateau into fertile fields, enormously increasing agricultural production and allowing a rapid growth in numbers which gave them – remarkably, in view of the apparent harshness and poverty of their homeland – the highest population density north of Mexico.

Partly, perhaps, because many of their *mesa*-top sites were extremely restricted, Anasazi communities tended to grow by becoming more concentrated and elaborate rather than by expanding over a larger and larger area. To begin with, individual houses were linked together in long terraces; later, they were extended upwards as well as outwards, creating tiered 'apartment houses' sometimes five storeys high, in which the roof of one level, reached by a ladder, became the entrance to the next. Some of these complexes grew to enormous size: the huge, semi-circular Pueblo Bonito, for instance, in Chaco Canyon, which was started around AD 900, eventually contained eight hundred rooms.

Anasazi civilization reached its 'Golden Age' in the Great Pueblo period, between around 1100 and AD 1300. With growing numbers, social and ceremonial life became more complex, and increasing specialization among craftspeople led to a spectacular flowering of weaving, pottery (including the distinctive black-and-white work still found among the Pueblos today), and jewellery-making. A sophisticated trading system brought goods and materials from many other areas into major Anasazi centres – Chaco Canyon stood at the hub of a vast network of carefully surveyed roads, strikingly similar to those found in Inca Peru, which is thought to have extended across an area of 60,000 square miles – and diffusing Anasazi ideas and technologies throughout the Southwest.

But in the second half of the thirteenth century, the Anasazi seem suddenly to have gone into decline. Civilizations in other parts of North America appear to have undergone a dramatic collapse at around the same time, leading to speculation that they were all affected by the same epidemic or natural catastrophe, but most scholars believe that the crisis of the Pueblo peoples was caused by local factors. Various explanations have been suggested: the Anasazi were driven out by invading nomads from the north; they depleted the limited supplies of wood in the area; their way of life was undermined by a long period of drought; or their communities simply became too large and, without any central control to weld them together, fell apart. Whatever the explanation, the tide of Anasazi expansion quickly ebbed. Some of the semi-nomadic groups in the Great Basin and elsewhere who had been on the fringes of their sphere of influence reverted to a hunter-gatherer way of life, while most of the Anasazi themselves, according to archaeologists, moved southwards to found new, smaller communities, some of which are still inhabited by their Puebloan descendants today.

Although Euro-American scholars are sometimes cautious about the link between the Anasazi and present-day peoples, many of the Pueblos themselves have detailed accounts which – like the Pimas' description of Casa Grande – connect them directly to the 'prehistoric' past. The most westerly of the Puebloan peoples, the Hopi, for example, believe that on their journey to their present home their ancestors had to make four migrations, during which they lived for a time at some of the now abandoned Anasazi communities. Striking evidence for this tradition comes from the 'signatures' used by modern Hopi to represent their different clans – a hunched flute player for the Flute Clan, an undulating serpent for the Snake Clan, and so on – which are remarkably similar to symbols painted on the walls of Anasazi sites. At Chaco Canyon, you can still see the image of a coyote next to two concentric circles, indicating that the Coyote Clan had only completed two of its migrations when it stopped there, but in a strikingly similar pictograph at the modern Hopi community of Oraibi there are four circles, showing that the cycle of journeys is now complete.

In the period immediately before European contact, the pattern was further complicated by the arrival of yet another major group, nomadic bands from the north who settled in the region and evolved into the peoples known today as Navajos and Apaches. The *Apacheans* are thought to have been originally inhabitants of the subarctic – their language, in which they call themselves *Dineh*, 'the people', suggests they are closely related to the *Dene-* or Athabascan-speakers of Northwest Canada and Alaska – who, over several centuries, gradually migrated southwards.

At the time of European contact, the *Dineh* had already begun to diversify into several culturally distinct peoples. All of them retained strong traces of their northern relatives' way of life – they continued to live in small, autonomous bands under the leadership of a dominant chief, to hunt and to practise a complex shamanic religion – but they had also started to absorb and adapt elements of their non-*Dineh* neighbours' cultures. In the east of the area, where the Southwest meets the southern plains, the Kiowa-Apache (*Dineh* who had joined the indigenous Kiowa but kept their own language and identity) and Lipan Apache adopted a way of life based on bison-hunting, while further west, in what is now Arizona, the Navajo and the western Apache had learnt agriculture from the Pueblos and cultivated maize, beans and squash as well as hunting and gathering wild plants. In between, the Jicarilla, Mescalero and Chiricahua Apache continued to live primarily as hunter-gatherers, but were still profoundly influenced by aspects of other cultures. The Jicarillas' origin legend, for instance, describes an emergence from the underworld strikingly similar to the Tewas' – although peopled with different animals, including the bison and the bear – and uses Pueblo-style masked dancers to represent the powerful *Gans*, or Mountain Spirits, that are central to the beliefs of most *Dineh* groups. (Significantly, non-Native Americans identified the *Gans* as devils, and still sometimes refer to the ceremonies in which they appear as 'Devil Dances'.)

This process of partial acculturation was the result of an uneasy symbiotic relationship between the Apacheans and the settled agricultural peoples which, by the time of the first Spanish expeditions, had developed throughout the region. Groups of *Dineh* would visit farming villages to exchange meat and hides for maize and other goods, acquiring, in the process, skills such as pottery and sand-painting, as well as a range of Pueblo myths and religious practices. Often, however, rather than trading, the Apacheans simply attacked Pueblo or Piman communities and took what they wanted – food, and sometimes slaves – by force. For the generally peaceful farmers, these raids were a terrifying intrusion which compelled them to fortify or move their settlements and engendered a deep hatred for the *Dineh*. The name 'Apache' itself comes from a Zuñi word which means simply 'enemy', and evidence of the same hostility can be found among virtually all the settled peoples.

This cultural diversity and survival means that there are still hundreds of different stories about the arrival of Europeans in the Southwest, each of which offers its own fascinating perspective on the encounter between Old World and New. One, however, stands out: the meeting of the Spanish with the Rio Grande Pueblos and the culturally related Acoma, Zuñi and Hopi communities further west. Here, the extremes of European and indigenous culture – the most fanatical Catholics, the most highly organized Native American societies – discovered each other. In the heat of the collision their two worlds fused, creating a relationship quite unlike any other in North America and shaping, to a great extent, the subsequent history of the area.

❀   ❀   ❀

At the beginning of all beginnings our ancestors came up out of the earth, until they were living beneath Sandy Place Lake to the north. The world under the lake was like this one, but dark. Spirits, people, and animals lived together, and death was unknown.

Among the spirits were the first mothers of all the Tewa, known as Blue Corn Woman Near to Summer and White Corn Woman Near to Ice. They asked one of the men to search for a path that would lead them away from the lake. When he reached the surface, all he could see was a misty haze in every direction, so he returned and reported that the earth was still ochu *(unripe).*

The mothers told the man to explore the world above. As he went, he came to an open place where all the tsiwi *(predatory mammals and carrion-eating birds) were gathered. When they saw him they all rushed towards him, knocking him over and mauling him. But then they said: 'It's all right! Get up! We are your friends,' and in an instant his wounds vanished. The animals dressed him in buckskins, painted his face black, tied feathers in his hair and gave him a bow and arrows and a quiver. Then they said: 'You have been accepted. From now on, you will use these gifts and be known as the Hunt Chief. Now you are ready to go.' And that is how the first Made Person, the Hunt Chief, came into being.*

So the hunt chief returned to the world beneath the lake. As he came near, he called out with a cry like a fox. When the people heard it they understood and rejoiced, saying: 'We have been accepted!' Then the Hunt Chief appointed two other men as leaders, giving each of them an ear of white corn. To the first he said, 'You are to lead and care for all of the people during the summer.' And to the second he said, 'You shall lead and care for the people during the winter.' That is how the second and third Made People, the Summer and Winter Chiefs, came into being.

Tewa origin account

For the Puebloans, even more than for other Native Americans, the origin account provides a template for understanding and organizing the world, pervading the individual's experience from the first moments of life. In the Tewa 'naming ceremony', a new-born child will receive two perfect ears of corn, one blue and one white, representing the two original mothers of the people, and the story continues to reverberate through all the rituals marking the child's induction into full membership of the community. At the 'water giving' ceremony, for instance, held during the first year of life, the Hunt Chief re-enacts his mythic predecessor's return to the people: announcing his presence with the bark of a fox, he appears dramatically at the door dressed – in a flowing buckskin, carrying a long bow, and with his face painted and his hair adorned with the feather of a carrion-eating bird – in the costume the animals gave the first Hunt Chief as a token of his acceptance.

Every Tewa is born into one of the two divisions created by the original Hunt Chief; the Summer and the Winter people. The distinction between the two groups is far more than social: 'Summer' is associated with the female principle – not merely with the world of women, who own the houses and dominate the domestic sphere, but also, by extension, with seeds, crops and the earth – while 'Winter' is associated with the male domain – hunting and warfare, sun, sky and lightning – which lies outside the village. The Corn Mothers who, in the origin account, send the men out to explore the earth thus prefigure the actual pattern of Pueblo social life.

Reconciling the polar opposites of male and female is a major preoccupation of Pueblo culture. The two principles meet most fundamentally, of course, in the act of procreation: just as the earth needs rain and sun from the sky in order to be fruitful, so a woman needs semen from a man in order to conceive children. By expressing and partaking in the fundamental processes of nature in this way, sexuality becomes closely linked to the sacred. Because all life depends on it, it is woven through the whole annual cycle of dances and ceremonies, which can only be carried out with the participation of both the Summer and Winter people and of all the different clans and societies making up the Puebloan community. The same concern is also embodied in the political structure: following the pattern laid down by the Hunt Chief at 'the beginning of beginnings,' the position of leader alternates between a Summer Chief, who presides over the community when the 'female' activities of planting and harvesting predominate, and a Winter Chief, who takes office when the crops have been gathered in and the men go to the mountains to hunt.

But that is only the beginning. The story goes on:

They still didn't know whether the earth could sustain them yet, so the chiefs sent six pairs of twins, the *Towa é*, to explore. The blue twins went North, the yellow twins went West, the red twins went South, the white twins went East and the dark twins went to the Zenith, but they all agreed that the ground was still too soft to walk on.

Finally, the all-coloured pair were sent out. They saw a rainbow in the sky and found that the earth was a little harder. Overjoyed, the people prepared to leave the lake. The Summer Chief led the way, but immediately sank up to his ankles in the mud. Then the Winter Chief strode forward and hoar-frost appeared, hardening the ground so that the people could walk on it.

And that is how the people began their journey southwards. But before they could complete it, they had to return to Sipofene [the lake]. Some of the travellers became ill, and the chiefs sensed that the people were not yet ready. When they reached their home beneath the lake, the Hunt Chief found that a witch had filled the hollow centre of one of the Corn Mothers with ashes, pebbles and cactus. This marked the beginning of evil in the world, and to combat it the Fourth Made Person, the *Ke* (medicine man), was created.

Three more times they had to return to the lake. On the first

occasion, the Clowns were created to entertain the people when they
grew tired and sad; on the second, the Scalp Chief was made to
ensure success in war; and on the third, the Women's society was
created to care for the scalps and to assist the Scalp Chief.

The different *kinds* of people created in this way remain the
fundamental categories of Tewa society. During the course of a lifetime,
a Tewa may move from being an ordinary citizen (one of the unnamed
mass of the 'people' who emerged 'at the beginning of beginnings') to
a *Towa é* (a political officer, who, like the original Twins, carries out
the chiefs' instructions by policing and protecting the community) to
one of the Made People, or *Patowa* (the religious and political leaders).
The origin legend permeates the ceremonies marking the induction of
a new *Patowa* or *Towa é*: each Made Person, for instance, receives an
elaborately decorated bowl representing the primordial lake. New
office-holders are also sometimes flogged with cactus spines or subjected to other tests of fortitude: for the Pueblos, like many other
agricultural peoples, blood has immense spiritual potency.

The impact of the origin story is not confined to the village and to
the society of the living. The heart of each Pueblo is the 'centre of
centres', the sacred 'mother earth navel' that connects the Tewa back
to the underworld from which they emerged. Radiating north, south,
east and west from this focal point are other sacred landmarks, arranged
in a series of concentric circles: the four dance plazas and the shrines
of the community itself; then, outside the village boundaries, a ring of
shrines to the four cardinal directions; beyond them, the *tsin*, a range
of four hills created by the original *Towa é*; and finally the four sacred
mountains which the first Twins discovered when they explored the
earth. This numinous landscape is inhabited by the spirits of the dead
and of all those who existed before emergence, who continue to
influence and interact with the Pueblo world, particularly by bringing
rain. At various times of year these ancestors are summoned by
feathered 'prayer sticks' – described by one early Spanish observer as
crosses with small sticks at the base 'adorned with plumes and many
withered flowers' – and reciprocate by leaving sticks of their own to
announce their impending arrival. Then they return to the community
in the form of fantastic masked figures – called *Oxua* by the Tewa, but

generally known by the Hopi name of *katsinas* or *kachinas* – who dance from plaza to plaza, to be greeted with offerings of cornmeal.

Finally, the Tewa story recounts, the people were ready for their journey from the lake:

> The Summer people travelled along the mountains west of the Rio Grande and supported themselves by farming and plant-gathering, while the followers of the Winter Chief travelled along the mountains east of the river and lived as hunters. On the way, they made twelve stops, and at each one they built a village which remains a sacred site for the Tewa today. At last, the two groups rejoined and built a village called Posi, where they remained a long time, until there was a serious epidemic and the elders decided to abandon it. The Tewa were divided into six groups, each with a mixture of Winter and Summer people so that the chiefs and other Made People could be replicated in every community. And that is how the six Tewa villages we know today came into being.
>
> In the very beginning we were one people. Then we divided into Summer people and Winter people, before coming together again as we are now. But you can see we are still Summer people and Winter people.

For the Puebloans, the journey from the underworld is not simply a physical migration but a metaphysical progression which parallels the spiritual development of both societies and individuals. This idea is perhaps most explicit among the Hopi, who believe that before its emergence into this world, humanity had progressed through three previous universes, each representing a different stage of consciousness. As well as being possibly the closest concept in a Native American culture to the Western notion of evolution, this belief has strong echoes of Asian philosophy. As the scholar Frank Waters put it in *The Book of the Hopi*: 'From the same mysticism the peoples of the Far East have created an empirical science, the Hopis a cosmic drama.'

The whole conceptual and ceremonial framework of Puebloan life, in fact, could be seen as a kind of 'cosmic drama', in which the origin story provides the cast, the stage, the themes and the narrative. Working simultaneously on many different levels, it brings together, through dance and ritual, male and female, human and animal, temporal and eternal, social and psychological. By reconciling differences in this way, it recreates the primordial harmony in which 'spirits, people, and animals lived together, and death was unknown.'

Where many Native American cultures were remarkably open-ended, freely adopting new knowledge and ideas and adapting their own explanations of the universe to accommodate them, the Puebloans' origin legends gave them a coherent, self-contained world-view into which they tried to fit every experience, however apparently unfamiliar. This tendency – which to a certain extent mirrors the way Christian Europeans tried to make sense of the 'New World' – was accentuated by the intricate nature of Puebloan societies. Although most Pueblo individuals are aware of the broad outlines of their peoples' origins, no single person knows the whole story in detail. Each episode, and the powers and rituals attached to it, forms part of the sacred knowledge possessed by one office-holder – such as the Hunt Chief – who passes it on to a member of his own society in the secrecy of the *kiva*. This interlocking structure makes the culture far less vulnerable to change, because no individual or group has the power to alter or abandon traditions single-handedly.

The distinctive nature of the Puebloans' civilization profoundly shaped how they saw the Spaniards and how the Spaniards saw them. Both sides had pre-existing categories into which they tried to incorporate the other. Perhaps most poignantly, the Hopi, like several Meso-american peoples, had a myth about a lost white brother, *Pahána*, whose return would usher in a period of peace and reconciliation. They had been eagerly expecting him for twenty years when, in 1540 by the Christian calendar, they saw the Spaniard Pedro de Tovar and a party of soldiers approaching them across the desert.

❊ ❊ ❊

In 1536, the authorities in New Spain were startled when four survivors from a failed expedition to Florida eight years before limped back into Mexico City. Describing their remarkable adventures among the Indians of what is now the Southwestern United States, Álvar Núñez Cabeza de Vaca and his three companions reported that, on the Rio Grande, they had heard stories about fabulously rich cities further north. In the hope of finding another Mexico or Peru, the Spanish set about organizing a new expedition to explore the area.

A reconnaissance party set out in March 1539, guided by a Moorish slave, Esteban (or Estevanico), who had been one of the four survivors, and led by the Franciscan Fray Marcos. Esteban – perhaps because his behaviour angered the friar – travelled separately, wearing bells, a crown of plumes and feather anklets and bracelets and escorted by a retinue of Indian allies.

In May, he reached the Zuñi community of Hawikuh. The people were just preparing to call the *katsina* to bring rain, and they were deeply disturbed by the arrival of the 'Black Mexican with the chili [ie swollen] lips' and his followers. When Esteban sent envoys carrying his symbol of authority, a 'calabash' decorated with red and white feathers, and the message that 'he was coming to establish peace and to heal them,' the head man reacted angrily. According to Zuñi tradition, he threw the rattle to the ground, saying that he 'knew what sort of people they were, and that the messengers should tell them not to enter the town, and if they did so, Esteban would be put to death.' He and his people reinforced the warning by symbolically barring the road with lines of cornmeal, but Esteban pressed on, threatening that the much larger force following him would destroy the community if any harm came to him. When he caused further offence by demanding turquoise and women, the Zuñi decided to kill him 'so that he would not reveal our location to his brothers.'

The impact of this incident can be gauged by the number of stories about it among not only the Zuñis but the other Pueblos. Many Pueblo people will tell you that 'the first *white* man we saw was a *black* man,' and at Jemez Pueblo on the Rio Grande there is an annual dance which, according to the Jemez historian Joe Sando, portrays Esteban and Fray Marcos: 'One figure wears a white skull cap, and his face is painted white. He wears a long black coat with a knotted white rope tied around his waist in the fashion of a Franciscan priest. A black sheep pelt covers the head of the other figure to indicate curly hair. His face is painted black, and he carries a snare drum that he plays whenever the friar walks about.'

Marcos himself finally reached Zuñi territory in June. He formally 'took possession' of the area for the King of Spain by erecting a cross on a mountain top, from which he caught a distant glimpse of Hawikuh. He then returned to New Spain to report that the 'very beautiful' Zuñi town was the legendary city of *Cíbola*, 'bigger than the city of Mexico' and surrounded by a 'land, which, in my opinion, is the largest and best of all those discovered.'

Enticed by this mouth-watering description, the Spaniards quickly assembled a new, larger expedition under the young and ambitious Francisco Vásquez de Coronado. As they passed through the frontier area, the soldiers met some resistance from victims of Spanish slave-hunting raids, but further north they found people who remembered Vaca and Fray Marcos and welcomed them with hospitality and gifts of food. For the Pueblos, again expectantly awaiting the ceremonial return of their own fantastically dressed ancestors, the spectacle of the Spanish cavalcade must have been full of disturbing images. Surrounded by the more familiar figures of Mexican Indians in full regalia were strange beings, their helmets swathed in feathers, their armour glowing with the light of the sun, mounted on monstrous beasts, carrying huge wooden crosses and driving a herd of unknown animals (pigs). Their immense power was confirmed by their guns, which dispensed unim-aginable destruction with a flash of lightning and a crack of thunder: the noise alone was enough to make the Indians fall to the ground in a daze. Not surprisingly, when they sent emissaries into the villages to announce their impending arrival, the Indians interpreted their crosses as prayer sticks and assumed that the Spaniards were *katsinas*.

The Spaniards were not slow to exploit these associations. Their experience in Mexico had already taught them the significance of the sun to the peoples of the area, and when Indians along the way called them 'gods' and asked if they had 'sprung from the water or earth or descended from the sky,' the soldiers had a ready answer. 'I came from the sun ... I am its son,' Pedro de Alarcón told a group of old men, and when they challenged him, asking how the sun could send him when 'it was high in the sky and never stopped,' he replied that 'they could see that at sunset and sunrise it came close to the earth where it dwelt ... [and] that the sun had created me in that land where it rose.' The old men immediately 'took maize and other grains in their mouths' and sprinkled Alarcón with them, telling him that this was how 'they offered sacrifice to the sun.'

Other Indians, according to the Spanish chroniclers, nervously approached each horse, speaking to it 'as if it were a person.' They 'rubbed their bodies against the animals' haunches, raising their hands to heaven and blowing toward the sky' in supplication. In front of the Spaniards' crosses they laid 'powders [sacred cornmeal] and feathers, some even the blankets they were wearing. They did it with such eagerness that some climbed on the backs of others in order to reach the arms of the crosses to put plumes and roses on them. Others brought ladders, and while some held them others climbed up to tie strings in order to fasten the roses and feathers.'

When Coronado reached Hawikuh, however, he found that the Zuñi, remembering their experience with Esteban the year before, were less welcoming. Hearing of his approach, the women and children had taken refuge on a nearby *mesa*, and the expedition was greeted by the men with 'coldness ... and mean faces.' The 'Outside Chief' – the political officer in charge of external relations – again tried to close the road with symbolic lines of cornmeal, but the soldiers quickly broke through with the battle-cry 'Santiago!' The warriors rained stones, arrows and lances on them, seriously wounding Coronado, who was carried away unconscious, but the better-armed Spaniards seized the town in less than an hour, forcing the Zuñi to flee. Coronado did not pursue them, but established himself at Hawikuh. Although bitterly disappointed to discover that 'Cibola' was merely a small pueblo 'all crumpled together' rather than Marcos's splendid city, the hungry soldiers found 'something we prized much more than gold or silver; namely plentiful maize and beans, turkeys larger than those in New Spain, and salt better and whiter than I have ever seen in my whole life.' The expedition remained at Hawikuh for four months, using it as a base to explore Hopi territory and the Grand Canyon and to search for 'Quivira', a mythic land supposedly rich in precious metals and silk.

By early December, however, the Spanish had almost exhausted the Zuñi's food supply, and Coronado moved his army east to the Rio Grande to spend the winter at a cluster of pueblos near the present-day Albuquerque which the invaders called Tiguex. While de Soto was pillaging his way through the area further east – at one point, although they didn't realize it, the two expeditions were less than 300 miles apart – Coronado was using identical methods to extract maize, blankets and

women from Tiguex. And when his desperate 'hosts' were finally driven
to take up arms, he responded with a ferocity that even de Soto might
have paled at: one hundred or more men were burnt at the stake, most
of the others fled or were killed in battle, and the bulk of the women
and children were taken as slaves.

The following spring, Coronado resumed the search for 'Quivira'.
They were led by two Native Americans: one – probably a Pawnee –
they called 'the Turk' ('because,' as one of them bluntly put it, 'he
looked like one'); the other was a Wichita named Sopete. The two
guides lured the soldiers out on to the Great Plains – presumably
because they would be more exposed to attack there – with tantalizing
tales of a fabulous chief who 'slept in the afternoons under a tree, lulled
by the music of golden bells run [sic] by the wind.' When, instead, they
discovered only a huge windswept grassland populated by vast herds of
bison and a few small Apache and Wichita communities, the Spaniards
garrotted the Turk in rage and frustration.

Finally, in 1542, Coronado returned to New Spain, bitterly complaining that Fray Marcos had 'not told . . . the truth in a single thing that
he said, but everything is the opposite of what he related,' and that the
area around the Rio Grande was virtually worthless. This sober
assessment effectively deterred further expeditions, and when, in 1548,
silver was discovered in northern Mexico, the colonists' energies
became focused on mining rather than exploration.

The Franciscans, however, continued to cherish ambitions for
another kind of conquest. Fired by an intense counter-Reformation
faith and a craving for union with Christ through martyrdom, they
hungered to bring the Gospel to the Pueblos. Like the Jesuits in South
America and Canada – and, to a much lesser extent, the founders of
'praying towns' in New England – they dreamed of creating ideal
Native American communities far from the corrupting influence of
settlers. Here, purged of their 'paganism' but retaining their ceremo-
nialism and 'simplicity', the Indians would 'spend their time marching
in processions and praising God with hymns and spiritual canticles.'

The friars were helped by a shift of mood in the Spanish court. In
1573, after eighty years in which his subjects had wrought almost
unimaginable destruction in the Americas, the king outlawed further
large-scale military expeditions like Coronado's. His new Ordinances of

Discovery declared: 'Discoveries are not to be called conquests. Since we wish them to be carried out peacefully and charitably, we do not want to use of the term "conquest" to offer any excuse for the employment of force of the causing of injury to the Indian.' Any future extension of Spanish power and settlement would be peaceful and directed by missionaries. (This change of policy makes an interesting comparison with the softening of British attitudes during the eighteenth century, which again took place a hundred years or so after the start of colonization.)

In the early 1580s, the Franciscans mounted two small expeditions to gather ethnographic and linguistic data which, they hoped, would help them to devise an effective strategy for converting and 'pacifying' the Pueblos. Their reports of the upper Rio Grande and its people were so enthusiastic that in 1595 the Crown authorized Don Juan de Oñate to colonize the area, instructing him that 'Your main purpose shall be the service of God Our Lord, the spreading of His holy Catholic faith, and the reduction and pacification of the natives of the said provinces.'

Oñate finally set out in January 1598. He had hoped to take the Indians by surprise, but many of them had learnt of his coming and fled to the mountains. The pueblo now known as Santo Domingo, however, was still inhabited, and when he reached it he gathered together the chiefs of thirty-one neighbouring communities for an elaborate ceremony in which they swore allegiance to the King of Spain. His aim – like Coronado's before him – was to use the knowledge he had gleaned of Native American culture to awe the Indians into submission through ritual and a show of force. Knowing that the Pueblos would have heard of the conquest of Mexico by word of mouth, his entourage consciously mimicked many of the details of Cortés' expedition against the Aztecs. The soldiers marched under an identical banner of the Virgin and were accompanied by Indian allies from the same people, the Tlascalan. Oñate's party included a group of Franciscans – exactly duplicating the twelve 'apostles of Mexico' on the earlier campaign – in front of whom, like Cortés before him, he publicly fell on his knees in order to show the 'proud and bellicose' natives 'the true veneration that they should show the friars.' For the Pueblos, who had never knelt before their own leaders or deities, this must have seemed an act of humiliating self-abasement, and one can only imagine what they must have felt as the Spaniards ordered them to follow Oñate's example. After they had done so, Oñate fell to his knees again and loudly prayed for the conversion of 'these infidels' and for 'the peaceful possession of these kingdoms.' His men then fired their harquebuses and erected a huge cross to symbolize the triumph of Christ.

The meaning of these rituals – which included, on occasion, not only scenes from the Spanish conquest of the Americas but also a medieval play called *The Christians and the Moors* – was not lost on a people whose own ceremonies resonated so deeply with historical and religious drama. Evidence of their profound impact can be found in the survival of some of the episodes and characters – such as Coronado and his horse, 'Santiago' – in Pueblo dances even today. Some scholars see the incorporation of these Spanish elements in native ceremonies as evidence of the conquistadors' success in colonizing not only the physical but also the psychological world of the native: by symbolically re-enacting their own defeat, Native Americans are tacitly – and, by now, perhaps unconsciously – acknowledging European domination. According to the Pueblo historian Joe Sando, however, the Spanish characters are figures of fun, included so that the Indians can 'gain a wry revenge upon their persecutors.'

For all its religious pageantry, the ostensibly spiritual aims of the Oñate expedition were undermined from the start by the very different motives of most of the settlers. Unlike the people of 'the middling sort' who made up the bulk of the British settler population, the majority of Spanish colonists were not seeking escape from religious persecution, commercial opportunities or a plot of land which they could work to provide for their own family. Many of them were ambitious or aspiring nobles who, far from turning their back on their homeland, were hoping to enhance their standing in the Spanish social order by gaining wealth, estates and military glory. Their status as *hidalgos* (gentlemen) precluded them from sullying their hands with physical labour or compromising their honour with trade: as Fray Gerónimo de Zárate Salmerón said in the 1620s, they were 'enemies of all kinds of work.'

This meant that – again unlike the British settlers – they envisaged a more or less permanent role for Native Americans in New Spain. Since land without labourers had little value, it made more sense to force the

Indians to work for their Spanish masters than to kill them or expel them as the English did. In fact, partly as a result of the staggering Indian death rate from disease and maltreatment, Spanish raiders kept up a ceaseless quest for new sources of indigenous slave labour that could be brought *into* colonized areas to fill the lowest ranks of hispanic society. The 130 soldier-settlers who accompanied Oñate took many times their own number of Indian, *mestizo* (mixed-race) and black slaves and servants to wait on them.

At the pinnacle of the New Mexican colonial hierarchy were the sixty or so *encomenderos*, who, in exchange for providing armed protection and assistance to the Franciscan missionaries, were granted a right to Indian tribute. The *encomienda* system was based on the same feudal principle underlying the division of England after the Norman conquest: each noble received a tract of land and the right to extract labour or produce from its inhabitants. From the *conquistadores'* point of view, the Pueblos were particularly well suited to the role of the Anglo-Saxon villagers in this arrangement. As one settler put it in 1599, New Mexico 'promises excellent returns because the native Indians are excellent and intelligent farmers; they are much given to commerce, taking from one province to another the fruits of their lands and the products of their labour.' Living – unlike many indigenous groups – in compact, fixed settlements, they were relatively simple to administer, and the *encomendero* or his agents would easily be able to collect his bi-annual 'tithes' of skins, cotton cloth and corn.

Oñate's efforts to establish this new relationship with the Indians quickly led to conflict. For the Pueblos, as for other Native Americans, gift-giving, both within and between communities, was an essential part of cultural life, and the *conquistadores* were initially often greeted with presents of food, clothing and – if their own accounts are to be believed – sexual favours from the women, who hoped, perhaps, through the gift of their bodies, to pacify the unpredictable and dangerously powerful Spaniards and reconcile the native and European worlds. When it became clear, however, that the Spanish gave little in return and expected further supplies as a matter of *right*, the Pueblos became increasingly aggrieved. In December 1598, less than two months after they had given Oñate a generous 'donation' of maize and turkeys, the people of Ácoma were asked to provide food, water and wood for his lieutenant, Captain Don Juan de Zaldívar, and thirty-one men. This time, the Indians seemed reluctant, although they promised to prepare some flour for the expedition. When the soldiers went to collect it, one of them stole two turkeys and sexually assaulted an Ácoma woman, and the enraged Indians killed Zaldívar and twelve of his men.

Determined to pre-empt further unrest, Oñate promptly sent a punitive force to wage 'war without quarter' against the Ácomans. After three days of fierce fighting, some 800 Indian men, women and children were dead, and almost 600 more had been taken prisoner. All the survivors over the age of twelve were condemned to slavery, and the children were given to the friars to be distributed as servants 'in this kingdom or elsewhere.' Every man over the age of twenty-five had one of his feet amputated, and two Hopis who had been at Ácoma during the battle lost a hand each and were sent back to their own people as a stern warning. Shortly afterwards, another group, the Tompiros, incurred Oñate's wrath for their reluctance to give him food and blankets. In a six-day battle, the Spaniards flattened three pueblos, killed nearly a thousand people and took four hundred prisoners.

These draconian – and, to the Indians, completely unaccountable – reprisals seem, as Oñate intended, to have persuaded the other Pueblos that they could not hope to defeat the colonists by force. It also, however, inevitably, left them still more fearful and suspicious of the Spaniards. When they saw the soldiers coming to gather tribute, many of them abandoned their homes and fled to the mountains, where thousands died from hunger and cold. As a result, the settlers' food supplies dwindled, exacerbated by a severe drought in 1600. When Oñate returned from yet another vain attempt to discover Quivira in September 1601, he found that most of the colonists, hungry, discontented with his leadership and disappointed at the absence of precious metals or other exploitable resources in the 'kingdom', had returned to Mexico. The Franciscans, anxious to prevent their missionary work from being undermined by the soldier-settlers' greed and brutality, added their own complaints against Oñate. They reported that, in addition to excessive cruelty towards the Indians, he had been guilty of sexual impropriety, living 'dishonourably and scandalously with women ... married and unmarried,' and allowing his men to abuse native women. This behaviour, according to the friars, was impeding the process of conversion: the Indians, they said, quite reasonably asked, 'if ... Christians cause so much harm and violence, why should [we] become Christians?'

In 1607, the Franciscans succeeded in forcing Oñate's resignation. Spanish commitment to New Mexico again wavered: the colony was troublesome, unproductive, and separated from the major centres of New Spain by a large unconquered territory where supply convoys and reinforcements were preyed on by bands of Native Americans. In 1609, however, under Franciscan pressure, the Crown agreed to retain the area as a field for missionary activity and appointed a new governor who, with a minimal force of fifty *married* soldiers, was to maintain order while the friars finally set about constructing their ideal Native American communities. For the next seventy years, cut off from developments elsewhere in North America, the Franciscans were to dominate and reshape the Pueblo world.

※　※　※

Their relative isolation from other Europeans was not the friars' only advantage: they also found a number of striking correspondences and echoes in Pueblo culture which helped them to gain a toehold. The Indians shared with the missionaries an intense spirituality (anthropologists calculate that Pueblo men spent half their waking life in religious activities); a belief in purification through fasting and flogging or flagellation; a ritual calendar full of brilliant ceremony; and an understanding of life as, in part at least, a spiritual journey. Unlike many Protestant missionaries, who tended to see the Devil at work in *every* aspect of native spirituality, the Franciscans did not scruple to make use of these parallels by, wherever possible, grafting Catholic meanings on to them. The 'prayer-stick' naturally translated into the central Christian symbol, the crucifix, and Fray Juan de Prada was so struck by the layout of Pueblo communities, which were also 'in the shape ... of a cross,' that he wondered if there was something providential about it. By the same token, you can still see, on the walls of Pueblo churches, Corn Mother Virgins clothed in ears of maize, or pictures of God surrounded by clouds, which – as the source of rain and the destination of the dead – are full of numinous significance for a Pueblo congregation.

The friars deliberately set out to create a Catholic ceremonial cycle to rival the natives' own: magnificent spectacles were needed to 'uplift the souls of the Indians and move them towards the things of God,' wrote Fray Alonso de Molina, 'because they are by nature lukewarm and forgetful of internal matters and must be helped by means of external displays.' The most solemn day of the year, Good Friday, with its penitential beatings and its re-enactment of the passion of Christ, had particular resonances for a culture so attuned to ritual blood-letting and to the idea, if not the practice, of human sacrifice. Evidence of how awe-inspiring the Indians found this display comes from the account of a friar who, after a group of *katsina* dancers had repeatedly ignored his instructions to stop, decided to assume the role of the reviled Jesus. Stripping himself naked, he scourged himself mercilessly with a whip and then put on a crown of thorns and a rope halter and dragged a cross through the village. Immediately the dancers stopped, many of them in tears and craving forgiveness.

But there were also many areas of native culture which the missionaries saw as enormous obstacles to conversion and which they tried to root out with ruthless fanaticism. First and foremost was the Indians' 'idolatry': their use of masks, dolls, fetishes and – in their unchristianized form – prayer sticks to venerate their ancestors and other more or less 'diabolical' spirits. The friars systematically confiscated and destroyed these 'wooden gods' – Fray Alonso de Benavides, for instance, claimed in the 1620s that he had seized and publicly burnt 'more than a thousand idols of wood' in a single day – and radically challenged the cosmology that gave them power by erecting crosses in the sacred *kivas*. Men who were caught 'invoking the devil' by continuing to practise their own rites were publicly beaten, sometimes to death.

A second issue on which the Catholic and Pueblo worlds seemed diametrically opposed was sexuality. Seeing procreation as a sacred activity which harmonized conflicting forces and ensured the well-being of the universe, the Pueblos were relatively relaxed and open about sexual experience. They regarded pre-marital sex, serial monogamy – a woman could 'divorce' her husband simply by putting his possessions outside her door, which compelled him to return to his mother's household – and polygamy as normal and acceptable. For the friars, all hopes of ecstasy were focused on the world to come, when, they believed, a life of rigorous self-denial would be rewarded by a quasi-sexual union with Christ. Even Catholics who had not taken a vow of chastity were expected to eschew all sexual relations outside the institution of lifelong monogamous marriage.

Again, the Franciscans used physical punishment – whipping, confinement in the stocks and hair-shearing – in an attempt to impose European standards of sexual behaviour, but found it 'difficult to extirpate this evil from among them.' On one occasion, an Indian 'witch' publicly denounced a friar for preaching about monogamy. All at once, 'A bolt of lightning flashed from a clear untroubled sky, killing that infernal agent of the demon right in the midst of those good Christian women who were resisting her evil teachings.' Much to the missionary's surprise and disappointment, however, the Indians interpreted the incident not as an act of vengeance by the Christian God but as an intervention from the sky world, which, by instantly transforming the woman into a cloud spirit, had validated what she was saying.

Like missionaries in other times and places, the Franciscans dealt with the persistence of native culture by trying to prevent it from being transmitted from one generation to the next. Through baptism (which directly rivalled the ceremonies inducting the child into his or her family and community), and then through gifts, education and training, they attempted to implant in the young their own, radically different view of the world. A key element to this process was making children see the priest, rather than the biological parents, as their father and mother. In 1626, for example, when a Zuñi man tried to win back his son from the missionary's influence, Fray Martín de Alvide told the boy: 'Son, I am more your father and I love you more than he, for he wants to take you with him to the suffering of hell, while I wish you to enjoy the blessings of being a Christian.'

Observing the central role of men in Pueblo religious life, and as the products of a male-dominated society themselves, the friars tended to concentrate their efforts on the boys, with the paradoxical effect that some women's societies and activities were less disrupted and, as a result, attained greater importance. The friars regularly humiliated men who stepped out of line by punishing them in front of their children, sometimes graphically demonstrating their impotence in the face of colonial power by grabbing and twisting their testicles. (In 1638, a Taos man complained that Fray Nicolas Hidalgo had 'twisted [his penis] so much that it broke in half.')

The emasculation of Pueblo men was not confined to the realm of the family. The missionaries radically redrew the boundaries between men and women in a host of other areas, skewing – in a culture in which the *idea* of male and female was such a crucial element – the balance of the whole society. To align the Pueblos more closely with the model of their own patriarchal culture, they vested ownership of the land and houses in men rather than women. At the same time, most of the activities traditionally regarded as being in the male domain – religion, hunting and warfare – were outlawed, and men were required instead to learn new occupations, such as herding domestic animals, or to take on roles previously reserved to women. This eroded their authority not only by closing the normal avenues for gaining knowledge, power and prestige, but also by exposing them to further ridicule: 'If we compel any man to work on building a house,' Fray Alonso de Benavides reported, 'the women laugh at him ... and he runs away.' As the ceremonies and responsibilities of the Winter (male) half of the year withered under this assault, the Summer, with its more acceptable sowing and reaping festivals, became relatively more important, with the result – according to the Tewa anthropologist Alfonso Ortiz – that today the Winter Chief governs for only five months and the Summer for seven.

In effect, the Franciscans created a whole parallel social order, using every device they could to marginalize the Pueblo leadership and assume its power for themselves. They rivalled the chiefs' ability to summon the rain-carrying *katsinas* by trying to time their arrival in communities to coincide with the onset of rain; they triumphantly flaunted their – to the Indians mind-boggling – power over domestic animals, which seemed to promise a far more reliable supply of meat than the rituals of the hunt chief. Where the traditional leaders used the *Towa é* and their equivalents to police the community and punish dissent, the friars used their own missionized church officials, the *fiscales*. And, perhaps most importantly, where the chiefs had tried

unsuccessfully to deter external aggression from settlers, the church-
men seemed to have their Spanish compatriots miraculously under
their control. On at least one occasion, the friars artfully colluded with
their armed escort to make this point by – yet again – staging a drama.
According to one soldier, just as the troops seemed about to execute
three Indians accused of horse-stealing, 'the friars came out in flowing
robes and removed the Indians from the block. As we pretended that
we were going to take them, the Indians who were watching immediately took hold of the said friars and Indians and carried them away to
their houses . . .'

Not surprisingly, the Pueblos seem to have been deeply divided and
confused by the missionary experience. Some individuals did, undoubtedly, undergo a genuine conversion to Catholicism: many more,
probably, accepted the outward form of Christianity and flocked to the
missions in order to gain access to food, European tools, domestic
animals and, above all, protection. (The Franciscans were always careful
to stress that they 'came to give rather than to ask of' the Indians,
underlining still further how different they were from the rapacious
encomenderos.) At the same time, the friars' assault on native culture,
and particularly the merciless beatings they administered to offenders,
left a legacy of bitterness and resentment. When the Church accused
settlers of corruption and of exploiting Indians economically and
sexually, the colonists riposted that the missionaries' excessively harsh
treatment of dissenters risked provoking a full-scale rebellion against
Spanish rule.

They were right. In 1680, exacerbated by a long period of drought
and an increase in raids by Apaches, the tensions in the Pueblo world
erupted in violence. The last straw was the trial for 'sorcery' of forty-
seven Pueblo people, four of whom were sentenced to death and the
rest to imprisonment or lashing. Led by one of the men who had been
whipped, Popé, the outraged Indians turned on the friars – who, by
some accounts, were given the choice of leaving peacefully – and killed
twenty-one of them. Then, in a well-planned campaign, they stole or
killed the horses and mules that were the conquerors' 'principal nerve
of warfare', and finally, after destroying most of the outlying Spanish
settlements one by one, they surrounded Santa Fe.

Unlike the Indians in King Philip's War, who, almost at the same moment, were desperately trying to expel the English from New England, Popé and his Pueblo and Apache followers still massively outnumbered their European enemies. At the time of the revolt, there were fewer than 2,500 people living in Spanish households in the whole of New Mexico, most of them servants or slaves, and only around 170 colonists who were capable of bearing arms. Against them were ranged some 8,000 Native American troops. As they tightened their hold on the 'kingdom's' capital by cutting off the water supply, the Indians were heard to exult, in words echoing the missionaries' jibes against their own deities: 'Now the God of the Spaniards, who was their father, is dead, and Santa Maria who was their mother, and the saints ... were pieces of rotten wood.'

After nine days, the Spanish survivors used their superior firepower to break out of Santa Fe and escape south towards Mexico. On the way, they found not only bodies, but, in the smoking ruins of churches, a mirror image of the desecrated *kivas*: statues smeared with excrement, chalices thrown into a basket of manure, a crucifix stripped of paint by a whip. And – a bizarre glimpse of how Christian symbolism had entered the Pueblo psyche – lying at the feet of the martyred Fray Pedro de Avila y Ayala, three lambs with their throats cut.

*   *   *

Like the nativists further east, the Pueblo rebels saw the conflict with Spaniards as a struggle between opposing spiritual forces. Their triumph showed that 'their own God whom they obeyed [had] never died,' and the victorious Popé and his lieutenants travelled from community to community, explaining that, in order to ensure a prosperous and peaceful future, the people must return 'to the state of their antiquity, as when they came from the lake ... that this was the better life and the one they desired, because the God of the Spaniards was worth nothing and theirs was very strong.' As well as destroying the churches and Christian images and sacred objects, the Indians must expunge all traces of Catholic belief in themselves, abandoning their baptismal names and washing themselves in the river, 'with the understanding that there would thus be taken from them the character of the holy sacraments.' Marriages solemnized by the friars were to be annulled, and the people were 'to burn the seeds which the Spaniards sowed and to plant only maize and beans, which were the crops of their ancestors.' To complete the inversion of the missionary regime, anyone who spoke Spanish or said the names of Jesus or Mary would be punished.

But the changes wrought to the Native American world by Spanish contact proved too widespread and too deep-rooted to be overturned wholesale. Exposure to Christian doctrine had profoundly affected the thinking even of cultural conservatives like Popé – it is significant, for instance, that he spoke of the missionaries' God being overcome by a single native deity rather than the multitude of spirits traditionally found in Pueblo culture – and had left a substantial minority of Catholics or Catholic sympathizers in most communities. Domestic animals and iron tools had become an essential part of the Pueblos' economy and had simultaneously made them more vulnerable to attack from their traditional enemies, the Apacheans, who, with the acquisition of horses, had become more mobile and aggressive. Outbreaks of disease, probably of European origin, continued to decimate the population.

To deal with the new situation, the Pueblos tried to develop new institutions. Under Popé's leadership they forged an inter-community alliance designed to protect them from both native and European enemies, but as the epidemics and the long drought continued and Apache raids, without the Spanish to deter them, intensified, internal rifts quickly opened up. In 1681, a Spanish expedition found the Pueblos still more or less united in their defiance, but by the end of that year some of the people had begun to doubt Popé's promises, complaining that they had had 'very small harvests, there [had] been no rain, and everyone [was] perishing.' By the start of the 1690s, according to the Indians' own tradition, discontent was so rife that a delegation from five Pueblos went to El Paso to ask the Spaniards to return.

In 1692, Don Diego de Vargas Zapata Luján Ponce de León led an expedition to reconquer New Mexico, and, in a four-month campaign, restored twenty-three Pueblos to Spanish control without – as he boasted – 'wasting a single ounce of powder, unsheathing a sword, or ... costing the Royal Treasury a single maravedi [*sic*].' The Indians' ambivalence and confusion is suggested by the reception they gave him, which ranged from armed resistance through sullen acceptance to rapturous rejoicing. At Zuñi, he was warmly welcomed and taken to 'a room on the second floor . . . finding there an altar with two large tallow candles burning' and a number of 'religious articles', including crucifixes, books and an oil painting of John the Baptist. De Vargas was flabbergasted at this evidence that a Catholic faction had survived in the community, apparently without a priest. (Intriguingly, according to the Indians' own tradition, a Spanish missionary known as Father Juan Greyrobe, who 'was very precious to the Zuñis,' was spared during the uprising and remained in the community, 'wearing Zuñi clothes' and taking a Zuñi wife. De Vargas makes no mention of meeting 'Father Juan', but a priest who had 'gone native' and married might well have chosen to conceal his identity from his fellow-Spaniards.)

Unlike the first conquest of New Mexico, the de Vargas expedition was not motivated primarily by missionary zeal. In the century since Oñate, Spain had lost her virtual monopoly in North America and was now facing increasingly serious competition from her johnny-come-lately colonial rivals, France and Britain. It was the alarming news of French incursions into Mississippi and Texas, rather than the supplications of the friars, that finally goaded her into action. The re-invasion effectively broke the area's hermetic isolation and began to open it, if only gradually, to the larger historical forces shaping the experience of Native Americans elsewhere.

For a few years after the re-conquest, there were further violent uprisings against colonial rule, but by the end of the century all the Puebloan peoples apart from the Hopi – who remained hostile, and were too remote and powerful to be subdued – had settled into an uneasy co-existence with the Spaniards. The over-riding need to extend and buttress the frontier led to several fundamental changes in Spanish policy, including the abolition of the hated *encomienda* (although the wage-labour system which replaced it, *repartimento*, was frequently abused by settlers, who still forced Indians to work for nothing) and made the military post, rather than the mission, the key European institution in New Mexico. While missionaries did return to the pueblos, they lost the dominant role as intermediaries between the natives and Spanish military power which had allowed them to rival and supplant the traditional leadership. Instead, they were forced to confine themselves primarily to the religious sphere, while the Crown appointed its own native 'governors' – whose symbol of authority, a silver-topped cane, is still in use in the pueblos today – to maintain order and implement Spanish policy.

The new system created frictions, as in other parts of North America, between cultural 'traditionalists', who rejected Spanish rule, and the governors and other 'progressives' who were prepared to collaborate with the colonists. Unlike the division, say, between Cherokee nativists and accommodationists, however, these differences seldom erupted into all-out conflict. While 'accommodation' in the English colonies generally meant accepting tribal dissolution and/or removal, the Pueblos were able to retain their identity as peoples and remain at the centre of the sacred topography which underpinned their culture. Spanish supervision was often intermittent, occurring only at specified times of year, and many of the more obviously 'pagan' ceremonies were able to continue – literally – underground, in the *kivas*. By avoiding the kind of open confrontations that had occurred during the seventeenth century, the Pueblos were able to preserve virtually their entire culture intact. 'Even at the end of so many years since their reconquest,' lamented a disheartened friar in 1776, 'the specious title or name of neophytes is still applied to them. This is the reason their condition now is almost the same as it was in the beginning, for generally speaking they have preserved some very indecent, and perhaps superstitious, customs.' As well as practising prohibited dances, he reported, the Indians openly used their baptismal names as terms of ridicule and entered the church, when they went at all, stark naked.

The result of this pragmatic arrangement has been that, over the centuries, the Pueblos have learnt to live simultaneously in two realities, each governed by its own calendar and its own understanding of the universe. In a way which is difficult for someone brought up in Western culture to understand, both of these worlds are valued and given their due: when a Pueblo person dies, for instance, a Catholic wake and Requiem Mass are followed by a traditional ceremony conducted by family members and clan and community officials. The Pueblos' acceptance of this duality was expressed very simply in a speech about the sacred Blue Lake made by the Governor of Taos, Severino Martinez, in New York in 1961:

We have visited St. Patrick's today. We have seen it and we had the privilege to kneel down and pray.

You have beautiful statues, beautiful figures of representative scenes which we now worship, you and I together. We don't have beautiful structures and we don't have gold temples in this lake, but we have a sign of a living God to who we pray – the living trees, the evergreen and spruce and the beautiful flowers and the beautiful rocks and the lake itself. We have this proof of sacred things we deeply love, deeply believe . . .

From the Spanish point of view, the *modus vivendi* with the Pueblos was a matter of practical politics rather than of philosophical reflection. With vast imperial ambitions but only a modest settler population – even by 1800, there were fewer than 20,000 colonists in New Mexico, mostly of mixed Spanish and native ancestry – Spain needed all the help it could get to protect its northern borderlands. For most of the eighteenth century, the most pressing threat was the ever-growing menace of Apache and Ute raiders, who indiscriminately attacked both settlers and sedentary Native Americans. This common danger, if nothing else, forged a link between colonists and Pueblos, and Pueblo auxiliaries regularly fought alongside Spanish forces patrolling the frontier.

Even though her grip on New Mexico was still, at best, tenuous, Spain decided to spread her scarce resources even more thinly by expanding into the vast desert area further west. Already, by the end of the seventeenth century, the southern part of what is now Arizona had been profoundly affected by a steadily advancing Spanish frontier in northern Mexico, with hundreds or perhaps thousands of native people being lured or taken as slaves to work in the rich gold and silver mines of Sonora. Here, and living in an essentially colonial *milieu*, they underwent an experience of Spanish rule very different from the Pueblos'. Valued primarily for their bodies rather than their souls, they were often brutally exploited and received little or no formal religious instruction. Missionaries were horrified at their treatment, which exposed them to – from the Church's point of view – the worst elements of settler society: '. . . in the first ranch of a mining settlement or Spanish town,' wrote Father Juan Nentuig, '. . . Indians meet with teachers of such a character, that in a couple of hours they are led into errors which corrupt them and cause the ruin of both body and soul . . .' Divorced from their own cultures and communities, many of them joined the ranks of detribalized Indians and *mestizos* who, by the end of the colonial period, had come to form the overwhelming majority in Spanish American society. (In modern Mexico, for example, while only about 15 per cent of the population identify themselves as Indian, scientists estimate that 90 per cent are of predominantly indigenous descent.)

In 1687, when the Italian Jesuit Father Eusebio Kino travelled north to begin mission work among the northern – or 'Upper' – Pimans, he was enthusiastically supported by Spanish miners and ranchers. Although most of the Pimans were agriculturalists, they were more widely dispersed than the Pueblos, living in scattered communities which the Spaniards called 'rancherías', and were regarded by the colonists as exceptionally 'savage'. The settlers expected that by following the Jesuit policy of 'reduction' – concentrating the Indians in mission communities where they could more easily be converted and controlled – Kino would open their land to economic development and, at the same time, transform them into a source of docile labour.

These hopes were quickly disappointed. Kino, by all accounts a gentle and kindly man, was generally welcomed by the Pimas and Tohono O'odham and seems to have been at pains to protect them from the worst effects of contact. He carried with him a written undertaking, signed by the viceroy, that the Indians would not be subject to forced labour and that they would not be expected to pay tribute during the missionary programme. When harsh or high-handed treatment by Spaniards sparked Indian resistance, moreover, Kino acted as a mediator rather than allowing the settlers to use the conflict as a pretext for declaring a 'just war' to seize more captives. This principled stand created widespread discontent among the settlers, who, from the early 1700s on, conducted a more or less constant campaign to have Kino's missions closed, but it was remarkably successful in winning the trust of the Indians. Although many Pimans retreated northwards to avoid the encroaching Spanish settlements, they continued, by and large, to accept – and sometimes even to ask for – Jesuit missionaries.

The power both of the Jesuits, however, and of the Spanish empire itself was starting to wane. As the eighteenth century developed, the forces unleashed by contact and conquest proved more and more difficult for either colonists or missionaries to control. As early as the 1620s, innovations introduced by the Spaniards had enabled one Athabascan group, called by the colonists 'Apaches de Navaju' (from a Tewa word meaning, apparently, either 'great planted fields' or 'takers from the fields') to develop a distinct way of life which, increasingly, posed a direct threat to Spanish rule. By building up large stocks of sheep, horses and cattle – originally acquired from settlers – the Navajos were starting to transform themselves from farmer-hunter-gatherers into farmer-pastoralists, running their herds over a huge area of arid grassland that was too dry for intensive agriculture. With a more plentiful supply of meat and little direct colonial pressure on their land, both their population – in a striking reversal of the post-contact pattern elsewhere in North America – and their land-base steadily increased. This process was given sharp impetus by the chaos in New Mexico during the 1680s and 1690s, when hundreds, or even thousands, of Pueblo refugees settled among the Navajos, swelling their numbers and bringing them new skills such as weaving, pottery and house-building.

In the first decade of the eighteenth century, Navajos started attacking the newly re-established Spanish settlements along the Rio Grande, and for the rest of the colonial period Navajo raids – primarily for livestock – remained a more or less constant feature of settler life. The Spaniards reciprocated with their customary slave-raids, killing men and seizing hundreds of women and children, but they were never able to deliver a decisive blow or establish a permanent presence in Navajo territory. As the other Apachean groups grew bolder, sweeping further south and west to plunder communities not only in southern New Mexico and Arizona but in Mexico itself, the Spanish authorities found themselves increasingly powerless. In 1751, just as they were trying to suppress an uprising of Piman peoples in the north, they were forced to abandon the provincial capital of Sonora.

In the 1760s, in an attempt to prevent its American empire slipping away, the Spanish Crown initiated a series of far-reaching changes. The Jesuits, who were thought to pose a serious threat to royal authority, were expelled in 1767, and two years later Franciscan missionaries and soldiers began to colonize southern California, founding their first mission at San Diego. Military posts were re-positioned to make them more effective, and in 1786 the newly appointed Viceroy of New Spain, Bernardo de Galvez, issued new instructions for governing the Frontier Provinces. After being eroded for more than a century by British and French rivalry, Spain's commercial position in North America was, he knew, perilously weak. To survive competition from the new, expansionist United States, he believed it was imperative to make trading alliances with Indians in the Plains and the Southeast. The main obstacle to this policy was the Apaches, who tied up manpower and resources that were urgently needed on the new frontier.

Galvez's response was to abandon the old ideology of conquest, with its ultimately religious justification, and adopt a purely pragmatic approach to 'pacifying' the Apachean tribes. In an aggressive, well co-ordinated campaign, parties of Spanish, Piman, Pueblo and Mexican Indian troops scoured 'Apachería', destroying houses and stocks of food, seizing herds of horses and killing or capturing hundreds of *Dineh*. When the survivors sued for peace, they were offered not 'the salvation of their souls' – which Galvez regarded as an impracticable aim in the short-term – but the chance to settle close to Spanish military posts, where they were plied with rations of food, tobacco and alcohol to remove their incentive for raiding and make them dependent on the colonists.

This approach was staggeringly successful. By 1800, the raids had almost stopped, a steady stream of settlers was returning to the Frontier Provinces – the first twenty years of the nineteenth century saw almost a 50 per cent rise in the Spanish population of New Mexico – and Spanish traders were doing a thriving business with the Comanches and other Plains peoples.

But these improvements on the margins of New Spain were not enough to avert the growing crisis at the heart of the empire. Throughout Spanish America, colonists were chafing at the government's unwillingness to grant them political power and economic freedom, and in 1809 and 1810, when Spain was caught in her own independence struggle against Napoleon, their discontent erupted in a series of local *coups* and uprisings. Initially, the revolutionaries claimed to be acting for the exiled King Ferdinand VII against the radical new parliament, the *Cortés*, which they felt had betrayed them, but when Ferdinand was restored in 1814 and tried to reassert the Crown's absolute power, they increasingly demanded complete separation from Spain.

In 1821, Mexico finally emerged from more than a decade of war as an independent republic. Like its Spanish predecessors, the new government believed that it had a duty to 'civilize' the Indians, but its definition of 'civilization' was sharply different. Where the Spanish authorities, at least until the final days of empire, had always seen their main purpose as the salvation of Indian souls, the republicans were guided by the secular ideals of the American and French Revolutions. Their mission, they believed, was to sweep away the intricate social, racial and religious caste system of Spanish America (New Spain, according to some theorists, had at least 128 different racial categories, each with its own place in the colonial hierarchy) and to draw *all* Mexicans into a liberal, property-owning democracy. At a stroke, therefore, the 'Indian' was abolished as a political concept, and Native Americans became merely *peasants*, who, through land-reform and education, could be freed from the shackles of ignorance and superstition.

Like parallel developments in the United States after independence, the removal of the Indians' special rights led to large-scale loss of indigenous lands, but in New Mexico and Arizona, far from the centres of power and population, it was the new government's conversion to free trade rather than its social policy that had the biggest impact. Dramatic industrial growth was rapidly transforming the burgeoning US into a world power, and Anglo-American entrepreneurs, with an impressive range of new goods and technologies to sell, had been covetously eyeing the lucrative Mexican market for years. With the abolition of Spain's restrictive trade barriers, Anglo merchants swarmed into the old Frontier Provinces along what quickly became known as the Santa Fé Trail. They were followed by 'mountain men', fur trappers and traders drawn by the abundance of fur-bearing animals in the Rockies, and then by land-hungry settlers and soldiers. At the same time, Anglo-immigrants flocked to Texas, where, under Mexico's liberal colonization policy, they were offered free land.

Many of the Anglo-Americans were less than impressed by their hispanic hosts. The trader Albert Pike described New Mexicans as 'a lazy gossiping people always lounging on their blankets and smoking cigarillos,' and thought they were 'peculiarly blessed with ugliness,' while Josiah Gregg wrote that they lived 'in darkness and ignorance,' and that they had 'inherited much of the cruelty and intolerance of their ancestors, and no small portion of their bigotry and fanaticism.'

The root of this disdain, in many cases, was the same sense of racial superiority and national destiny that, in a different context, underlay the Indian Removal policy in the US. Most New Mexicans were not merely Spanish Catholics – reason enough for suspicion and hostility – but 'mongrels', with a long history of ethnic inter-marriage even among the aristocratic élite who claimed descent from *conquistador* ancestors. Lurking beneath the hispanic affectation of European breeding, many Anglos thought they discerned unmistakable flashes of atavistic indolence and savagery. The New Mexican character, according to an observer in the 1850s, was a compound of 'all the vices of those whose homes are washed by the blue waters of the Mediterranean Sea' and 'the cunning and deceit of the Indian.'

With the rapid growth of literacy in the US, these kinds of views were starting to reach a mass audience – most of whom would never venture west of the Mississippi – through patriotic newspapers and a spate of popular books about life on the frontier. J. Ross Browne's *Adventures in Apache Country*, for instance, confidently asserted that: 'Every generation the population grows worse, and the [Mexicans] may now be ranked with their natural compadres – Indians, burros, and coyotes.' As 'Yankees' – as the hispanics called them – continued to flood into northern Mexico, a mood of feverish nationalism quickly developed in the United States. It was unthinkable that free-born Anglo-Saxons should live under the sway of a people, who, as well as being corrupted by miscegenation, had reduced themselves to servility by three centuries of craven obedience to the Church and the Spanish Crown. Only through annexation by the United States could hispanics hope to escape the downward spiral of degradation and kindle a spirit of liberty and independence. They had become, as the *Illinois State Register* put it, 'reptiles in the path of progressive democracy,' and they 'must either crawl or be crushed.'

Texas, which had already become predominantly Anglo by 1830, blazed the trail. In 1836 it declared itself an independent republic and then, almost immediately, pressed for admission to the United States. The Texans' campaign won enormous popular support in the US – 'Man and woman,' wrote one newspaper editor, 'were not more formed for union, by the hand of God, than Texas and the United States are formed for union by the hand of nature' – and became the key issue in the 1844 Presidential election. In 1846, Congress voted to annex Texas, and sent a new ambassador to Mexico City to negotiate the purchase of New Mexico and California as well.

The Mexicans angrily rejected the suggestion and openly threatened war, but the United States was undeterred. No human law, not even the law of nations, could be allowed to impede the pre-ordained march of Progress. 'Away, away with all these cobweb tissues of rights of discovery, exploitation, settlement, contiguity, etc. . . .' John O'Sullivan had written the year before, ' [Our claim] is by the right of our manifest destiny to overspread and to possess the whole of the continent which Providence has given us for the development of the great experiment of liberty and federative self-government entrusted to us.'

In this mood, President Polk ordered General Zachary Taylor to occupy the north bank of the Rio Grande, a disputed area claimed by both governments. When Mexican and US troops clashed, Polk reported that 'Mexico has passed the boundary of the United States, has invaded our territory, and shed American blood on American soil,' and Congress promptly declared war. During the ensuing desperately unequal struggle, US troops entered Mexico City and hoisted the Stars and Stripes over 'the halls of Montezuma.' There was excited talk of annexing the whole of Mexico, but the idea was rejected, in part because it would have meant absorbing a large, biologically Native American population which, it was thought, would threaten US institutions. Finally, in 1848, under the Treaty of Guadeloupe Hidalgo, the Mexican government was forced to cede not only Texas but also New Mexico, California and all the land in between.

Two hundred and fifty years after Don Juan de Oñate marched up the Rio Grande, the Pueblos and the other Native Americans of the Southwest had to face a new invasion of alien people and ideas. Like the Spaniards before them, the newcomers proclaimed themselves the vanguard of civilization and then promptly set about robbing, raping and brutalizing the indigenous population. To people as conscious of their own history as the Pueblos, there must have been a grim sense of *déja vu* when the Missouri volunteers sent to occupy their homeland started stealing crops and livestock and kidnapping native women. In 1847, while the war with Mexico was still going on, the people of Taos and a number of Indian and Mexican allies were finally provoked into retaliation, and, in a series of attacks, they killed the first US governor of the Territory of New Mexico and twenty other Anglo-Americans. The authorities responded with a massive show of arms, killing some 200 Indians and destroying much of Taos in a heavy artillery bombardment.

Yet, for all its echoes of Ácoma and Tiguex, the US conquest of the Southwest ushered in a very different era for the Indians. Unlike the Spanish, Anglos did not view civilization primarily as something you imparted to other *people* – who were, almost certainly, racially incapable of it – but rather as something which, through settlement, you transposed into other *areas*. They had little interest in either Indian labour or – to begin with, at least – Indian souls, but only in Indian land, in which, through their own efforts, they planned to plant an ethnically and culturally Anglo community.

Where Spain, therefore, had always envisaged some kind of permanent future for Indians in America, if only as detribalized, Christianized servants, the new government viewed them as at worst an obstacle and at best an irrelevance to the long-term development of the country. As it set about containing and segregating the Native Americans of the Southwest to make their territory safe for settlement, it at last drew them into the epic struggle for North America which, by now, extended from the Atlantic to the Pacific.

8. The Far West

The burning world

Lively, lively, we are lots of people.
Maidu song

The western rim of the continental United States is, in many ways, a mirror image of the east. In the north of the region, there are still a few concentrations of Native American population – the Yakima reservation in Washington State, Warm Springs in Oregon – but California denies its Indian origins as completely as New England. The valleys, hillsides and sprawling suburbs are strewn with Spanish colonial-style houses that hint vaguely at a hispanic past, but with a few exceptions – Shasta, Yosemite – the Native American presence has been banished even from the map, crowded out by the names of Catholic saints and Anglo pioneers. 'We're vapours, we're ghosts,' says a contemporary native Californian, Lauren Bomellyn. 'When I was at school, I remember in the California history book that we [Native Americans] would get just a page in the front. The last time the book was published they wanted to wipe even that out. They wanted to start California history with the Spanish missions and just skip that there were Indians here at all . . .'

Yet at the time of Columbus, the West coast was probably the most heavily populated region north of Mexico, an intricate patchwork of cultures, languages and ways of life stretching from Baja California to the Alaska panhandle. In present-day California alone, there were six major language families and 150 different societies with a combined population of perhaps 700,000 – around 10 per cent, according to recent estimates, of the total for the whole of what is now the United States and Canada.

What makes these numbers so remarkable is that – with a handful of exceptions along the Colorado River – none of the peoples of the far west practised agriculture. The early development of the area seems to have paralleled the rest of North America, with a big game hunting phase giving way, at the end of the Ice Age, to a way of life based increasingly on foraging, gathering wild plants, fishing and hunting small animals. While the Southwest and Southeast were starting to cultivate crops, however, the West coast nations continued to refine their economy.

For peoples like the Yokut, Miwok, Maidu, Pomo and Wintu, the key discovery – as important as the acquisition of horticulture elsewhere – was a crushing and leaching process which enabled them to live by harvesting acorns from the prolific oak forests covering much of what is now California. The nuts were stored in large baskets and then, when they were needed, pulverized, treated to remove the bitter tannic acid that made them unpalatable, and made into gruel or bread. The diet was supplemented with berries, roots, deer, fish, wildfowl and small game such as rabbits and gophers.

While subsistence activities in other parts of North America were often sharply divided between seasons and sexes – women harvesting in the summer and autumn, for instance, and men hunting in the winter – native Californians generally worked together all the year round. With a temperate climate, fish and game could be taken at any time, using techniques and materials similar to those needed for gathering: the same skills in basketry produced beaters, winnowers and seed carriers and weirs, traps, pots and nets. The natural bounty of the region, and their ingenuity in exploiting it, meant that, unlike many other hunter-gatherers, most Californian groups were able to subsist within a relatively small, defined territory. They built permanent communities of brush- or bark-covered houses in sheltered valleys and alongside rivers, making short expeditions to nearby mountains, streams and woods to gather food.

The settlement – often of no more than a hundred or so people – was the focus of social and political life. With few exceptions, native Californians identified themselves as coming from a *place* rather than belonging to a *'tribe'*. Above the level of the (generally hereditary) village headman, there was little political organization, although in some areas several neighbouring bands grouped themselves together into larger 'moieties' such as the 'Coyotes' and the 'Wildcats'. Since a

'Wildcat' could only marry a 'Coyote', and *vice versa*, this arrangement created ties of kinship and obligation between different peoples who might otherwise have been enemies.

For the Californian Indians, like the clan-based societies further east, the *idea* of kinship was crucially important. Strangers would be interviewed to discover whether they were related, however remotely, to a member of the group. If they could establish even a symbolic connection, they were accepted, literally, as one of the family; if they failed, remaining beyond the horizon of the community's own, inner world, they were treated with suspicion and even hostility. (In case this seems very alien, it is worth remembering that the English words *kin* and *kindness* have the same root.)

Some scholars have suggested that California remained in the 'hunter-gatherer stage' because it was so isolated. They argue that, while a series of migrations brought Mexican agriculture to Arizona, Mississippi and other areas, the desert and the continental divide effectively cut California off from developments elsewhere in North America. In fact, however, it is clear that the West coast was penetrated by a whole range of outside cultural influences. Trade networks carried shells from the Gulf of California eastwards as far as the Great Plains, and brought pottery and other goods into the area from the Southwest. The Kuksu religion, found among several peoples in central California, shows strong Puebloan characteristics – including the impersonation of spirits by dancers – which suggest prolonged contact with the Anasazi. If Californian natives did not adopt agriculture along with other Southwestern cultural traits, it was probably because it did not seem to offer them any obvious advantages over their highly sophisticated hunter-gathering economy. Indeed, as the historian Alvin Josephy Jr. points out in *The Indian Heritage of America*, 'If agriculture had been introduced . . . it would have been so unproductive in its initial stages as to have caused widespread starvation among the dense population.'

Along its northern and eastern fringes, California merged almost imperceptibly with adjacent culture areas. From close to the present-day Oregon border northwards, along the lush, mist-shrouded Pacific shore, stretched a string of nations – Yurok, Coos, Chinook, Chehalis, Quileute, Makah and others – whose way of life was profoundly influenced by the great 'Northwest coast' cultures of western Canada and southern Alaska. Where the staple in central and southern California was acorns, the Northwest coast peoples lived primarily by harvesting the vast quantities of salmon that swarmed up their rivers every spring to spawn. By smoking or drying the bulk of the catch to provide food for the rest of the year, they were able to live in permanent communities and to develop a complex ceremonial and artistic life. They built substantial plank houses (some as large as sixty feet long), wove blankets, clothes and baskets out of plant fibres, and – particularly in what is now British Columbia – developed an extraordinary, quite distinctive style of wood-carving. Their intricate, brightly coloured wooden masks, boxes, house fronts and 'totem poles', decorated with the figures of animals and supernatural beings like the thunderbird, are perhaps the best-known and most recognizable images in North American Indian art.

Unlike their neighbours to the south (and most other North American Indian groups), Northwest societies were strictly hierarchical. At the top of the social scale were 'chiefs' or 'nobles' and their families; then 'commoners'; and finally, at the bottom, 'slaves' (usually captured from other tribes), who in some villages made up nearly a third of the population. Prosperous 'nobles' owned not only material possessions like canoes, blankets and ornately decorated clothing, but also names, songs or powerful guardian spirits. In the north of the area, high-ranking individuals regularly held a kind of ritual feast called a *potlatch* (from the Nootka word *patshatl*, meaning 'giving') in which – in the belief that 'the more you give, the richer you are' – they gave away and sometimes even destroyed their property. The northern Californian peoples tended to display their possessions less flamboyantly, but shared many of the same values. The Yurok, for instance, had an intricate legal code, in which the victim of an offence received recompense according to his or her wealth.

Moving east, the Northwest coast culture area blends gradually into the Columbia Plateau, an upland region of fast-flowing streams and rivers, flanked by the Cascade and Rocky mountain ranges, which covers interior Oregon and Washington State and parts of Montana, northern California, Idaho and British Columbia. Like the coastal nations, the two dozen or so peoples of the area – Modoc, Klamath, Spokane, Palouse, Kalispel, Nez Percés and others – subsisted primarily by salmon-fishing, but their social life echoed the more egalitarian societies of central California. Under the leadership of a 'headman' selected for his abilities, they built riverside villages of circular, earth-roofed houses, making regular trips into the surrounding area to hunt and gather roots and berries.

Further south, eastern California touches the sparsely populated Great Basin of Utah, Nevada and parts of neighbouring states, where small bands of Utes, Paiutes, Shoshoni and other Uto-Aztecan-speakers followed a way of life essentially unchanged from the 'desert foraging' culture of the prehistoric Southwest. With low rainfall and an extreme climate – the summer temperature in Death Valley can reach 140° Fahrenheit – most of the area was only lightly covered with sagebrush, juniper and piñon trees, and the Great Basin peoples were almost constantly on the move in search of food. They caught insects, lizards, snakes and rabbits, gathered nuts and seeds and used sticks to dig up roots (which led Anglo-American settlers to give them the contemptuous name 'Digger Indians').

Finally, in its Southeastern corner, California met the Southwest culture area. In a narrow strip along the Colorado River on the border with Arizona lived a string of farming peoples – the Uto-Aztecan Chemehuevis and Yuman-speakers such as the Mohaves, Maricopas and Yumas – who continued to subsist like the prehistoric Mogollons and early Hohokams further south. Living in small communities close to rivers, they planted their plots of corn, beans, pumpkins, tobacco and gourds in the rich bottom lands where they would be naturally irrigated by floodwater.

There has been a great deal of archaeological work on the *material* remains of Californian Indian cultures, but, because the people themselves were overwhelmed so quickly, it is very difficult to reconstruct their pre-contact life from the *inside*. Perhaps the best glimpses we have come from northern groups like the Hupa, the Tolowa and the Wintu, who were studied by ethnologists in the late nineteenth century and who still retain at least some oral traditions today.

The surest guide to their view of the world – because it embodies their deepest values, and is less likely to be changed by contact than other aspects of their culture – can again be found in their origin legends. At the heart of their cosmology was the belief that:

There was a world before this one ... the world of the first people, who were different from us altogether. Those people were very numerous, so numerous that if a count could be made of all the stars in the sky, all the feathers on birds, all the hairs and fur on animals, all the hairs on our own heads, they would not be so numerous as the first people.

This central idea runs through the long myth-cycles found among all the northern Californian nations, which recount, in intricate detail, how the first world was transformed into the reality we know today. Often, the genesis of the new order was a cataclysmic fire or flood, in which most of the 'first people' were turned into the animals and birds, rocks and stars. According to the Wintu, for instance:

Olelbis [the creator] looked down into the burning world. He could see nothing but waves of flame; rocks were burning, the ground was burning, everything was burning. Great rolls and piles of smoke were rising; fire flew up toward the sky in flames, in great sparks and brands. Those sparks became *kolchituh* (sky eyes), and all the stars that we see now in the sky came from that time when the first world was burned. The sparks stuck fast in the sky, and have remained there ever since the time of the *wakpohas* (world fire). Quartz rocks and fire in the rocks are from that time.

But, beneath their new appearances, the 'first people' retain their primal power, which remains the driving force of the universe. Shamans can harness it to heal (or harm), summoning their spiritual assistants with songs of striking poetic beauty, such as the Wintu *Song of Waida Werris* (the Pole Star):

> The circuit of earth which you see,
> The scattering of stars in the sky which you see,
> All that is the place for my hair [i.e., rays of light].

The same concept underlies the northern Californians' central ceremony, the annual (or, occasionally, bi-annual) 'world renewal dance', when the people gather at the *axis mundi* to 'restrengthen' the earth and celebrate the start of a new cycle. In a series of complex rituals – rebuilding the sacred wooden 'dance house', kindling a new fire, gathering the first acorns or salmon of the season – the religious leaders revitalize the universe by recalling the words and actions of the pre-human spirit people. Virtually the entire nation was drawn together in the dance, which could involve forty or more communities and last for up to sixteen days.

Describing the 'World Renewals', the ethnographer and anthropologist A. L. Kroeber wrote: '. . . they want their world stable; they dread its tilting and slipping, its shaking by earthquake, its flooding, its invasion by famine or by epidemics advancing like clouds. It is the warding off these threats that is the formal motivation of their greatest rituals . . .' Ironically, when contact finally came in the mid-nineteenth century, it was their practice of peacefully gathering together to stabilize the world that made the northern Californians so peculiarly vulnerable to the forces of chaos and destruction.

✿   ✿   ✿

> *At the time of death,*
> *When I found there was to be death,*
> *I was very much surprised.*
> *All was failing.*
> *My home, I was sad to leave it.*
>
> *I have been looking far,*
> *Sending my spirit north, south, east and west.*
> *Trying to escape death,*
> *But could find nothing,*
> *No way of escape.*

Luiseño song

In 1540, Hernando de Alarcón sailed up the Colorado River with shiploads of supplies for the Coronado expedition, while Melchior Diaz travelled overland to meet him. In their unsuccessful attempts to find each other, both parties encountered 'large and well-formed' Yumans, whose initial friendliness quickly turned to hostility when Diaz captured and tortured some of them as a 'preventive' measure.

Two years later, Rodriguez de Cabrillo made the first recorded European voyage along the Californian coast. He was followed, in 1579, by Sir Francis Drake, who landed north of the present-day San Francisco and was enchanted by the natives he found there. His effusive account is full of images of the Golden Age: the Indians were 'people of a tractable, free and loving nature, without guile or treachery,' who not only plied him with basket-loads of 'an herb which they called Tabacco' (almost certainly not tobacco) but also – conveniently enough – gave him a large chunk of western North America. According to the brass plate he set up, their 'KING AND PEOPLE FREELY RESIGNE THEIR RIGHT AND TITLE IN THE WHOLE LAND UNTO HER MAJESTIES KEEPING.' As the historian Angie Debo points out, 'It was not the first time nor the last when Indians gave away their land without knowing it.'

For almost the next two centuries, California remained marginal to European ambitions, with only occasional Spanish and British incursions along the coast and around the Colorado River (although it is possible that, as in other regions, epidemics of Old World diseases spread far in advance of direct contact). The Spanish invasion in 1769, however, brought systematic and traumatic change, transforming native life in the southern part of the area and eventually affecting peoples as far north as Alaska.

Just as Drake had expected to find joyful, open-handed Arcadians, so the Spaniards expected to find natives living in 'ignorance, infelicity and misery.' Not surprisingly, they found them. The missionaries' reports, even allowing for their deep religious convictions and genuine moral outrage, are often curiously blinkered. According to Pedro Font, for instance, the agricultural Yumans, living 'twenty or thirty or more' to a house 'like hogs,' were not only sexually 'shameless and excessive' but also 'very fond of smoking, and . . . very lazy, and if this were not so they would reap much larger harvests; but they are content with what is sufficient to provide themselves with plenty to eat . . .' Among friars, presumably, being satisfied with enough would have been considered a virtue, but in Native Americans it was clearly a vice. Similarly, although the Yumans were 'as a rule . . . gentle, gay and happy,' it was because they were 'like simpletons' who 'marvelled as if everything they saw was a wonder to them, and with their impertinent curiosity they made themselves troublesome and tiresome . . .'

The missionaries, following the model already established in other parts of Hispanic America, set out to concentrate the Indians in European-controlled settlements where they could be converted to Catholicism and transformed into a labour force for the Spanish-speaking *gente de razon* ('people of reason') – many of whom were themselves detribalized Mexican *mestizos* and natives. Small parties of priests and soldiers scoured the country, using a mixture of gifts, threats and outright force to bring unconverted *'gentiles'* into the missions.

Remarkably, we still have a 'wild' Indian's account of his capture and incarceration. In 1878, when he was an old man, a Kamia called Janitin told an interviewer:

> I and two of my relatives went down ... to the beach ... we did no harm to anyone on the road, and ... we thought of nothing more than catching and drying clams in order to carry them to our village.
>
> While we were doing this, we saw two men on horseback coming rapidly towards us; my relatives were immediately afraid and they fled with all speed, hiding themselves in a very dense willow grove ...
>
> As soon as I saw myself alone, I also became afraid ... and ran to the forest ... but already it was too late, because in a moment they overtook me and lassoed and dragged me for a long distance, wounding me much with the branches over which they dragged me, pulling me lassoed as I was with their horses running; after this they roped me with my arms behind and carried me off to the Mission of San Miguel, making me travel almost at a run in order to keep up with their horses, and when I stopped a little to catch my wind, they lashed me with the lariats that they carried, making me understand by signs that I should hurry; after much travelling in this manner, they diminished the pace and lashed me in order that I would always travel at the pace of the horses.
>
> When we arrived at the mission, they locked me in a room for a week; the father [a Dominican priest] made me go to his habitation and he talked to me by means of an interpreter, telling me that he would make me a Christian, and he told me many things that I did not understand, and Cunnur, the interpreter, told me that I should do as the father told me, because now I was not going to be set free, and it would go very bad with me if I did not consent in it. They gave me *atole de mayz* [corn gruel] to eat which I did not like because I was not accustomed to that food; but there was nothing else to eat.

One day they threw water on my head and gave me salt to eat, and with this the interpreter told me that I was now Christian and that I was called *Jesús*: I knew nothing of this, and I tolerated it all because in the end I was a poor Indian and did not have recourse but to conform myself and tolerate the things they did with me.

The following day after my baptism, they took me to work with the other Indians, and they put me to cleaning a *milpa* [cornfield] of maize; since I did not know how to manage the hoe that they gave me, after hoeing a little, I cut my foot and could not continue working with it, but I was put to pulling out the weeds by hand, and in this manner I did not finish the task that they gave me. In the afternoon they lashed me for not finishing the job, and the following day the same thing happened as on the previous day. Every day they lashed me unjustly because I did not finish what I did not know how to do, and thus I existed for many days until I found a way to escape; but I was tracked and they caught me like a fox; there they seized me by lasso as on the first occasion, and they carried me off to the mission torturing me on the road. After we arrived, the father passed along the corridor of the house, and he ordered that they fasten me to the stake and castigate me; they lashed me until I lost consciousness, and I did not regain consciousness for many hours afterwards. For several days I could not raise myself from the floor where they had laid me, and I still have on my shoulders the marks of the lashes which they gave me then.

As well as being subjected to hard labour and military discipline, 'Mission Indians' were forced to assume a new social and cultural identity as part of a European – and still essentially feudal – household. 'The Fernandino Father is like a king,' reported one convert, Pablo Tac. 'He has his pages, alcaldes, majordomos, musicians, soldiers, gardens, ranchos, livestock, horses by the thousand, cows, bulls by the thousand, oxen, mules, asses, 12,000 lambs, 200 goats, etc.' Within a few years, Indian neophytes – and some unconverted natives – were providing servants for the *gente de razon* not only in the Missions themselves but also in *presidios* (forts), ranches and civilian towns such as Los Angeles. Their labour, in fact, built and supported virtually the whole of Hispanic California.

Following the pattern elsewhere in North America, a minority of the 'Mission Indians' do appear to have become genuine converts both to

Catholicism and to the 'civilized' way of life. The Luiseño Pablo Tac, for example, seems eagerly to have embraced the missionary view: '. . . we lived among the woods,' he wrote, 'until merciful God freed us of these miseries through Father Antonio Peyri, a Catalan, who arrived in our country in the afternoon with seven Spanish soldiers.' (This enthusiasm was rewarded with a trip to Rome, where Tac became ill and died at the age of nineteen.) For the majority, however, the mission experience was a catastrophe. Disorientated, depressed and weakened by harsh physical conditions and an unfamiliar diet, they were reduced to a state of apathetic lethargy in which tens of thousands died from European diseases. In 1818, Governor Vicente de Sola reported that, of 64,000 baptized natives, 41,000 were now dead. By the 1830s, the coastal Indian population had fallen from perhaps 70,000 to around 15,000.

For much of the colonial period, the Spanish presence provoked violent unrest. In 1783, after a bitter two-year conflict, the warlike Quechans forced the Spaniards to withdraw permanently from the Colorado River area. The smaller, less aggressive groups further west were less successful, although several of them fought heroically, quickly adopting tactics – such as digging huge defensive pits – which made them more effective against the mounted invaders. The Spaniards had effectively ended most organized opposition in the coastal area by about 1810, but captured Indians continued to resist the missions by plotting to kill the priests or by running away to live outside Spanish control in – as a Franciscan described one settlement – 'a republic of hell and diabolical union of apostates.' Alarmed at the haemorrhaging of the mission population from breakouts and disease, the authorities mounted a series of major military operations to recapture *cimarrones* (runaways) and find new sources of *gentiles*. Parties of soldiers not only scoured almost the whole of present-day California and Utah but also forayed as far up as Alaska, further undermining many Northwest coast nations that were just starting to feel the impact of Russian, Spanish, British and American traders.

But although the Spanish invasion brought disruption and a fall in population to a wide area, it did not result in the kind of wholesale destruction caused by the English settlements in New England. By 1845, there were still no more than about 4,000 *gente de razon* in California, clearly not enough – even with firearms, military organization and the systematic use of terror – to control the whole region. With the help of information gleaned from *cimarrones* and from occasional brushes with Spanish troops, some groups outside the mission area quickly learnt how to make themselves less vulnerable to attack. Peoples such as the Yokuts, Miwok and Wappo abandoned their peaceful, sedentary way of life to become semi-nomadic guerrillas, ambushing parties of soldiers and then retreating into swamps or forest where their knowledge of the terrain enabled them to avoid capture. Although they were often defeated in individual skirmishes, they held their ground so tenaciously that Spain was unable to expand permanently beyond the coastal region.

Mexican independence in 1821 loosened the Hispanic grip still further. Without either the Spaniards' military power or their religious zeal, the Mexican authorities found themselves fighting a losing battle to keep control of large parts of California. True to its liberal ideals, the new republic declared that indigenous people were free and equal citizens, but in practice the situation for many Californian natives – like their counterparts in New Mexico – grew markedly worse. Although the missions were secularized and turned into 'Indian Towns' in the 1830s, the system of forced Indian labour was retained – without it, the authorities realized, hispanic California would have collapsed overnight – and most of the best land quickly ended up in the hands of powerful Mexican families. Their new masters, the neophytes soon found, were often even more brutally exploitative than the Church. Not surprisingly, thousands of *cimarrones* fled to Mexican towns, where they could merge with the *mestizo* population, or swelled the ranks of hostile groups in the interior.

From the late 1820s onwards, the 'wild' Indians proved increasingly effective against Mexican forces. An escaped neophyte called Estanislao – described by one scholar as 'a real genius' for his brilliant use of trenches, breastworks and military strategy – organized a band of runaways and *gentiles* who, in 1829, repelled an assault by troops armed with a swivel gun. Although he was later forced to retreat, his success seems to have encouraged a spate of Indian unrest in California, with more and more bands moving away from purely defensive action and starting to go on the offensive. By the mid-1830s, hostilities had spread from the interior into areas that had been under Spanish control for decades. Frequent raiding drove many Hispanos from their homes and undermined Mexico's fragile hold over the whole region: at one point, natives even seemed on the point of capturing San Diego. But while a few leaders did aim to expel Europeans altogether, the majority were prepared to settle down into a kind of live-and-let-live co-existence with Hispanos once their own rights to local autonomy had been won. Unable to re-impose their authority by force, Mexicans in much of the region had to accept an informal *modus vivendi* – strengthened by frequent intermarriage between the two groups – with more or less self-governing native communities.

But for all their success in containing, and even pushing back, the frontier, California's native people were critically weakened by eighty years of hispanic rule. The mission system had destroyed the independence and sapped the cultural vitality of many groups, and – as in other parts of North America – European disease had taken a horrific toll: in one epidemic alone, in 1838, an estimated 70,000 Indians died of malaria. By the mid-1840s, their population had fallen from perhaps as much as 700,000 to less than 200,000. In this enfeebled state they were forced to confront an unimaginably greater cataclysm: Mexico's loss of California to the US, and, simultaneously, the discovery of gold there.

*   *   *

Just then I peeped round my mother to see . . . [the white men]. *I gave one scream, and said, –*

'Oh, mother, the owls!'

I only saw their big white eyes, and I thought their faces were all hair . . .

I imagined I could see their big white eyes all night long. They were the first ones I had ever seen in my life.

Sara Winnemucca, Paiute

My grandpa, before white people came, had a dream. He was so old he was all doubled up. Knees to chin, and eyes like indigo. Grown son carry him in great basket on his back, every place.

My grandpa say: 'White Rabbit' – he mean white people – 'gonta devour our grass, our seed, our living. We won't have nothing more, this world. Big elk with straight horn come when white man bring it.' I think he meant cattle. 'Nother animal, bigger than deer, but round feet, got hair on his neck.' This one, horse, I guess.

My aunt say: 'Oh, Father, you out your head, don't say that way.'

He say: 'Now, Daughter, I not crazy. You young people gonta see this.'

Lucy Young, Wintun, 1939

The Anglo-American world had already begun to impinge on the far West decades before the US–Mexican War. As early as the 1770s, sailors from passing ships – like their English counterparts on the Atlantic seaboard in the late sixteenth century – were trading more or less informally along the coast, and in 1792 an American craft sailed up the Columbia River. Eleven years later, President Jefferson sent Meriwether Lewis and William Clark to explore the territories acquired by the United States under the Louisiana Purchase, and, in an epic journey overland from St. Louis to the Pacific, they made contact with some fifty native nations, including the Shoshones, Nez Percés and Cayuses. In their wake came fur-traders and Mountain Men, missionaries and a trickle of settlers along the Oregon Trail, bringing new influences to the ferment already created by Spanish slave raids. By the 1830s, the lives of many Northwestern groups had been transformed by trade and – particularly on the Plateau – the acquisition of the horse; the Nez Percés, for instance, had quickly become expert horsemen, raising large herds of appaloosa ponies and using their new-found mobility to extend their hunting range on to the Plains.

In the years following Mexican independence, growing numbers of Anglo-Americans, attracted by the authorities' generous land-grants policy, also moved into California itself. Rather than following the US practice of forcibly removing Indians, many of them adapted to local conditions by adopting a more Mexican approach, making alliances with neighbouring Indians and using their labour to create personal fortunes for themselves. John Sutter, for instance, whose settlement at Sacramento, founded in 1839, became a focus for US immigrants, employed native workers not only to build his fort, hunt, fish and grow crops, but also to raid other communities for captives who could then be sold to Hispano rancho owners at a substantial profit.

This pattern continued, to begin with, when gold was found at Sutter's sawmill in January 1848. Many of the first prospectors and miners were natives, sometimes from as far away as the coast, hired by Sutter and other prosperous Anglo-American settlers. Ironically, their very success proved to be their downfall. Fired by reports of the Indians' discoveries, tens of thousands of Anglo-Americans started flooding west to prospect on their own account, and by May 1849 there were 5,000 wagons on the California trail. By late 1850, when the state was admitted to the union, the non-Indian population had reached 92,000 – an increase of 1,000 per cent or more in only five years – and by 1860 it had soared to 380,000.

This sudden influx was probably the single most destructive episode in the whole history of Native/Euro-American relations. The miners flocked, by and large, not to the existing hispanic settlements along the coast but to the mountains and forests of the interior which, since the arrival of the Spanish, had become the Indians' heartland. Native groups had no time to adapt and nowhere to escape to as, sometimes within a matter of days, their last refuges were completely overrun.

But it was not simply the scale of the Anglo-Americans' invasion but also their attitude that made it so lethal. The profound contrast between Spanish and Anglo approaches towards the native, already evident in New Mexico and elsewhere, appeared at its most extreme in California. Many of the miners seem to have been driven by a deep-rooted racial hatred, seeing Indians as, at best, a source of women and saleable captives – between 1850 and 1863 an estimated 10,000 California Indians, many of them children, were sold or indentured – and at worst simply an obstacle to be eliminated. As native people faced the usual horrifying problems of disease, dispossession and starvation, they also found themselves having to contend with armed bands of Anglo murderers who, on the slightest pretext or no pretext at all, would exterminate whole communities. More Indians probably died as a result of deliberate, cold-blooded genocide in California than anywhere else in North America. With uneasy irony, the nineteenth-century historian H. H. Bancroft wrote:

the California valley cannot grace her annuals with a single Indian war bordering on respectability. It can boast, however, a hundred or two of as brutal butchering, on the part of our honest miners and brave pioneers, as any area of equal extent in our republic. The poor natives of California had neither the strength nor the intelligence to unite in any formidable numbers; hence, when now and then one of them plucked up courage to defend his wife and little ones, or to retaliate on one of the many outrages that were constantly being perpetrated upon them by white persons, sufficient excuse was offered for the miners and settlers to band and shoot down any Indians they met, old or young, innocent or guilty, friendly or hostile, until their appetite for blood was appeased.

The long catalogue of atrocities against Californian Indians makes dismal reading. A fairly typical example is the case of Stone and Kelsey, two American trappers who established a ranch in the Clear Lake area in the late 1840s. Following the Mexican pattern, they forced a band of Pomos to work as cowboys and servants. According to Pomo oral tradition:

> . . . only those herds [cowboys] got anything to eat. Each one of these herders got four cups of wheat for a day's work. This cup would hold about one and a half pints of water. The wheat was boiled before it was given to the herders. And the herders shire [shared it] with their families. The herders who had large families were also starving. About twenty old people died during the winter from starvation. From severe whipping, four died. A nephew of an Indian lady who was living with Stone was shoot to death by Stone . . . [the Indians suffered] whipping and tieing their hands together with rope. The rope [was] then thrown over a limb of a tree and then drawn up until the Indian's toes barly touch[ed] the ground and let them hang there for hours. This was common punishment. When a father or mother of young girl was asked to bring the girl to his house by Stone or Kelsey, if this order was not obeyed, he or her would be whipped or hung by the hands. Such punishment occurred two or three times a week. And many of the old men and women died from fear and starvation.

Finally, in the autumn of 1849, the Pomos could bear this treatment no longer. After long debate, they killed Stone and Kelsey and then took 'what wheat and corn they could pack ... to a hiding place, where they could not be found by the whites ... The men went out to kill cattle for their use, and every man who was able to ride caught himself a horse ... So the Indians lived fat for a while.'

But after a few weeks, a party of US soldiers found the refugees. One morning the Pomo lookouts saw a long boat coming up the lake with:

> ... [a] pole on the bow with [a] red cloth. And several of them came. Every one of the boats had ten to fifteen men ... The next morning the white warriors went across in their long dugouts. The Indians said they would meet them in peace. So when the whites landed, the Indians went to welcome them but the white man was determined to kill them ...
>
> One old lady, a Indian told about what she saw while hiding under a bank in under a cover of hanging tuleys [bulrushes]. She said she saw two white men coming with their guns up in the air and on their guns hung a little girl. They brought it to the creek and threw it in the water. And a little later two more men came in the same manner. This time they had a little boy on the end of their guns and also threw it in the water. A little ways from her she said lay a woman shot through the shoulder. She held her little baby in her arms. Two white men came running torge [toward] the woman and baby. They stabbed the woman and the baby and threw both of them over the bank in to the water. She said she heard the woman say, 'O my baby'; she said when they gathered the dead, they found all the little ones were killed by being stabbed, and many of the women were also killed [by] stabbing. She said it took them four or five days to gather up the dead: And the dead were all burnt on the east side of the creek ...
>
> The next morning the soldiers started for Mendocino County ... The Indians wanted to surrender. But the soldiers did not give them time. The soldiers went in the camp and shot them down as if they were dogs. Some of them escaped by going down a little creek leading to the river. And some of them hid in the brush. And those who hid in the brush most of them were killed ... They killed mostly women and children ...

Similar incidents occurred again and again in the decades following the acquisition of California by the United States. The 2,000–3,000

Yana, for example, most of whom had adapted to the invasion of their land by becoming labourers, were virtually exterminated between 1850 and 1872, largely in revenge for the theft of cattle and horses by other, half-starving Native American peoples. (It should be said that a few of the handful of survivors were saved by their Anglo employers, who protected them or helped them to escape.) The Yuki, who may have numbered as many as 12,000 or more at the time of contact, were systematically reduced in three decades to fewer than 200 by a sustained campaign of genocide. According to one early settler, parties of Anglo men went out 'two or three times a week' to kill 'on average, fifty or sixty Indians on a trip.'

The social life of Northwestern people like the Wintu, Yurok and Hupa, with their elaborate 'world renewal' rites, made them particularly vulnerable. The modern Tolowa Lauren Bomellyn explains:

In December of each year the Tolowa people gathered together at the Axis Mundi to celebrate the creation of the earth. It's a ten day celebration beginning at the winter solstice, the shortest day of the year ... It would take days for people to arrive and as the population grew, the new Anglo settlement in Crescent City became a little worried, they thought that the Indians were maybe gathering to ... wipe them out or something. Since they had only been in the area less than a year, the settlers didn't realize that this was a normal annual thing.

So the Tolowa people all across the area and the Yurok further south gathered together at the centre of the world, to dance and celebrate ... They danced all night until morning, and then they rested during the day and prepared food and so forth and then in the evening the dance started again ... And each night the dance became a little more elaborate than the night before ... On about the sixth night ... the local militiamen got together, and they drank some whisky and got a good buzz going, and then they got on their horses and went out and surrounded the village, which was one of the larger towns in the area. And of course we all lived in plankhouses made from redwood then.

They lined up along a slough which lies in front of the village and then they began to set the buildings on fire, and as the people were trying to escape they were killed. Anybody who jumped into the slough to get away was gunned down into the water. And it happens that I have a great-great-uncle who survived, he was in the sweat house and he slid out and went into the slough and got away, and then he pushed himself southward in the slough. In the morning the entire village was set aflame, and hundreds of people were burned and killed outright. He said the slough was literally red with the blood of the people, and the babies that were found crying were just tossed into the flames to destroy them as well. So several hundred people perished there at . . . Yan'daak'ʉt, and later the place was called Burnt Ranch. And the local people still know where Burnt Ranch is . . .

The next year, because Axis Mundi was destroyed, the dance was moved to 'Eechuulet, and they started to dance there and they were attacked again and my great-grandmother said that there were seven layers of bodies in the dance house when they burned it. They just stacked them in and torched the house down and . . . burned them up there. The next year, 1855, there was . . . a battle at the mouth of the Smith River, where about seventy of our people were killed. But by this time our numbers were drastically reduced . . .

Although many of these attacks were carried out by gangs of civilians or self-appointed 'volunteers', they were often encouraged and supported by the wider population. A Marysville newspaper announced in 1859 that:

A new plan has been adopted . . . to chastise the Indians for their many depredations during the past winter. Some men are hired to hunt them, who are recompensed by receiving so much for each scalp, or some other satisfactory evidence that they have been killed. The money has been made up by subscription.

Two years later, the Shasta *Herald* reported that 'A meeting of citizens was held a day or two ago at Haslerigg's store, and measures taken to raise a fund to be disbursed in payment of Indian scalps for which a bounty was offered.' Another article drily noted after a particularly violent massacre that 'To defray the expenses of this heroic work, enormous claims were presented to the Legislature.'

But at the same time, even in California itself, there was a strong current of unease and disgust at the behaviour of the 'lowest and most brutal of the border population.' The anguished accounts of regular army officers and other more 'educated' Americans make it clear that many of them understood – and were appalled by – the magnitude of what was happening. In 1860, for instance, Major G. J. Raines reported to the Assistant Adjutant General at Fort Humboldt:

> I have just been to Indian Island, the home of a band of friendly Indians between Eureka and Uniontown, where I beheld a scene of atrocity and horror unparalleled not only in our own Country, but even in history, for it was done by men self acting and without necessity, colour of law, or authority – the murder of little innocent babes and women, from the breast to maturity, barbarously and I can't say brutally – for it is worse ... Volunteers, calling themselves such, from Eel River, had employed the earlier part of the day in murdering all the women and childen of the above Island ... midst the bitter grief of parents and fathers ... I beheld a spectacle of horror, of unexampled description – babes, with brains oozing out of their skulls, cut and hacked with axes, and squaws exhibiting the most frightful wounds in death which imagination can paint – and this done ... without cause ... as far as I can learn, as I have not heard of any of them losing life or cattle by the Indians. Certainly not these Indians, for they lived on an Island and nobody accuses them.

The national and metropolitan press often echoed this shocked tone. In June 1860, under the headline 'Indian butcheries in California', the San Francisco *Bulletin* gave a grisly account of 'the murderous outrages committed on the aboriginal inhabitants of California ...' Like Major Raines, the writer 'can bring to light no circumstance to palliate or extenuate them in the slightest degree.' He goes on: 'In the Atlantic and Western States, the Indians have suffered wrongs and cruelties at the hands of the stronger race. But history has no parallel to the recent atrocities perpetrated in California. Even the record of Spanish butcheries in Mexico and Peru has nothing so diabolical.'

Yet what the writer clearly finds so appalling is that, while the victims were 'of the Digger tribes, known as friendly Indians, the most degraded and defenceless of the race, entirely destitute of the bold and murderous spirit which characterizes other tribes of red men,' the perpetrators were 'men with white skins.' The text is full of images of racial shame:

> In one of the settlements an aged and feeble chief collected the women around him, when they were about flying on the approach of the human bloodhounds, assuring them that white men did not kill squaws and that they would be safe. But they all perished together . . .
>
> We have spoken of the authors of this butchery as men – white men. So they were. We can invent no logic that will segregate them from our own species. Would that it were possible to do so . . .
>
> Civilized humanity will scarcely believe it possible for human beings to be degraded so far below savages . . .

Ultimately, the sense of outrage at 'the murder of Indians by wholesale' – while clearly genuine – is rooted in much the same assumption of 'white' racial supremacy as the massacres themselves. Throughout the second half of the nineteenth century, as science was pressed into service to provide a rational justification for Anglo expansion, belief in the biological superiority of the 'Anglo-Saxon race' became increasingly commonplace in intellectual circles as well as in popular culture. Already, in 1839, in *Crania Americana; or, a Comparative View of the Skulls of Various Aboriginal Nations of North and South America*, Samuel George Morton had put forward the idea that the different races of mankind had been created separately – a theory that curiously parallels some nativist beliefs – and were destined to remain permanently unequal. This thesis was enthusiastically developed by Morton's followers in the 'American school' of ethnology. In 1854, for instance, *DeBow's Review* neatly vindicated both slaveowners and frontiersmen by comparing 'the negro' with 'the Indian':

> The former, in the state of slavery for which he is created, under the favouring care of a superior race, cannot be civilized or made a white man by any length of culture, but his condition can be ameliorated, and he indirectly enjoy the benefits of civilization. But the stern, proud Indian cannot be enslaved. The type of the savage beasts among whom he lives, like them he will disappear before the new tide of human life now rolling from the East, and with the buffalo, will have vanished the red man of America.

The following year, Oliver Wendell Holmes took up the same theme when he memorably described Native Americans as 'this sketch in red crayons of a rudimental manhood[,] to keep the continent from being a blank until the true lord of creation should come to claim it.'

Charles Darwin's *The Origin of Species*, published a decade after the Gold Rush, gave scientific racism a new intellectual authority. Subtitled *Or The Preservation of Favoured Races in the Struggle for Life*, it seemed to offer a purely *biological* explanation for the global 'success' of northen Europeans at the expense of other peoples. Where seventeenth-century Puritans believed that God had chosen them to populate the New World, nineteenth-century Americans could now feel confident that Nature had selected them for the same purpose. Within only a few years, references to Darwin and the theory of Evolution were commonplace in writing about Native Americans. In 1871, for instance, Mark Twain described the Gosiutes of the Great Basin as:

> ... the wretchedest type of mankind I have ever seen up to this writing ... The Bushmen and our Goshoots are manifestly descended from the self-same gorilla, or kangaroo, or Norway rat, whichever animal-Adam the Darwinians trace them to.

Twain was not alone in seeing the California and Great Basin Indians as being the lowest of the low, several rungs down the evolutionary ladder even from other Native American groups. H. H. Bancroft, normally a more sympathetic observer, wondered: '... why the Digger Indians ... were so shabbily treated by nature; why with such fair surroundings they were made so much lower in the scale of intelligence than their neighbours.'

It is, perhaps, not surprising that Anglo-American commentators – including some who felt a genuine compassion for the Indians – should have seized on Darwin to explain the genocide of native Californians as an inevitable, biological process in which the morals and intentions of individual settlers were largely irrelevant. As late as the 1940s, Shelburne Cook was describing Californian history in purely ecological terms, as an unequal contest between a weaker and a stronger 'race'. His account is full of the kind of scientific vocabulary – *habitat, organism, species* – which would normally be used to discuss microbes rather than people:

When the California Indian was confronted with the problem of contact and competition with the white race, his success was much less marked with the Anglo-American than with the Ibero-American branch ... [Under Spanish rule] the valley and northern tribes were evincing a fair capacity for adaptation ... to the new environment imposed by the entrance of a new biological group ...

[But] when the Indian was forced to withstand the shock and impact of the Anglo-Saxon invasion, his failure ... was virtually complete. In the physical and demographic spheres his competitive inferiority was such as to come very close to bringing about his literal extermination ... The present study undertakes to describe some of the processes involved in this racial failure ...

[A] factor of significance here is that of numbers. Other things being equal, the intensity of conflict and the weight thrown against the primitive group will roughly follow the numerical strength of the new or invading species. This general principle has been demonstrated repeatedly with the lower organisms in their parasite-host or predator-prey relationships, and it holds similarly for human beings.

Although Darwinism was clearly not directly responsible for the near-extermination of Californian Indians, it sprang from, and contributed to, an intellectual climate in which genocide was seen as natural and unavoidable. Evolutionists might distance themselves from the intemperate tone of popular culture, but it is easy to see how their theory of 'Favoured Races' succeeding in 'the Struggle for Life' could feed into the work of writers like Horace Bell, who ringingly declared in 1881:

We will let those rascally redskins know that they have no longer to deal with the Spaniard or the Mexican, but with the invincible race of American backwoodsmen, which has driven the savage from Plymouth Rock to the Rocky Mountains, and has headed him off here on the Western shore ... and will drive him back to meet his kindred fleeing westward, all to be drowned in the Great Salt Lake.

The peoples of the far west – even the supposedly 'degraded and defenceless' natives of central and western California – did not simply accept this fate passively. From the late 1840s to the late 1860s a succession of different groups, including Cayuses, Hamakhavas,

Miwoks, Shoshones, Hupa and several bands of Paiutes, put up stiff resistance to the invasion of their land. As late as 1873, the Modoc leader *Kentipoos* (known to the settlers as Captain Jack) was holding out against US forces in the lava beds of northern California. But the odds were overwhelmingly against them. By 1870, in just over two decades of US rule, the number of Indians in California had dropped from 100,000 to only 31,000 and was still falling rapidly, while the non-native population had rocketed to more than half a million.

Even after the far west had been 'pacified' militarily, the atmosphere of intense racial hatred and contempt continued to shape Anglo attitudes towards native people. Under the Treaty of Guadeloupe Hidalgo, the United States had undertaken to continue the Mexican policy of recognizing indigenous rights, but in practice Indians were regarded as 'trespassers on the public domain' and remained subject to dispossession, enslavement, massacre and murder. They were not accorded citizenship in the new state and – although many native women were forced into prostitution and 'concubinage' – were forbidden to marry Anglo-Americans. They could not testify in court, so they had no legal recourse when settlers occupied their territory, kidnapped women and children or carried out vigilante attacks on their villages. 'On good authority,' wrote T. T. Waterman in 1917, 'I can report the case of an old prospector-pioneer-miner-trapper of this region who had on his bed even in recent years a blanket lined with Indian scalps . . . The Indians he had killed he had killed purely on his own account. No reckoning was at any time demanded of him.' Waterman describes one attack in vivid, angry detail:

A party of whites, in April 1871, pursued a band of Indians with dogs. They located them in a cave across a narrow gulch, and shot a number of them, finally entering the cave itself. Here they found a lot of dried meat, and some small children. The hero of the occasion, being a humane man, a person of fine sensibilities and delicacy of feeling, could not bear to kill these babies – at any rate, not with the heavy 56-calibre Spencer rifle he was carrying. 'It tore them up too bad.' *So he shot them with his 38-calibre Smith and Wesson revolver.*

The federal authorities did make some attempt to regulate relations with the Indians and to control the acquisition of Indian land, but –

like their British counterparts in the Southeast a century before – they
found they were powerless to stem the flood of settlers. In 1851 and
1852, three commissioners negotiated treaties with native groups in a
large part of California who, they reported, were eager for peace and
willing to cede the bulk of their territory and accept US jurisdiction in
exchange for secure reservations. Under the agreements, a total of 7.5
million acres was 'set apart forever for the sole use and occupancy of
the aforesaid tribes,' and the United States undertook to provide the
Indians with rations and assistance in learning agriculture. By the end
of 1852, many bands had already left their ancestral homes and
gathered on the new reservations.

But the Commissioners, establishing a precedent that was to be
followed by later generations of Indian agents, creamed off a large part
of the supplies intended for native people. (Often, for example, they
gave Indians only half a blanket each, thereby creating a surplus that
could be sold for their own profit.) At the same time, Anglo settlers
organized a vigorous campaign against the treaties, and Congress,
under immense pressure, finally refused to ratify them. Further
attempts were made during the 1850s to establish new, smaller
reservations, but most of them were again undermined by official
corruption and opposition from local Anglos. The result, as J. Ross
Browne pointed out in a report at the time, was to leave the Indians
still more vulnerable and exposed:

> A very large amount of money was annually expended in feeding
> white men and starving Indians ... it invariably happened, when a
> visitor appeared on the reservations, that the Indians were 'out in the
> mountains gathering nuts and berries...' Very few of them, indeed,
> have yet come back ... In the brief period of six years, they have
> been nearly destroyed by the ... government. What neglect, star-
> vation, and disease have not done, has been achieved by the
> co-operation of the white settlers in the great work of extermination.

By 1860, the government had more or less abandoned the uphill
struggle to protect Indian land in California, leaving only a handful of
reservations and 'farms'. During the next few years, small areas were
set aside in the Hoopa Valley and Colorado River regions – in both
cases, significantly, to 'pacify' groups that had offered serious military

resistance – but the majority of Indians found themselves virtually landless. Many of them could only live by stealing livestock, thereby provoking still more murderous 'reprisals'. Others took work as labourers on Anglo ranches, but even here, as the Yana experience shows, they were not safe from attack.

As Californian natives were reduced to a marginal existence on the fringes of settler communities, newspapers began publishing heavily ironic articles ridiculing their attempts to speak English and to adapt to Euro-American clothes and customs. Readers were amused by arch accounts of native people 'sporting the cast-off toggery of a white man,' or 'promenading the levee ... in a brand new fitout ... to the great admiration of the beholders, with the air of an upper-ten young lady through the New York Broadway ...' In 1863, for instance, the Marysville *Appeal* reported:

> A tall, corpulent, pox-marked Digger, with bones half an inch thick through his ears, and a shocking bad hat on his head, stalked into the *Appeal* sanctum yesterday and informed us in a solemn manner as follows: 'Me bluth'n-law – Wahketaw – Captain Yuba Ingin – he mucha dead...' Saying this, and uttering several mournful grunts, John Digger helped himself to a seat and gazed wonderingly at our active scissors ... He stuck to his story that the Chief of the Yubas was dead ... Wahketaw was a 'good Ingin,' and the sorry remnants of his tribe have been for many years the inoffensive aboriginal bummers of this city and vicinity.

The following year, the same paper, under the headline 'Big Ingin Mr.', drolly recounted that:

> Captain Sutter alias Lampacker, the Indian Chief of the Yubas, called yesterday to pay his respects to the editor – same as other big injins sometimes do. The Captain is always in trouble – always in want – family all dead, as usual – no coat or shoes – and very cold nights.

Accounts like this, which seem to prefigure the grunting comic Indian of the twentieth century, introduce a new tone into Anglo writing about native people. Less than a hundred years after the Spanish invasion, and as the United States' conquest of the west neared its end, indigenous Californians had ceased to be figures of mystery or menace: they had become figures of *fun*.

* * *

We had a good country until the white people came and crowded us ... My ancestors were glad to see the white strangers come. My people made no trouble. Never thought about making trouble. Never held anything against the white race. I am telling you, my people made no trouble, although the whites killed many of them! Only when they want to put us in one small place, taking from us our home country, trouble started.

Hemene Moxmox (Yellow Wolf), Nez Percé

Further north, however, the collision between the indigenous and Anglo worlds was taking a different, more familiar course. The native peoples of the 'Oregon country' seemed to fit the Anglo-Americans' favoured image of the proud, unyielding 'savage' far more closely than the peaceable 'Diggers' of California and the Great Basin. And, without either a significant hispanic presence or the kind of mass invasion which – as a result of the Gold Rush – had coincided with the United States' acquisition of California, the federal government was more successful in imposing its authority on the area before large-scale settlement began.

In 1853, the Oregon country was divided into Oregon and Washington Territories, and the new governors soon made treaties with the coastal nations, many of whom had already been drastically reduced by disease. They then called the Nez Percés, Yakimas, Umatillas and other peoples of the interior, who had acquired horses (and, in the case of the Nez Percés, cattle and Christian missionaries) from the Anglos, but still retained their land and independence, to a treaty-making council at Walla Walla in 1855.

Contemporary accounts of the meeting give a vivid sense of the Anglos' mingled admiration, apprehension and disdain. A thousand Nez Percé warriors appeared 'mounted on fine horses and riding at a gallop, two abreast, naked to the breech-clout, their faces covered with white, red, and yellow paint in fanciful designs, and decked with plumes and feathers and trinkets fluttering in the sunshine.' The Indians put on a spectacular display, 'charging at full gallop ... firing their guns, brandishing their shields, beating their drums, and yelling their war-whoops . . .' On Sunday, when the Christianized Indians held a service, 'Every thing was conducted with the greatest propriety,' but the overall effect was an 'odd mixture' of 'the wildest Indian traits with a strictness in some religious rites.'

Despite deep opposition from Chief Kamiakim of the Yakimas and some of his followers, the US commissioners negotiated three separate treaties, guaranteeing the usual reservations, annuities, schools and economic help in exchange for the bulk of the Indians' land. Almost at once, however, conflict developed. Governor Stevens of Washington told the Yakimas that they would not have to surrender their territory until 'our chief the President and his council sees this paper and says it is good, and we build the houses, the mills and the blacksmith shop' – a process which he thought would take two or three years. In fact, however, he announced within twelve days that the area was open to settlement. As Anglo-Americans poured in, the Indians – many of whom had been deeply unhappy about the treaty – started killing them. Following the pattern established more than two centuries before in New England, when the Narragansetts had helped the fledgling colony of Connecticut to destroy the Pequots, some Nez Percés honoured their own agreement with the United States by enlisting in the army, and in 1858 the 'hostiles' were defeated at Spokane.

But, like so many others before them, the Nez Percés quickly discovered that friendship towards the Euro-Americans was no guarantee of special treatment: the incessant hunger for land shattered old loyalties and transformed allies into enemies almost overnight. In the early 1860s, a new gold rush brought thousands of settlers to Oregon, many of whom decided to stay in the lush Wallowa Valley area at the heart of the Nez Percé reservation. The authorities called a new council and persuaded a small faction of the tribe to conclude a new 'thief' treaty surrendering 90 per cent of its remaining land, including Wallowa, but the Christianized *Tuekakas* (Old Chief Joseph) refused to sign the agreement and tore up his Bible in disgust. He and his people stayed in their homeland, doggedly following a policy of passive resistance towards the growing tide of Anglos settling around them.

In 1871, Old Joseph died. On his deathbed he made a plea to his son *Hin-mah-too-yah-lat-kekht* (Young Joseph) which – in the rather flowery English version published in a magazine a few years later – quickly became a classic statement of Native American feeling for the land:

My son, my body is returning to my mother earth, and my spirit is going very soon to see the Great Spirit Chief. When I am gone, think of your country. You are the chief of these people. They look to you to guide them. Always remember that your father never sold his country. You must stop your ears whenever you are asked to sign a treaty selling your home. A few years more, and white men will be all around you. They have their eyes on this land. My son, never forget my dying words. This country holds your father's body. Never sell the bones of your father and your mother.

In 1873, after a formal inquiry had upheld the Nez Percés' right to the area, the President proclaimed the Wallowa Valley a reservation, but settlers continued to abuse and murder Indians and threatened to exterminate them altogether if they stayed. Finally, in 1877, in an abrupt *volte face*, Washington gave the Joseph band thirty days to relocate to Idaho and told them that failure to comply would be regarded as an act of war. Young Joseph and his brother Ollokut (or Ollicut), anxious to avoid a conflict, reluctantly agreed, but while they were away butchering their cattle a young Nez Percé was provoked into killing a settler who had murdered his father. The rage and frustration which the Nez Percés had held stoically in check for years suddenly erupted in attacks on 'white' homesteads across the region in which fifteen or so men were killed.

Young Joseph and Ollokut joined their people in hiding and tried to negotiate peace terms with the US troops sent to round them up, but when the soldiers shot at a party of Nez Percés under a flag of truce and the Indians fired back, killing two buglers, they realized that war was inevitable. Hoping to find refuge in Canada, *Hin-mah-too-yah-lat-kekht* led his people on a heroic 1,700-mile journey in which he repeatedly outmanoeuvred and defeated the pursuing army while – like Tecumseh and Joseph Brant before him – scrupulously avoiding unnecessary killing. Finally, however, having lost virtually all his chiefs, including Ollokut, and hundreds of his followers, he was forced to surrender only thirty miles from the Canadian border. Through an interpreter, he told General Howard:

> I am tired of fighting. Our chiefs are killed ... The old men are all dead.
>
> It is the young men who say yes and no. He who led on the young men is dead. It is cold and we have no blankets. The little children are freezing to death.
>
> My people, some of them, have run away to the hills, and have no blankets, no food; no one knows where they are – perhaps freezing to death.
>
> I want to have time to look for my children and see how many I can find. Maybe I shall find them among the dead.
>
> Hear me, my chiefs. I am tired; my heart is sick and sad.
>
> From where the sun now stands I will fight no more forever.

Hin-mah-too-yah-lat-kekht's fate highlights the contrast with the experience of Californian native people. Where tens of thousands of 'Diggers' were simply driven to oblivion, Joseph became a national hero. His dignified eloquence, his chivalry and his superb generalship won him real admiration, making him – along with Crazy Horse, Sitting Bull, Geronimo and Cochise – one of the handful of genuinely famous Native Americans in history. He was widely interviewed and photographed – including, on at least once occasion, with his old adversary General Howard – and his surrender speech became a widely read testament of nobility in defeat.

Yet, however heartfelt the feelings he inspired, Joseph was venerated not as a man but as the romantic emblem of a 'doomed race'. Public acclaim did not translate into personal sympathy and understanding: away from the cameras and the journalists, he and his people were quietly subjected to a grim mixture of vindictiveness, interference and neglect. While the defeated 'hostiles' who were prepared to accept Christianization and 'civilization' were allowed to join those members of the tribe who had remained at peace with the United States on the Nez Percé reservation in Idaho, Joseph and a few hundred diehard supporters who refused to abandon their own beliefs were exiled to the bleak, arid Colville reservation in Washington State, surrounded by the remnants of scores of other little bands. His descendants are still there today, desperately trying to cling on to their own culture and identity. Every summer, they return to the town which bears his name in the Wallowa Valley – where, until recently, they were regularly subjected to racist abuse – and hold a 'Friendship Feast' with other Nez Percés and local non-Indians to try to heal the deep wounds which still divide their people.

Hin-mah-too-yah-lat-kekht himself, despite constant pleas, was never allowed to go back to Wallowa. When he died in 1904 a doctor gave the cause of death as 'a broken heart.'

❊   ❊   ❊

At dawn on 29 August 1911, butchers at a slaughterhouse near Oroville, California, were woken by the sound of barking dogs. In the corral outside they found a 'wild man', clearly terrified, crouching against the fence. He was:

> ... emaciated to starvation, his hair was burned off close to his head, he was naked except for a ragged scrap of ancient covered-wagon canvas which he wore around his shoulders like a poncho. He was a man of middle height, the long bones, painfully apparent, were straight, strong, and not heavy, the skin colour somewhat paler in tone than the full copper characteristic of most Indians. The black eyes were wary and guarded now, but were set wide in a broad face, the mouth was generous and agreeably moulded. For the rest, the Indian's extreme fatigue and fright heightened a sensitiveness which was always there.

Now that its native people had almost disappeared – by 1900 there were only some 15,000 left – California, like New England a century before, was beginning to view them with a kind of wistful curiosity. The 'wild man' became a celebrity, with crowds pressing in to the local jail to see him, and soon news of his capture had reached San Francisco. A professor in the new discipline of Anthropology, T. T. Waterman, promptly travelled to see him. 'This man is undoubtedly wild...' Waterman reported to his colleague, A. L. Kroeber. 'He will be a splendid informant, especially for phonetics, for he speaks very clearly.'

The 'wild man', it emerged, was Ishi, the last of a group of southern Yana who had fled the massacres of the 1860s and 1870s and had been living in hiding ever since. Waterman and Kroeber took him to San Francisco where – apparently without irony – they gave him a room in their museum. For the remaining four and a half years of his life, Ishi worked unstintingly to provide them with ethnological data on the Yana way of life.

Under the influence of the German-born scholar Franz Boas, anthropology was already moving away from scientific racism towards a view of human differences based on *culture* rather than *biology*, and this more open, less bigoted approach helped to form Kroeber's and Waterman's relationship with Ishi. They clearly became deeply devoted to the 'wild man', regarding him as a close personal friend. After he died in 1916, Waterman wrote a moving tribute to him:

He convinced me that there is such a thing as a gentlemanliness which lies outside of all training, and is an expression purely of an inward spirit. It has nothing to do with artificially acquired tricks of behaviour. Ishi was slow to acquire the tricks of social contact. He never learned to shake hands but he had an innate regard for the other fellow's existence, and an inborn considerateness, that surpassed in fineness most of the civilized breeding with which I am familiar ... He contributed to science the best account he could give of the life of his people, as it was before the whites came in. To know him was a rare personal privilege, not merely an ethnological privilege. I feel myself that in many ways he was perhaps the most remarkable personality of his century.

Yet for anthropology, just as for earlier ways of understanding 'the Savage', Ishi's final significance is that he represents the *past* which, for better or worse (and to Waterman, at least, it was patently for better) has been swept away by 'civilization'. Ishi's fame – his story has formed the basis of books, films and a meditation by the Catholic mystic Thomas Merton – stems from his role as 'the last wild Indian in North America, a man of Stone Age culture subjected ... to twentieth-century culture.' When Kroeber died, the eminent French anthropologist Claude Lévi-Strauss commented, remarkably: 'He is the last of the North American ethnologists to have known the Indians [i.e., Ishi] ...

With Kroeber it is truly the America before Christopher Columbus
which has died completely.'

For all the academic trappings, Ishi's life and death – like those of
the smallpox victims in New England and so many other Indian people
before him – seemed ultimately to prove only that the Native American
was destined to vanish from the face of the earth.

9. The Great Plains

The heart of everything that is

A long time ago my father told me what his father told him, that there was once a Lakota holy man, called Drinks Water, who dreamed what was to be; and this was long before the coming of the Wasichus. He dreamed that the four-leggeds were going back into the earth and that a strange race had woven a spider's web around the Lakotas. And he said: 'When this happens, you shall live in square grey houses, in a barren land, and beside those square grey houses you shall starve.' They say he went back to Mother Earth soon after he saw this vision, and it was sorrow that killed him. You can look about you now and see that he meant these dirt-roofed houses we are living in, and that all the rest was true. Sometimes dreams are wiser than waking.

Black Elk, Lakota

The Plains – a huge wedge of grassland, roughly divided into 'prairie' in the east and the drier 'high plains' of the west, driven through the heart of North America from Canada to Texas – was the last major area in the continental United States to be settled by Euro-Americans. It is easy to see why. Apart from a few isolated pockets of higher ground – the Ozarks in Missouri, the Black Hills and Badlands in South Dakota – and clusters of cottonwood, willow and chokecherry trees along sheltered creeks and rivers, the same flat, open landscape stretches nearly unbroken from the Mississippi Valley to the Rockies. Exposed to almost Saharan heat in summer and subarctic cold in winter, swept by high winds and sudden violent storms, it seemed so repellent and worthless that some early nineteenth-century maps refer to it as the 'Great American Desert'. For emigrants used to the domestic agricultural landscape of Europe or East coast America and yearning for a farm of their own, it must have appeared no more than a desolate

wilderness, a final test of their faith and endurance before they reached
the lush, temperate promised land of Oregon or California.

Because it was the final military conflict in the long struggle for
possession of North America, the war for the Plains, when it did come,
has attained a unique place in the national mythology of the United
States – and, since America so powerfully dominates the global
imagination, in the mythology of the world. It was recorded by
photographers, dramatized by popular novelists and – first through
spectacles such as Buffalo Bill's *Wild West Show* and then through the
new medium of film – transformed into the most potent symbol of the
triumph of Manifest Destiny. In popular culture and the popular
imagination, it came to represent the ultimate, archetypal encounter
between the timeless, unchanging, elemental Savage and the dynamic,
thrusting European. It was the defeat of the Plains tribes that seemed
to consign the Indian irreversibly to history and finally put the stamp of
'civilization' on the entire continent.

There is something deeply ironic – though somehow strangely fitting
– about this. To begin with, far from pre-dating contact, the Plains
Indian culture of the nineteenth century was a relatively recent
phenomenon which depended, in part, on innovations introduced by
Europeans. It would be difficult, in fact, to find a native group which
better exemplified cultural change and adaptation, or one that gave a
less accurate image of pre-Columbian America. Rather than disappearing at the end of the 'Indian Wars', moreover, native people remain a
strong and a growing presence, at least in the Western part of the area,
while the non-Indian population is falling steadily as more and more
young people migrate to more prosperous parts of the country. If
current trends continue, Native Americans could actually become a
majority again in North and South Dakota at some point in the next
century.

You get a sense of how tenuous the Euro-American grip is if you
drive across the west today. Large swathes of the region are littered
with deserted farmsteads and dying towns – crumbling stores, bars and
gas stations, dilapidated little houses gradually taking on the bleached
colours of the surrounding landscape – that look as if they have just
been dropped there for no particular reason and then abandoned.
When you cross into a Native American reservation, the communities

have much the same impoverished, improvised appearance, but the atmosphere is far more vital and energetic, with bustling shops and hordes of children playing in the street. You get the unmistakable impression that, unlike their nomadic Anglo neighbours, who stay for a generation and then move on, these are people who feel they belong and have a future here.

This situation is nothing new. Recent research by two academics at Rutgers University, Frank and Deborah Popper, found that some 140,000 square miles of the Great Plains, with a total non-Indian population of around 400,000 (a lower population density than aboriginal societies in many parts of North America had achieved by the time of Columbus), had been fiscally insolvent since the land had been taken from Native Americans more than a century ago. The study concluded – in the words of the Native American writer Ward Churchill – that it was impossible

> ... to maintain school districts, police and fire departments, road beds and all the other basic accoutrements of 'modern life' on the negligible incomes which can be eked from cattle grazing and wheat farming on land which is patently unsuited for either enterprise ... Without considerable federal subsidy each and every year, none of these counties would ever have been viable. Nor, on the face of it, will any of them ever be. Put bluntly, the pretence of bringing Euroamerican 'civilization' to the Plains does little more than place a massive economic burden on the rest of the United States.

Without, apparently, any irony, the Poppers suggested that the experiment of the last 150 years should simply be abandoned, and that these areas should be returned to the herds of bison which had occupied them before 'the West was won.'

✵   ✵   ✵

[Sweet Medicine] travelled a long way, deep into the heart of the Black Hills country, where he seemed to be called by some great power. At last he reached a mountain known ever since by the Cheyennes as Noahvose, the Sacred or Holy Mountain; today it is called Bear Butte. Here he entered and found a place like a big

lodge or tipi. Old women were sitting along one side and old men along the other. But they were not really people, they were gods. And he saw four arrows there, which were to become the Four Sacred Arrows of the Cheyenne tribe.

The old ones called him Grandson and began instructing him in many things he should take back to the people. They taught him first about the arrows, because they were to be the highest power in the tribe. Two were for hunting and two for war. Many ceremonies were connected with them, and they stood for many laws. He was taught the ceremony of renewing the arrows, which must take place if one Cheyenne ever killed another. The arrows had to be kept by a special priest in a sacred tipi, covered at all times unless the Arrow Ceremony was under way.

Sweet Medicine learned next that he was to give the people a good government, with forty-four chiefs to manage it, and a good system of police and military protection, organized in the four military societies – the Swift Foxes, Elks, Red Shields, and Bowstrings. There was so much more to learn besides these things that he was there for most of the four years, before he was sent forth again to carry the laws to the people. One of the old ones came out before him, burning sweet grass as incense to purify the air for the arrow bundle. And with it in his arms he started for home.

John Stands In Timber, Cheyenne

Before European contact, the cultural development of the Plains seems to have paralleled the pattern in other areas of North America, with a big game hunting economy evolving, at the end of the Ice Age, into a way of life based on foraging and hunting smaller animals. By around 2,500 years ago, the mound-building 'Hopewellian' Culture of the Ohio Valley had begun to reach the region, and over the next millennium or so a limited form of horticulture, based on maize and bean cultivation, penetrated much of the prairies and even – where tentacles of fertile land spead west along river valleys – into parts of the arid high plains. This 'Plains Woodland' phase was replaced, in turn, after about AD 800 by a more intensively agricultural way of life, as the burgeoning 'Mississippian' civilization to the south and east brought new ideas and techniques into the area.

By the end of the fifteenth century, the eastern Plains was occupied by a string of prosperous farming nations – mostly Caddoan-speakers like the Wichita, Caddo and Pawnee, or Siouan-speaking peoples such as the Osages, Kansas, Omahas, Iowas, Poncas and Missouris – who lived, in many ways, much like their Iroquoian and Muskogean neighbours to the east. They built villages of circular earth- or grass-covered houses close to creeks and rivers, cultivated fields of maize, squash, beans and tobacco, and ventured on to the open prairie for part of every year to hunt the bison (or buffalo).

The peoples further west, by contrast – perhaps because of a prolonged drought – seem to have abandoned agriculture altogether in favour of full-time hunting. When members of the Coronado expedition reached what is now Texas in 1541, they encountered small groups of 'Querechos' (probably Apaches) who:

> ... subsist ... entirely on cattle [bison], for they neither plant nor harvest maize. With the skins they build their houses; with the skins they clothe and shoe themselves; from the skins they make ropes and also obtain wool. From the sinews they make thread, with which they sew their clothing and likewise their tents. From the bones they shape awls and the dung they use for firewood, since there is no other fuel in all that land. The bladders they use as jugs and drinking containers ...
>
> They are a gentle people, not cruel, faithful in their friendship, and skilled in the use of signs. They dry their meat in the sun, cutting it into thin slices, and when it is dry they grind it, like flour, for storage and for making mash to eat. They cook it in a pot, which they always manage to have with them. When they put a handful in the pot, the mash soon fills it, since it swells to great size ... they have no permanent residence anywhere, since they follow the cattle to obtain food.

This early description contains some recognizable elements of the later Plains way of life – the dependence on the bison, the use of a *travois* (a hide sling hung between two poles and dragged by a dog) to carry goods – but little of its scale and flamboyance. The 'gentle, faithful' Apaches lived in bands of, at most, a few families, travelling everywhere on foot and unable to move far from rivers and waterholes.

Since they could not outrun the much faster bison, they either had to stalk their prey or stampede them into a pound or over a cliff.

During the next three hundred years, the forces unleashed by the European invasion transformed this apparently simple nomadic existence into the 'classic' Plains culture. The single most important factor, at least in the early stages, was the 'equestrian revolution'. The Spaniards, knowing that the cavalry gave them huge military and psychological advantages over native people, tried at first to prevent horses falling into Indian hands, but it was a losing battle. As Spanish slave-raids and punitive expeditions increasingly destabilized the borderlands of New Spain, non-agricultural peoples like the Apaches responded by attacking and pillaging colonial settlements – which, unlike the migrating herds of bison, could be relied upon to stay in one place. At first they merely took livestock for meat, but many of them soon realized that by adopting the very different European relationship with the horse they could enormously increase their own power and mobility.

This process was accelerated by the Pueblo Revolt in 1680, when huge Spanish herds were captured by the Indians and traded far beyond the colonial borderlands to groups who, in many cases, had never seen a European. Just as the fur trade further east had provoked an increasingly desperate struggle for guns, so now the peoples west of the Mississippi found themselves in an intense competition for horses. By the middle of the eighteenth century, Native American societies in much of southwestern and central North America had become equestrian.

The change was most spectacular and far-reaching in the Plains. The acquisition of horses liberated hunters from the need to remain close to rivers and allowed them to range more or less at will. Instead of having to wait for game to pass their camp, they could now actively seek it out. And when they had located a herd, they could ride close to kill as many bison as they needed rather than relying on hit-and-miss techniques that might startle the animals prematurely and drive them out of reach.

The shift to an equestrian way of life, rather like the advent of agriculture elsewhere, sparked a population explosion in the Plains. A previously almost uninhabitable area suddenly offered an accessible, dependable and – with an estimated total of sixty million or so bison – apparently boundless food supply. As the constraints that had kept the nomadic bands no larger than thirty or forty people dissolved virtually overnight, numbers started to grow dramatically. At the same time – in an interesting reversal of the supposed direction of social development – many of the farming peoples on the eastern fringes abandoned their fields and villages and took to hunting full-time. They were joined, as the reverberations from European settlement spread deeper and deeper into the continent, by growing numbers of migrants from outside the area altogether, driven – or choosing – to move away from the dislocation and disruption of the frontier.

By 1800, the Plains was a checkerboard of more than thirty different societies and six distinct language families. Across the north, in the Canadian prairies and the present-day states of Montana, the Dakotas and Minnesota, were Algonquian-speaking Blackfoot, Gros Ventres (Atsina) and Plains Cree and Ojibway; Caddoan Arikara and Siouan Crow, Assiniboine, Mandan, Lakota and Dakota. The central heartland was dominated by Algonquian Arapaho and Cheyenne and Caddoan Pawnee, while the eastern fringes were peopled by a string of Siouan-speakers – Osage, Kansa (Kaw) and Oto – and the Caddoan Iowa. In the south, bordering the southwestern culture area (and to some extent influenced by it), were Kiowas, eastern Apaches and Shoshonean Comanches. Several more marginal groups, including the Utes and Shoshones of the Rockies and even, on occasion, plateau nations like the Nez Percés, did not migrate permanently to the Plains but visited the area regularly to hunt.

Because the 'classic' Plains culture developed so recently, we can, in some cases, directly contrast Native American and European under-standings of how it evolved and what it meant. The Cheyenne, for instance, are thought by anthropologists to have migrated over many generations from the Great Lakes region of eastern Canada. One version of their own origin story, written down in the 1960s, records that they were created:

> ... in another country, where great waters were all around them ...
> it could have been an island in the ocean. They lived mostly on fish
> and birds there, and they had a hard time as they were often hungry.

But they were able to travel, and at last they came to a place where they found large animals. That encouraged them to go on farther to find a better country where they could live.

One time two young men disappeared for many months. When they returned they told the people they had found a bigger and better land, and the people moved toward it.

Historical and archaeological evidence and the Indians' own oral tradition agree that the Cheyennes lived for a while in a wooded area, perhaps present-day Minnesota, where they built villages, cultivated crops and learnt to make pottery. A story thought to date from that time describes how, 'Many generations after the Creation,' a young man dreamed that he was 'shooting at a buffalo, but his arrow turned and hit another one standing far away, striking it in the side.' After having the same dream four times:

he made up his mind ... to find out what it meant, so he got up before sunrise and took his bow and arrows and started out. Before long he found some buffalo and thought to kill one ... As they drew near he shot at one, but the arrow turned and hit another, a young cow, and he thought to himself that the dream had come true.

But his arrow had not badly hurt her. She turned around two or three times, with the arrow hanging from her side, and started out walking.

The man followed her trail, but saw only a lone *tipi* in the distance. As he came close:

... a little boy came running out to meet him, calling him father. 'My mother is ready,' said the boy. 'She has your meal prepared, and you are to come in and eat.'

He took the little boy's hand and went with him into the tipi. A young girl greeted him, as if she were his wife and the little boy their son. The tipi was furnished with a bed, and fine willow rests, and cooking pots made of clay – a kind he had never seen. They showed him how to make such pots out of dirt mixed with water, shaping it with his fingers, then putting it by the fire until it was black, and then on top of the fire until it hardened like a kettle. And he was the man who later showed his people how to make pots to cook food.

... And they went to bed that evening like any family, planning to move early the next day. But when the young man awoke he was lying on his back, looking up at the sky. There was no tipi, and no sign of the girl or the little boy ...

At last he found the tracks of a woman and a little boy. They led him on in the same direction as the buffalo had gone the day before, and he followed them ...

Finally, the trail led him to a vast herd of bison, and one of the calves trotted up and greeted him as 'father'. With the help of the calf–boy, the man won a race against all the other animals, and the 'old men buffalo' told him:

'From now on everything will be done by the outcome of this race. You are on top now, above every animal and everything in the world. All we animals can do is supply the things you will use from us – our meat and skins and bones. And we will teach you how to give a Sun Dance.'

So they all gathered at a place where a Sun Dance lodge was fixed and made ready, and the young man was taught to perform the ceremony. The place where that was held can still be seen in the Black Hills. And the path where the race was run is still there also, going right around the Hills.

By the end of the eighteenth century, most of the Cheyenne had pushed west on to the Plains, and the Black Hills and the bison had become the centre of their world. Within a few generations they, their Sioux neighbours – to whom, according to both peoples' traditions, they introduced the horse – and most of the other societies of the region had adopted much the same way of life. For most of the year the members of each 'tribe' lived as separate bands, following game during the spring and autumn and moving to sheltered and – if possible – well-wooded areas for the winter, but in the summer they congregated to socialize, perform religious ceremonies and conduct a huge communal hunt. Their encampments of conical, buffalo-hide *tipis*, arranged in a vast circle to represent, as the Lakota put it, the 'sacred hoop' of the nation, became one of the archetypal images of 'the Indian' recorded by nineteenth-century artists and photographers.

Although this instant community – which could number several thousand people – might appear from the outside little more than a random collection of families and individuals, it was in fact a tightly woven pattern. Just as an Iroquois, for example, recognized a clan brother or sister in another village as a relative, so an intricate network of affiliations cut across the different Plains bands, preserving their identity as part of the larger 'tribe' when they were apart and giving everyone a defined role when they met. The most important were generally the many *sodalities* or societies which – like clubs or professional associations in Western cultures – brought people together around shared interests and activities. There were feasting and dancing societies, societies for people who had undergone the same spiritual experience, craft guilds, women's societies (which were sometimes also open to homosexual men) and, most crucially, male soldier societies. All these organizations had their own officers, insignia, ceremonies and rules: the Cheyennes' élite warrior society the Contraries, for instance, famously reversed normal behaviour, shivering on the hottest day, saying 'yes' when they meant 'no' and even riding into battle backwards.

Anthropologists explain the central importance of *sodalities* in Plains life – and the relative unimportance of lineages – as the result of rapidly changing conditions: rising numbers, migration and the adoption of a new way of life, they argue, shattered old patterns of kinship and residency, necessitating new institutions to ensure social cohesion. The Plains peoples themselves – as the Cheyenne story of Sweet Medicine's journey to the Black Hills suggests – saw them as part of a sacred order, established so that the nation could live harmoniously and well. The soldier societies, in particular, embodied and upheld many of the highest ideals of the culture. As well as demonstrating their courage by raiding enemies and defending the tribe against external aggression, they also acted as a kind of police force, maintaining discipline in the community and ensuring that hunters followed the prescribed regulations for killing and distributing meat. Standing Bear of the Lakota remembered:

> The soldier bands went first when they started out to kill buffalo. They went in formation – everyone was to go behind the soldier band. If they went ahead of the soldier band they would be knocked unconscious. The soldiers went twenty abreast and the hunters followed four or five abreast. Everyone had to respect the soldiers,

for whenever they said they would do something they meant it – they kept order. We were started toward the herd and everyone was to hunt alike. If a man went around ahead after the buffalo he would get knocked off his horse and would not get a buffalo.

The advisor [councillor] would ... go around and find the best men in the bunch with good horses and bring them forward and [he] said to them: 'Good young warriors, my relatives, your work I know is good. What you do is good always, so today you shall feed the helpless and feed the old and feeble and perhaps there is a widow who has no support. You shall help them. Whatever you get you shall donate to the poor.'

The idea of *interdependence*, both between individual human beings and between people and the rest of creation, lay at the heart of Plains cultures. Like the Cheyenne's Algonquian relatives in the Northeast – and many other societies – they did not see hunting as a one-way, predatory process in which one species simply exploited another: they understood it, instead, as a sacred reciprocal relationship between relatives. At a profound level, the animals *gave* themselves to their human relations, who had to respond by showing their gratitude and love through ritual and – since the gift was intended to benefit *all* the people – by sharing the meat with the same open-handed generosity.

Just how closely the Plains tribes identified themselves with their prey is shown by the multiplicity of stories in which – like the Cheyenne legend of the young man who dreams of shooting a buffalo – bison turn into human beings and *vice versa*. One of the most beautiful Lakota myths, giving the origin of many of their most important rituals and beliefs, describes how a mysterious woman visits the people. She takes a bundle from her back and tells the chief:

'Behold this and always love it! It is *lela wakan* [very sacred], and you must treat it as such. No impure man should ever be allowed to see it, for within this bundle there is a sacred pipe. With this you will, during the winters to come, send your voices to *Wakan-Tanka*, your Father and Grandfather.'

After the mysterious woman said this, she took from the bundle a pipe, and also a small round stone which she placed upon the ground. Holding the pipe up with its stem to the heavens, she said: 'With this sacred pipe you will walk upon the Earth; for the Earth is your Grandmother and Mother, and She is sacred. Every step that is taken upon Her should be as a prayer. The bowl of this pipe is of red stone; it is the Earth. Carved in the stone and facing the centre is this buffalo calf who represents all the four-leggeds who live upon your Mother. The stem of the pipe is of wood, and this represents all that grows upon the Earth. And these twelve feathers which hang here where the stem fits into the bowl are from *Wanbli Galeshka*, the Spotted Eagle, and they represent the eagle and all the wingeds of the air. All these peoples, and all the things of the universe, are joined to you who smoke the pipe – all send their voices to *Wakan-Tanka*, the Great Spirit. When you pray with this pipe, you pray for and with everything.'

The sacred woman gives the people many more instructions and then, 'moving around the lodge in a sun-wise manner,' leaves.

... but after walking a short distance she looked back towards the people and sat down. When she rose the people were amazed to see that she had become a young red and brown buffalo calf. Then this calf walked farther, lay down, and rolled, looking back at the people, and when she got up she was a white buffalo. Again the white buffalo walked farther and rolled on the ground, becoming now a black buffalo. This buffalo then walked farther away from the people, stopped, and after bowing to each of the four quarters of the universe, disappeared over the hill.

The spiritual world communicated with peoples like the Lakota above all through *visions*. Looking at the vast rolling landscape of the Plains – buttes, bone-coloured rocks tortured into impossible shapes by the wind, huge vistas of yellow-green grassland that stir and shimmer like the flank of an animal under the endlessly changing sky – it is easy even for a non-Indian to feel that this is a place poised for some extraordinary event. Adolescents would seclude themselves for days and nights in an isolated spot and fast and pray until they were visited by a spirit guardian, usually an animal or bird, that could be called upon for guidance and protection.

The yearning for a vision, for a direct disclosure from the spiritual world, also drove people to mortify, and sometimes even torture, themselves in the most important religious ritual in most Plains tribes, the summer Sun Dance. During the course of the ceremony, which was held to give thanks for the gifts of the past year and to start a new cycle of life, participants pledged to go without food and water for days at a time as they danced under the relentless heat of the sun. In some tribes, the 'pledgers' attached themselves to the central 'sacred tree' by long strips of leather skewered through deep slits in their chests: they then pulled away until the flesh ripped and the thongs broke free. This habit caused particular revulsion among some of the earliest Europeans and Euro-Americans to witness it, but a twentieth-century Lakota spiritual leader, Frank Fool's Crow, explains (with typical Native American inclusiveness) that:

The Sioux received the Sun Dance from *Wakan-Tanka*, and we honour Him by doing it as He told us to. Since the White man has come to us and explained how He sent his own son to be sacrificed, we realize that our sacrifice is similar to, or in memory of Jesus' own. As to how the White Man feels, there was a far more terrible thing done by Jesus Christ. He endured more suffering, more pain, was even stabbed here [pointing to his side], and died . . . the Sioux feel a special closeness to God in the dance and piercing . . . the pledgers seldom lose a particle of their flesh if they are pierced and tied properly – and even if they do, it is considered as a thank offering returned to the God from whom it came.

The spiritual fervour and visual brilliance of 'classic' Plains culture, with its visions and fasts, its spectacular head-dresses and ornately decorated costumes, harnesses and *parfleches*, seem, in retrospect, to match the hot-house intensity of its short life. The horses – and, later, the guns – that made its meteoric rise possible were symptoms of the very changes which, paradoxically, would just as abruptly destroy it. From the beginning, the Lakota, the Cheyenne and others had to be more or less permanently on a war footing, as more and more tribes crowded on to the Plains, increasing pressure on the peoples already there. War parties regularly raided other groups to steal their horses or drive them away from contested areas. Joining a soldier society and taking part in attacks on enemies was the surest way for a young man to gain prestige: according to at least one Lakota source: 'No boy was a full-fledged man until he had been out with a war-party and not until then was he considered eligible for marriage.'

Yet, while Plains Indians were, unquestionably, more warlike than most other Native American groups, and thousands of them died in inter-tribal conflicts, their *idea* of war had little in common with the European concept. Fighting was still, largely, a matter of show and symbolism, an opportunity for individuals to demonstrate prowess and settle scores. In some ways, it was closer to a sporting contest than to total war: the greatest honour went to the warrior who *counted coup* on his enemy – touched him with a weapon without being hurt himself – rather than killing him. And, like members of a sports team, men took part in war-parties ultimately because they *chose* to rather than because they were *told* to. They might be under immense pressure to fight, but no one could punish them if they refused. As Luther Standing Bear eloquently describes it:

> The Lakotas were self-governors, and the rules and regulations that governed the conduct of people and established their duties as individuals, families, and bands came from a great tribal consciousness. Deep within the people, mingling with their emotions, was an inherent sense of solidarity – a tie between one and all others that the nation might be expressed.
>
> Though each person became individualized – could be as truthful, as honest, as generous, as industrious, or as brave as he wished – could even go to battle upon his own intiative, he could not consider himself as separate from the band or nation. Tribal consciousness was the sole guide and dictator, there being no human agency to compel the individual to accept guidance or obey dictates, yet for one to cut himself off from the whole meant to lose identity or to die.

This combination of custom and individualism meant that 'it was harder to break laws than to keep them,' and consequently 'there were few law-breakers.' But it left the Plains peoples quite unprepared for their encounter with a conformist society in which a soldier obeyed orders or faced the firing squad.

✿   ✿   ✿

Many generations ago, Iktome the Spider Man, trickster and bringer of bad news, went from village to village and from tribe to tribe. Because he is a messenger, Spider Man can speak any language, so all tribes can understand what he says.

He came running into the first camp, shouting: 'There is a new generation coming, a new nation, a new kind of man who is going to run over everything. He is like me, Ikto, a trickster, a liar . . .

. . . this man will misname you and call you by all kinds of false names. He will try to tame you, try to remake you after himself . . .

. . . Watch the buffalo: when this new man comes, the buffalo will go into a hole in a mountain. Guard the buffalo, because the White Long-legs will take them all. He will bring four things: wicocuye – sickness; wawoya – hate; wawiwagele – prejudice; waunshilap-sni – pitilessness . . .

. . . You shall know . . . [this man] as washi-manu, steal-all, or better by the name of fat-taker, wasichu, because he will take the fat of the land. He will eat up everything . . .'

Itkome left, and slowly people forgot about that White Long-legs coming, because for a while things were as they had always been. So they stopped worrying. Then one morning two Sioux women were out gathering chokecherries, and suddenly a black smog covered the place where they were.

And out of this blackness they saw a strange creature emerging. He had on a strange black hat, and boots, and clothes. His skin was pale, his hair was yellow, and his eyes were blue. He had hair growing under his nose and falling down over his lips; his chin was covered with hair; he was hairy all over. When he spoke, it did not sound like human speech. No one could understand him. He was sitting on a large, strange animal as big as a large moose, but it was not a moose. It was an animal no one knew.

This strange creature, this weird man, carried in one hand a cross and in the other a fearful firestick which spat lightning and made a noise like thunder. He took from his black coat something hard, shiny, glittering, and transparent which served him as a water bag. It seemed to contain clear water. He offered it to the women to drink, and when they tried it, the strange water burned

*their throats and made their heads swim. The man was covered
with an evil sickness, and this sickness jumped on the women's
skin like many unnumbered pustules and left them dying. Then
they realized that the* wasichu *had arrived, that finally he was
among them, and that everything would be changed.*

Leonard Crow Dog, Lakota

No one knows when the northern Plains peoples first encountered
Europeans. In 1680, in present-day Illinois, the French explorer Robert
Cavelier de La Salle met a band of 'Chaa' Indians, who may have been
Cheyenne (the name comes from the Sioux *Shar'ha*) still making their
westward migration, and by the 1730s Mexican and French traders
were regularly visiting some groups around the Black Hills, exchanging
metal arrowheads, sheet metal and other articles for hides. But when
Standing All Night, an Arikara, met two men with fair faces and beards
in the late eighteenth century, he was still so startled that he ran away,
thinking that they must be 'mysterious people, who perhaps had come
out from the ground or out of a hill.'

By the start of the nineteenth century, many Plains peoples were
already partially dependent on trade: in 1806, for example, Alexander
Henry the Younger reported that some of the Cheyenne were wearing
dresses of 'Spanish manufacture' after being visited by a Spanish boat
'loaded with goods.' With a few exceptions, most notably the Blackfoot,
they welcomed the Lewis and Clark expedition (1803–6) as an
opportunity to acquire still more goods, and the trail west from St.
Louis was soon dotted with trading posts. The growing availability of
guns, in particular, was starting to transform both hunting and warfare,
fuelling even more intense inter-tribal competition.

Increased trade also – following the now familiar pattern – brought
new and lethal diseases. Some oral traditions about 'the great sicknesses'
still survive, giving a vivid glimpse of the Indians' bewilderment and
terror. One Cheyenne account, for instance, records that, around 1800,
the tribe was struck by an epidemic (probably of cholera) in which:

> . . . a person could be standing or walking along, and all at once his
> arms and legs would jerk up, and he dropped as if he had been shot
> and never came out of it but died soon afterwards.

. . . one warrior, a brave man . . . came walking along the camp circle during this time singing a war song. 'I cannot see the enemy who is killing us,' he cried. 'When I see an enemy I never stay back, but I cannot protect the people from this thing; they just fall and die.' He was singing and talking that way in between times, and when he walked back to his own tipi the sickness struck him too, and he dropped as if he had been shot, dead.

In the first forty years of the nineteenth century, three smallpox pandemics swept through the Plains, drastically depleting the population and taking some tribes close to extinction. The Mandans, for instance, thought to have numbered some 15,000 a century before, had already been reduced to fewer than 2,000 people when they were struck by the disease in 1837. The artist George Catlin, who had painted them a few years earlier, gave a graphic account of what happened:

It seems that the Mandans were surrounded by several war-parties of their more powerful enemies the Sioux, at that unlucky time, and they could not therefore disperse upon the plains, by which many of them could have been saved; and they were necessarily inclosed within the piquets of their village, where the disease in a few days became so very malignant that death ensued in a few hours after its attacks; and so slight were their hopes when they were attacked, that nearly half of them destroyed themselves with their knives, with their guns, and by dashing their brains out by leaping head-foremost from a thirty foot ledge of rocks in front of their village. The first symptom of the disease was a rapid swelling of the body, and so very virulent had it become, that very many died in two or three hours after their attack, and that in many cases without the appearance of the disease upon the skin. Utter dismay seemed to possess all classes and all ages, and they gave themselves up in despair, as entirely lost. There was but one continual crying and howling and praying to the Great Spirit for his protection during the nights and days; and there being but few living, and those in too appalling despair, nobody thought of burying the dead, whose bodies, whole families together, were left in horrid and loathsome piles in their own wigwams, with a few buffalo robes, etc. thrown over them, there to decay and be devoured by their own dogs . . .

So have perished the friendly and hospitable Mandans, from the best accounts I could get; and although it may be *possible* that some few individuals may yet be remaining, I think it is not probable; and one thing is certain, even if such be the case, that, as a nation, the Mandans are extinct, having no longer an existence.

The Plains way of life was also coming under pressure from the growing traffic of traders and emigrants across the continent. As early as 1825, under the terms of a 'friendship treaty' with the US, several Plains nations, including the Lakota and the Cheyenne, agreed to let wagon-trains pass through their territory. The trail cut a barren strip across the middle of the hunting grounds, dividing the buffalo into two herds and splitting several tribes – among them the Cheyenne and the Arapaho – into 'southern' and 'northern' branches.

At the same time, reverberations from the Euro-American frontier were increasingly felt along the southern and eastern borders of the Plains. By 1832, when the defeat of the celebrated Sauk and Fox leader Black Hawk in Iowa and Wisconsin effectively ended armed Native American resistance east of the Mississippi (except for a few Seminole diehards in the Florida Everglades), the tide of settlement had already begun to encroach on the rich grasslands of the eastern prairies. Missouri had become a state in 1821, and by 1848 Iowa, Wisconsin, Arkansas, Michigan and Florida had also joined the Union. Peoples indigenous to the new states, such as the Osage and the Oto, together with Delaware, Wyandot (Huron) and other groups who had already been removed from their ancestral homelands further east, were shunted closer and closer to the newly transplanted 'Five Civilized Tribes' in what is now Oklahoma. Most of them were given 'permanent' homes in parts of modern Kansas and Nebraska, with the usual promises of annuities and agricultural assistance, and the map was hastily redrawn to include their reservations in the 'Indian Territory'.

But almost immediately the new boundaries were breached by settlers from Missouri and Kansas, who cut down the Indians' timber, stole their cattle and murdered them with impunity. During the early 1850s, as Kansas and Nebraska prepared for territorial government, there were increasingly vociferous demands – echoing the fervent anti-Native American feeling in Georgia and Alabama twenty years before

– that all the 'cumberers of the soil' within their borders should be removed altogether. Congress authorized the President to negotiate with the Indians to 'extinguish' their title, and the Commissioner of Indian Affairs promptly obtained land cessions from fourteen tribes, reducing their combined territory from eighteen million to just over one million acres. Even this pitifully diminished land-base was quickly eroded, as Indians were driven from their homes or defrauded of individual allotments, and most of the Kansas tribes ended up moving south into the remaining Indian Territory.

The scale of westward migration in the years following the Treaty of Guadeloupe Hidalgo – which would have been unimaginable only a decade before – posed an increasing threat even to the peoples of the 'barren Plains'. In 1849, the federal government established Fort Laramie in Wyoming, and two years later held a great council of the northern tribes – some eight to twelve thousand in all – to try to allay their fears about the proliferation of trails and wagon trains. Most of the Indians left reassured and committed to peace. 'I will go home satisfied,' said Cut Nose of the Arapahos. 'I will sleep sound, and not have to watch my horses in the night, or be afraid for my women and children. We have to live on these streams and in the hills, and I would be glad if the whites would pick out a place for themselves and not come into our grounds.'

In 1853 the government made similar promises of peace and friendship to the Comanches, Kiowas and other southern Plains peoples, but in Washington it seemed clear that their way of life was doomed. In the same year, the Chairman of the House Committee on Indian Affairs declared, in poetic vein, that:

> The whites can no longer be kept out of the Indian country. The plains and prairies to the Rocky mountains have nearly ceased to echo the lowing of the buffalo; the crack of the emigrant's whip, the merry jest and joyous laugh of the Caucasian man, now ring through the vast wilderness.

In 1855 the federal government leased the western portion of the Indian Territory from the Five Civilized Tribes as a possible home for the Plains tribes, and over the next ten years the Wichitas and a few smaller groups from Texas moved there. The very idea of an 'Indian

Territory', however, was itself being increasingly called into question. As early as 1848, the missionary David Lowry had warned that removing Native Americans to a separate country was no longer a practicable solution to 'the Indian Problem', because it would inevitably be engulfed as the flood of settlers pouring west met 'the tide rolling eastward from the Pacific,' and in less than a decade events seemed to be bearing him out. In 1857, the governor of the new territory of Kansas was voicing an increasingly widespread view when he suggested that the Five Civilized Tribes should again be displaced and their lands opened to settlement. 'The Indian treaties will constitute no obstacle,' he said tersely, 'any more than precisely similar treaties did in Kansas.'

The Five Civilized Tribes, yet again, were victims of their own success. The suffering of removal had left deep wounds – leading, in the case of the Cherokee, to a prolonged civil war – but they were now painfully reconstructing their world. By the 1850s the Cherokees, in particular, had entered a Golden Age which earned their nation the admiring *sobriquet* 'the Athens of the West'. Their new capital, Talequah, boasted elegant neo-classical public buildings, a national newspaper, the *Advocate*, and thriving presses producing a torrent of books and pamphlets in their own language. John Ross and his family and other members of the 'mixed-blood' élite owned elegant, well-furnished mansions nearby, fuelling the criticism – often heard from grumbling Anglos – that they were exploiting the impoverished, apathetic 'full-blood' masses living in log cabins and cultivating plots of maize and potatoes.

The missionary Samuel Worcester, who had moved west with the Cherokee, explicitly rebutted this charge: '. . . it will be asked, is the improvement which has been described general among . . . full-blooded Indians . . . or only the half-bloods? I answer that . . . I have spoken of the mass of people, without distinction . . . though those of mixed blood are generally in the van, yet the whole mass of the people is on the march.' Even the poorest Cherokee, in fact, seem to have enjoyed a standard of living that would have been the envy of many of their Anglo neighbours in Arkansas, Missouri and Kansas. With 126 public schools and opportunities for both men and women to go to college, they had far higher levels of education and literacy, and since every citizen had a right to land – which, like the other 'Civilized Tribes', the

Cherokee held in common – there was almost no homelessness or poverty.

The elderly John Ross and other leaders argued, as they had before removal, that, since they were so clearly making 'progress', the Five Civilized Tribes should be left in peace. But every glowing report and impressive statistic only added to the excitement of land speculators, and, thirty years after Jackson's Removal Act, removal was once more on the national agenda. In the presidential election campaign of 1860, William Seward publicly declared that: 'Indian Territory south of Kansas must be vacated by the Indian.'

The outbreak of the Civil War the following year, however, abruptly halted this plan, at least temporarily. Overnight, the Five Civilized Tribes seemed to have reverted to an earlier phase of their history: instead of being treated as obstacles to settlement, they had suddenly become pawns, once again, in a Euro-American conflict. John Ross staunchly advocated neutrality, writing to one secessionist:

> I am – the Cherokees are – your friends and the friends of your people but we do not wish to be brought into the feuds between yourselves and your Northern Brethren. Our wish is for peace. Peace at home and Peace among you.

But as officials from both sides set out to woo the Five Civilized Tribes, this policy became increasingly unrealistic. The Confederacy argued that the Union had merely split in two, leaving the Indians in the southern half, and that from now on their dealings would therefore naturally be with the new government. This impression was reinforced by the government agents in Indian Territory, almost all of whom were secessionists: the Union appointed new agents of its own, but they were based in Kansas where the Indians could not reach them.

The Confederate authorities eagerly exploited their advantage. Commissioner Albert Pike of Arkansas was sent to warn the Five Civilized Tribes of the Union's predatory intentions – not difficult, given that William Seward had become President Lincoln's Secretary of State – and to organize a 'United Nations of the Indian Territory' to resist 'the invading forces of Abolition.' He also offered the tribes favourable new treaties, guaranteeing their autonomy and giving them the right to send delegates to the Confederate Congress, before going on to the Leased

District to sign agreements with the Wichita, Comanche, Kickapoo and other southern Plains groups.

For all his posturing as a champion of Indian rights, Pike's correspondence shows that his long-term aims were not very different from Seward's: in a letter to President Jefferson Davis extolling the wealth and beauty of the Indian Territory, he defended the 'concessions' he had made on the grounds that they 'are really far more for *our* benefit than for *theirs*; and that it is *we* . . . who are interested to have this country . . . opened to settlement and made into a State.' Many Indians, however, grasped at his promise of a secure future and enthusiastically backed the Confederate cause, to which – as the Choctaw council put it – their 'affections, education, institutions, and interests' naturally bound them.

But the influential John Ross, with his long and bruising experience of Anglo duplicity, still resisted. When Brigadier Ben McCulloch demanded the right to raise companies of Indian volunteers to fight for the South, Ross angrily – and presciently – wrote back:

> Our country and institutions are our own. However small the one or humble the other, they are as sacred and valuable to us as those of your own populous and wealthy State to yourself and your people. We have done nothing to bring about the conflict in which you are engaged with your own people, and I am unwilling that my people shall become its victims.
>
> I am determined to do no act that shall furnish any pretext to either of the contending parties to overrun our country and destroy our rights . . .

But Ross was quickly overtaken by events. His old pre-removal opponent Stand Watie raised his own Cherokee regiment, which entered Confederate service on the same day that the Choctaws and Chickasaws signed a treaty with Pike. Ross immediately called a mass meeting in Talequah. Concerned above all to avoid another Cherokee civil war, he finally, against his own better judgement, advocated an alliance with the Confederacy on the grounds that: 'Union is strength, dissension is weakness, misery and ruin!' He told friends:

> We are in the situation of a man standing alone upon a low naked spot of ground, with the water rising all around him . . . The tide carries by him, in its mad course, a drifting log . . . By refusing it he

is a doomed man. By seizing hold of it he has a chance for his life. He can but perish in the effort . . .

Within months, however, the tribe's fragile unity had been swept away. Under conflicting pressures, the Cherokees and their neighbours quickly fragmented into pro- and anti-Union factions. As Ross had foreseen only too clearly, the war brought them 'misery and ruin' and gave a pretext for Anglo-Americans, yet again, 'to overrun our country.' During four years of fighting, the Five Civilized Tribes lost most of the farms and communities they had worked so hard to build and perhaps as much as 25 per cent of their population. In the ensuing peace treaties, even those who had sacrificed most for the Union were forced to sign confessions of 'war guilt', and to 'punish' them the whole western part of Indian Territory was confiscated. They also, ominously, had to agree to the construction of railways across their land. Although they narrowly avoided being forced to accept a territorial government, the Commissioner of Indian Affairs insisted that they should be administered by a federally sponsored inter-tribal council that would quickly 'lead to that result.'

The Civil War also had profound repercussions for Indians on other parts of the 'frontier'. In 1862, having routed their greycoat opponents, the Union forces sent to occupy New Mexico turned their attention to 'pacifying' the bands of Navajo and Apache who were still raiding settlements. The celebrated Mimbreño Apache leader Mangas Colorado was captured under a flag of truce and subsequently murdered, and, in a relentless war of attrition, the Mescaleros were finally forced to surrender and accept a reservation at Bosque Redondo, an arid area in the Pecos River Valley chosen 'for the concentration and maintenance of all captive Indians from the New Mexico territory.' Colonel 'Kit' Carson, determined to show that 'wild Indians could be tamed,' then set out to conquer the Navajo with an aggressive scorched-earth campaign, destroying *hogans*, fields and orchards, seizing herds of sheep and horses and finally taking the sacred stronghold of Canyon de Chelly by force. Most of the Navajos, half-starving and dejected, were driven on the 'Long Walk' – the Southwest's equivalent of the Trail of Tears – to join the Mescaleros at Bosque Redondo. So many died, however, from disease and poor conditions that they were eventually allowed to return to the Chuska mountains, which became the heart of their present-day reservation.

The grasslands to the north, by contrast, seemed at first to escape the destructive currents sweeping back and forth across the continent. In the early months, the US government, clearly showing how strategically unimportant it considered the Plains, withdrew virtually all its troops from the area, leaving fewer than three hundred men to garrison the four widely scattered forts along the emigrant trails. This actually led to a decline in the number of Indian attacks, suggesting that, left to themselves, the supposedly bloodthirsty Sioux and other tribes were prepared to co-exist peacefully with the travellers passing through their territory and were more interested in hunting than in killing Americans.

But an uprising of Santee Sioux in Minnesota in 1862 set off a chain reaction across the region that eventually drew the United States into the bloodiest and hardest-fought 'Indian Wars' in her history. The Santee were Dakota, or eastern Sioux, who had continued their farming way of life in Minnesota when their close relatives, the Lakota, had become hunters on the Plains to the west. In the 1850s some 150,000 settlers poured into the area, and by 1862 the Santee had surrendered nine-tenths of their territory and were confined to a narrow 1,500 square mile strip along the Minnesota River. Even this last refuge was rapidly being eroded: in April 1861 thirty-two illegal settlers on the Santees' land wrote to President Lincoln to ask for protection.

The usual abuses – fraudulent land deals, exploitation by traders, outright theft and sexual assaults on women – had already strained relations between the Indians and their Anglo neighbours almost to breaking point when, in July 1862, the Santee were told that their annuity payments would be delayed. The warehouse at the agency on their reservation was full of supplies, but the new agent, Thomas Galbraith, would not distribute them until the Indians had the money to pay for them.

With the loss of their land and game, the Santee could no longer support themselves, and they were by now desperately hungry. Not to share food when you had it was, in terms of their culture, inexplicably cruel (as the Lakota Luther Standing Bear put it: 'For one man with a full stomach to heap more misery upon one with an empty stomach is savage beyond compare.') and a crowd of angry Santees gathered at the agency. Their leader, *Ta-oya-te-duta* (Little Crow), told Galbraith:

> We have waited a long time. The money is ours, but we cannot get it. We have no food, but here are these stores, filled with food. We ask that you, the agent, make some arrangement by which we can get food from the stores, or else we may take our own way to keep ourselves from starving. When men are hungry they help themselves.

Galbraith asked some of the traders for advice, and one of them, Andrew Myrick, replied: 'So far as I am concerned, if they are hungry let them eat grass or their own dung.' The Santee were stunned for a moment: then, furious and humiliated, they stormed out of the meeting.

In this tense atmosphere, it took only a minor incident to spark off a major confrontation. Returning from an unsuccessful hunt, four young Santee found some eggs laid by a settler's chicken. When one of them warned that they should not take them, his companions goaded him: 'You are a coward. You are afraid of the white man. You are afraid to take even an egg from him, though you are half-starved.' These taunts erupted into a heated argument, and finally, to demonstrate their courage, the hunters killed five settlers.

When he heard the news, *Ta-oya-te-duta* was appalled. A long-standing accommodationist, he had worked hard to make himself acceptable to his Anglo neighbours, taking a plot of land for a farm and joining the Episcopalian church, and was convinced that violence against them could only result in disaster. When the killers and their followers, knowing that there would be reprisals, demanded a pre-emptive war, he replied:

> You are full of the white man's devil water. You are like dogs in the Hot Moon when they run mad and snap at their own shadows. We are only little herds of buffalo left scattered; the great herds that once covered the prairies are no more. See! – the white men are like the locusts when they fly so thick that the whole sky is a snowstorm. You may kill one – two – ten; yes, as many as the leaves in the forest yonder, and their brothers will not miss them. Kill one – two – ten, and ten times ten will come to kill you. Count your fingers all day long and white men with guns . . . will come faster than you can count.
> . . . Yes: they fight among themselves, but if you strike at them

they will all turn on you and devour you and your women and little children just as the locusts in their time fall on the trees and devour all the leaves in one day.

But knowing that no Indian would now be safe, and conscious that his own reputation was at stake, he reluctantly agreed to fight. 'Ta-oya-te-duta is not a coward,' he told his people. 'He will die with you.'

Taking the settlers off guard, Little Crow was at first – perhaps to his own surprise – strikingly successful. The Santee attacked the agency, killing ten men, including the trader Myrick – who was found, in a strange echo of Virginia 250 years before, with grass stuffed in his mouth – and then ambushed a column of soldiers, killing half of them. For a few days, they had the initiative, destroying outlying settlements and besieging Fort Ridgely and the town of New Ulm, but as US reinforcements poured into Minnesota they were gradually beaten back. Finally, after little more than a month, they were defeated by General Sibley and a force of 1,500 men at Wood Lake. Hundreds were captured, and thirty-eight prisoners were hanged in December 1868 in the largest mass execution in US history.

'Little Crow's War' sent tremors across the West. Some of the Santee, including *Ta-oya-te-duta*, managed to escape to Canada: others fled on to the Plains and tried to persuade their relatives there to go on the offensive. 6,000 soldiers followed the 'hostiles' into North Dakota in a vain attempt to capture them, raising tensions still further. At the same time, understandably terrified that events in Minnesota might be repeated further west, settlers and travellers urgently demanded additional troops to protect them.

Since the US army was stretched to capacity by the Civil War, the government sent bands of Volunteers to reinforce the forts. Many of these 'citizen soldiers' were frontiersmen with a deep hatred and contempt for Native Americans: on one occasion, for instance, a group of them fired shells into a friendly Sioux camp for artillery practice. Not surprisingly, the Indians responded by increasing their raids on wagon trains and cattle herds. By the summer of 1864 the situation was so serious that T. I. McKenney, a regular US army officer, reported:

I think if great caution is not exercised on our part, there will be a bloody war. It should be our policy to try and conciliate [the Indians]

... and stop these scouting parties that are roaming over the country, who do not know one Indian tribe from another and who will kill anything in the shape of an Indian. It will require only a few more murders on the part of our troops to unite all these warlike tribes.

McKenney was right. In 1861, the Governor of Colorado, John Evans, had persuaded two Southern Cheyenne 'peace chiefs', Black Kettle and White Antelope, who had always been friendly to the Anglos, to sign an agreement surrendering a large tract of hunting territory close to the burgeoning city of Denver. The other Cheyenne chiefs, however, rejected it (something which, as autonomous band leaders, they were perfectly entitled to do), and in the spring and summer of 1864, hoping for a pretext to take the land by force, members of the Colorado militia launched a series of indiscriminate raids against Cheyenne camps. They were commanded by Colonel John Chivington, a Methodist preacher and rabid Indian-hater who was notorious for publicly advocating the murder of Native American children on the grounds that 'nits make lice.' In terms that echoed the ferocious rhetoric of Captain John Mason during the Pequot War more than two centuries before, he declared: 'Damn any man who sympathizes with Indians! I have come to kill Indians, and believe it is right and honorable to use any means under God's heaven to kill Indians.'

When Chivington ordered his men to 'kill Cheyennes whenever and wherever found,' the US commander of Fort Lyon, Major Edward Wynkoop, invited Black Kettle and White Antelope to move their bands close to his garrison, partly for their own safety and partly to prevent them being provoked into joining the 'hostiles' in an all-out war. Chivington promptly had Wynkoop removed on the grounds that he was too 'conciliatory'. His replacement, the hard-line Major Scott Anthony, encouraged the Indians to stay near the post not in order to protect them but rather – in the words of the historian Angie Debo – 'to have them available for a massacre.'

Early on the morning of 29 November 1864, Chivington and several hundred men attacked Black Kettle's camp at Sand Creek. According to Cheyenne oral tradition:

As soon as he saw the soldiers coming, early in the morning, Black Kettle called out to them and tried to talk, and raised an American flag up on a pole and moved it back and forth hoping the soldiers would stop. But they did not. The soldiers charged in and started shooting, women and small ones as well as warriors. They spared no one, and they cut up and scalped the dead afterwards. All the tribes heard about it. Gray Blanket told later how some of them grabbed three children and took them back to some officers, the oldest eight and the youngest four or five, and a lieutenant said, 'Orders are to kill small and big.' And he shot one in the head with his pistol and then the other two, though they cried and begged for mercy. He said his own little boy came out of a tepee crying, and one officer aimed and missed him twice but another set his gun on his knee and knocked him over at the second shot.

Old man Three Fingers' mother put her baby on her back and grabbed Three Fingers' hand – he was just a little boy – and ran for the creek. The soldiers kept firing at her and one hit her in the shoulder, but she made it down below a bank to a safe place. Then she took the baby off her back and it was dead, shot through the body. Her husband was killed at the same time. Afterwards she lived with the Northern Cheyennes for many years, and she never stopped telling about it.

Another woman, Black Bear's wife, had a scar where she had been shot. They called her One Eye Comes Together because of it. She told terrible things about the soldiers killing children, and carrying some of the women away and mistreating them. They shot most of them afterwards, but a few lived to tell about it.

The following day US Lieutenant James Connor rode through the massacre site:

I did not see a body of man, woman or child but was scalped, and in many instances their bodies were mutilated in the most horrible manner – men, women and children's privates cut out, &c; I heard one man say that he cut out a woman's private parts and had them for exhibition on a stick ... I also heard of numerous instances in which men had cut out the private parts of females and stretched them over their saddle-bows and wore them over their hats while riding in the ranks.

Estimates of the number of dead vary between 105 and around 200, but there is no question that the figure would have been much higher if Chivington's men had been professional soldiers rather than undisciplined – and often drunk – civilian volunteers. As it was, many Indians escaped – including Black Kettle, who was subsequently killed in another massacre – to alert other bands to what had happened. At the end of December, angry Sioux, Arapaho and Cheyenne joined forces to avenge Black Kettle's band, and Chivington had his war.

Early in 1865, 1,000 warriors attacked the South Platte trail, plundering a military post, burning ranches and stations, capturing livestock and wagon trains and killing more people than had died at Sand Creek. The following summer, after a successful spring hunt, an even larger force raided the North Platte trail and wiped out a military wagon train. The United States sent General P. E. Connor and more than 3,000 men to encircle the 'hostiles', with orders not to 'receive overtures of peace or submission' and to 'kill every male Indian over twelve years of age,' but the Indians managed to escape to their hunting-grounds, forcing Connor to withdraw empty-handed.

But, almost immediately, still more serious threats crowded in. The flood of travellers to the west, temporarily slowed by the Civil War, started to swell again, and regular troops returned to the Plains to protect them. Work began on a rail route across the region, and forts were built along the newly made Bozeman Trail to the Montana minefields, which cut directly through the heart of the Sioux' hunting territory. At the same time, the Homestead Act of 1863 had opened the way for Anglo-American settlement of the high Plains, and communities were already starting to spring up along its eastern rim.

Rather than trying to fight the tribes to a standstill, which had proved singularly unsuccessful, the government decided on a new, two-pronged policy: to reduce the Indians to the verge of starvation by encouraging hunters like Buffalo Bill Cody to destroy their bison herds; and to bribe them to settle on reservations with promises of food and annuities. In practice, however, it proved impossible to unpick the pattern of suspicion, racial hatred and violence that, in the aftermath of Sand Creek, had come to dominate relations between Anglos and Native Americans.

In 1867, as Indian 'depredations' continued, Major General Winfield Scott Hancock determined to make an example of one of the tribes in order to cow the rest into submission. He chose the unfortunate

Cheyenne, on the grounds that they 'would appear to be as deserving of chastisement as any other.' Despite Wynkoop's protests, he provoked a war by marching 1,400 men to a Cheyenne and Sioux encampment. When the women and children, remembering the Chivington massacre, ran away, he took this as evidence that they were 'a nest of conspirators' and burnt their village. He then sent Lieutenant-Colonel George A. Custer to pursue the 'hostiles', sparking off yet another spiral of raids and reprisals.

As their bison herds dwindled and the war of attrition against them intensified, most of the southern tribes – Kiowas, Comanches, Southern Cheyennes and Arapahoes and others – were forced, by the end of the 1860s, to accept reservations in the western half of Indian Territory. The Five Civilized Tribes and other, more recent, arrivals sent assurances of their 'friendship and kind feelings' to the Plains peoples and invited them to join their regular 'Okmulgee Council'. Despite the diversity of their linguistic and cultural backgrounds, the different Indian Territory nations quickly showed a remarkable ability to work together, and were soon developing plans for an Indian state where all the native people of the US could eventually live together.

But further north, the Sioux and their allies, under the Lakota war leader Red Cloud, were continuing to hold out. In 1866, they turned back from a council called to discuss the Bozeman trail when they realized that the army had already begun building forts, and began a heroic fight against overwhelming odds for their land, their way of life and the bison on which they depended. Three Lakota, interviewed in the 1930s when they were old men, gave a rare and fascinating Indian perspective on the conflict which makes it clear how deeply they felt the threat to their survival.

> ... I felt that the white men would just simply wipe us out and there would be no Indian nation ... We wouldn't have fought the white men if they hadn't fought us. We would have allowed them to live among us in peace.
>
> When I was ... about fourteen, I remember that the white men were coming and that they were going to fight us to the finish and take away our land, and I thought it was not right. We are humans too and God created us all alike, and I was going to do the best I

could to defend my nation. So I started out on the warpath when I was sixteen years old.

From what I heard from old people, I thought I would just have to do my part. We roamed the country freely, and this country belonged to us in the first place. There was plenty of game and we were never hungry. But since the white men came we were fighting all the time. The white man was just going to kill all of us. I was so scared that I rode one horse all night just guarding ... The band I was in got together and said they were not going to let the white men run over them and down deep in my heart I was going to defend my fellow men to the last. At the age of ten or eleven I had a six-shooter and a quiver full of arrows to defend my nation.

Although they were massively outnumbered and outgunned, the Lakota were able to elude or defeat the army time and again. Standing Bear gives a vivid account of their tactics:

We went into battle naked because it is more handy. You can get around quickly and are more swift in every way. With clothes on you would be much slower. We had the pony's bridle fastened to our belt to keep the pony from getting away when the rider would fall off.

... The white cavalry did not know how to fight. They stuck together and thus made an easy target for us. When we started fighting, we would probably be under the horse's belly and after we were on the ground we would jump around, and it was pretty hard to hit us. We'd zigzag toward them. It was open order fighting. We fought in circles because when we go around them it would scare the soldiers and then we would charge on them ... Some would go one way and the others would go another way, thus disorganizing the soldiers. We would hang on our ponies at times with one leg. This is a real trick to know how to do. Then we would shoot under the horse's neck, while the other leg is cramped up on the side.

Red Cloud besieged the government's forts, quickly choking off traffic along the Bozeman trail, and in December 1866 annihilated a force of eighty men under Captain William J. Fetterman (who, ironically, had boasted that he could ride through 'the whole Sioux nation' with precisely that number of soldiers). Incensed by the Indians' audacity and the failure of his own men to contain them, General

Sherman broke out angrily: 'We must act with vindictive earnestness against the Sioux, even to their extermination, men, women, and children.'

But, despite the public blustering, it quickly became clear that a military solution was simply not practicable. The cost of the campaign against the Sioux and their allies – President Grant's Secretary of the Interior, Carl Schurz, estimated it at almost $1 million per Indian killed – was an unsustainable expense for a country recovering from the ravages of civil war. Finally, in 1868, the government had to concede defeat – perhaps the only instance in history of the United States losing an Indian war and having to accept the enemy's peace terms.

Under the Fort Laramie treaty of 1868, the government agreed to close the hated Bozeman trail and to leave a vast area – including the whole of western South Dakota – as 'unceded Indian territory.' Red Cloud, suspecting that this might be yet another worthless promise, withheld his signature until he saw the US forts evacuated and burnt to the ground by his joyful followers.

✿   ✿   ✿

But Red Cloud's victory was short-lived. As the tide of settlement carried Anglo-Americans into the last unconquered parts of the United States, the mood of the country moved against making treaties with Native American nations altogether. In his annual report for 1869, the Commissioner of Indian Affairs, Ely S. Parker, declared:

> The Indian tribes of the United States are not sovereign nations, capable of making treaties, as none of them have an organized government of such inherent strength as would secure a faithful obedience of its people in the observance of compacts of this character. They are held to be wards of the government, and the only title the law concedes them to the lands they occupy or claim is a mere possessory one. But because treaties have been made with them, generally for the extinguishment of their supposed absolute title to land inhabited by them, or over which they roam, they have become falsely impressed with the notion of national independence. It is time that this idea should be dispelled, and the government

cease the cruel farce of thus dealing with its helpless and ignorant wards . . .

From a modern perspective, this seems a remarkable conclusion. Since colonial times, British and US officials had consistently agreed that Indian treaties were almost invariably broken not by Indians but by settlers, generally because the Crown or the federal government had lacked the strength or the will to restrain their own people. In the ninety years since independence, the United States had made more than 370 treaties, *every single one of which* had been violated by US citizens. The Five Civilized Tribes, moreover, had shown that even in Euro-American terms, Native Americans were capable of organizing a 'government of such inherent strength as would secure a faithful obedience of its people.' To add to the ironies, Parker was himself a Seneca Indian – a member of the Iroquois confederacy which had so excited the admiration of European and Euro-American political thinkers.

But few people were struck by these contradictions at the time. The decision to end treaty-making with Indians – which was finally enacted by Congress in 1871 – seemed inescapable good sense. With the inferiority of Native Americans widely accepted as proven historic and scientific fact, it was clearly preposterous for the United States to feign an equal relationship with them. The only question was: what should the *new* relationship be?

This issue was debated with growing intensity during the last third of the nineteenth century. It revolved, essentially, around the old conundrum that had exercised Europeans and Anglo-Americans for three centuries: could native people be saved by 'civilization', or were they doomed to melt away 'like snow before the sun'? Powerful voices were raised on both sides. 'Humanitarians' like Parker believed that they were savable, provided that 'such legislation should be granted to them as a wise, liberal, and just government ought to extend to subjects holding their dependent relation.' In practice, this meant:

. . . plac[ing] the Indians upon reservations as rapidly as possible, where they could be provided for in such manner as the dictates of humanity and Christian civilization require. Being thus placed upon reservations, they will be removed from such contiguity to our frontier settlements as otherwise will lead, necessarily to frequent outrages, wrongs, and disturbances of the public peace. On these reservations they can be taught, as fast as possible, the arts of agriculture, and such pursuits as are incident to civilization, through the aid of the Christian organizations of the country now engaged in this work, co-operating with the Federal Government.

The government ethnologist Garrick Mallery sought to give this approach, known as the 'peace policy', some scientific weight, arguing that the belief that Native Americans were 'withering' was 'absolutely false.'

... though some temporary retrogradation must always be expected among individual tribes at the crisis of their transition from savagery or barbarism to more civilized habits, yet now, the number of our Indians is on the increase and will naturally so continue, unless repressed by causes not attributable to civilization, but to criminal misgovernment, until their final absorption into the wondrous amalgam of all earth's peoples, which the destiny of this country may possibly effect. Neither from views of the physiological, religious or sociological characteristics should they be regarded as an exceptional or abnormal part of the human race, or so treated in our national policy.

The opposing view, however, was more in tune with the popular mood. Sensational dime novels and pictures of scalped and mutilated massacre-victims in the mass-circulation press had helped to create an almost hysterical anti-Indian feeling. 'A dead Indian is a pleasing picture ...' wrote the humorist Bill Nye in 1881. 'The picture of a wild free Indian chasing the buffalo may suit some, but I still like life in art. I like the picture of a broad-shouldered, well-formed brave as he lies with his nerveless hand across a large hole in the pit of his stomach.' It was, as always, gratifying to believe that such queasy genocidal fantasies enjoyed the sanction of a higher power. Colonel John Gibbon clearly struck a chord (his essay won the gold medal in an army competition) when he wrote in 1880:

Philanthropists and visionary speculators may theorize as they please about protecting the Indian ... and preserving him as a race. *It cannot be done.* Whenever the two come in contact ... the weaker *must* give way, and disappear. To deny this is to deny the evidence of our own senses, and to shut our eyes to the facts of history.

Advocates of the 'peace policy' received a serious setback when, in the mid-1870s, war erupted, yet again, on the Plains. The trigger, all too predictably (but virtually ignored at the time), was the failure of the United States government to hold its own citizens to the terms of a treaty. In the spring of 1874, General Custer and a party of 1,200 soldiers, scientists and newspapermen set out to explore the Black Hills of South Dakota, where, reportedly, parties of illegal miners had found gold. The area, known to the Lakota as *Paha Sapa*, was the sacred centre of the Sioux universe, 'the heart of everything that is,' and well inside boundaries of the 'Great Sioux Reservation' recognized by the Fort Laramie Treaty.

When the expedition confirmed that there was 'gold at the roots of the grass,' it precipitated an invasion of miners and prospectors. At first the government made a half-hearted attempt to remove the trespassers, but it soon decided that it would be easier to remove the Indians. A commission was sent to offer $6 million for the Hills, but it was quickly surrounded by 7,000 armed warriors and forced to withdraw. The Sioux then held their own council and sent a message rejecting the government's offer.

Illegal settlers, nonetheless, started laying out towns in the Black Hills, demanding that the army should protect them against possible Native American reprisals. In November, the United States issued an ultimatum to the Indians, ordering them to come into the government agencies on the 'Great Sioux Reservation' by the end of the following January or be brought in as 'hostiles'. Since it would have been impossible for the bands to comply in the depths of a Great Plains winter, this was tantamount to a declaration of war.

The following spring, a three-pronged campaign was launched against the Lakota and their Cheyenne allies. It ended in yet another catastrophe for the United States. General Crook, with 1,300 men (including Crow and Shoshone auxiliaries), was forced to withdraw after a fierce battle on 17 June. Just over a week later came perhaps the most famous engagement of the 'Indian Wars', the Battle of the

Little Bighorn, when General Custer and his men were wiped out by a large Indian force under Crazy Horse, Sitting Bull and other leaders.

The news that a US general and 225 soldiers had been annihilated by Indians reached Washington on 5 July 1876, the day after the conclusion of the nation's centennial celebrations. Smarting from the humiliation, and driven by a storm of public outrage, the government poured thousands of troops into the Plains to put an end, once and for all, to Native American resistance. One by one, fighting to the last, the half-starving Sioux bands were brought in and confined around the agencies that had served their vast reservation. The Northern Cheyenne were moved down to Indian Territory to join their southern relatives, but hundreds of them died of disease and despair. Finally, after a heroic breakout and an epic trek back to their homeland, they were allowed to remain on the Montana reservation where they live today.

During the 1880s, as the last bands of Apaches and other 'hostiles' were being rounded up, the argument about what should be done with the Indians continued. Already, however, it was increasingly tinged by a new mood – or, rather, a resurgent mood – of maudlin sentimentalizing about 'the Vanishing Race'. Even as the guns fell silent, the callous drollery of writers like Twain and Nye was giving way, yet again, to tearful nostalgia. At the Chicago World's Fair in 1893, an elderly Potawatomi, Simon Pokagon, did brisk business selling copies of his book *A Red Man's Greeting*, which was printed on birch bark and prefaced with a short poem:

> Alas for us! our day is o'er,
> Our fires are out from shore to shore;
> No more for us the wild deer bounds;
> The plow is on our hunting grounds;
> The pale man's ax rings through our woods,
> The pale man's sails skim o'er our floods;
>   Our pleasant springs are dry.
> Our children – look by power oppressed! –
> Beyond the mountains of the West,
>   Our children go to die.

Although some of his readers believed that Pokagon had written this verse himself, it was, in fact – all too appropriately – part of a classic of

New England wistfulness, Charles Sprague's *Ode, Pronounced at the Centennial Celebration of the Settlement of Boston, September, 1830*. Pokagon had done nothing more than replace the word 'their' with 'our'.

The hunger for a colourful past was also being served by a genuinely new phenomenon: the Wild West show – and, by the end of the century, the Wild West film. For decades, real-life characters like Wild Bill Hickok and Buffalo Bill Cody had been the subject of fictional adventure stories. Now, five years after the Little Big Horn, Buffalo Bill was travelling the country with Sitting Bull and other former 'hostiles', thrilling audiences with simplified reconstructions of 'how the West was won.' Just as policy-makers were striving to frame a lasting, rational solution to the 'problem' of the defeated tribes, this blurring of history and showbusiness contributed yet one more element to the swirl of powerful, deeply contradictory ideas and feelings about 'the Indian' in the American psyche.

❖ ❖ ❖

The emotions of Native Americans themselves are hard to imagine. In under four centuries, disease, warfare, hunger, massacre and despair had reduced their population from an estimated 7–10 million to less than 250,000. As well as costing them their independence and more than ninety per cent of their land, the long struggle against Europeans and Euro-Americans had ruptured their sense of reality.

For the Plains nations, the extermination of their vast bison herds – by 1895 there were fewer than *1,000* animals left – had not only driven them to starvation and defeat but had destroyed the core of their spiritual and ceremonial world. And the desperate quarrels over how to respond to the Anglo threat – to sign or fight, to accommodate or resist – had left them bitterly divided. The Lakota, for instance, were split between followers of Red Cloud, who had finally been induced to sign a fraudulent treaty (later found by the US Supreme Court to be illegal) selling the Black Hills, and Crazy Horse, who had held out to the last and died on a soldier's bayonet. The legacy of their mutual hostility and suspicion still persists in the deep fault-lines running through Lakota society today.

As they struggled to come to terms with the scale of their defeat, tribes across the west were suddenly offered a new hope which promised to repair the lost meaning and cohesion of their universe. Followers of the messianic 'Ghost Dance' cult believed that by wearing 'ghost shirts' and performing powerful songs and dances they would bring back their dead loved ones, the vanished bison and the old way of life.

Starting among the Paiutes of the Great Basin, the Ghost Dance quickly swept through the Plains, and by the winter of 1890 it had reached the Lakota. In remote camps across the remnants of the 'Great Sioux Reservation', thousands of Native Americans were fervently dancing and singing for deliverance. Fearing another 'uprising', the government – yet again – sent troops to 'pacify' the Indians.

On 14 December, Sitting Bull and seven ghost dancers were shot dead in a scuffle with police on the northernmost reservation, Standing Rock. Some of his followers then fled to join another leader, Big Foot, who was leading his own people towards Pine Ridge, hundreds of miles to the south. It was here that both Red Cloud's and Crazy Horse's bands had settled, and, according to Charlotte Black Elk, a contemporary authority on Sioux history and culture, Big Foot's mission was to try to heal the rift between the two groups:

> There was fear that as Crazy Horse's followers were beginning to get more involved in the Ghost Dance they would be prepared to go to war again. And there was still a lot of division between Red Cloud's followers and Crazy Horse's followers. So the people in our community made the decision that a peace had to be arbitrated.
>
> We have a position called 'The Keeper of the White Wing.' The Trumpeter Swan is the bird of the north, its message is reconciliation: you have to throw away everything that's finished its time and then go forward clean again. And so the wing of the Trumpeter Swan signified this office. Big Foot was that person among our people.

Big Foot and some 400 men, women and children arrived at Pine Ridge on 28 December 1890. They were met by members of the Seventh Cavalry – George Custer's unit – and ordered to camp at Wounded Knee Creek. That night, the soldiers cracked open barrels of whisky, and some of the Indians heard them drunkenly boasting that they would avenge the Little Big Horn.

The following day, the Sioux were disarmed. Soldiers then conducted a tent-by-tent search for any remaining weapons. As a deaf Sioux called Black Coyote was struggling to hold on to his rifle a shot was heard (it is still not clear which side it came from) and the nervous cavalry opened fire. About three hundred Indians were killed outright or fatally wounded. Thirteen soldiers died, apparently caught in crossfire from their own side. Several cavalrymen received Congressional medals of honour for heroism.

'Our story says, no minister would come and bury these people,' says Charlotte Black Elk:

And there was a gentleman on his way to Wyoming, a Congregationalist minister, and he left the train and came in and performed Christian rites so they could bury these people. When our people went down there to the grave site, they'd buried them in a mass grave. One of the women saw the wing: it was shattered, it was covered with blood. She ran to get it and the contract gravedigger pushed her aside and grabbed the swan's wing and threw it into the grave.

For Anglo-Americans, the massacre at Wounded Knee, with its desolate images of twisted Indian corpses frozen into the snow, has become a deeply significant moment. It poignantly represents the end of the 'frontier', the three-century process of continuous expansion that had carried their country from a few tiny trading posts to potentially the most powerful nation on earth. The 'Indian' who had barred the way, the Indian who *was* in some sense the unpossessed, unconquered continent, was finally defeated. Whether child of Eden or the wild beast in the wilderness, he was, at last, banished to his natural home: the past.

But for Native Americans, the massacre has another layer of meaning. While it is remembered as the last major military confrontation of the 'Indian Wars', it also marks the beginning of a new struggle against – in some ways – an even more destructive and demoralizing enemy.

Part III

INTERNAL FRONTIERS

10. Kill the Indian to Save the Man

Assimilation

*A long time ago I lived free among the buffalo on the Staked Plains
and had as many wives as I wanted, according to the laws of my
people. I used to go to war in Texas and Mexico. You wanted me
to stop fighting and sent messages all the time: 'You stop, Quanah.
You come here. You sit down, Quanah.' You did not say anything
then, 'How many wives you got, Quanah.' Now I come and sit
down as you want. You talk about wives; which one I throw
away? You pick him? You little girl, you go 'way; you got no papa
– you pick him? You little fellow, you go 'way; you got no papa –
you pick him?*

Quanah Parker, Comanche

For most Native Americans, the new phase had already, in fact, begun
well before the massacre of Big Foot and his band. As early as 1849,
the Committee on Indian Affairs, recognizing that the United States
was fast running out of land to which native people could be permanently removed, had proposed that the only 'alternative to extinction'
was to settle 'our colonized tribes' on government-run 'reservations',
where they could be protected against dispossession and extermination
until they were 'sufficiently advanced in civilization ... to be able to
maintain themselves in close proximity with, or in the midst of, a white
population.' Two years later, the Secretary of the Interior saw the
options still more starkly: 'The policy of removal ... must necessarily
be abandoned; and the only alternatives left are, to civilize or exterminate them.'

Throughout the 1850s and 1860s, an increasingly vociferous body of
philanthropists, appalled at the government's continuing inability to
prevent a spate of massacres in the West, demanded that it should
wholeheartedly embrace the course of 'civilization'. From the earliest

days of independence, critics of government policy had argued that the popular view that Indians could not be 'civilized' was, in the words of George Washington's Secretary of War, Henry Knox, 'probably more convenient than just.' Now, as the nation reached maturity and seemed close to fulfilling its continental destiny, reformers like Bishop Henry Whipple of Minnesota (who after Little Crow's War successfully appealed for clemency for hundreds of Indian prisoners) insisted that the United States must at last accept its moral responsibility to 'save' the remaining Native Americans both from physical obliteration by its own citizenry and from the 'errors' of the Indians' own culture. In 1864, Whipple gave a resounding reply to the question of whether native people were 'capable of receiving a Christian civilization': 'We answer, unhesitatingly, Yes.' All that was required, he believed, was the political will to establish an effective system of reservations where the Indians would be safe while devout Christians conscientiously prepared them for life 'in close proximity' to Anglo-Americans. In 1869, this idea became the cornerstone of President Grant's 'peace policy'.

There was, of course, a long tradition of trying to 'civilize' the Indian, from the 'praying towns' of seventeenth-century New England to the 'demonstration farms' advocated by Thomas Jefferson 150 years later, but for most of the colonial and post-Independence period the 'improving' impulse had only played a small part in official dealings with native people. The overriding motive had always been to open more of the continent to Euro-American settlement and to protect settlers against Indian 'depredations' rather than to 'raise up' the Indians themselves, and although treaties routinely paid lip-service to the idea of native 'improvement' by promising tribes schooling and agricultural training in exchange for their land, these commitments were seldom fully honoured. (As late as 1877, the Congressional appropriation for 'Indian education' was a mere $20,000.) Although some officials and missionaries did make earnest efforts to implement them, many Americans shared Governor Gilmer's opinion – expressed during the removal era – that treaties need not be taken too seriously because they were merely 'expedients by which ignorant, intractable, and savage people were induced without bloodshed to yield up what civilized people had the right to possess.' The sorry history of California in the 1850s – a catalogue of unratified agreements, disappearing reservations and systematic corruption which had spectacularly failed to halt the destruction of the Indians – was only the latest evidence that this cavalier attitude was not confined to the 'lowest and most brutal of the border population' but was also widespread among federal officials and legislators. In 1867, President Grant's Peace Commissioners reported:

> The records are abundant to show that agents have pocketed the funds appropriated by the government and driven the Indians to starvation. It cannot be doubted that Indian wars have originated from this cause. The Sioux war, in Minnesota, is supposed to have been produced in this way. For a long time these officers have been selected from partisan ranks, not so much on account of honesty and qualifications as for devotion to party interests and their willingness to apply the money of the Indian to promote the selfish schemes of local politicians.

The Commissioners were determined to root out the incompetence, fatalism and dishonesty in the Indian Service. They were partially successful – their proposal, for example, that agents should be nominated by missionaries in the field led to a reduction in corruption – but only, paradoxically, by drastically diminishing the legal position of Indians. The treaty-making process might, in practice, have often been no more than a cynical ploy, but in theory it had accepted that Native American communities were – in the words of Chief Justice John Marshall – 'domestic dependent nations' with distinct rights. As well as acknowledging that Indian land belonged to the Indians – if it didn't, after all, how could the United States buy it from them? – treaties also generally recognized that an Indian nation retained at least limited sovereignty within the boundaries of any territory which it had not surrendered. Some agreements had specifically provided that tribes would be able to continue governing themselves according to tribal custom: rather than surrendering wrongdoers to the federal government, for example, they could impose their own punishment and then – when the victim was a US citizen or a member of another tribe – simply pay an indemnity to the United States.

But for the reformers, as we have seen, treaties were only a 'cruel farce' which impeded progress by encouraging Native Americans to harbour delusions of 'national independence'. In reality, Indians were no more than 'helpless and ignorant' dependants of the United States, who were incapable of concluding binding agreements and whose title to the land was 'a mere possessory one'.

In the period following the suspension of treaty-making in 1871, this far more restricted view of Native American rights and powers came to predominate. Reservations – from the reformers' perspective – were not unsurrendered areas of a tribe's ancestral homeland, but simply parts of the 'public domain' which the United States had 'set aside' for the use and protection of its wards. There was therefore no need for the federal authorities to continue – or even to pretend to continue – to recognize most tribal governments, and Indian Office officials increasingly tried to establish their own, rival power structures on the reservations, organizing courts and appointing native policemen whose first loyalty was to them rather than to tribal and clan leaders. At the same time, the agents – now often driven more by moral fervour than by the profit motive – assumed an almost unlimited authority over the life of the individual Indian which effectively reduced him – or her – to the status of a child. Since the time of Columbus, Europeans had seen Native Americans as children – pastoral innocents or feckless, thoughtlessly cruel delinquents: now, at last, Anglo-America was consciously accepting the role of guardian.

By the 1870s, even the most fervent 'friends' of the Indian accepted that this unprecedented extension of government control was justified and unavoidable. In 1878, the reformer Captain Richard Pratt told an audience:

> The mass of the Indians in our land have with few tribal exceptions remained until very recently in the enjoyment of their savage life, but now a change has come, the advance of our civilized population from the East has reached the heart of the continent . . . The dawn of a great emergency has opened upon the Indian . . . He is in childish ignorance of the methods and course best to pursue. We are in possession of the information and help and are able to give the help that he now so much needs.

Four years later, the Reverend George Ellis was even blunter:

> We have a full right, by our own best wisdom, and then even by compulsion, to dictate terms and conditions to them [the Indians]; to use constraint and force; to say what we intend to do, and what they must and shall do ... This rightful power of ours will relieve us from conforming to, or even consulting to any troublesome extent, the views and inclinations of Indians whom we are to manage ... The Indian must be made to feel that he is in the grasp of a superior.

But the crucial issue was: how should this 'rightful power' be used? What – even backed by the vast military and economic resources of a modern industrial state – could it be expected to achieve with a gaggle of 'ignorant savages'? In the decade before Wounded Knee, this question came to dominate discussion of the 'Indian Problem'.

❖   ❖   ❖

You see this barren waste ... Think of it! I, who used to own rich soil in a well-watered country so extensive that I could not ride through it in a week on my fastest pony, am put down here! Why, I have to go five miles for wood for my fire. Washington took our lands and promised to feed and support us. Now I, who used to control 5,000 warriors, must tell Washington when I am hungry. I must beg for that which I own. If I beg hard, they put me in the guard-house. We have trouble. Our girls are getting bad. Coughing sickness every winter carries away our best people. My heart is heavy. I am old, I cannot do much more ...

Red Cloud as an old man, recorded by Warren K. Moorhead

The terms of the debate were established, to a great extent, by a single – on the face of it improbable – event. In 1877, the Poncas, a small tribe in Nebraska who had already adopted a largely Euro-American farming way of life, had become one of the last Native American groups to be selected for removal to Indian Territory. When they protested that they did not want to leave, soldiers were sent to round them up. According to the Ponca leader, Standing Bear:

The soldiers collected all the women and children together; then they called all the chiefs together in council; and then they took wagons and went round and broke open the houses. When we came back from the council, we found the women and children surrounded by a guard of soldiers.

They took our reapers, mowers, hay rakes, spades, ploughs, bedsteads, stoves, cupboards, everything we had on our farms, and put them in one large building. Then they put into the wagons such things as they could carry. We told them that we would rather die than leave our lands; but we could not help ourselves. They took us down. Many died on the road. Two of my children died. After we reached the new land, all my horses died. The water was very bad. All our cattle died; not one was left. I stayed till one hundred and fifty-eight of my people had died.

Finally, when his young son died, Standing Bear refused to bury the body in the alien soil of Indian Territory. With thirty followers and a single horse-drawn wagon carrying the dead child, he set out for home.

We were three months on the road. We were weak and sick and starved. When we reached the Omaha Reserve the Omahas gave us a piece of land, and we were in a hurry to plough it and put in wheat. While we were working, the soldiers came and arrested us. Half of us were sick. We would rather have died than have been carried back [to Indian Territory]; but we could not help ourselves.

The Poncas' story was far from unique – many peoples in California and elsewhere had suffered as much or worse – but it was taken up by T. H. Tibbles, a Nebraska newspaperman, who used the growing power of the press to turn it into a *cause célèbre*. Public-spirited citizens, horrified to read of the cruelty and incompetence of their own soldiers and bureaucrats, raised money to apply for Standing Bear's release from detention on a writ of habeas corpus. When the case was heard in 1879, the whole court – including the judge and General Crook – was moved to tears by Standing Bear's eloquence.

The government claimed that an Indian was ineligible for the writ because he was not 'a person' within the meaning of the Constitution, but, in an historic decision, the judge rejected this argument and ordered that Standing Bear should be freed. Leader-writers across the country were elated: San Francisco's *Alta California* hailed the decision as the 'only case now recollected where a court of this country has rendered justice to the Indian as if he were a human being.' The newly released Standing Bear himself became a national celebrity (it is interesting to compare his fate with the treatment meted out to the equally famous Nez Percé Chief Joseph at roughly the same time), addressing crowded East coast lecture halls on the need for constitutional guarantees to be extended to Native Americans. Finally, he and 170 of his followers were allowed to return to Nebraska, where some of their descendants still live today.

The treatment of the Poncas – and the 'Ute War' of the same year, in which an insensitive federal agent sparked an outbreak of violence among the Utes of Colorado – helped to fuel mounting criticism of government policy and to transform 'the Indian question', for a while, into an important national issue. In the years following the disasters of 1879, no fewer than three new philanthropic organizations sprang up to campaign for Native American 'rights', and in 1883 their leaders began meeting annually at Lake Mohonk in New York State to forge a common strategy.

The new 'friends of the Indian' shared with the Peace Commission reformers who had preceded them a profound conviction that the aim of government policy should be to 'civilize' Native Americans, but they took a subtly different view of how this should be achieved. In particular, they saw the reservation system – regarded by Bishop Whipple and his colleagues as key to 'saving the Indian' – as part of the problem rather than the solution. Isolating Native Americans under federal control, they believed, would only encourage dependence and 'backwardness' and prevent the tribal child from maturing into a civilized adult. What was needed was an intensive programme of 'civilization' to 'raise' the Indian to the level where he (it was always 'he') could be released – in the words of a *Chicago Tribune* editorial on the Standing Bear case – 'from the arbitrary control of the Indian Bureau and allowed all the rights and immunities of a free man.'

This new approach was, in part, a direct response to the recent failures of government Indian policy, but it also reflected shifts in the wider political and intellectual climate. By the 1880s, many Americans were troubled by what they saw as the growing threat to their national character and cohesion posed both by rapid social and economic change and by large-scale immigration. The dramatic burgeoning of huge, polyglot industrial cities teeming with newcomers from Ireland and southern and eastern Europe challenged the United States' idea of itself as a landscape of farms and small towns, predominantly populated by hardy, self-reliant Anglo-Saxons. At the same time, Euro-Americans were having to rethink their relationship with non-European minorities, particularly with the recently emancipated African-Americans and with the tens of thousands of Chinese labourers who were flocking to the Pacific coast. It seemed clear that if the country was to survive and to retain its identity, it had to move away from the simple association between race and culture which had sustained it and justified its actions during the most intense period of westward expansion. Anglo-Saxon 'civilization' could no longer be the exclusive preserve of Anglo-Saxons: some means would have to be found of grafting its values – Protestant individualism, a belief in hard work, private property and the law – on to people of very different ethnic and cultural backgrounds.

For several reasons, Native Americans seemed a good test-case for this experiment. Southern politicians were effectively blocking the extension of full civil rights to black Americans, and hostility towards Asians on the West coast was so intense that in 1882 Congress passed a Chinese Exclusion Act. Native Americans, by contrast, were widely scattered and still generally thought to be a 'vanishing race' who could pose little long-term threat to the majority. The likeliest opponents of any attempt to 'save' them – the non-Indian population of the western Territories where most native people now lived – had no representation in Congress and consequently little political influence in Washington.

At the same time, as peace gradually settled over the west, many Americans elsewhere were beginning to take a positive – and more sympathetic – interest in 'the Indian'. With the final defeat of the last 'wild' tribes, the pendulum was starting to swing back once again towards a more romantic image of the 'savage': even as the vicious enemy of Progress slowly shuffled out of the public imagination under armed guard, the helpless victim began to take his place. The old feelings of poignancy and loss were heightened by a growing recognition that the United States' treatment of native people had been less than honourable. Books like Helen Hunt Jackson's *A Century of*

Dishonor – a kind of early *Bury My Heart At Wounded Knee*, published in 1881, which painted a devastating picture of American treachery and cruelty – made uncomfortable reading for a nation that believed it had a unique destiny as the standard-bearer of Christian civilization. Many – mostly East coast – philanthropists feared that the country's shameful record of brutality and duplicity towards its own first people would cast a permanent shadow over its claim to the moral leadership of mankind. As the Commissioners negotiating with the Sioux for the 'sale' of the Black Hills put it in 1876:

> We cannot afford to delay longer fulfilling our bounden duty to those from whom we have taken that country, the possession of which has placed us in the forefront of the nations of the earth. We make it our boast that our country is the home of the oppressed of all lands. Dare we forget that there are also those whom we have made homeless, and to whom we are bound to give protection and care? . . .
>
> A great crisis has arisen in Indian affairs. The wrongs of the Indians are admitted by all. Thousands of the best men in the land feel keenly the nation's shame. They look to Congress for redress. Unless immediate and appropriate legislation is made for the protection and government of the Indians, they must perish. Our country must forever bear the disgrace and suffer the retribution of its wrongdoing. Our children's children will tell the sad story in hushed tones, and wonder how their fathers dare so trample on justice and trifle with God . . .

Four years later, in the wake of the Standing Bear case, the *New York Tribune* made the same point in strikingly similar terms:

> The original owner of the soil, the man from whom we have taken the country, in order that we may make of it the refuge of the world, where all men should be free if not equal, is the only man in it who is not recognized as entitled to the rights of a human being.

The glorious story of America would not be complete unless, somehow, it included a happy ending for Indians too.

This did not mean, of course, 'turning the clock back' by restoring Native Americans to their land and their independence: it meant sharing with them the self-evidently superior life of their conquerors.

In 1880, Major John Wesley Powell, director of the newly established Bureau of Ethnology, wrote that the 'major portion' of the debt which the government owed Native Americans could 'be paid only by giving to the Indians Anglo-Saxon civilization, that they may also have prosperity and happiness under the new civilization of this continent.'

Evidence that this transformation might be possible seemed to be offered by Powell's colleagues in the newly emerging social sciences. In 1877, the 'father of American anthropology', Lewis Henry Morgan, published his influential *Ancient Society, or Researches in the Lines of Human Progress from Savagery Through Barbarism to Civilization*, which argued – as the subtitle suggests – that all human societies are on a single, unalterable evolutionary ladder. Native Americans, at the time of 'discovery', had been clustered on the middle rungs, from 'Upper Savagery' to 'Middle Barbarism', but would inevitably, in the course of history, progress to 'civilization'. The only question – much debated at successive Lake Mohonk conferences – was whether, with appropriate help from the United States, they could now skip the intervening 'ethnical periods' and move in a single step to the 'civilized' level. (This oddly parallels Lenin's discussions with Karl Marx – who was also heavily influenced by Morgan – about whether Russia could undergo a workers' revolution without first passing through the stage of 'bourgeois capitalism'.)

Although there were dissenting voices, most of the 'friends of the Indian' believed that, with the right policies, Native American evolution could be hastened. The key, they thought, could be found in Morgan's – breathtakingly confident – assertion that:

> It is impossible to overestimate the influence of property in the civilization of mankind. It was the power that brought Aryan and Semitic nations out of barbarism into civilization ... Governments and laws are instituted with primary reference to its creation, protection and enjoyment ... With the establishment of the inheritance of property in the children of its owner, came the first possibility of the strict monogamian family.

It is important to realize just what a deep chord this idea struck in the social and political élite from which the bulk of the reformers were drawn. By closely identifying 'civilization' with private property, it simultaneously vindicated their own economic system – which was already being challenged by the rise of European socialism – and offered a straightforward, decent solution to the 'Indian question' which left their wealth, power and world view intact. It seemed so incontestably right that Merrill Gates, President of the Lake Mohonk Conference, could declare, with a certainty matching Morgan's own:

> *We need to awaken in him* [the Indian] *wants.* In his dull savagery he must be touched by the wings of the divine angel of discontent. Then he begins to look forward, to reach out. The desire for property of his own may become an intense educating force. The wish for a home of his own awakens him to new efforts. Discontent with the tepee and the starving rations of the Indian camp in winter is needed to get the Indian out of the blanket and into trousers, – and trousers with a pocket in them, and with a *pocket that aches to be filled with dollars!* ...
>
> There is an immense moral training that comes from the use of property. And the Indian has had all that to learn. Like a little child who learns the true delight of giving away only by first earning and possessing what it gives, the Indian must learn that he has no right to give until he has earned, and that he has no right to eat until he has worked for his bread ... We have found it necessary, as one of the first steps in developing a stronger personality in the Indian, *to make him responsible for property*. Even if he learns its value only by losing it, and going without it until he works for more, the educational process has begun. To cease from pauperizing the Indian by feeding him through years of laziness, – to instruct him to use property which is legally his, and by protecting his title, to help him through the dangerous transition period into citizenship, – this is the first great step in the education of the race.

From this perspective, even the Five Civilized Tribes, for all their accommodation and 'progress', had failed to release the genie of self-improvement which alone could carry them to the pinnacle of human achievement. After a visit to the Cherokees in 1885, Senator Henry Dawes – perhaps the single most influential campaigner – reported at Lake Mohonk:

The head chief told us that there was not a family in that whole nation that had not a home of its own. There was not a pauper in that nation, and the nation did not owe a dollar. It built its own capitol, in which we had this examination, and it built its schools and its hospitals. Yet the defect of the system was apparent. They have got as far as they can go, because they own their land in common. It is Henry George's system, and under that there is no enterprise to make your home any better than that of your neighbours. There is no selfishness, which is at the bottom of civilization. Till this people will consent to give up their lands, and divide them among their citizens so that each can own the land he cultivates, they will not make much more progress.

But the reformers knew that 'ignorant savages' would not 'give up their lands' willingly: they must be forcibly harnessed to the engine of human advancement by an enlightened government. Dawes and his colleagues proposed an ambitious programme of social engineering to prise the individual Indian from the 'degrading' grasp of the 'tribe' and elevate him to the plane of the citizen. First, since tribal land represented, in Powell's words, 'everything most sacred to Indian society,' the tribe's collective relationship with it must be systematically broken. Dividing it into individual holdings would undermine the kinship structure and 'traditional modes of inheritance,' breaking the old web of mutual obligation which impeded personal achievement and helping to foster self-reliance. Any 'surplus' could then be sold to 'whites', whose presence would bring 'uplift' and further weaken tribal bonds. At the same time, Indian children would be removed from the 'pernicious influence' of the home to mission or government schools where they could be prepared to take their place – if only at a fairly humble level – in mainstream America. Finally, when he had become sufficiently 'civilized', the adult native would receive the ultimate prize: US citizenship.

It would be quite wrong to suggest that the reformers advocated this policy for purely cynical reasons: some of them, such as the indefatigable Alice Fletcher, clearly believed that it was the only humane course for native people. It is probably true, however, that they would not have won the backing they needed unless their agenda had also served other, powerful – and far from altruistic – interests. At the start of the

1880s, even after all the losses of the previous three centuries, Native Americans still controlled lands with a total area one and a half times the size of California, allowing most tribes to be – like the Cherokees – economically self-sufficient. For speculators, railroad companies and populist politicians, the campaign to 'free' and assimilate the Native Americans offered a convenient – and morally unimpeachable – means of securing these last refuges for Anglo-American settlement and development. Striking evidence of how successfully businessmen learnt to clothe their demands in the language of philanthropy comes from a convention held in 1888, which urged the opening of Indian Territory in a ringing declaration that could have been written by Dawes himself:

> The highest obligation of a government towards a helpless, conquered people, penned in a tract of country . . . is to teach them the arts by which they alone can endure, and to infuse into them the spirit of self-reliance and industry which underlies all civilization and all permanent prosperity.

Even with such a powerful following wind, the reformers encountered strong opposition. The belief that Native Americans were 'uncivilizable' still had its advocates, and an influential group of Congressmen, mostly from the west, argued that the assimilation campaign was a waste of time and money. James Belford of Colorado railed against appropriating 'millions . . . for the support of an idle, vagrant, malevolent, malicious race,' and the Kansan John J. Ingalls claimed that trying to educate Indians was 'as absurd' and 'futile' as taking 'a herd of Texas broadhorn steers and endeavouring to turn them into Durhams and thoroughbreds by reading Alexander's herd book in their cattle-pens at Dodge City or Wichita.' The National Indian Defense Association, alone among the 'friends of the Indian', questioned whether enforced assimilation was in the best interests of Native Americans themselves. Remarkably, a minority report of the House Indian Affairs Committee even charged that:

> The real aim . . . [of this policy] is to get at the Indian lands and open them up to settlement . . . If this were done in the name of greed it would be bad enough; but to do it in the name of humanity, and under the cloak of an ardent desire to promote the Indian's welfare

by making him like ourselves, whether he will or not, is infinitely worse.

And Senator Henry Teller of Colorado, himself not above a little corruption at the native's expense, presciently declared:

If I stand alone in the Senate, I want to put upon the record my prophecy in this matter, that when thirty or forty years will have passed and these Indians shall have parted with their title, they will curse the hand that was raised professedly in their defence to secure this kind of legislation, and if the people who are clamouring for it understood Indian character, and Indian laws, and Indian morals, and Indian religion, they would not be here clamouring for this at all.

But the appeal of helping 'the Indian' by divesting him of his remaining land and resources proved too powerful. 'A moral obligation rests upon the United States,' argued John Kasson of Iowa, 'to change by proper and humane methods the system by which the Indians formerly lived, a system of which we deprived them, into the system of the white man which we are urging upon them.' A glimpse of the enormous significance with which some Congressmen invested this responsibility can be found in an extraordinary outburst by Representative Henry Johnson: when Richard Holman of Indiana urged a reduction in Indian spending, Johnson told him that if the Indians who had met Columbus had been able to see into the future, nothing they saw would have appalled them:

... until they saw the apparition of the gentleman from Indiana in the noonday of the nineteenth century, standing up in the American House of Commons with his well-known face begrimed all over with the war paint of economy, holding in one hand his scalping knife and in the other that instrument of still worse torture, his contemptible, penurious Indian appropriations bill.

By the time of the Wounded Knee massacre, the broad spectrum of support for 'civilization' had allowed the reformers to put in place a comprehensive programme to 'save the Indians'. Yet, for all its attractions for members of the élite, the idea that Native Americans were being steadily turned into sober citizens never really dented the popular belief that they were 'disappearing'. In 1912, a newspaper editor described the discovery that the Indian population was no longer falling as 'a considerable jolt to the current sentiment, which pictures the red man as a tragic figure expatriated and fast vanishing from his native plains and woods.'

*   *   *

The attempted transformation of the Indian by the white man and the chaos that has resulted are but the fruits of the white man's disobedience of a fundamental and spiritual law. The pressure that has been brought to bear upon the native people, since the cessation of armed conflict, in the attempt to force conformity of custom and habit has caused a reaction more destructive than war . . .

True, the white man brought great change. But the varied fruits of his civilization, though highly coloured and inviting, are sickening and deadening. And if it be the part of civilization to maim, rob, and thwart, then what is progress?

Luther Standing Bear, *Land of the Spotted Eagle*

Native Americans themselves were in no doubt that a new, and even more relentless, campaign had been launched against them. To begin with, a sustained assault on their land-base deprived them – in the fifteen years following Standing Bear's trial alone – of almost half their remaining territory. Much of the initial loss came from seven major land cessions involving only a relatively small number of tribes – in 1880, the Utes of Colorado, for instance, were forced to surrender twelve million acres at a stroke – but the passage of the General Allotment Act in 1887 opened the way for a broader offensive.

The Allotment Act – often called the 'Dawes Act', after its main sponsor – was the legislative cornerstone of the assimilation pro-gramme. Described by Theodore Roosevelt as a 'mighty pulverising engine to break up the tribal mass,' and hailed by philanthropists as the Indian 'Magna Carta' or 'Declaration of Independence', it established a clear mechanism for implementing the reformers' vision: when the President (rather than the people themselves) considered that a tribe was sufficiently 'advanced', its members would be told to select individual allotments – generally 160 acres per nuclear family – and the remainder of the reservation would then be sold. Under the original act, the allottees would automatically become citizens and their property would be held in trust for twenty-five years to prevent them losing it – as so many native people had before – to unscrupulous non-Indians. In 1906, however, the law was amended to allow the trust restrictions to be lifted early in the case of 'competent' individuals, and to delay the granting of citizenship until the trust period had expired.

To the dismay of the bill's philanthropic supporters, it soon became clear that tribes were as likely to be selected for the quality of their 'surplus' land as for the degree of 'civilization' they had attained. The first allotment began in 1887 on the one million-acre Sisseton and Wahpeton Sioux reservation in South Dakota, which eventually yielded a 'surplus' of 660,000 acres, and before the end of year work had begun on other communities in the Dakotas, Nebraska and Oregon. By 1891, the commissioner of Indian Affairs was able to report that more than twelve million acres – 11.5 per cent of all reservation land – had been 'restored to the public domain' in just two years.

The government tried to persuade Native Americans that allotment would be in their own best interests, and some Indians – even if they were not entirely convinced – certainly ended up believing that they had no choice but to accept the division of their land. Many tribes, however, put up stiff resistance. In 1888, in response to a plea for help from the peoples of southwestern Indian Territory, the Five Civilized Tribes (who, with their neighbours the Osages, were exempt from the provisions of the Dawes Act) convened a council of twenty-two Indian nations to try to forge a common strategy. One by one, delegates from the newly settled tribes appealed (in terms which suggest how deeply, by the end of the nineteenth century, Euro-American concepts of 'savagery' and 'civilization' had penetrated the consciousness even of 'wild' Indians) for guidance and support from their hosts. 'The white people see a great deal further than we do,' said White Man, a Kiowa-Apache. 'This may be something that will prove our ruin. We come to you as more intelligent Indians and ask your advice.' His anxiety was echoed by White Wolf, a noted Comanche war leader: 'We urge you, civilized brothers, use all your wisdom on the road for safety for our lands. With that safe, there is hope of perpetuation.'

The Indian Territory tribes decided – like Tecumseh and his followers almost a century before – that their best hope lay in uniting 'as one family under one Indian government.' 'If we combine,' said Macopia, a Potawatomi, 'we shall then be like an island in the waters. We should not be carried away, but should stand. I think if we do our best God will help us.' Even though his own people were not immediately threatened, the Creek leader Pleasant Porter agreed: 'The civilized tribes cannot escape if they fail to help you,' he told the delegates. 'The weak will fall, but not alone.' It was, he said, a 'policy untried,' but:

> All past policy has been death to the Indian. I believe this policy must come from us; from within ourselves; from our own minds. All natures grow from within. Communities have the same growth from within, not from without ... This is an important question – one of life or death.

The council appointed a committee to draft a constitution for an 'Indian union' and agreed to meet again twelve months later to finalize the plan, but it was overtaken by events. Before the next council could be held, Congress had forced the Five Civilized Tribes to sell two million acres of land and had opened it to Euro-American settlement. The following year, the area was organized as Oklahoma Territory and given power to extend its authority over the reservations of the 'wild' tribes to the west, effectively cutting the Indian Territory in half and ending all hopes of an Indian state. The Five Civilized Tribes still survived as a fragile, isolated enclave, but, as Pleasant Porter had foreseen, they could not hope to stand for long against the tide that had eroded their own land-base and swept away their neighbours.

Native American resistance in other parts of the country is more difficult to gauge, but the patchy evidence we have suggests that it was widespread and often intense. Six days before the Allotment Act was passed the Commissioner of Indian Affairs, apparently worried that tribes in the Northwest might unite in opposition to the bill, ordered federal agents in the area to prevent Native Americans leaving their reservations without permission. The next year, the Chippewa of Minnesota demonstrated their support for the idea of an Indian union by sending a message of friendship and gifts of tobacco and strings of *wampum* – another echo of the nativist movement – to the 1888 council in Indian Territory.

But, like Tecumseh and so many others before them, the Indians fighting allotment found that they were ultimately impotent: neither protests nor appeals to the US courts could avert the systematic dismemberment of their lands. Although the reform movement had been driven, in part, by concern over the 'despotism' of federal officials – Standing Bear's champion, T. H. Tibbles, memorably described them as 'a horde of minor but absolute monarchs over a helpless race' – it now used the same power to impose its own programme. As the Indians' ability to provide for themselves was progressively undermined by the loss of their land, their game and their self-confidence, the Bureau of Indian Affairs (BIA) was increasingly able to enforce its will by arbitrarily withholding government rations – an entitlement under most treaties – from 'recalcitrant' individuals. When even this failed, agents could call in the army to cow the Indians into submission.

Native Americans had been losing ground to Euro-American society for three centuries, but they had generally been able to escape the full impact of cultural collision – when they had been able to escape at all – by retreating into areas where they could continue to live, at least partially, according to their own traditions. Even now, a few groups tried the same tactic: conservative Kickapoos in western Indian Territory, for example, refused to divide up their reservation. When they were finally tricked into making allotments they gave all their money to an attorney, who promised to buy them a tribal territory in Mexico and then, in a scandal involving several prominent public figures (including at least one Senator) defrauded them utterly and left them destitute. Later still, the White River Utes left their allotted reservation *en masse* and set off for South Dakota, vainly looking for a new home where they could pursue their tribal life.

But most tribes, for whom withdrawal was no longer an option, now saw the invader's very different cultural order, with its written rules, its legal and military sanctions and its fixed boundaries of time, space and identity, carried into the very heart of their own communities. The Lakota, Luther Standing Bear, gives a glimpse of how horrifying they found it:

The [Lakota] word for custom and habit, *wouncage*, had its traditional meaning of simply following tribal usage without enforcement of any sort; so with the coming of the white man and his treaties and written declarations of various sorts, the word *woope* was coined to meet the situation. *Woope* conveyed the meaning of armed soldiery, guns, cannon, policemen, ball and chain, jails and guards, and all the cruel equipment of war that has come out of the night of life. The apparent thing to the Lakota was that the written word was in itself ineffective and without power, and *woope*, or what the white man called law, designated not order but force and disorder. Force, no matter how concealed, begets resistance.

The process of 'Americanization' began with the legalistic 'tribal rolls' drawn up by federal agents, which undermined the Indians' own sense of who they were – derived from the oral tradition and a common knowledge of clan and band affiliations – by registering them according to Anglo-American notions of family and individuality. The Northern Cheyenne, John Stands in Timber, a small child at the time of the Dawes Act, remembered:

> I got my name in the old Indian way, partly by accident. I was with my mother at Pine Ridge [a Sioux reservation] when they made the first census roll at Tongue River [the Northern Cheyenne agency], so we missed it. Otherwise I would have had my father's name, Stands Different. The government wanted to cut down on names, so at the census they called people in by families. The father would give his Indian name, which was translated, and then the rest had to use it too, with a first name to go beside it. That was how my grandfather became George Wolf Tooth and his wife Lucy Wolf Tooth. Before then all the names were different and they could change as well. My father's brothers were White Man Bear and John Crazy Mule, and George American Horse's father was American Horse but his brother was Austin Texas. I don't know how he got that one.

Just as the tribal rolls imposed an alien, rigid pattern on the fluid social life of the tribes, allotment laid a simplistic grid on the landscape, often with unforeseen consequences. (Among the Hopi, for instance, the allocation of lands customarily used by one clan to members of another heightened the traditional rivalry between them.) At the same time, the assumption of bureaucratic control over every aspect of the Indians' lives had the paradoxical – but predictable – effect of reducing many of them to the very condition of childish dependency from which it was intended to free them. According to the Lakota, Charlotte Black Elk:

> Many times families were denied rations, there were also other rules. People were put on allotments, so instead of living altogether in a community we all of a sudden were divided up. Now I come from Crazy Horse's people and so our people, because we were viewed as the hostiles, we were the first people that left the agency compound and moved on to the reservation area and we picked the Wounded Knee area and all of a sudden we were involved in the Ghost Dance. So our people, when the allotment period came, we were scattered all over the reservation, whereas Red Cloud got to keep all of his people together, American Horse got to keep all of his people . . .
>
> You were told that when once you received an allotment you shall live on that allotment and if you leave it you will no longer be an Indian if you're not tied to that allotment. And if you want to marry someone . . . let's say you lived in Wounded Knee district . . . and you wanted to marry someone in Pass Creek district, you had to go to the BIA agent and get permission to live with your spouse and leave your allotment. If you left the reservation you were denied your allotment. After being sent off to school, if it was viewed you had a sufficient amount of education you were called 'competent' and the rest of the Indians were 'incompetent'. And once you were viewed as competent then your Indian rights were removed from you, you were severed from the tribe. And so there was this whole process of enforcing, this whole wiping us out. It was a bureaucratic genocide.

In the first thirteen years of the Dawes Act alone, the government forced through nearly 33,000 allotments and 'released' some 28,500,000 acres of 'surplus' land – an achievement of which Andrew Jackson himself might have been proud. But that was only the first step on the road to 'civilization'. Under a kind of lottery system, each reservation was assigned to one or other of the Christian denominations, who could then send missionaries to lead the assault on 'paganism'. At the same time, many of the Indians' own religious and cultural practices – such as the Plains tribes' Sun Dance – were suppressed, often with the kind of wholesale brutality used by the Franciscans in seventeenth-century New Mexico. Charlotte Black Elk recalls:

> All of a sudden we were told: 'Not only will you not be able to practise your religion, but you shall also bring all of your sacred objects – sacred pipes, spirit bundles, everything that we had that was sacred – into the agency and there we shall have a grand bonfire.'
>
> Every little thing that told us we were Lakota and that was tied into our culture, our social fabric, was outlawed. The boys had their hair clipped short. We have long hair, we cut our hair only when we're in mourning, so if someone has short hair it's a sign that they have lost a loved one and you behave a certain way around them. Only practising homosexuals had their hair cut short into what's now a fashionable man's haircut, the short layered haircut.
>
> . . . It was just saying what you are is bad, everything about you is bad, your women can no longer pierce their ears, because to pierce our ears is a sign that we're entitled to hear sacred knowledge. We were told that women will no longer have the role in society that they enjoyed, that they were to become like white women, they were to be chattels, they were to be owned by men, you had to take your husband's name. So every thing about our culture was systematically to be destroyed.

As well as separating Native Americans from each other physically, the assimilation process also – and perhaps even more destructively – generated bitter social and political divisions. By using its immense power to reward and promote tribal members who collaborated – albeit often reluctantly – with the government, and to punish those who clung to their own culture, the BIA created opposing 'progressive' and 'traditional' camps which further undermined the already fragile cohesion of Indian communities. These splits were a continuation, in some respects, of the old conflict between 'nativists' and accommodationists, and tended to run along existing fault lines, such as the rift between the followers of Red Cloud and Crazy Horse among the Lakota.

In a few cases, the 'progressive/traditional' battle became deeply entangled with the tribe's own cultural system and took on a new, mythological meaning. The Hopi, for instance, whose expectation of their long-lost white brother *Pahàna* returning to bring universal peace had initially led them to welcome the Spaniards, now turned to the same tradition for an explanation of their current problems. Loloma, leader of the 'progressive' camp, who had reluctantly allowed Protestant missionaries to start working with his people, became increasingly obsessed by a sacred tablet showing the figure of a headless man. According to the *Book of the Hopi* by Frank Waters, Loloma believed it prophesied that 'a time would come when the Hopis would be forced to develop their land and lives at the dictates of a new ruler. They were not to resist, but to wait for Pahàna ... But if the Hopi leader accepted any other religion he must assent to having his head cut off. This would dispel the evil and save his people.'

For years, Loloma agonized over whether he, or his 'traditional' rival Yukioma, was the chief who had to be beheaded. Finally, in 1905, the two factions met in a ritual confrontation, which led to Yukioma and his followers being driven out and starting a new community, but neither leader was killed. As Loloma's grandson described it:

> All the Hopis know that Loloma and Yukioma were to test one another as to who would be the one with strong faith and is good for the good people ... If Loloma had been willing to have his head cut off, he would be the highest and respected man of our time and of this world. Because there was a principle behind what he said he understood, and that is the writing on the tablet he possessed. Since neither man was willing to have their head cut off, it was the beginning of other trials for the Hopi people. It was this shame or disgrace that killed him.

Probably the deepest ruptures were caused by the school system, which carried the war not only into tribal communities but into families and individuals. From the start, many of the most idealistic reformers had seen Anglo-American education as the ultimate solution to the 'Indian problem', believing that even individual ownership would not work if it only succeeded in modifying the Native Americans' external circumstances. For the three-century struggle against 'savagery' to be really successful, its final phase had to transform the inner savage, too. In 1891, Merrill Gates fervently told the Lake Mohonk conference that 'the time for fighting the Indian tribes is passed' and that what was needed now was an 'army of Christian school-teachers.'

> That is the army that is going to win the victory. We are going to conquer barbarism, but we are going to do it by getting at the barbarism one by one. We are going to do it by the conquest of the individual man, woman, and child which leads to the truest civilization. We are going to conquer the Indians by a standing army of school-teachers, armed with ideas, winning victories by industrial training, and by the gospel of love and the gospel of work.

This was not simply rhetoric. The pioneer of Native American education was Captain Richard Pratt, an army officer who had fought in the 'Indian campaigns' and had tried – with some success, according to his supporters – to 'civilize' Indian prisoners of war. In 1879, hoping to demonstrate that he could achieve even more dramatic results by applying the same methods to Native American children, he founded the Carlisle Indian School in Pennsylvania, which quickly became the model for other institutions across the country.

Pratt was a devout and sincere man whose experience commanding a contingent of black troops and a Cherokee scout detachment had led him to believe, like Whipple and the other reformers, that 'race' was a largely meaningless concept: all significant human differences, he thought, could be explained by environment alone. He liked to illustrate the point by telling the story of a 'white' child who had been captured and brought up by the Sioux. When he arrived at Carlisle, Pratt said, the boy was 'in blanket, leggings and moccasins. His hair was long and matted. He was as dirty and as much covered with vermin as any in the party. He spoke no word of English, but could speak the Sioux language with as much fluency as the others.' Although his teachers considered the child intelligent, they found that 'he learned English with less readiness and made slower progress than many of the Indian boys who came with the same party and under like circumstances.'

But although he dismissed the idea that Native Americans were *racially* inferior, Pratt shared the common conviction that their *cultures* were worthless relics from an earlier stage of development which must be destroyed. From the violent terms in which he often talked about Indian education, it is quite clear that he saw it as a continuation of armed conflict by more high-minded and effective means. When General William T. Sherman opposed his work, for instance, he angrily – and with astonishing self-confidence – wrote to President Hayes:

> I know I am at this time 'fighting' a greater number of 'the enemies of civilization' than the whole of my regiment put together, and I know that I am fighting them with a thousand more hopes of success. Knowing as I do that I am supremely right, it would be wicked to falter, even though pressure to that end came in threats from the General of the Army.

In the same vein, explaining where he differed from those who – like General Philip Sheridan – thought that 'the only good Indian was dead,' Pratt gave the assimilation movement its own brutally simple slogan: *his* aim, he said, was to 'kill the Indian and save the man.'

At Carlisle (established, appropriately enough, in an abandoned barracks), Pratt set out to achieve this transformation with ruthless efficiency. From the beginning, children were left in no doubt that they were to be stamped with a new identity. When they arrived, as well as receiving new 'American' names, the boys had their hair cut (often a deeply traumatic experience, because in many tribes long hair symbolized manhood) and were forced to put on stiff uniforms, while the girls were squeezed into Euro-American dresses. Pupils then quickly had to adapt to a strict, quasi-military régime, under which – in addition to learning English, US history and other 'American' subjects – the boys were drilled like army recruits and the girls were taught the domestic skills thought appropriate for 'civilized' wives (and servants). They were forbidden to speak their own languages, and all mention of their Native American background was discouraged.

In fairness to Pratt and his followers, this approach did not strike most contemporary observers as cruel: on the contrary, it seemed to demonstrate the generosity of an enlightened government. Carlisle was not, in many respects, very different from the expensive boarding schools to which thousands of upper-class and upper-middle-class British children were being sent at the time, and much of Pratt's language – about the need to 'mould character', for example – would have been immediately recognizable to the kind of Victorian educationalist for whom all children were 'savages'. But whereas the casualties of

English public schools – men who were permanently cold, repressed, or unable to grow up – were products of a culture that was *theirs* and that told them they were destined to rule the world, Native American schoolchildren were thrown into a hostile universe in which everything that made them what they were was systematically ridiculed and condemned. Not surprisingly, many did not survive – and many who did survive were scarred for life by the experience.

Luther Standing Bear, one of Pratt's first pupils, gives a vivid account of his time at Carlisle which is worth quoting at some length:

One day [in 1879] there came to the agency a party of white people from the East. Their presence aroused considerable excitement when it became known that these people were school teachers who wanted some Indian boys and girls to take away with them . . .

I could think of no reason why white people wanted Indian boys and girls except to kill them, and not having the remotest idea of what a school was, I thought we were going East to die. But so well have courage and bravery been trained into us that it became part of our unconscious thinking and acting, and personal life was nothing when it came time to do something for the tribe . . . in giving myself up to go East I was proving to my father that he was honoured with a brave son . . .

On our way to school we saw many white people, more than we ever dreamed existed, and the manner in which they acted when they saw us quite indicated their opinion of us. It was only about three years after the Custer battle, and the general opinion was that the Plains people merely infested the earth as nuisances, and our being there simply evidenced misjudgement on the part of Wakan Tanka. Whenever our train stopped at the railway stations, it was met by great numbers of white people who came to gaze upon the little Indian 'savages.' The shy little ones sat quietly at the car windows looking at the people who swarmed on the platform. Some of the children wrapped themselves in their blankets, covering all but their eyes. At one place we were taken off the train and marched a distance down the street to a restaurant. We walked . . . between two rows of uniformed men whom we called soldiers, though I suppose they were policemen. This must have been done to protect us, for it was surely known that we boys and girls could do no harm . . . the white people [stood] craning their necks, talking, laughing, and making a great noise. They yelled and tried to mimic us by giving what they thought were war-whoops. We did not like this, and some of the children were naturally very much frightened ... Back on the train the older boys sang brave songs in an effort to keep up their spirits and ours too. In my mind I often recall that scene – eighty-odd blanketed boys and girls marching down the street surrounded by a jeering, unsympathetic people whose only emotions were those of hate and fear; the conquerors looking upon the conquered. And no more understanding us than if we had suddenly been dropped from the moon.

At last at Carlisle the transforming, the 'civilizing' process began. It began with clothes. Never, no matter what our philosophy or spiritual quality, could we be civilized while wearing the moccasin and blanket ... Our accustomed dress was taken and replaced with clothing that felt cumbersome and awkward. Against trousers and handkerchiefs we had a distinct feeling – they were unsanitary and the trousers kept us from breathing well. High collars, stiff-bosomed shirts, and suspenders fully three inches in width were uncomfortable, while leather boots caused actual suffering. We longed to go barefoot, but were told that the dew on the grass would give us colds. That was a new warning for us, ... for in that time colds, catarrh, bronchitis, and *la grippe* were unknown. But we were soon to know them. Then, red flannel undergarments were given us for winter wear, and for me, at least, discomfort grew into actual torture ... My niece once asked me what I disliked most during those first bewildering days, and I said, 'red flannel.' ... I still remember those horrid, sticky garments which we had to wear next to the skin, and I still squirm and itch when I think of them. Of course, our hair was cut ... in some mysterious way long hair stood in the path of our development. For all the grumbling among the bigger boys, we soon had our heads shaven. How strange I felt! Involuntarily, time and time again, my hands went to my head, and that night it was a long time before I went to sleep. If we did not learn much at first, it will not be wondered at, I think. Everything was queer, and it took a few months to get adjusted to the new surroundings.

Almost immediately our names were changed to those in common use in the English language. Instead of translating our names into English and calling Zinkcaziwin, Yellow Bird, and Wanbli K'leska,

Spotted Eagle, which in itself would have been educational, we were just John, Henry or Maggie, as the case might be. I was told to take a pointer and select a name for myself from the list written on the blackboard. I did, and since one was just as good as another, and as I could not distinguish any difference in them, I placed the pointer on the name Luther . . .

Of all the changes we were forced to make, that of diet was doubtless the most injurious, for it was immediate and drastic. White bread we had for the first meal and thereafter, as well as coffee and sugar. Had we been allowed our own simple diet of meat, either boiled with soup or dried, and fruit, with perhaps a few vegetables, we should have thrived. But the change in clothing, housing, food, and confinement combined with lonesomeness was too much, and in three years nearly one half of the children from the Plains were dead and through with all earthly schools. In the graveyard at Carlisle most of the graves are those of little ones.

But the outside world was virtually unaware of the sufferings of the Carlisle students. The school's public image, bolstered by the reports of enthusiastic visitors and Pratt's own skilful use of publicity, suggested that it was making remarkable 'progress' with its 'savage' charges. To ram this point home, Pratt cannily commissioned a series of 'before and after' portraits showing the same pupils, first on their arrival at Carlisle, with long hair, wild eyes and 'outlandish' costumes, and then a few years later, after they had been transformed into docile likenesses of Euro-American students. Here, it seemed, was living proof that the experiment was working. Seeing the pictures, the ever-flowery Merrill Gates gushed:

The years of contact with ideas and with civilized men and Christian women so transform them that their faces shine with a wholly new light, for they have indeed 'communed with God.' They came children; they return young men and young women; yet they look younger in the face than when they came to us. The prematurely aged look of hopeless heathenism has given way to that dew of eternal youth which makes the difference between the savage and the man who lives in the thoughts of an eternal future.

To a modern eye, the photographs seem to tell a different story: with the benefit of hindsight, the 'wholly new light' in many of the faces looks like dazed confusion or outright unhappiness. At the time, however, they potently conveyed the welcome message that it really *was* possible to 'kill the Indian and save the man.' Pratt had showed, once and for all, said the reformer Herbert Welsh, that 'we need no longer ask the question, Can the Indian be civilized?' What was clearly needed now was a massive extension of Indian education so that *all* Native American children, and not just a select few, could be led – in the words of the Carlisle motto – 'from Savagery into Civilization'.

The last twenty years of the nineteenth century saw a sustained effort to meet this 'urgent need, and by 1900 there were more than 300 Indian schools across the country, with a combined enrolment of nearly 22,000 – close to 10 per cent of the entire Native American population at the time. Because Pratt and the bulk of the other reformers believed that Indian children could only be effectively educated away from the 'degrading' influence of the home, the overwhelming majority of pupils – almost 18,000 – were at boarding establishments modelled, to a greater or lesser extent, on Carlisle.

The scale of the Indian education campaign makes generalizations difficult. Some institutions were run directly by the government and others by missionaries; some were located on reservations and others, like Carlisle itself, in the midst of Anglo-America. Children could find themselves being taught by – at one extreme – selfless idealists who genuinely believed that they were sacrificing their lives for a noble cause and, at the other, bullying sadists who took out their inadequacies on their pupils. There was also a wide range of expectations about what Native American children were capable of achieving. Pratt saw no reason why able Indians, like their Anglo-American counterparts, should not grow up to become lawyers or doctors – a confidence that was vindicated by Carlisle graduates such as the Dakota Charles Eastman, who went to medical school – but many principals assumed that native people were fit only for manual labour and should be trained as mechanics, farmers or shop assistants. (Pupils were often required to spend half the day working on farms or in workshops, which not only taught them supposedly useful skills but also, by making them part of the workforce, reduced the school's running costs.)

But, for all their variety, the schools all ultimately pursued the same assimilationist aim, and most of them were prepared to resort to more or less brutal measures to achieve it. In 1890, for instance, the government, impatient at the slow progress being made in eliminating the use of Native American languages, instructed them that 'Pupils must be compelled to converse with each other in English, and should be properly rebuked or punished for persistent violation...' The schools implemented this rule with – in some cases – astonishing cruelty. During a series of interviews with a later generation of pupils, most of whom had been at school in the 1930s, one elderly woman, Celene Not Help Him, recalled:

> We talk Indian in the classroom, they'll ... bend a ruler and hit you in the mouth, that really hurts but I keep forgetting ... I talk Indian, and that's when they took me in a room and hit me on the back with – I don't know what it is, I think it's a razor strap, it really hurts.

Tim Giago, a graduate of a Catholic school, described a more imaginative approach:

> One of the favourite punishments of some of the Jesuits was to take the young people if they were caught speaking their language and force them to bite down on a very large rubber band ... as tight as they could. And then the rubber band would be stretched out as far as they could stretch it without it popping from his mouth and then released and it was smashed back into his face, or her face, and that was one way they tried to break us from speaking our own language.

For many Native American children, used to warm and loving homes with little or no physical punishment, the harshness of the boarding-school régime was simply incomprehensible. 'Everything was done in the military system,' recalls a Lakota, Harry Bird.

> Your bed's got to be made in military system, and your fingernails got to be clean, you got to be trim. Your shoes got to be polished, your buttons got to be shined. And they start counting: one, two, three, four ... They'd come out and say: 'Fall in! Eyes right! Forward march!' Work was the same way, that's how they trained us. And if you miss roll call they're going to ask you why, and if you don't give them the right answer they're going to put you to work. They'll give you a toothbrush to clean the bathroom with ... Or they're going to

take you out in the playground and drill the heck out of you. I thought they were crazy. They think I'm crazy, too!

If we forget and speak Indian, they kick us and whip us . . . It was cruel . . . I couldn't understand at first, I thought I come here to learn and they come and use a whip on us.

Asked about his strongest memories of boarding school, another elderly man, Harry Charger, said:

I remember the hunger, I remember the fear, I remember the loneliness and I remember the cold . . . I've seen young men's backs broke. I've seen young men's necks broke. I've seen a young man's hip-bone kicked out of place, it healed like that . . . so he couldn't move it. He ran with the rest of us like that and they called him 'Stiffy.'

Hundreds of children ran away, and some schools offered a $5 reward – like the bounty on Indian scalps during the colonial period – to anyone who rounded them up and brought them back. Thousands were killed by the now all too familiar epidemics of Euro-American diseases – particularly flu and TB – that swept through the schools. Some died for no discernible medical reason: Harry Bird remembers one friend, for instance, who baffled the doctors by simply wasting away: 'I think if you come right down to it he didn't have no kind of sickness except he is lonesome. He died of loneliness. At that time it was really rough.'

But the school experience did not merely tear Native American children away from their families and subject them to harsh physical conditions: it shifted the clash between 'savagery' and 'civilization' from the outer to the inner world, creating, for thousands of American Indians, a permanent internal frontier that could never be entirely pacified. An insight into how it affected the individual's sense of him or her self comes from the autobiography of Don C. Talayesva, a Hopi student who was sent to the Sherman Institute (named, ironically, after Pratt's old opponent, William T. Sherman) in Riverside, California, in 1906. While he never lost the liberal Pueblo attitude towards sex – despite the rules, he successfully made assignations with a series of girlfriends – he tried hard in other ways to win the teachers' approval. At YMCA meetings, he recalled:

... we were expected to stand on our feet and testify for Jesus Christ. I prepared a little sermon which I could get up and repeat: 'Well, my partners, I am asked to speak a few words for Jesus. I am glad that I came to Sherman and learned to read and cipher. Now I discover that Jesus was a good writer. So I am thankful that Uncle Sam taught me to read in order that I may understand the Scriptures and take my steps along God's road. When I get a clear understanding of the Gospel I shall return home and preach it to my people in darkness. I will teach them all I know about Jesus Christ, the Heavenly Father, and the Holy Ghost. So I advise you boys to do your best and pray to God to give us a good understanding. Then we will be ready for Jesus to come and take us up to heaven. I don't want any of my friends to be thrown into the lake of hell fire where there is suffering and sorrow forever. Amen.' At that time I was half-Christian and half-heathen and often wished that there were some magic that could change my skin into that of a white man.

But then Talayesva had an experience that permanently changed his life. Like thousands of other boarding school students, he became seriously ill and was taken to the infirmary, where his condition rapidly deteriorated. As he lay there, so close to death that the nurses combed his hair and washed his face in readiness for his funeral, he saw, he remembers, 'a tall human being standing by my bed in Katcina costume...'

[The figure] said: 'Now, my boy, you are to learn a lesson. I have been guarding you all your life, but you have been careless. You shall travel to the House of the Dead and learn that life is important. The path is already made for you. You had better hurry; and perhaps you will get back before they bury your body. I am your Guardian Spirit (*dumalaitaka*). I will wait here and watch over your body; but I shall also protect you on your journey.'

Then, Talayesva records, he was lifted out of the room and carried back to his homeland. In a sacred landscape deeply shaped by Hopi myths and beliefs, he encountered both members of his own family and a succession of potent *katcinas*. Their message was always the same: he had failed to take life seriously and had neglected his own culture. Finally, he met the leader of the clowns, who told him:

Now, my nephew, you have learned your lesson. Be careful, wise and good, and treat everybody fairly ... Your Guardian Spirit has punished you so that you may see and understand ... We are your uncles and will see that no harm comes to you. You have a long time to live yet. Go back to the hospital and to your bed. You will see an ugly person lying there; but don't be afraid. Put your arms round his neck and warm yourself, and you'll soon come to life. But hurry, before the people put your body in a coffin and nail down the lid, for then it will be too late.

Talayesva recovered, convinced that he must follow the 'Hopi Way' for the rest of his life. Reflecting later on his school days, he listed all that he had learnt:

I could talk like a gentleman, read, write, and cipher. I could name all the states in the Union with their capitals, repeat the names of all the books in the Bible, quote a hundred verses of Scripture, sing more than two dozen Christian hymns and patriotic songs, debate, shout football yells, swing my partners in square dances, bake bread, sew well enough to make a pair of trousers, and tell 'dirty' Dutchman stories by the hour. It was important that I had learned how to get along with white men and earn money by helping them. But my death experience had taught me that I had a Hopi Spirit Guide whom I must follow if I wished to live. I wanted to become a real Hopi again, to sing the good old Katcina songs, and to feel free to make love without fear of sin or a rawhide.

Talayesva was able to reintegrate himself in the Hopi community, but others were not so lucky. Some – like the minority of genuine converts among the Californian missions a century before – fulfilled the schools' expectations by successfully making the transition into the Euro-American world; at the other extreme, a few children were hidden by their parents and did not fall into the educationalists' hands at all. For the great majority, however, school was a deeply traumatic experience. Of those who survived, many were deeply confused and divided against themselves. Luther Standing Bear recalled seeing:

... the sad sight, so common today, of returned students who could not speak their native tongue, or worse yet, some who pretended they could no longer converse in the mother tongue. They had become ashamed and this led them into deception and trickery. The boys came home wearing stiff paper collars, tight patent-leather boots, and derby hats on heads that were meant to be clothed in the long hair of the Lakota brave. The girls came home wearing muslin dresses and long ribbon sashes in bright hues which were very pretty. But they were trying to squeeze their feet into heeled shoes of factory make and their waists into binding apparatuses that were not garments – at least they served no purpose of a garment, but were bordering on some mechanical device. However, the wearing of them was part of the 'civilization' received from those who were doing the same things. So we went to school to copy, to imitate; not to exchange languages and ideas, and not to develop the best traits that had come out of uncountable experiences of hundreds and thousands of years of living upon this continent.

It does not take great psychological insight to realize that, for all but an exceptional few, this drastic experiment in social engineering must have been crippling. Its subjects were systematically taught to despise everything they loved – parents, relations and culture – as 'primitive' and 'dirty', and to believe that their only hope lay in being 'made over' into a replica of the conquerors who daily tormented them. Not surprisingly, many of them ended up hating both the 'savage' and the 'civilized' – and hating, above all, themselves, the battlefield where the two sides struggled endlessly for supremacy. Caught in limbo, feeling that they were full members neither of the 'tribal' world nor of the developing Anglo-American society around them, thousands of them sank into apathy, alcoholism and despair, helping to create the cycle of abuse, dependency and self-destructive behaviour that still haunts Native American communities today. As an elderly Lakota woman puts it, reflecting on her own life:

> We never received any good from these Christians, their teaching, their beatings, they don't understand what they done to me was really made me unsure of myself . . . As I was growing up I could never participate in public because of my low self-esteem. I was afraid . . . They hurt our young and as we grew up we in turn learnt to beat our kids, which is not a good way to be . . .

I seen children being hit and forbidden to speak their language, I went through the same thing at the mission, it's left a permanent scar, I'll never forget it ... It still influences how I live every day.

*   *   *

It is not so much a question of capacity as it is of time ... You are the evolution of thousands of years, and we the evolution of thousands of years, perhaps ... We both probably started at the same point, but our paths diverged, and the influences to which we were subjected varied, and we see the result. Who can say but that we would finally have reached a stage of civilization toward which we were progressing slowly, but none the less surely, which would have suited our life better than the civilization which has been so violently and suddenly thrust upon us – a civilization which in the matter of the care and disposition of property would have suited us far better than the cumbrous and intricate methods which you have of adjusting property interests among you.

Pleasant Porter, Creek

As the government campaign against reservations in the Plains and the far west gathered pace, there was still some reluctance in Washington to launch a final assault on the remaining territory of the Five Civilized Tribes. Even so bullish a patriot as Theodore Roosevelt felt that respecting their unique status, solemnly guaranteed by successive administrations, was a matter of national honour: in a withering attack on 'foolish sentimentalists' like Helen Hunt Jackson, who dared to criticize the United States' record on Indian affairs, he conceded that:

... every good man or woman should do whatever is possible to make the government treat the Indians of the present time in the fairest and most generous spirit, and to provide against ... the wrongs with which the civilized nations of the Indian Territory are sometimes threatened.

But, in face of the mounting clamour for their land to be 'opened', such principled opposition quickly crumbled. During the 1890s, a series of measures progressively extended federal control over the internal affairs of the tribes, and, with every year, Washington came closer and closer to liquidating them altogether. The Indians lobbied tirelessly to rally their dwindling band of supporters, but in 1898 Congress finally passed the Curtis Act, which provided for the termination of their governments and the allotment of their land. It had taken just ten years for Pleasant Porter's prophecy that the Five Civilized Nations could not stand alone to be fulfilled.

The United States' action threw the tribes, yet again, into turmoil, opening up old wounds that could be traced back to the removal era and before. On the one side were the largely 'mixed-blood' 'progressives', who saw defeat as inevitable and favoured negotiation to extract the best possible terms; on the other were predominantly 'full-blood' traditionals – the 'irreconcilables' – who insisted that their treaties were sacrosanct and that the federal government would uphold them even against its own agents. Creek, Choctaw, Cherokee and Chickasaw 'irreconcilables' formed an inter-tribal 'Four Mothers Society', said at one time to number 24,000 members, to oppose dissolution, and 'full-blood' Creeks established an alternative national Council to restore the tribal régime. According to its leader, Chitto Harjo:

> He [the US government] told me that as long as the sun shone and the sky is up yonder these agreements will be kept ... He said as long as the sun rises it shall last; as long as the waters run it shall last; as long as grass grows it shall last ... He said, 'Just as long as you see light here, just as long as you see this light glimmering over us, shall these agreements be kept, and not until all these things cease and pass away shall our agreement pass away.' That is what he said, and we believed it ... We have kept every turn of that agreement. The grass is growing, the waters run, the sun shines, the light is with us, and the agreement is with us yet, for the God that is above us all witnessed that agreement.

Harjo's followers – known as 'the Snakes' – instructed their fellow-Creeks not to accept allotments or rent land to non-citizens, on pain of being arrested and whipped by a company of 'light-horsemen', and by 1901 they had become so influential that the 'progressive' tribal

government asked the federal authorities for protection against them.
When US marshal Leo Bennet seized ninety-four of the 'irreconcilables' at a meeting, they sent a letter to President McKinley which
shows their unquestioning trust in the treaties and reflects the depth of
the cultural gulf separating them from Anglo-America:

Presitent McKinley,   Hickory-town, I. T.
Washington D. C.   Jan. 26, 1901

DEAR SIR:

As I want you to hear from me Hickory-town Muskogee Indian as
we full-bloods as we held a meeting there as this the treaty between
U. S. government & Indians was made long along a I am under the
treaty raise my children a I have already told to you. I have made
elect the chief and also light horsemen ready all together made my
sign through the Indian nation but your citizen is what trouble me
so. cause my citizen in trouble your citizen arrest my citizen without
any cause, I know of. I am doind perfectly right as what treaty was.
I am not disturb any U. S. government nor break any law whatever. I
am right line. but your citizen what trouble me so I am you said to
let know what cause you to trouble so. I wrote to you about it but it
is your citizen. you have perfecly right to tend right away, as I ask to
you. as you said any-one bother in your nation I would tend to that
clear out of my nation as you said as this gentleman what bothers so
his name Dr. Bennett. U. S. marshall suppose to be. As you see this
letter to please answer it right away.

I am friendly worker for Muskogee Nation

LARTER MEKKO

As it gradually became clear, however, that the government no
longer had any intention of honouring its treaty obligations and was
determined to push ahead with liquidation at all costs, some of the
'irreconcilables' began to see removal, once again, as the only means of
ensuring their survival as nations. They pleaded with Congress for
permission to sell their allotments and use the proceeds to buy a new
territory in South America or – like their erstwhile western neighbours,
the Kickapoos – in Mexico. As the Choctaw Jacob B. Jackson eloquently
put it to a Senate committee in 1906 (again echoing the language of
the nativists a century before):

Surely a race of people, desiring to preserve the integrity of that race, who love it by reason of its traditions and their common ancestors and blood, who are proud of the fact that they belong to it may be permitted to protect themselves, if in no other way by emigration. Our educated people inform us that the white man came to this country to avoid conditions which to him were not as bad as the present conditions are to us; that he went across the great ocean and sought new homes in order to avoid things which to him were distasteful and wrong. All we ask is that we may be permitted to exercise the same privilege. We do not ask any aid from the Government of the United States in so doing. We do ask that we may be permitted, in a proper way, by protecting our own, to dispose of that which the Government says is ours, and which has been given us over our protest against the distribution . . .

. . . our social, political and personal conditions [have changed]. There is nothing left for us to do but accept conditions as they are. There is no remedy for us except removal.

If the Choctaw and Chickasaw people as a whole were willing to lose their racial status, to become by a slow process of blood mixture, and through changed conditions, white men in fact . . . we do not oppose the carrying out of their desires; but, in addition to the reasons given, we believe that the Great Father of all men created the Indian to fill a proper place in this world. That as an Indian he had certain rights, among which is a right to exist as a race, and that in the protection of that right . . . we are fulfilling the purpose of the Divine Creator of mankind.

But Jackson's appeal was ignored, perhaps because, as the historian Angie Debo perceptively suggests:

It is doubtful if the white man's conscience could have permitted the Indians to be driven a second time into exile. He could convince himself that by allotment he was conferring a real boon on the Indians, but to save his own self-respect he could not permit them to flee from his benefactions. He was happier not to be confronted with the spiritual wastage that he had wrought.

But even with the option of removal closed, many of the 'irreconcilables' clung to their treaties and steadfastly resisted dissolution. As late as 1912, for example, almost 2,000 Cherokees, despite being forced to live in abject poverty, refused to claim their allotments or to accept the per capita payments to which they were entitled from the enforced sale of tribal land, and three years later it was reported that 'seventy or eighty' Creek 'Snakes' were regularly returning cheques mailed to them by the government agent. Many other Native Americans simply sank into a state of quiet despair. The transcript of a meeting between Pleasant Porter (who, as a 'progressive', had reluctantly collaborated with the liquidation of the Five Civilized Tribes) and members of a federal commission sent to investigate the allotment process gives a revealing analysis of their predicament:

PLEASANT PORTER: ... It was a mistake to have changed these people's relations with the government ... The Indians ... haven't had time to grow up to that individuality which is necessary to merge them with the American citizen. The change came too soon for them ... There will be a remnant that will survive, but the balance is bound to perish, do what you may for them. There is that sense of right and wrong which will bind men together and preserve the peace and maintain virtue and provide for offence without. That is the institution out of which a nation grows. Each of these groups [the Five Tribes] must have had that; but you rub that out, you transplant them into what they have no knowledge of ... there is no life in the people that have lost their institutions. Evolving a thing out of itself is natural, transplanting it is a matter of dissolution, not growth. There may be a few that will grow ... but the growth will not be natural; and I don't see anything now that it has gone this far but to come to it heroically and pay no regard now to our prejudices or sentiment; do the matter up in a businesslike way, for every delay changes conditions ...

If we had our own way we would be living with lands in common, and we would have these prairies all open, and our little bunches of cattle, and would have bands of deer that would jump up from the head of every hollow, and flocks of turkeys running up every hillside, and every stream would be full of sun perch. Those things are what we were used to in our early life. That is what we would have; and not so much corn and wheat growing, and things of that kind. But we came up against it; this civilization came up against us and we had no place to go.

Q: You told us a moment ago they were dying off pretty fast?

A: Yes, sir, the old people are.

Q: Is there any special cause for that?

A: Nothing; there is no new disease; I don't see anything other than the want of hope.

But despite such evidence, few politicians were prepared to risk their careers by seriously opposing the despoliation of the Five Civilized Nations: it was, quite simply, proving far too popular and profitable. The tribes' combined estate – 19.5 million acres, or nearly half of present-day Oklahoma, with rich farmland, large pine forests, working coal-mines and untapped oil reserves – presented probably the most tempting opportunities for parting Native Americans from their property in US history. When the Curtis Act put most of this wealth up for grabs, tens of thousands of non-Indians poured into Oklahoma to get their share, either legally, through the purchase of tribal 'surpluses', or illegally, through the kind of methods used to defraud Indian allottees in the Southeast and Kansas. Within a few years, a thriving new industry had sprung up, popularly known as 'grafting off the Indians.'

From the start the 'grafters' – they seem to have accepted the title themselves – were helped, wittingly or otherwise, by actions of the federal government. For example, the President (the selfsame Theodore Roosevelt, incidentally, who, a decade earlier, had urged the prevention of 'wrongs' to the Five Civilized Tribes) vetoed a plan by the Choctaw authorities to send a commission to every settlement to assist in the selection of allotments. This effectively left tribal members open to systematic abuse by unscrupulous Euro-Americans. Resourceful scouts rounded up parties of 'full-bloods' and auctioned them to grafters – sometimes for as much as $30 a head – who helped the Indians to choose their allotments and made them sign fraudulent contracts to lease and – eventually – to sell their holdings.

When land was required urgently, the authorities could be persuaded to remove holdings from trust status by issuing blanket certificates of 'competency' to their owners; when it was more profitable to perpetuate restrictions – generally because Native Americans with property in trust needed paid legal 'guardians' – perfectly capable Indians could be declared unfit. The burgeoning oil economy, which made a small minority of holdings fabulously valuable, encouraged the growth of an entire community of professional guardians, who could be assigned by conniving judges to 'supervise' lucrative trust properties. In one case, less than nine weeks after the death of a Creek man in an accident, no fewer than eight guardians had been appointed to administer his estate – from which, of course, they were handsomely paid. The Five Civilized Tribes' immediate neighbours, the Osages, who had retained the mineral rights to their reservation when the surface was allotted, were particularly big business for racketeers. By the early 1920s, their land was generating an annual oil income of $20 million, 90 per cent of which was creamed off by non-Indians through various forms of corruption, including the murder of Osage adults to gain guardianship of their children. Between 1921 and 1925, there were twenty-four unsolved homicides in the Osage community.

Fuelled in part – especially during the Prohibition era – by the involvement of large-scale organized crime, the plunder of the Five Civilized Nations proceeded at an astonishing pace. By 1930, a century after the start of the removal process that had brought them to Indian Territory and supposedly guaranteed their survival for ever, many members of the 'liquidated' tribes, particularly among the 'full-blood' diehards, had become exiles in their own land, eking out a living – when they could live at all – in remote and unproductive areas where it took twenty acres to support one cow. More than three thousand families were receiving weekly assistance from the Red Cross to prevent them from starving to death. One Cherokee told a visiting Senate committee:

> We have not very much land left now. If we keep on selling it piece by piece, after a while the Indians will not have any land in this country, not one piece left. Now what are we going to do? Are we going to be turned out like hogs or something like that? ... If we do not have but one acre, we could live there till we starved to death or just die.

He was not exaggerating. In 1956, less than sixty years after the Curtis Act, it was found that members of the Five Civilized Tribes retained just 316,902 acres of trust land – a mere 1.6 per cent of the territory they held 'in perpetuity' in 1898.

Reviewing the whole impact of the allotment policy in 1948, a Task Force under ex-President Hoover reported:

> The practice of allotting land and issuing fee patents obviously did not make the Indians 'competent'. It proved to be chiefly a way of getting Indian land into non-Indian ownership . . .
>
> The rationalization behind this policy is so obviously false that it could not have prevailed for so long a time if not supported by the avid demands of others for Indian lands. This was a way of getting them, usually at bargain prices.

It is hard to disagree.

11. New Deal and Termination

'Let none but the Indian answer'

All sorts of feeble excuses are heard for the continued subjection of the Indian. One of the most common is that he is not yet ready to accept the society of the white man – that he is not yet ready to mingle as a social entity.

This, I maintain, is beside the question. The matter is not one of making-over the external Indian into the likeness of the white race – a process detrimental to both races. Who can say that the white man's way is better for the Indian? Where resides the human judgement with the competence to weigh and value Indian ideals and spiritual concepts; or substitute for them other values?

Then, has the white man's social order been so harmonious and ideal as to merit the respect of the Indian, and for that matter the thinking class of the white race? Is it wise to urge upon the Indian a foreign social form? Let none but the Indian answer!

Rather, let the white brother face about and cast his mental eye upon a new angle of vision. Let him look upon the Indian world as a human world; then let him see to it that human rights be accorded to the Indians. And this for the purpose of retaining for his own order of society a measure of humanity.

Luther Standing Bear, Lakota

Senator Teller was right: it was forty years before the government was finally forced to concede that compulsory assimilation had failed. Throughout the decades following the Dawes Act, the reformers stuck doggedly to their guns, insisting – in the face of growing evidence that allotment and the school system were leaving thousands of Native Americans impoverished and demoralized – that the fault lay not in the policy itself but in the way in which it was being implemented. To begin with, they found a convenient scapegoat in a series of major financial scandals involving federal agents: how could anyone expect the 'civilization' process to work if millions of dollars intended for Indian welfare and education were being systematically siphoned off by non-Indians? In 1905, however, the government effectively staunched this haemorrhage by giving the Indian Service yet another major overhaul, which finally succeeded – except in a few areas, most notably in the former Indian Territory – in rooting out widespread official corruption.

But far from bringing about an improvement, the 'purification' of the régime seemed only to hasten the dispossession and marginalization of native people. Growing numbers of Indians, bullied, cheated or bribed out of their homes, were driven to take refuge with relatives who still owned allotments and who, according to tribal tradition, could not refuse to offer them food and shelter. As a result, not only the 'feckless' landless families but also many of the 'property-owners' who were meant to spearhead the transformation of Native Americans into thrifty, prosperous citizens lived in chronic poverty. No longer able to blame dishonest government agents for this disaster, many reformers reverted to the old belief that Indians must be inherently inferior. As Walter M. Camp wrote in a report to the US Board of Indian Commissioners in 1920:

> ... I am minded to express ... my own conclusion as to the fundamental difference between the so-called 'civilized' man and the so-called 'savage,' ... The savage is concerned only with the imme-diate necessities of life, while the civilized man looks not only to the future, but beyond mere subsistence. In other words, the Indian is not a capitalist. It matters not which way this fact is stated. One might say that he is lacking in industry, and that the dearth of capital is an effect and not the cause of his poverty. Whichever way one puts it, the fact remains that it has not been in the nature of the Indians to accumulate either property or stores of goods as a reserve against adverse conditions. It has not been the way of the Indian to fortify himself against temporary failure of effort, as is the habit of the more sagacious element of civilized peoples. We thus see a difference of mental attitude as between the two races that, fundamentally, accounts for all of the industrial differences.

A small handful of critics, however, were starting to look elsewhere for an explanation of the failure of assimilation. Perhaps, they argued, the problem was neither a deficiency in the Indian's 'nature' nor the 'individual corruption' of government personnel, but a fundamental flaw in the most basic Euro-American assumptions about Native Americans. As John Collier – later Franklin Roosevelt's Commissioner of Indian Affairs – put it:

> It was not individual corruption but collective corruption; corruption which did not know it was corrupt, and which reached deep into the intelligence of a nation. It was such a collective corruption that dominated the ... Indian record of the United States. Collective corruption is more effectually carried into deed through agents not personally corrupt.

For several reasons, this idea became increasingly influential during the 1920s. The political and commercial vested interests that had so vociferously demanded the break-up of the reservations fifty years before had already had their reward – the bulk of the most valuable land and resources owned by Native Americans in 1880 was now in non-Indian hands – and there was consequently less pressure to continue the allotment policy which had made this massive transfer of wealth possible.

At the same time, the slow shift of public opinion towards a more sympathetic view of 'the Indian' was continuing. More than a generation after the massacre at Wounded Knee, there was, once again, a growing sense of nostalgia – expressed in the burgeoning conservation movement – for the romance of 'the frontier' and the beauty of the 'unspoiled wilderness'. Native Americans, far from still being seen as a military threat, had, in fact, demonstrated their 'patriotism' by volunteering in their thousands to fight *for* the United States during the First World War, even though most of them, as non-citizens, were not eligible for the draft. In 1924 the government acknowledged this contribution by granting citizenship to all Indians, irrespective of whether or not they had proved their 'competence'. (In the event, many Native Americans – particularly those who, like the Iroquois, jealously defended their own sovereignty – were less than delighted with this 'gift', which they saw as something of a poisoned chalice.)

The Great War also affected attitudes in another, less definable way. Although the United States was generally less traumatized by the experience than most of the other combatants – it suffered far fewer casualties, and emerged from the conflict an undisputed world power – it was to some extent touched by the same mood of melancholy self-examination that gripped many European countries following the Armistice in 1919. The slaughter of the Western Front – in which, according to Allied propaganda, even 'racially advanced' Germans had behaved like 'savages' – and the turmoil of the Russian Revolution raised disturbing doubts about the superiority of European civilization and the power of capitalism.

In the United States, this pessimism was, to begin with, only a muted counterpoint to the 'ballyhoo' of the Twenties, when frenetic economic growth, the rise of mass entertainment and a string of dazzling technological achievements gave most Americans an unprecedented feeling of national wellbeing. It was strong enough, however, to make a small but influential minority – including writers such as the fashionably nihilistic F. Scott Fitzgerald and the social moralist Sinclair Lewis – question what they saw as the greed and empty materialism of American life. During the post-war decade, this general sense of unease became increasingly focused on 'the Indian question', thanks largely to the efforts of one man: John Collier.

Because he was such a pivotal figure, whose personality and achievements still generate immense controversy and whose legacy, even today, continues to dominate the debate over the place of Native Americans in US society, it is important to look briefly at Collier's background and career. His disenchantment with 'modern' civilization, and his interest in more 'traditional' cultures, were deeply rooted in his own early experience. In the 1890s, while he was still a teenager, his prosperous Atlanta family was ruined by a financial scandal which drove his mother to death through laudanum addiction and his father to suicide. Reduced to a state of 'deep physical and spiritual depression,' the young Collier vowed never to seek 'success in the society' that had destroyed his parents. He sought solace in long camping trips to the Appalachian mountains, where he found a sense of 'cosmic consciousness' in his own solitude and the beauty of the landscape that was to stay with him for the rest of his life.

In 1902, Collier entered Columbia University, and for the next two decades he restlessly explored the ideas of a range of writers – Nietzsche, Kropotkin, William Morris – who shared his distrust of industrial society and his hunger for a world of small communities based on some richer and more satisfying values than the aggressive individualism of *laissez-faire* capitalism. But although he was attracted by the backward-looking idealism of the Arts and Crafts movement (he wrote several *faux* pre-Raphaelite poems, modelled on Morris, crammed with images like 'dawn flowery sky meadows' and 'pungent fog-wreaths cold'), Collier did not simply reject modernity altogether. While he disliked the biological determinism of Social Darwinists such as Herbert Spencer, he passionately believed that Science, if it were controlled 'by the collective mind of society,' could be a force for good, enabling humanity to direct its own evolution.

Collier drew these disparate strands into a personal philosophy that directly challenged the prevailing assimilationist ideology of the time. Concerned that the melting pot and unbridled industrialization were creating an 'unplanned and inhuman urban America,' in which a mass of rootless individuals, connected to each other only by economic ties, were no more than slaves of the machine, he argued that immigrants to the United States should preserve and celebrate their own cultural traditions. Only by continuing to practise their languages, dances and social customs, he thought, could they avoid losing the 'ancestral' knowledge of how human beings can live together as true members of a society.

For almost two decades, Collier moved from project to project, working as a journalist, a social worker and an educator, looking for a cause that would allow him to implement his ideas. The results were almost always unsuccessful and sometimes farcical: in 1915, for example, his plan to hire the New York city armoury to teach '1000 working-class girls' how to dance misfired when a drunken Isadora Duncan made sexual advances to the mayor. A close friend of Collier's, Mabel Dodge, gives a vivid picture of him at the time as 'a small blond Southerner, intense, preoccupied,' who, 'Because he could not seem to love his own kind of people, and . . . was full of a reformer's enthusiasm for humanity . . . turned to other races and worked for them.' She describes, with some wonderment, his quixotic efforts to turn the tide

of Americanization by urging immigrants to 'keep their national dress
. . . their diets, their religion, and all their folk ways.'

It was Mabel Dodge who finally introduced Collier to the 'race' that
became the grand passion of his life. When he was on his way to
Mexico after yet another professional setback (this time with immigrants in California), she invited him to visit her in the artists' colony
that had sprung up around Taos Pueblo in New Mexico. Watching a
group of Taos Indians performing the spectacular Red Deer Dance, he
was 'storm-shaken' by an almost mystical revelation:

> . . . through a multitudinous, stern, impassioned collective outgiving,
> the tribe's soul appeared to wing into the mountain, even to the
> Source of Things.
>
> . . . a whole race of men, before my eyes, passed into ecstasy through
> a willed discipline, splendid and fierce, yet structural, an objectively
> impassioned discipline which was a thousand or ten thousand years old,
> and as near to the day of first creation as it had been at the prime.
>
> Here was a reaching to the fire-fountain of life through a deliberate
> social action employing a complexity of many arts. Here was the
> psychical wonder-working we think we find in Greek drama as lived
> out in Athens four hundred years before Christ. And here it was a
> whole community which entered into the experience and knew it as
> a fact. These were unsentimental men who could neither read nor
> write, poor men who lived by hard work, men who were told every
> day in all kinds of unsympathetic ways that all they believed in and
> cared for had to die, and who never answered back. For these men
> were at one with their gods.

Here, at last, it seemed, was what Collier had been looking for: a
'Red Atlantis' that still retained the primordial secret of communal life.
Through all the 'long, remorseless course of events, the social destruction piled on biological destruction which the white man [has] wrought
upon the Indian,' Native Americans had 'kept the faith' by holding on
to the 'most profound of their spiritual possession':

> That possession is a way of life at once simple, since it is disciplined,
> and complex: it involves world-view and sentiment of self; institution-
> alized tradition and symbol-invested belief, which implicitly or
> explicitly realizes man as a co-partner in a living universe – man and

nature intimately co-operant and mutually dependent. It is a way of life which realizes the individual and his society as wholly reciprocal and both of them as drawing value and power from the racial and cosmic past and transmitting value and power to the racial and cosmic future, and past and future are not only that which in linear time-sequence has been or is yet to be, but are propulsive, efficient, living reality here and now.

Collier's response to Native Americans belongs, undoubtedly, to the long European tradition of seeing the 'Indian' as living in a 'Golden Age': his description of aboriginal Californians, for instance – 'peoples joyously hospitable who seemed as free as birds, whose speech and colours were like the warbling and plumage of birds' – strikingly echoes Sir Francis Drake's account almost four centuries before. But unlike earlier generations (as well as most of his own contemporaries), Collier did not believe that the 'Indian spirit' was, for all its attractions, inevitably doomed to extinction: on the contrary, he thought that it could and must be preserved, not only as a belated act of justice to Native Americans themselves, but because it was what 'our sick world most needs.' Convinced that 'Could we make it our own, there would be an eternally inexhaustible earth and a forever lasting peace,' he solemnly dedicated himself, with the evangelical determination of the convert, to keeping it alive for the benefit of *all* humanity. His fervour prompted D. H. Lawrence, who was living at Taos at the time, to warn – some would say presciently – that Collier could destroy the Indians by 'setting the claws of his own benevolent volition into them.'

After the false starts and disappointments of his earlier career, Collier had finally found a cause that enlisted all the contradictory elements of his complex nature – visionary mysticism and prophetic zeal, bureaucratic efficiency and analytical intelligence, a passion for justice and a politician's gift for propaganda and in-fighting – and he embarked on his self-appointed crusade with unflagging, monomaniacal energy.

❖   ❖   ❖

Collier's first major test came in 1922, when Congress attempted to defuse a tense situation in New Mexico by passing the Bursum Bill, which effectively deeded 60,000 acres of Pueblo land to Anglo and Hispanic squatters. This move was a flagrant breach of the Treaty of Guadeloupe Hidalgo, which committed the United States to respecting Spanish and Mexican land 'grants' to the Indians, and threatened to destroy the Pueblos' desert-farming way of life.

Collier immediately set about rallying opposition. Travelling from village to village, he alerted the Indians to the danger they faced and encouraged them to unite as – in the words of one leader – 'we did long ago when we drove the Spaniards out.' Together with a handful of other non-native advisers, he helped the Pueblos to draft a moving response to the bill which cannily appealed directly to 'the people of the United States':

> We the Pueblo Indians, have always been self-supporting and have not been a burden on the government. We have lived in peace with our fellow Americans even while we have watched the gradual taking away of our lands and waters. Today, many of our pueblos have the use of less than an acre per person of irrigated land, whereas in New Mexico ten acres of irrigated land are considered necessary for a white man to live on. We have reached a point where we must either live or die.
>
> Now we discover that the Senate has passed a bill, called the Bursum Bill, which will complete our destruction ... this bill will deprive us of our happy life by taking away our lands and water and will destroy our Pueblo government and our customs which we have enjoyed for hundreds of years, and through which we have been able to be self-supporting and happy down to this day.
>
> . . .
>
> The Pueblo, as is well known, existed in a civilized condition before the white man came to America. We have kept our old customs and lived in harmony with each other and with our fellow Americans.
>
> This bill will destroy our common life and will rob us of everything which we hold dear, our lands, our customs, our traditions.
>
> Are the American people willing to see this happen?

Collier used his immense flair for publicity to carry this message to a broad public, addressing meetings, dashing off indignant articles and exploiting his personal connections with organizations such as the General Federation of Women's Clubs to create a formidable pro-Pueblo alliance. When, partly at his instigation, seventeen Pueblo delegates travelled to Washington to testify before the Senate Committee on Public Lands and Surveys, Collier arranged for them to stop *en route* in Chicago and New York, where – like Standing Bear more than a generation before – they drew large and enthusiastic audiences. At the stock exchange, because of a rule forbidding speeches, they sang and played their drums, driving their listeners 'wild' and prompting a flood of 'kill the Bursum bill' telegrams to Congress.

In the face of this relentless campaign, the Secretary of the Interior, Albert Fall, was unable to secure passage of the bill, and in March 1923, already buffeted by the financial scandals of the Harding administration, he resigned. (He was later tried and imprisoned for corruption.) The following year, Congress passed the Pueblo Lands Act, a compromise measure which offered the Pueblos greater legal protection and 'reimbursed' them for any land lost.

But the assault on the Pueblos was not over. Forced to back down over the land issue, the Bureau of Indian Affairs turned its fire on the 'pagan' dances and rituals at the heart of their social and political life. As early as 1920, the veteran founder of the strongly assimilationist Indian Rights Association, Herbert Welsh, had suggested that the government should act to lift the Pueblos 'out of a stone-age condition of human society by the spiritual force of the Christian religion.' Most Pueblo Indians were, of course, Catholics, but Welsh, a staunch protestant from the Dawes era, felt that the Spanish missionaries had not done enough to stamp out their 'heathen' customs. On the basis of a report by a clergyman working for the Interior Department, he claimed that secret ceremonies such as the Hopi Snake Dance involved obscene sexual practices which transgressed the 'moral and legal restraints imposed by marital obligations' and which must be suppressed.

At a time when the United States was being swept by successive waves of paranoia and moral panic – the 'Red Scare', anxiety about immigration and widespread demands for the prohibition of alcohol – this idea struck a popular chord. As the Bursum Bill began to flounder, the Bureau attempted to discredit both the Indians themselves and the 'agents of Moscow' who supported them by circulating a lurid account of Pueblo ceremonies, accompanied by what Collier called 'unprintable pornographic exihibits.' In February 1923, the Commissioner of Indian Affairs, Charles Burke (who a few years later publicly told the people of Taos that their religion made them 'half-animals') sent a warning to the Pueblos:

> I could issue an order against these useless and harmful perform-ances, but I would much rather have you give them up of your own free will and, therefore, I ask you now in this letter to do so. If at the end of one year the reports which I receive show that you are doing as requested, I shall be very glad, but if the reports show that you reject this plea, then some other course will have to be taken.

Once again, Collier was at the forefront of the campaign against the BIA. In May 1923 he founded the American Indian Defense Association (AIDA), a new, radically different 'Indian rights' organization pledged to preserving rather than destroying Native American cultures and beliefs, and became its first Executive Director. The same month, he helped the Council of All the New Mexico Pueblos to prepare a 'Declaration, addressed to the Pueblo Indians, to all Indians, and to the People of the United States' in which they vigorously defended their religion:

> We have met because our most fundamental right of religious liberty is threatened and is actually at this time being nullified. And we make as our first declaration the statement that our religion to us is sacred and is more important to us than anything else in our life. The religious beliefs and ceremonies and forms of prayer of each of our pueblos are as old as the world, and they are holy. Our happiness, our moral behaviour, our unity as a people, and the peace and joyfulness of our homes, are all a part of our religion and are dependent on its continuation.
>
> To pass this religion, with its hidden sacred knowledge and its many forms of prayer, on to our children, is our supreme duty to our ancestors and to our own hearts and to the God whom we know. Our religion is a true religion, and it is our way of life.

The Declaration went on to rebut, 'as untrue, shamefully untrue and without any basis of fact or appearance, and contrary to the abundant testimony of White scholars who have recorded our religious customs,' the accusation that the 'secret dance is ... little less than a ribald system of debauchery.' It concluded with another well-judged appeal to 'the citizens of the United States' and to other Native Americans:

> We are but a few people, in the pueblos. We have inherited and kept pure from many ages ago a religion which, we are told, is full of beauty even to White persons. To ourselves at least, our religion is more precious than even our lives. The fair play and generosity of the American people came to the rescue of the Pueblos when it was proposed to take away their lands. Will the American people not come to our rescue now, when it is proposed to take away our very souls?
>
> Most of all we say to all the Pueblos whom we represent – to all of the ten thousand Pueblo Indians, and likewise to the Hopi and Navajo Indians: This is the time of the great question. Shall we peacefully but strongly and deathlessly hold to the religion of our fathers, to our own religion, which binds us together and makes us the brothers and children of God? There is no future for the race of the Indians if its religion is killed. We must be faithful to each other now.

But the Pueblos and their allies soon learnt that it was easier to generate popular support over the Bursum Bill, which could be presented as a straightforward question of property rights, than over the far murkier and more emotive issue of religious freedom. The greater public sympathy for Native Americans was not, in general, accompanied by deeper understanding of their problems: indeed, for most non-native people, 'the Indian' had already become an almost invisible figure, represented only by the simplistic images of films like Richard Dix's *The Vanishing American*, which – clearly echoing novels such as *The Last of the Mohicans* and anticipating the later direction of Hollywood – placed him squarely in a disappearing past. For the vast majority of Americans, 'helping' Native Americans still meant easing their transition into the mainstream rather than encouraging them to hope for a 'future for the race of the Indians.' The opponents of the Pueblos, a powerful coalition of government and churches, were able to tap a rich seam of prejudice and fear among people who believed that to question the country's 'civilizing' mission was, in some way, to challenge the idea of the United States itself. Borrowing some of Collier's own tactics – they arranged, for instance, for 'progressive' Christian Indians to speak at public meetings – they managed to whip up widespread public concern about the perpetuation of 'pagan superstition' in 'modern' America.

Almost alone, Collier stuck resolutely to his very different – and, in retrospect, genuinely modern – vision of a plural, multi-cultural United States in which distinct Native American societies would have a permanent and important place. Convinced that religion was even more crucial to the Indians' survival than land, he argued that it was unconstitutional for the government to interfere with their beliefs and practices, a view which pitted him not only against old-style, evangelical 'friends of the Indian' like Herbert Welsh – who had actually opposed the government over the Bursum Bill – but also against many of his supporters in organizations such as the General Federation of Women's Clubs.

Undaunted, Collier tightened his grip on the American Indian Defense Association by (sometimes ruthlessly) driving out less radical members, and, over the next ten years, forged it into a formidable political assault weapon. Rather than simply responding piecemeal to individual policies, he relentlessly criticized the whole apparatus of Indian Affairs for failing to protect Native Americans and for systematically denying them rights that other US citizens took for granted. He started his own magazine, *American Indian Life*, to publicize the case for reform, and became a consummate lobbyist in Washington, where his passionate, well-researched testimony won him growing Congressional support. By 1926, he and his allies had not only defeated the government's attempts to suppress Pueblo religion but had also exposed such glaring deficiencies in its handling of Native American health, education and resources that the Secretary of the Interior asked Lewis Meriam, director of the Institute for Government Research, to conduct a full-scale investigation into the Indian Service.

In 1928, Meriam published his findings in *The Problem of Indian Administration*. The first detailed analysis of what had happened to Native Americans since the end of the 'Indian Wars', it made shocking reading for those who still believed that 'the Indian' was somewhere out west, happily maturing into a 'modern citizen' under the guidance of a benign government. It revealed that most Indians were poor and many were destitute; that their diet, housing, sanitation and health were appalling, with high infant mortality rates and epidemics of tuberculosis and trachoma on many reservations; that 'no sanatorium in the Indian Service meets the minimum requirements of the American Sanatorium Association'; that the care and education of native children in boarding schools were 'grossly inadequate' and that Native Americans generally were discontented, unhappy and lacking in hope and initiative. Meriam laid much of the blame on inadequate funding, but he also conceded that the allotment policy had not recognized 'the strength of the ancient system of communal ownership' and had consequently:

> ... largely failed in the accomplishment of what was expected of it. It has resulted in much loss of land and an enormous increase in the details of administration without a compensating advance in the economic ability of the Indian ... It almost seemed as if the government assumed that some magic in individual ownership would in itself prove an educational civilizing factor, but unfortunately this policy has for the most part operated in the opposite direction.

Ideologically, the Meriam Report was a strange hybrid, lurching uneasily between the assimilationist views of old-style reformers like Herbert Welsh and the very different vision of Collier and his supporters. On the one hand, it declared that 'the fundamental requirement' of Indian policy was to enable Native Americans to be 'absorbed into the prevailing civilization or be fitted to live in the presence of that civilization at least in accordance with a minimum standard of health and decency'; on the other, it urged 'more understanding of and sympathy for the Indian point of view,' even acknowledging that:

> Leadership will recognize the good in the educational and social life of the Indians in their religion and ethics, and will seek to develop it and build on it rather than to crush out all that is Indian. The Indians have much to contribute to the dominant civilization ...

Although Collier cavilled at some of the report's findings – he thought, in particular, that it was far too lenient to Burke and other members of the government – he welcomed it as clear evidence that his American Indian Defense Association and its allies had at last begun to achieve a 'provisional revolution' in Indian Affairs. The most damning indictment of government policy since Helen Hunt Jackson's *A Century of Dishonor* almost forty years before, it 'blasted apart', he believed, the 'dungeon' surrounding 'the Indian question' and opened the way to far-reaching reform. When Herbert Hoover became President a few months later, Collier was hopeful that conditions were at last 'favourable to a large reorganization' of the system.

The Hoover administration did adopt some of Meriam's recommendations, but its attempts at change were frustrated by continuing corruption and by the assimilationist Secretary of the Interior, Ray Lyman Wibur, who thought that rather than bolstering Native American societies, the government should treat 'the Indian' like a dependent child, giving it 'a pickle and let[ting] it howl.' Collier found Wilbur's old-fashioned view that 'the redman's civilization must be replaced by the white man's' and 'the Indian must give up his role as a member of the race that holds aloof, while all other races enter into our melting pot' profoundly disappointing, and by 1930 he and the American Indian Defense Association were once again on the offensive, defiantly harrying the BIA at every turn. In 1932, he supported the Democratic presidential candidate, Franklin D. Roosevelt, 'a liberal in thought and heart' and a believer in 'scientific government'.

Roosevelt rewarded this confidence by appointing as Secretary of the Interior Harold L. Ickes, a founder member of the American Indian Defense Association, who promptly – in the face of implacable opposition from more 'moderate' Indian Rights organizations and from a host of powerful political and commercial enemies – nominated Collier as Commissioner of Indian Affairs. To his own surprise (even he, realizing that his record might make him a liability, had originally favoured looking for a less contentious and 'politically stronger' contender for the job), Collier finally found himself, after more than a decade of tireless campaigning, with his hands on the levers of power.

His appointment could not have come at a more opportune time. With the Wall Street collapse of 1929, the nagging sense that there was something amiss with American civilization was no longer the preserve of a privileged few: it had become part of the daily experience of families across the country. If the United States, the land of opportunity, could not provide jobs for millions of people who yearned only to work, then the 'American Dream' itself had failed.

Many members of the intelligentsia, such as John Steinbeck (whose *Grapes of Wrath* created some of the most enduring images of the Depression), as well as hundreds of thousands of workers and the unemployed, turned to socialism or communism for a solution. Some writers and thinkers went even further, questioning the whole basis of Euro-American history itself. For perhaps the first time since the start of English settlement, they began to see the despised and almost-exterminated cultures of Native America not merely as doomed relics of the past – whose destruction, however sad, was the inevitable price of Progress – but as a possible salvation for the increasingly bewildered civilization that had supplanted them. In Nathanael West's wild satire *A Cool Million*, for instance, published in 1934, the Native American character Israel Satinpenny incites his fellow-Indians to rebel against 'that abomination of abominations, the paleface':

> In our father's memory this was a fair, sweet land, where a man could hear his heart beat without wondering if what he heard wasn't an alarm clock, where a man could fill his nose with pleasant flower odours without finding that they came from a bottle. Need I speak of springs that had never known the tyranny of iron pipes? Of deer that had never tasted hay? Of wild ducks that had never been banded by the U.S. Department of Conservation?
>
> In return for the loss of these things, we accepted the white man's civilization, syphilis and the radio, tuberculosis and the cinema. We accepted his civilization because he himself believed in it. But now that he has begun to doubt, why should we continue to accept? His final gift to us is doubt, a soul-corroding doubt. He rotted this land in the name of progress, and now it is he himself who is rotting. The stench of his fear stinks in the nostrils of the great god Manitou.

And two years later, in *The Redman's Message*, Ernest Thompson Seton proclaimed:

> The Civilization of the Whiteman is a failure; it is visibly crumbling around us. It has failed at every crucial test . . .

Our system has broken down ... Wherever pushed to a logical conclusion, it makes one millionaire and a million paupers ...

We offer you the Message of the Redman, the Creed of Manhood. We advocate his culture as an improvement on our own, if perchance by belated repentance, remorse, restitution, and justification, we may save ourselves from Divine vengeance and total destruction ... so that we may have a chance to begin again with a better, higher thought.

This climate of doubt and confusion created, almost overnight, a receptive audience for Collier's ideas. It is hard to think of another period in US history when a senior political figure could have publicly declared, as Collier did in 1934, that, 'We – I mean our white world in this century – are a shattered race – psychically, religiously, socially and esthetically shattered, dismembered, directionless,' and that, as a result, Western civilization should:

... examine with a wondering and tender concern, and with some awe, these Indian communities which by virtue of historical accidents and their own unyielding wills are even today the expressions, even today the harborers, of a great age of integrated, inwardly-seeking life and art. What seed are they keeping, for the soil and climate of a future age of our own which may become a possible soil and climate for them? ... We may be helped through knowing them, and even through trying to help them, in their desperately unequal struggle for continued existence.

Determined to seize the opportunity which this unique moment had given him, Collier set out to challenge the whole thrust of North American history over the past 450 years.

✻ ✻ ✻

The Indians were descendants of peoples who knew, before the onslaught of a foreign culture, the freedom of the eagle on wing all across the North American continent. Under Crazy Horse they beat the pants off Custer on the Little Big Horn in a final attempt to preserve it. They won the battle but lost the war. They died mercilessly with Chief Big Foot at Wounded Knee because they did not have that freedom.

The 1930s held a ray of hope that they would again see some of the freedom reappear . . .

Benjamin Reifel, Sioux

The unique events of two generations, culminating in a crisis of political necessity, catapulted this man into a position of historic importance. He rode to office on the wings of those events. He stood on the shoulders of many who had gone before and made himself into a figure of national importance and influence. But John Collier betrayed us. His autocratic administration and repressive administration damned him before the Indians, creating that fault line in historic estimates of Collier and his works which finally cast him from his seat at the side of the white man's Jesus Christ, where some historians have mistakenly placed him.

Rupert Costo, Cahuilla

My common sense tells me that John Collier is a member of the White Race, but my heart tells me John Collier is an Indian. Yes, indeed, John Collier is an Indian with a heart as big and broad as the day is long. This Indian is as capable as any class of people on earth – the only trouble is we haven't had the chance to prove it to the white man. We have been like a smudge. The blanket has been put over us and the smoke couldn't be seen, but through the provisions of [Collier's reforms] . . . we see a new day dawning.

Reverend C. Aaron, Stockbridge Indian (Mahican), 1934

For all his high-flown rhetoric, Collier was astute enough to know that his vision could only be implemented through a carefully managed programme of pragmatic, politically acceptable measures. While inveighing against earlier reformers like Dawes and Pratt, he hoped to win support for overturning their legacy by appealing, as they had, to a mixture of philanthropy and financial self-interest. Ending forcible assimilation, he argued, would not only be better for Native Americans but would also, in the long term, cost the United States less than any of the alternatives – a claim that was strengthened by the revelation that, despite Dawes' extravagant promises, the country was now actually spending more on Native Americans than it had before the Allotment Act. He shrewdly outlined his goal as being:

> . . . so productively to use the monies appropriated by the Congress for Indians as to enable them, on good, adequate lands of their own, to earn decent livelihoods and lead self-respecting, organized lives in harmony with their own aims and ideals, as an integral part of American life. Under such a policy, the ideal end result will be the ultimate disappearance of any need for government aid or supervision. This will not happen tomorrow; perhaps not in our lifetime; but with the revitalization of Indian life due to the action and attitudes of this government . . ., that aim is a probability.

The centrepiece of Collier's policy was the Indian Reorganization Act (IRA), an ambitious package of interrelated reforms designed to halt and reverse the destruction of Native American communities. To stem the continuing erosion of the Indian land-base, all further allotment was prohibited, the trust status on existing holdings was extended indefinitely and $2 million a year was appropriated for the purchase of additional land. At the same time, to help them regain at least some measure of autonomy and self-sufficiency, tribes were encouraged to organize their own governments and to establish business corporations, and – since most reservations were chronically poor and undeveloped – a revolving loan fund of $10 million was set up to provide capital for plant and equipment.

Perhaps inevitably, given that it seemed a kind of roadblock across the path of 'Progress' – an ideal still cherished by millions of Americans even in the depths of the Depression – the IRA encountered stiff opposition, and steering it through Congress took all Collier's formidable skills of persuasion and compromise. A comparison of his initial proposals – forty-eight pages, with four major titles and numerous subdivisions – with the much slimmer and more modest measure that was finally enacted throws his intentions into sharp relief and starkly reveals what some people see as the fatal paradox at the heart of his policy. His original version was both simultaneously more generous and more restrictive than the final bill: it would have given the tribes far greater freedom – amounting, in effect, to home rule – but then promptly snatched it away by making almost every important decision subject to approval by the Secretary of the Interior. Critics were quick to seize on this as evidence that, for all his vaunted liberalism, Collier was fundamentally just as arrogant and dictatorial as Dawes had been: he wanted the tribes to have democracy, but only if he could ensure that they used it to do what he considered best.

There was, undoubtedly, an authoritarian streak in some of Collier's provisions, particularly those dealing with land. He was absolutely convinced that a communal land-base was essential to tribal survival, but the Dawes Act had left many reservations hopelessly chequer-boarded and fragmented. Often, the best land had been removed from trust status and sold, and where restrictions had remained in force there were sometimes so many heirs to a particular allotment after one or two generations that it could not be divided up and had to be leased to non-Indians (with the rental, in some cases, amounting to less than the cost of the stamp required to send it). On the Oglala Sioux' reservation at Pine Ridge in South Dakota, for instance, more than a quarter of the allotted land had been sold, and a further 36 per cent was in heirship status and rented out on a more or less permanent basis to Anglo-American ranchers. To repair this kind of damage, Collier thought the Commissioner of Indian Affairs should have the power to buy individual allotments, even when the owners did not want to sell, so that they could be reconsolidated into coherent tribal holdings.

But in other respects, the comparison with Dawes seems profoundly unjust. While the reformers of the 1880s had believed – in the words of the Reverend George Ellis – that the United States had the right 'to say what we intend to do, and what they must and shall do' and need not consult 'to any troublesome extent, the views and inclinations of Indians whom we are to manage,' Collier was determined that Native Americans should understand and assent to the policies that affected them. Unlike any previous Commissioner of Indian Affairs, he had the courage – and the self-confidence – to argue his case before native people themselves, organizing a series of regional 'Indian Congresses' at which he explained his proposed legislation and invited comments and suggestions from tribal representatives. Some of the modifications to the original 'Collier Bill' – including the removal of the contentious clause allowing the mandatory reincorporation of allotments into the tribal land-base – were made in direct response to Indian concerns raised at these meetings.

For Collier, in fact, the whole direction of post Civil War policy, with its assumption that Native Americans were merely individual 'wards' to be treated as the United States saw fit, had been an aberration. Historically, both the colonial authorities and the federal government had always considered 'Indian nations' to be – in the words of Chief Justice John Marshall's celebrated decision a century before – 'distinct, independent political communities, retaining their original natural rights, as the undisputed possessors of the soil, from time immemorial,' and this status had not been diminished by the tribes' enforced acceptance of US domination, because 'a weak state, in order to provide for its safety, may place itself under the protection of one more powerful, without stripping itself of the right of government, and ceasing to be a state.' This idea was not simply a matter of legal theory: as men like Sir Edmund Andros and Sir William Johnson had been quick to grasp, its echoes of the way the weaker members of a confederacy allied themselves to a powerful *sachem* had made it a natural template for European–Native American relations during the colonial and post-revolutionary period, and it was the basis for most of the hundreds of treaties by which the United States had acquired much of North America. Collier hoped that the Indian Congresses would be a first step towards restoring this bilateral relationship – in which both sides, in theory, at least, had a legitimate voice – which had effectively been in abeyance since the suspension of treaty-making in 1871.

But he also had another, more immediate motive for taking his message directly to the Indians. As news of his proposals spread, enemies from the Coolidge and Hoover eras, gleefully seizing the opportunity to attack him as relentlessly as he had attacked them, joined forces with old-style 'friends of the Indian', missionaries, disgruntled Indian Service personnel and racketeers to condemn his policy as a return to 'degrading tribalism'. Their more or less malicious – and often wildly inaccurate – rumours about his intentions found a receptive audience not among Anglo-Americans but also in many Native American communities, whose long experience of 'white' duplicity and betrayal had left them understandably suspicious of any new initiative by the government. Collier believed that by talking to them in person and demonstrating his willingness to listen he could persuade the majority of Native Americans to support him, thus undermining one of his critics' central arguments: that he was imposing his own ideas on Indians against their will.

It was a formidable task. Collier's description of the first Congress, at Rapid City in South Dakota, gives a vivid sense of the problems he faced. It started, he reported:

> ... amid a cloud of grimly silent fears. The lands of the landed Indians were to be confiscated, they feared, and given to the landless ones. The Indians were to be deprived of their citizenship and of the franchise. The Indians were to be interned, fenced in like buffaloes, compelled back into some (they were told) ancient and outmoded life. The Commissioner, it was said, had bribed a tribal leader, by offering him four sections of land, to support the Indian Reorganization Act.

Collier dismissed these ideas as irresponsible scaremongering, but countered them by playing on Indian anxieties himself. 'In the history of countries and peoples,' he told his listeners, 'there comes a time when everything is possible,' and with a passion that led critics to accuse him of emotional blackmail, he implored them not to let their 'moment of destiny' pass by 'unused.' As he explained to the troubled Oklahoma meeting:

> If there ever will be a time when the Indians of the United States can get what they need, now is the time. Now is the time when the government is doing big things in a generous way, making fundamental changes through the country. Three or four years from now conditions may have changed. There may not be the same spirit at work ... It may prove to be a case of now or never, and surely it is a time for every Indian to think seriously. Surely it is a time for every Indian to think of his children as well as of himself.

Although he could not allay all the Indians' fears – some 'progressives' remained convinced that he was trying to drive them 'back to the blanket', while at the other extreme a number of 'traditionals' clung to the belief that the IRA was just another strategy for extending 'white' control over their lives and land – Collier's evident sympathy, sincerity and grasp of the issues seem to have won over a majority of the delegates. As one of them, the Winnebago Mitchell Red Cloud, put it: 'Justice may be blind, but Mr. Roosevelt and Mr. Collier are excellent eye doctors.' His remarkable success in turning the tide of Native American opposition is reflected in a pre-ratification straw poll taken after the Indian Congresses: seventy-four tribes, with a total population of 158,279, voted to support his Bill, while only eighteen, with a population of 21,884, voted against. As he had calculated, this overwhelming endorsement helped him to swing the House and Senate Indian Affairs Committees behind reform.

Undaunted by his bruising struggle over the IRA, Collier energetically embarked on a whole series of other measures to strengthen native societies and to help define a permanent place for them in American life. In the face of bitter hostility from missionaries, he insisted that Indians were entitled to the same religious freedom as other US citizens and that native schoolchildren should no longer be forced to attend Christian services if they or their parents objected. At the same time, concerned that the boarding schools were disrupting family life and sapping native culture, he slashed their enrolment (from 22,000 to 14,000 in the first two years alone) and progressively shifted responsibility for Indian education to reservation day schools or, where possible, to local public schools. To promote pride in 'Indianhood', he commissioned texts on Native American history and achievements, and encouraged tribes to preserve and use their own languages as well as English. Under his auspices, the lawyer Felix Cohen compiled a forty-six volume collection of laws and treaties and published the *Handbook of Federal Indian Law*, perhaps the most authoritative attempt ever made to clarify and codify the special legal standing of 'Indian tribes' within the United States.

As well as trying to create a more favourable political and cultural climate, Collier also took practical steps to help native people improve their communities. The Roosevelt administration's ambitious attempt to generate new jobs through a massive programme of public works gave him the opportunity to establish Indian Emergency Conservation Work – part of the national Civilian Conservation Corps – which, over the next nine years, employed some 85,000 native people on projects such as road-building and constructing storage dams to prevent erosion. Seeing greater native involvement at every level of Indian Affairs as a crucial element in promoting self-government, he took steps to increase the number of Native Americans employed by the BIA. To stimulate neglected tribal arts and crafts, he hired Indians to decorate Indian Service buildings and set up a board to develop new markets for Native American artists and protect them against non-Indian imitators. He also tried to implement his vision of 'scientific government' by allowing the Bureau of Indian Affairs to contract with other federal agencies, such as the Public Health Service, for the provision of specialist services, and drafted in experts in conservation, land management and other disciplines to give the tribes professional advice. In the same vein, convinced 'that in the ethnic field research can be made a tool of action essential to all the other tools, indeed, that it ought to be the master tool,' he established an applied anthropology unit within the BIA to build up a more accurate picture of native societies and identify ways of bolstering them. Like so much of Collier's thinking, this idea came to be widely accepted only a generation or more later: to an academic community still heavily dominated by Morgan's model of cultural evolution, in which ethnography was seen primarily as a means of recording dying cultures, the belief that anthropologists should serve the people they studied – and even help them to survive – was a radical new departure.

The effects of all this frenetic activity varied widely from community to community. Despite putting Native Americans under immense pressure to accept the Indian Reorganization Act – to the understand-able outrage of his critics, he ordered that abstentions should be counted as 'yes' votes, and forbade tribes that voted 'no' to reconsider their decision at a later date – he failed to translate the support he had received from the Indian Congresses into the overwhelming endorse-ment he had hoped for. In the event, 181 tribes, with a combined population of nearly 130,000, voted to accept the IRA, while 77, totalling just over 86,000, rejected it. Groups voting 'no' ranged from the fiercely independent Iroquois Six Nations, who saw the act as an infringement of their cherished sovereignty, to peoples like the Five Civilized Tribes in Oklahoma, many of whose members were already largely assimilated and whose tribal institutions were so fractured – the

Cherokees, for example, owned less than 400 acres – that they could not be pieced together. (Because of their unique history, in fact, all the Oklahoma tribes were exempted from most of the IRA's provisions, although a separate measure two years later gave them some of the same benefits, such as access to a revolving credit fund.) The bitterest blow for Collier was the loss of the largest tribe, the Navajos, who rejected the act by a majority of less than 500 votes, largely through the influence of a 'progressive' tribal leader who sided with Collier's missionary opponents.

The impact of Collier's policies was also to some extent blunted by the broader political and economic situation. Because of the tight financial constraints imposed first by the Depression and then by the Second World War, many of his proposals were never fully funded: he received little more than half the $10 million he requested for the revolving credit fund, for instance, and was only able to help the tribes increase their landholdings by less than 20 per cent of the additional 25,000 million acres he estimated that they required.

At the same time, the debate over the Indian New Deal was inevitably touched by the larger ideological currents polarizing American and European society in the 1930s. Increasingly, in their campaign against the Indian Reorganization Act, leaders of the 'progressive' American Indian Federation found they were able to enlist the support not only of the kind of old-style conservatives who had opposed Collier in the past but also of overtly fascist and Nazi organizations which regarded his promotion of cultural and racial tolerance and his rejection of unbridled capitalism as anathema. Elwood A. Towner, for instance, an assimilated urban 'mixed-blood' who called himself Chief Red Cloud and sported a war-bonnet decorated with a swastika, forged links with the German-American Bund and attacked Collier as a 'Jew-loving Pink Red' for employing Felix Cohen and other Jews. (The Nazi attitude towards Native Americans – as to so much else – was deeply contradictory. Racial theorists drew heavily on nineteenth-century American 'scientific racism' to justify their belief in Teutonic superiority, and Hitler seems to have seen the 'Nordics of North America, who had ruthlessly pushed aside an inferior race to win for themselves soil and territory for the future' as a model for his own policy of national expansion. On the other hand, the 'Noble Savage' was a potent figure in German popular culture – the Führer himself was one of millions of fans of Karl May's wildly romantic *Old Shatterhand* novels – and the Nazi regime eventually solemnly declared American Indians to be members of the 'Aryan race'.)

Collier tried to discredit the idea that he was attempting 'to turn the clock back' or that his programme was connected with 'communism, socialism, and paganism' by arguing – with some ingenuity – that his reforms, far from being inspired by 'Russia or Karl Marx', were in fact wholesomely all-American. Freed from its atavistic connotations, he claimed, the 'tribe' could be seen as no more than 'a legally recognized holding corporation – a holder of property and a holder of tangible rights granted by treaty or statute,' and Indian business corporations were comparable to the Empire State Building, which existed only because 'a great many people had pooled their investments.' His record, however (as far back as the 'Red Scare' of the early 1920s, he had been placed under government surveillance because of his interest in the Bolshevik 'experiment') and the relentless onslaught against him meant that he was unable to shake off the 'red' label, which dogged him throughout the rest of his career.

Yet, despite all these limitations, the Indian New Deal still achieved some remarkable results. During his eleven years in office (the longest tenure of any Commissioner of Indian Affairs) Collier not only halted the apparently ineluctable process of Native American land loss but actually – probably for the first time in history – reversed it. Under his policies, the total area of Indian lands in the continental United States rose from some 47 million to 51 million acres – roughly the level at which it remains today. (This figure disguises the fact that, as a result of the sale of allotments and other measures, large areas of many reservations are now controlled by non-Indians, but it is only fair to point out that if Collier had been able to implement his original land consolidation proposals a far higher proportion would still be in Native American hands.) He was also at least partially successful in liberating Indian communities from the endemic powerlessness and dependency that had sapped their hope and initiative. During his Commissioner-ship, the government lent the tribes a total of $12 million, fuelling an explosion of economic activity: Native American beef-cattle herds, for instance, increased by 105 per cent, their yield of animal products by

2,300 per cent, and their total agricultural income from $1.85 million to $49 million. (Collier later boasted that less than $4,000 of loans had to be cancelled as uncollectable, a record which made Indians 'the best credit risk in America.') In 1948, the BIA was able to announce that 'since the beginning of agricultural extension work on Indian reservations, more than 12,000 families [perhaps 10 per cent or more of the entire Native American population] have been completely or partially rehabilitated and are now wholly or nearly self-supporting.'

These composite statistics, impressive though they are, distort the overall picture because they blur the enormous variations between different groups. A substantial minority of tribes, including many of those which had voted against it, derived little benefit from the Indian Reorganization Act, while a few others – most of them, unsurprisingly, communities which still retained a communal land-base and a strong tribal identity – did spectacularly well under it. Groups such as the Apaches, with their long tradition of adapting to new conditions and exploiting new possibilities, were especially successful. One San Carlos Apache leader recalled:

> Conditions were deplorable on the San Carlos Reservation before the Indian Reorganization Act. There was no economic development of any kind. I heard about the IRA when the superintendent came to our CCC [Civilian Conservation Corps] camp and explained the contents . . . I remember that a prominent Indian stood up and said, 'This is what we have been waiting for. The white man has driven us around like cattle for many years. We need to take advantage of the opportunity to form our own government and run our own business.' I think the IRA was the best thing that ever happened to Indian tribes . . . For many years, the San Carlos Apaches held a celebration on June 18 to commemorate the birth of this legislation.

Another Apache tribe, the Jicarillas, took advantage of the Act to return their allotments to tribal control, start the first Indian-operated 'Tribal General Store' and establish a flock of sheep to provide for 'aged and incapacitated' tribal members; while their relatives the Mescaleros borrowed $242,000 to rehouse the residents of a slum camp, increase their farm production eightfold, expand their co-operative cattle operation and start a tribal warehouse.

The Indian New Deal also brought significant, if less dramatic, improvements in apparently less promising areas. In 1937, a BIA agricultural expert suggested that a community of impoverished Cherokee 'full-bloods' should start growing strawberries in the rocky hills around their homes in eastern Oklahoma, and twelve of them borrowed $2,800 to start their own co-operative. They quickly paid off the loan and increased their average income more than 1,000 per cent to $600 a year, and by 1949 the business had expanded to provide a living for 150 families.

It is relatively easy to measure the economic results of this ferment of energy: far harder to gauge its psychological impact on individuals and communities. The anecdotal evidence, however, suggests that Collier's reforms did give many Native Americans not only a more adequate livelihood but also, after generations in which their sense of themselves and their view of the world had been systematically undermined, new hope and self-respect. According to Henry Roe Cloud, a Winnebago, during the New Deal Indians could once again hold their heads high 'instead of looking down all the time,' because they knew that they had 'a great history, and great thoughts, and great ideas and inspirations in our hearts.' Joseph W. Hayes, a Chickasaw, put it more simply when he praised Collier for helping to ensure that 'every morning our children will be Indians.'

Yet despite all these achievements, Collier is still vilified by many people, both native and non-native, today. This apparent paradox stems, in part, from the very scale of his success: even now, five decades after he left office, he remains a potent figure, the man who, more than any other Commissioner of Indian Affairs in history, shaped the landscape of 'Indian Country'. As a result, many Native Americans, understandably, hold him at least partially responsible for the conditions in which they live their daily lives. He is criticized, in particular, for the bullying tactics he sometimes used to try to secure acceptance of the Indian Reorganization Act (it is important to remember that, in most Native American cultures, domineering behaviour is still seen as deeply offensive) and for the legacy of factionalism which he left in many communities. They argue that by forcing tribes to adopt a Western-style elective form of government, in which rival candidates have to compete for public support, he created political frictions where none had existed before. As Elmer Savilla, Director of the National Tribal Chairmen's Association, put it:

> The IRA destroyed the Indian way of doing things ... Most tribal elections ... are contested the minute they are over. In the old days, when we selected leaders by consensus, there was not that kind of situation. The Crow [who rejected the Indian Reorganization Act] are a good example of how consensus works. They have a general council where all the tribal members attend and make their decisions. When they come out with a decision, there is nobody to blame, because everybody had a hand in it.

Many Indians resent the IRA not only on the grounds that it is culturally alien, but also because they see it as a colonial imposition which denies their sovereignty and keeps power firmly in the hands of the Commissioner of Indian Affairs. As a result, in some communities, such as Pine Ridge, cultural 'conservatives' sometimes boycott the elections altogether, further fuelling the tensions between 'traditionals' and 'progressives' which have been festering since before the start of the reservation era.

While Native American critics often blame Collier for arrogantly disregarding Indian culture, non-Indians tend to accuse him of romanticizing and idealizing it. His formative experience in the Southwest, they claim, had duped him into thinking that all Native American groups were similar to the Pueblos. His passion for the communal life he found at Taos blinded him not only to the enormous diversity of Native American cultures, but also to the fact that, as a result of Euro-American contact, most tribes had lost far more of their own traditions than the Pueblos and some had changed so much that, in the words of the anthropologist Fred Eggan, they 'had almost disappeared in a cultural sense.' He tried, consequently, to apply policies designed for Taos or Acoma to a whole range of peoples whose needs were often radically different. As a former colleague of Collier's recalled in a moving but clear-sighted tribute: 'Sometimes he saw communities, it seemed to me, where communities did not exist ... decisions made on assumptions of community when only its social fragments exist lead to bitter disappointments. So it was with John Collier.'

But even some of Collier's critics concede that – in the words of a prominent Native American lawyer – he 'tried to build upon the strength of the Indian people. Whether you like the IRA or not, it was a significant reversal of federal Indian policy. To that extent, ... [he] deserves credit.' Almost single-handedly, in fact, Collier challenged some of the most deep-rooted orthodoxies of his society by trying to derail the apparently 'inevitable' course of history. His attempt to find another way for Native and non-native Americans to live together was arguably, in its way, as radical as the 'Five Civilized Tribes' experiment a century before. What makes it so remarkable is that the initiative this time came not from the Indians themselves but from Euro-Americans – finally, from the very federal government which, since independence, had consistently undermined the viability of native societies, and over the past fifty years had tried unrelentingly to destroy them. It is hard to see how, given the political, economic and cultural realities of the time, anyone could have done more: it is extraordinary that he did as much as he did.

In the end, perhaps Collier's biggest fault was that he misjudged the enormous power of the interests ranged against him. Just as men such as Dawes had underestimated the durability and strength of the tribal system and tried to deal with Native Americans as individuals without a past or a culture, Collier underestimated the fundamental forces in the non-Indian world which had always worked against the survival of distinct tribal societies. By 1947, when he wrote his classic *Indians of the Americas: the Long Hope* and optimistically called the chapter on the New Deal 'Final Struggle Commences and Prevails', these forces were once again starting to gain the upper hand.

*　*　*

The Indians believed that when the dark clouds of war passed from the skies overhead, their rising tide of expectations, though temporarily stalled, would again reappear. Instead, they were threatened by termination ... Soaring expectations began to plunge. Termination took on the connotation of extermination for many.

Benjamin Reifel, Sioux

I have spoken with many people who were touched by termination. They have bitter feelings toward the government. These people are angry because they have not been identified in the eyes of the government as Indian, even though everyone would readily recognize what they are.

... We have looked at termination as a policy that lasted from approximately the mid-1940s into the 1960s. I submit to you that termination has been around a lot longer than that, and you can expect to see it in the future. Maybe the descriptive word has changed, but the thrust of the policy is there. From the time of Indian removal, through the creation of the reservations, through the enactment of the Major Crimes Act in 1885, to the General Allotment Act in 1887, you can see the work of the United States Congress in trying to dismantle tribal government and Indian rights.

Larry EchoHawk, Pawnee

I have been involved in resisting or fighting some form of termination all my life. Ever since the European people arrived on this continent, we have been in the process of termination. But you do not learn much about it in books that people read.

... Because of these problems, I do not think that termination has ended. It will always be with us.

Joe De La Cruz, Quinault

There is an eerie sense of *déjà vu* about the post-Collier era. In the space of only a few years, all the old familiar ingredients of Indian Affairs, which the New Dealers thought they had banished forever, re-emerged from the shadows to create a kind of distorting-mirror image of earlier policies.

Partly, as always, this shift reflected broader changes in US society and the world at large. Just as the Great War had helped to generate a more receptive climate for Collier's philosophy, so the Second World War undermined it. With all available resources being diverted to the war effort, Indian programmes were starved of funds, virtually stalling further progress in implementing the New Deal. At the same time, 25,000 Native Americans – including many of the most able leaders –

left their homes to serve in the armed forces, while thousands more migrated to non-Indian communities to work in war-related industries. This double blow was a severe setback for reservation communities which, under Collier, had painfully begun edging their way towards a more viable social and economic life.

The impressive contribution made by Native American servicemen to the war effort – Indian 'code-talkers', using their own languages to baffle enemy interceptors, played a crucial role in military communications, and a Pima, Ira Hayes, became a national hero for his part in raising the US flag on Iwo Jima – once again created greater public appreciation for *individual* native people, but not, by and large, for their distinctive cultural needs and differences. Instead, in the mood of national unity created by the war itself and the increasingly conformist atmosphere of the Truman and Eisenhower years, it resuscitated the old feeling that Indians must be 'freed' to live like other Americans – a feeling heightened by the sense that, at a time when the United States was leading the growing international movement for the decolonization of European empires, it was unacceptable for her to retain any 'colonial' peoples of her own. In 1946, partly to prepare the way for this ultimate 'liberation', Congress established the Indian Claims Commission to settle all outstanding Native American complaints of government fraud, theft or mismanagement with a final cash payment. Whatever the original motives of the bill's sponsors, it gave the BIA – as the Commissioner of Indian Affairs menacingly pointed out in 1952 – 'the means of removing a major Indian objection to any move' towards a change in policy.

The ill-informed but well-intentioned 'humanitarian' impulse was quickly harnessed, as it had been during the Dawes era, by interest groups with their own reasons for wanting to resume the assault on 'tribalism'. Speculators and developers were once more casting a hungry eye on the remaining Indian lands and resources, which, with the growth of agriculture during the war and the 'improvements' of the New Deal, suddenly seemed far more tempting. A conservative Congress, meanwhile, rife with ancient – and partly justified – suspicions of bureaucratic extravagance, was eagerly looking for ways to cut expenditure and 'get the government off the taxpayers' backs.' By 'liberating' Native Americans from the 'degrading wardship' of federal supervision and coaxing or forcing them back on to the path of assimilation – all in the unimpeachable name of 'Indian civil rights' – right-wing politicians believed they could neatly kill several birds with one stone.

Although this strategy was given a new name, 'Termination', its supporters made no secret of the fact that it marked a return to what they saw as the historic norm. As one of its principal advocates, Senator Arthur V. Watkins of Utah, put it:

> Unfortunately, the major and continuing congressional movement toward full freedom was delayed for a time by the Indian Reorganization Act of 1934, the Wheeler-Howard Act. Amid the deep social concern of the depression years, Congress deviated from its accustomed policy under the concept of promoting the general Indian welfare. In the post-depression years Congress – realizing this change of policy – sought to return to the historic principles of much earlier decades.

Collier and his supporters tried to refute the charges against the Indian New Deal. Indians, they pointed out, were not 'wards' but enjoyed all the rights of citizenship except – like other Americans – where these were limited by local laws, and the 'tribe', the 'only presently feasible type of local self-government they can share in and use for their advancement,' was simply exercising the powers and functions of a municipality. The expense of Indian administration, moreover, was largely the result of precisely the kind of assimilation policy Congress was now proposing, which had created 'a permanently dispossessed and impoverished group' of welfare-dependents. Like Senator Teller's prophecy, however, these warnings were ignored: the allure of a few years' cheap land and cheap government proved too strong to resist. In 1947, the BIA's Acting Commissioner, William Zimmerman Jr., was subpoenaed by the House Sub-Committee on Indian Affairs and told to produce a set of guidelines which could be used to determine whether or not a particular tribe was ready for the withdrawal of Federal services. He – rather reluctantly, it seems – suggested several factors which should be taken into account, including the tribe's degree of acculturation, its economic circumstances and its willingness to be relieved of supervision.

In 1950, the Truman administration clearly signalled its new hard-line approach when it appointed Dillon S. Myer, who had been in charge of the wartime internment and resettlement of Japanese Americans, as Commissioner of Indian Affairs. Myer's forceful methods – which included interfering in tribal elections, selling Indian land without the tribe's consent, removing a BIA superintendent who had upheld Indian rights and supporting a bill which would have allowed Indian Service employees to carry guns and arrest Native Americans without warrant – set the tone for the next decade. He was under no illusion that native people would universally welcome 'liberation', but he insisted that 'We must proceed, even though Indian co-operation may be lacking in certain cases.'

The definitive statement of the Termination policy was HCR (House Concurrent Resolution) 108, adopted in August 1953, which declared Congress's intention to make Native Americans 'subject to the same laws and entitled to the same privileges and responsibilities as ... other citizens of the United States' by 'freeing' them from 'all Federal supervision and control.' A few days later, Congress passed Public Law 280, which extended state control over all the Indians – with a few specified exceptions – in five states, and empowered other states to enact similar legislation for themselves. From 1954 to 1960 some fourteen recognized tribes with reservations were terminated, often without their consent. Most were small, impoverished communities who had little idea of what was happening to them, but a few – most notably the Menominee of Wisconsin and the Klamath of Oregon – were large, wealthy tribes with considerable natural resources who fought the government's decision for some years.

The fate of the Klamath is particularly significant, not only because of the amounts of land and money involved but because they were seen as the most crucial test-case for Termination: as Tom McCall, later Governor of Oregon, wrote in 1958: '... tribes not yet on a termination schedule realize that the Federal policy of eventual termination will be implemented unless the "pilot" process at Klamath degenerates into a distinct, nationally acknowledged failure.' It is important, therefore, to look at their experience in some detail.

Superficially, the Klamath seemed ideal candidates for the removal of federal protection. Their 1.3 million-acre reservation, rich in timber and ranchland, made them one of the most prosperous Indian groups in the United States, producing enough revenue to give each tribal member a modest per capita income of about $800 a year and to pay the entire cost of the services – including a hospital with a full-time medical team – which they received from the BIA. They had intermarried to some extent with the local non-Indian population and sent their children to local public schools.

Those who knew them well, however, realized that this situation gave an altogether misleading impression of the tribe's adjustment to non-Indian society. True self-sufficiency for the Klamath had ended in 1864, when they had signed a treaty ceding 21.3 million acres, and since then, far from teaching them how to stand on their own feet, the government had reduced them virtually to the status of pensioners. By the mid-1940s the Bureau of Indian Affairs Superintendent estimated that only 35 per cent of the tribe were capable of surviving without their per capita payments.

The Tribal Council recognized the dangers of this unhealthy situation and had for some time been pressing for an opportunity to take more responsibility for managing the tribe's affairs, but they also knew that the change could not be made overnight. The Acting Commissioner of Indian Affairs agreed. In identifying them as a tribe for whom Termination could eventually be considered, he warned that they were completely unprepared for it at that point and would need an interim period of up to fifty years if they were to make the transition to full independence successfully.

But Watkins and his colleagues in Congress ignored him. They argued that Zimmerman's view was based on the assumption that the Klamath wanted and would be able to survive as a tribe, whereas the whole intention of the Termination policy was that Indian communities should be dispersed as quickly as possible. The loss of their land, which Zimmerman and others thought almost certain to ensue from immediate withdrawal of supervision, would only hasten this process.

When hearings on the Klamath termination bill were held early in 1954, the tribe desperately sent two elected delegates, Jesse Kirk and Boyd Jackson, to Washington to appeal for a stay of execution. 'Why should we at this moment get in a hurry?' asked Jackson. 'What have we done? What do the Klamath Indians owe to this Federal Government? We pay our own way as we go along.' His prime concern was that some way should be found of holding the tribe and the reservation together, and he thought they needed perhaps fifteen or twenty years to develop a plan that would enable them to do this without Federal protection. '. . . when you put a person to do things, and you find that he can do them, through experience – then he is ready to go on his own. We haven't been given that experience.'

But Jackson was up against Senator Watkins, a wily professional politician whose absolute conviction that he was right – he saw Termination as comparable to the Emancipation Proclamation – made him a ruthless and unscrupulous opponent. The record of their exchanges gives a revealing – and unedifying – insight into Watkins' character and the combination of bullying and cajolery he used to get his way. At first he tried to disarm the Indians, calling them by their first names and answering their complaints that the tribe was unready by saying 'I think you are a lot wiser than you want to let on,' but as this approach failed to move them he became increasingly cold and hostile. Even though he had already accepted testimony from Wade Crawford, a pro-Termination tribal member who had no official status (because of his unpopular views, Crawford had failed to win a seat on the Tribal Council, but Congress had forced the tribe to pay his travel expenses to Washington anyway), Watkins now tried to discredit Kirk and Jackson as unrepresentative because they had not submitted the issue to a referendum. 'You don't believe in that sort of government, do you, that such a few people can determine the policy for all the rest of them?' he asked Jackson. 'That falls in line with the practice that we find is carried on here,' Jackson replied. 'What you do here represents the thinking for 160 million people. And why couldn't we, in our group, operate in the same manner?' This response seems to have angered Watkins, who walked out a few minutes later while Jackson was in mid-sentence. Finally, after several days of this treatment, the delegates were told that if they did not agree to Termination a substantial sum of money awarded to the tribe by the Indian Claims Commission would be withheld by Congress.

The legality of this ploy – which was also used successfully against the Menominee – is questionable, but it had the desired effect. Kirk and Jackson reluctantly capitulated and put their signatures to the bill – sowing the seeds of a widespread belief that the 'greedy' Klamath *wanted* to be terminated in order to 'get rich quick'. Their action was never ratified by the Tribal Council, nor was it put to a vote of the tribe as a whole, but for Watkins it was enough: promptly forgetting his misgivings about the delegates and his earlier insistence on a referendum, he quickly steered the Klamath termination bill into law, despite warnings from BIA personnel and other qualified observers that it would be a disaster.

Within only a few months, there was clear evidence that they were right. A team of three management specialists, appointed by the government to implement the Act, sent back increasingly desperate reports about the situation on the reservation. They found that nearly half the tribe belonged to families in which the adults were completely or partially unfit to handle money, and that even among those considered competent there was widespread misunderstanding of what Termination meant. Like the Tribal Council before them, the management specialists asked for more time to prepare the Indians for what was to happen to them. They were granted a three year extension, but despite their best efforts they found this totally inadequate and finally, amidst growing chaos, they were fired.

Even at this point, Congress failed to read the warning signs. Plans for the disposal of the reservation went ahead. In 1958 the Klamath were given their first and only chance to vote: on whether they wanted to take their individual shares of the tribe's assets at once or leave them in a private trust for a further ten years. In neither instance could they choose to take land rather than money. Contemporary documents show that the tribal members were utterly bemused by the choice before them. '...I am thoroughly convinced,' wrote Rex Putnam, Superintendent of Public Instruction, to the Area Director of the BIA, 'that the Indian people do not understand the implications of the trust agreement, the appraisal of the reservation nor how their property might be managed in the future ... in our opinion, the Klamath people are probably more unsure, uncertain and confused than they were two years ago.' Finally, largely because local officials told them that the private trust was a dangerous option, 77 per cent of the tribe voted to withdraw their money at once rather than risk losing everything.

'The idea that the Klamath were ready to run their own lives is the biggest lie ever written on a piece of paper,' says Chuck Kimbol, a contemporary tribal leader. The government finally exposed it in 1961 when it came to give the withdrawing members their shares of $43,000 each. Almost 75 per cent of the money had to be paid straight into some kind of trust, guardianship or conservatorship for Indians too young or too incompetent to handle it themselves.

In the same year, Federal supervision was withdrawn. The government took most of the reservation and left the Klamath to the mercies of the state authorities, the various individuals who had effectively inherited the BIA's trust responsibility, and local businessmen. Gordon Bettles, a tribal member who grew up during Termination, recalls:

> I would liken it to a dream time. Salesmen used to show up and take everything out on the lawn. Vacuum salesmen, furniture salesmen, people selling everything you can put in a house. The Indian way is to feel sorry for people like that. My aunt, she bought just a token from all of them – a plate here, a spoon there. She ended up with a house full of junk she couldn't use.

Dishonest selling methods and overpricing became so blatant and widespread that in 1972 the Federal Trade Commission had to send a team to investigate the abuses.

Salesmen were not the only beneficiaries of the bonanza. The local bar association set a fee for administering Indian trusts that was three times the normal rate, and even this was not enough for a few enterprising souls, who contrived to defraud their Klamath charges of hundreds of thousands of dollars. With the extension of state law into Indian communities, the Klamath found not only that they were suddenly liable to taxation, but also that their families were likely to be forcibly broken up by the authorities. Children were placed in non-Indian foster homes and forced to pay for it from their own trust fund.

The really big winnings from Termination, however, went to the federal government. For $90 million it acquired land and timber worth, by its own, very conservative reckoning, $120 million. In the twenty-five years following Termination, the former reservation, now largely incorporated in the Winnema National Forest, earned the United States close to $200 million.

By the middle of the 1960s, the boom was over. The money of the withdrawing members was largely dissipated and the Klamath were further from mainstream America than ever. A survey carried out in 1965 showed that most of them had tried to spend their shares wisely on housing, medical expenses, cars and other general maintenance. Some had invested in small businesses, most of which failed for lack of expertise. Many Klamath who had moved away and tried to make it in the cities had returned to the area round Chiloquin hurt and bewildered. Involvement with the non-Indian community, far from increasing, had actually declined. By one of the many ironies in the Klamath situation, the policy which had been designed to make them like other Americans had in reality simply reduced them to the conditions of other Indians.

Dream time now turned to nightmare. Without the tribal clinic and with no more funds to pay for medical care and insurance, the health of the Klamath worsened dramatically. Discrimination against Indians hardened in the public schools and the local welfare department: in 1965 there was only one Klamath receiving welfare, even though a full 40 per cent of them had no money left. Tensions and divisions in the community intensified, leading to violence, family breakdown and a threefold increase in juvenile delinquency. Withdrawing members envied remaining members whose money was still to come; remaining members blamed withdrawing members for 'selling out'. A third group, by now quite large, consisted of children born after the closure of the tribal rolls in 1954, who had received nothing from the sale of the reservation and often bitterly resented the older members of their own families. A Senate Committee, visiting the area in 1969, reported that 'the Termination of the Klamath reservation in Oregon has led to extreme social disorganization of that tribal group. Many of them can be found in state penal and mental institutions.'

While the government was terminating 'advanced' tribes like the Klamath, it also tried to sap the economic vitality of other communities by freezing the Rotating Loan Fund, scrapping development projects, running down federal services and resuming the old policy, abandoned by Collier, of removing restrictions from individual allotments so that they could be sold. The aim was not only to save money but to force tribespeople to leave the reservations to look for work in non-native towns, where, it was assumed, they would quickly be absorbed in the general population. To encourage this process, 'Relocation centres' were established in a number of cities and potential Indian wage-earners were offered removal expenses for themselves and their families. As it became clear that a substantial proportion of the migrants quickly gave up and returned home – 32 per cent in 1953, for example – larger and larger sums were appropriated to give Native American workers longer and more comprehensive cover. In 1956, $1 million was used to relocate more than 12,500 people: the following year the figure jumped to $3.5 million.

There is no question that some kind of programme to help Native Americans subsist away from the reservations was necessary. With improving medical facilities, the native population, though still far more prone to disease than non-Indians, was at last starting to rise rapidly again – between 1940 and 1960 it increased from 355,000 to 509,000 – and it was obvious that even in the most favourable conditions most tribes could not hope to support all their members on their own lands. The relocation policy, however, was a blatant and more or less heavy-handed attempt to destroy Indian communities rather than to strengthen them: the reservations were deliberately undermined, and migrants were often resettled as far away from home as possible in order to weaken their family and tribal ties. In fact, as a survey conducted in 1956 showed – and anyone with a modicum of psychological insight would have predicted – it was precisely those Native Americans with a secure background, and the knowledge that they could return to the reservation whenever they wanted, who adapted best. Those, by contrast, who were anxious about their home base tended to keep running back to make sure it was still there.

Like so many other policies, relocation also set up unnecessary tensions among the Indians themselves. By making life on the beleaguered reservations such a test of faith and courage, the government encouraged people who 'stuck it out' to regard the migrants as traitors who had abandoned their 'Indianness' under pressure. Those who returned, moreover, according to the Sioux leader Gerald One Feather, often 'brought back problems that they inherited from urban communities. For instance, we have established reservation ghettos, which we never had before.'

Some Native Americans did successfully make the transition into the non-Indian world, but for many others the experience was a disaster.

According to a study of relocated Indians carried out by the Community Welfare Council of Minneapolis in the mid-1950s, most migrants arrived poorly dressed, with inadequate funds and little idea of how to set about finding and keeping suitable work. Their housing conditions were deplorable: 'One Indian family of five or six, living in two rooms, will take in relatives and friends who come from the reservations seeking jobs until perhaps fifteen people will be crowded into the space,' and in one case sixteen Indians of all ages were found crammed into one unventilated attic. Problems of maladjustment and unease in an alien culture were acute: during a test period of thirteen days, some 450 cases were heard in the police court, seventy-two of which involved Native Americans who were all, with one or two exceptions, charged with drunkenness. The symptoms of Indian distress created hostility among the larger population, who easily dismissed native people as 'drunk Indians' without investigating why they should behave as they did. The average age of death among Minneapolis Native Americans in 1955 was thirty-seven years, as against forty-six years for all Minnesota Indians and sixty-eight years for Minneapolis residents.

By the end of the 1950s, Termination and Relocation seemed set to repeat the drearily familiar pattern of destruction seen during the Dawes era. But the political climate had changed, and a vital new factor had started – to begin with, almost unnoticed – to emerge: organized, and highly effective, opposition from Native Americans themselves.

12. The New Indians

Most [of us] ... can remember when we were children and spent many hours at the feet of our grandfathers listening to stories of the time when the Indians were a great people, when we were free, when we were rich, when we lived the good life. At the same time we heard stories of droughts, famines and pestilence. It was only recently that we realized that there was surely great material deprivation in those days, but that our old people felt rich because they were free. They were rich in the things of the spirit, but if there is one thing that characterizes Indian life today it is poverty of the spirit. We still have human passions and depth of feeling (which may be something rare in these days), but we are poor in spirit because we are not free – free in the most basic sense of the word. We are not allowed to make those basic human choices and decisions about our personal life and about the destiny of our communities which is the mark of free mature people. We sit on our front porches or in our yards, and the world and our lives in it pass us by without our desires or aspirations having any effect.

We are not free. We do not make choices. Our choices are made for us; we are the poor ... We have many rulers ... They call us into meetings to tell us what is good for us and how they've programmed us, or they come into our homes to instruct us and their manners are not always what one would call polite by Indian standards or perhaps by any standards. We are rarely accorded respect as fellow human beings. Our children come home from school to us with shame in their hearts and a sneer on their lips for their home and parents. We are the 'poverty problem' and that is true; and perhaps it is also true that our lack of reasonable choices, our lack of freedom, our poverty of spirit is not uncon-nected with our material poverty.

Clyde Warrior, Ponca, President, National Indian Youth Council,

1967

The attitude that non-Indians, and some Indians, have is that someday the Indians are just going to disappear and that we should be working to make Indians disappear is very wrong. We are not going to disappear. We have got to educate the American public and also our leaders that we are here to stay and that in staying here we have got to find a place for resolving our problems that will give us a life that has meaning for us and our Indian children and that there is a real hope that a complete life can be realized.

Mel Thom, Paiute, President, National Indian Youth Council, 1964

UNITED NATIVE AMERICANS BUY
MONTANA STATE

The United Native Americans (UNA) is proud to announce that it has bought the State of Montana from the whites and is throwing it open to American Indian settlement. UNA bought Montana from three winos found wandering in Glendive. The winos promptly signed the treaty, which was written in the Northern Cheyenne language, and sold Montana for three bottles of wine, one bottle of gin and four cases of beer.

The Honourable George E. Little Bear, the new Commissioner of Caucasian Affairs, has announced the following new policies:

The Indians hereby generously give the whites four enormously huge reservations of ten acres each at the following locations: in the middle of Makoshika Park, in the Bad Lands of South Dakota, in the Utah Salt Flats and in the Yukon. These reservations shall belong to the whites for as long as the sun shines and the grass grows, or until such time as the Indians want them back.

All land on the reservations, of course, will be held in trust for the whites by the Bureau of Caucasian Affairs, and any white who wants to use his land in any way must secure the permission of Commissioner Little Bear.

Of course, whites will be allowed to sell trades and handicrafts at stands by the highway. Each white will be provided annually with one blanket and one pair of tennis shoes, a supply of Spam, and a copy of My Life Among the White People. The latter was written as an exposé by a former Indian student at an all white high school.

If an American Indian proves incompetent enough, he may qualify to be superintendent of any of the above-mentioned Bureau of Caucasian Affairs reservations that have been so generously set aside by the United Native Americans. Applicants for the Superintendents' jobs must have less than a year of education, must not be able to understand the Caucasian languages or customs, must have an authoritarian personality, have proof of dishonesty and must have a certificate of incompetence. Of course, no whites need apply.

Commissioner Little Bear also announced the founding of four boarding schools to which white youngsters will be sent at the age of six. 'We want to take those white kids far away from the backward culture of their parents,' the commissioner said. The schools will be located on Alcatraz Island, the Florida Everglades, Point Barrow, Alaska, and nearby Hong Kong.

All of their courses will be taught in the Indian Languages, and there will be demerits for anyone caught speaking English. All students arriving at the school will immediately be given IQ tests to determine their understanding of Indian languages and hunting skills . . .

In honour of the whites, many cities, streets, cars and products will be given traditional Caucasian names. One famous Indian movie director has even announced that in his upcoming film, 'Custer's Last Stand,' he will use many actual whites to play the parts of the soldiers, speaking real English; although of course, the part of Custer will be played by Tonto.

Certain barbaric white customs will not be allowed. Whites will not be permitted to practice their heathen religions, and will be required to attend Indian ceremonies. Missionaries will be sent from each tribe to convert the Caucasians of the reservations. White churches will either be made into amusement parks or

*museums, or will be torn down and the bricks and ornaments sold
as souvenirs and curiosities.*

From: *The Colville Tribal Tribune*, 20 December 1973

There was, of course, nothing new about Native Americans fighting
back: from the time of the earliest settlements, they had struggled as
best they could to protect themselves against the increasingly powerful
forces that threatened their survival. But their final military defeat at
the end of the nineteenth century and their confinement on reservations had not only sapped their strength, it had also undermined
their freedom of movement and their ability to forge effective alliances.
Such resistance as there had been – a few local outbreaks of violence,
a handful of law suits and widespread non-co-operation – had simply
been too patchy and spasmodic to make much impact nationally.

In 1944, however, members of some forty tribes – many of them
employees in John Collier's more liberal BIA, whose experience of
being posted to different parts of the country had broadened their
knowledge and understanding of other native communities – came
together in Washington to create a new lobbying organization, the
National Congress of American Indians. By drawing together Native
Americans from across the country in a truly national, pan-Indian body,
they aimed to give tribes the kind of leverage that they could not hope
to exercise in isolation.

The NCAI faced enormous problems, particularly in its early years.
As well as trying to operate with only a shoestring budget in an
increasingly hostile political climate, it suffered serious internal difficulties: probably the most ambitious attempt at a grand coalition since
the War of 1812 (in fact, it was arguably trying to unite even more, and
more diverse, groups than Tecumseh had, although admittedly in less
fraught circumstances), it was riven by long-standing intra- and inter-
tribal frictions and regional rivalries that made it perilously hard to
develop common strategies and speak with a united voice.

Nonetheless, within a decade the fledgling organization was strong
enough to challenge the new direction of government policy. In 1953,
when Joseph Garry, a Coeur d'Alene from Washington State, was
elected President and Helen Peterson, a Lakota, became Executive
Director (thereby establishing a long tradition of power-sharing

between the Sioux and the Northwest tribes which was to dominate the NCAI for much of the next four decades), they immediately set about responding to the looming threat of Termination. It was, Helen Peterson remembers, an uphill struggle:

> We had little understanding of what termination really meant, except that it struck terror into the hearts of people . . .
>
> In the NCAI office we did all we could to support, encourage, and back up those people who dared to question termination, but it was pretty much a losing battle. The NCAI was in a tough spot. We were deeply committed to respecting the sovereignty of a tribe. Did the NCAI want to oppose termination even when the people involved wanted it? We never really came to a final answer on that question.
>
> The NCAI mobilised at a convention in Phoenix, Arizona, in December 1953. Before that time, its office had been closed. It was really in no position to act as a national organisation. But we managed to raise a little money, and an emergency conference concerning American Indian legislation was held two months later. This conference was the beginning of sobering up some of the congressmen. It launched our effort to slow down and stop further implementation of the termination policy.

For all its feelings of powerlessness and frustration, the NCAI was, in fact, already having a serious impact. Like the advocates of previous policies, Watkins and his backers had packed the Congressional hearings with carefully selected tribal members – such as the Klamath Wade Crawford – who had given the impression that most Indians actually supported Termination, and the discovery that there was concerted, deeply felt Native American opposition did, indeed, have a 'sobering' effect on many non-Indians. For a Washington establishment accustomed to seeing Indians as electorally insignificant, moreover, the new generation of leaders showed an alarming political sophistication: during the 1954 congressional campaign, for example, they discussed mobilizing the Indian vote *en masse* against pro-Termination candidates – a genuine, if limited, threat to congressmen from western states such as New Mexico with a large Native American population, and striking evidence that Indians were starting to adopt the kinds of tactics that, in the past, land speculators and other interest groups had used so successfully against them.

As well as underestimating their Native American opponents, Watkins and his followers seem also to have misjudged the direction of the country as a whole. Even as they demanded a return to 'traditional American values' – self-reliance and low taxes – the US was being transformed into a complex industrial empire which, every day, looked less and less like the predominantly agricultural, small-town idyll of their imagination. It had emerged from the Second World War not only as the most formidable military power on earth but also – with much of Europe and Japan in ruins – as the engine of the world economy. With the Cold War intensifying and its international commitments burgeoning, the United States' defence budget alone made the ideal of a cheap, unobtrusive federal government a fantasy.

Despite the undoubted emotional appeal of their message, moreover, in practice the conservatives found it difficult to push back the frontier of state intervention even in domestic life. During the New Deal and the Second World War, millions of Americans had come to accept that Washington had a legitimate role in helping disadvantaged communities, and now, as living standards for the majority soared, there was a growing feeling that some of the country's massive resources should be used to help marginalized social groups share in the 'American Dream'. Although the *historic* 'Indian' retained a vital symbolic place in US culture as the primordial adversary – as evidenced by the popularity of Hollywood Westerns and TV shows such as *The Lone Ranger and Tonto* – contemporary Native Americans, in the eyes of most of their fellow-citizens, had largely lost their air of menace and begun to look more and more like just another ethnic minority who needed – and deserved – help. This was not the time to fire the public with another campaign to 'pulverize the tribal mass' and leave thousands of detribalized Indians to their fate.

Partly because of this shift of mood, the new policy failed to yield either the political or the financial dividends that Watkins had promised. As terminated tribes disintegrated, many of their members ended up on state welfare rolls or receiving special federal assistance, which often more than cancelled out any savings made to the Indian Affairs budget. Before Termination, for example, the Menominee – who, like the Klamath, paid for virtually all their own services – cost Washington a mere $144,000 a year; by 1966, five years after withdrawal, the federal and state governments between them had spent a total of more than $6 million implementing the new policy and trying to deal with the chaos it had created.

The growing evidence that withdrawal was not working and that most Native Americans were bitterly opposed to it weakened the impetus for an aggressive extension of Termination, particularly during the second half of the 1950s, when – in the wake of Senator Joe McCarthy's downfall – a more liberal national mood blunted the ideological fervour for a rapid winding-down of the BIA. Few congressmen were willing to argue that the policy should be completely abandoned, however. Instead, Democratic opponents of withdrawal backed a measure, enacted in 1955, to allow non-Indian companies to take out long leases on Indian lands in order to develop deposits of coal and other natural resources. By giving corporate America such a compelling interest in the survival of the reservations, they hoped, they would further dissipate pressure for immediate tribal liquidation.

But these gradual changes came too late to save tribes like the Klamath and the Menominee, and even during the 1960 presidential campaign, although both the major candidates said they would not 'force the issue,' neither of them was prepared to come out explicitly against Termination. 'Eventual withdrawal' remained official policy, giving bureaucrats a potent weapon in their dealings with the increasingly politicized Indian leadership. As the Sioux activist Vine Deloria Jr. angrily complained:

> When it is known nationally that Congress is considering termination once again, bureau employees use this threat to keep tribes in line. Whenever a tribe begins to show a bit of independence, a BIA official will throw broad 'hints' that the tribe had better forget it or be recommended for termination.
>
> Recommendation for termination is no idle threat. As we have seen, in the 1950s the bureau offered every possible excuse for terminating tribes. No Indian is so foolish as to believe that it can't happen again. So the tribe generally gives in and follows the bureau line. The risk of total destruction of the Indian community is too great to treat lightly.

When I was Director of the National Congress of American Indians, the bureaucrats would tell me that the NCAI was advocating termination by following a course opposite to the BIA. Fortunately we always had an active tribal membership that thrived on combat and never took the threats seriously. But had I been leading a small tribe in western Washington, Wisconsin or Nevada, the threat would have been enough to stop me cold.

The Blackfoot tribal chairman, Earl Old Person, appealing for the policy to be repealed, vividly conveyed how the dread of Termination blighted and paralysed life in many Native American communities:

> It is important to note that in our Indian language the only translation for termination is to 'wipe out' or 'kill off.' . . . You have caused us to jump every time we hear this word . . . how can we plan our future when the Indian Bureau threatens to wipe us out as a race? It is like trying to cook a meal in your tipi when someone is standing outside trying to burn the tipi down.

The election of John F. Kennedy in 1960 led many Native Americans to hope for a more understanding approach, but to begin with the new administration, anxious to avoid alienating powerful pro-Termination senators like Henry Jackson of Washington, temporized, merely stating that its policy was to help the tribes 'prepare' for withdrawal. In less than a year, however, the powerful social and political currents that were to sweep across the United States over the next decade had started to reach 'Indian Country'. In 1961, Kennedy asked Philleo Nash, a sympathetic liberal with wide experience of working with Native Americans, to conduct a wide-ranging investigation into Indian policy, and a few months later appointed him Commissioner of Indian Affairs. As well as continuing to encourage the commercial exploitation of reservations, Nash immediately saw that some of the government's 'New Frontier' programmes – in particular, the Area Development Administration (later Economic Development Administration), established to develop poor communities and regions – could be used to help Native Americans, bypassing the BIA and channelling funds directly to the tribes themselves. As Vine Deloria Jr. and Clifford Lytle put it in *The Nations Within*:

The ARA-EDA inclusion of tribal governments on the same basis as counties and local governments was a major breakthrough for the cause of self-government and may have been the watershed event of the century. Even the best of the New Deal programmes had not regarded Indians as sufficiently responsible to subcontract large sums of money with them.

In the same year, still more momentously, the NCAI and a group of anthropologists brought together representatives of some seventy tribes in Chicago for an 'American Indian Conference' which, despite some internal frictions – 'traditionals' on some reservations, for example, feared that tribal members who had relocated to the cities might press for Termination in order to claim their share of tribal assets – issued an unprecedented 'Declaration of Indian Purpose'. It began with a resolution which asserted that: 'We ... [have] a right to choose our own way of life. Since our Indian culture is slowly being absorbed by the American society, we believe we have the responsibility of preserving our precious heritage . . .' It went on:

... the history and development of America show that the Indian has been subjected to duress, undue influence, unwarranted pressures, and policies which have produced uncertainty, frustration, and despair. Only when the public understands these conditions and is moved to take action toward the formulation and adoption of sound and consistent policies and programmes will these destroying factors be removed and the Indian resume his normal growth and make his maximum contribution to modern society.

The Declaration then outlined a series of proposals to strengthen Native American communities and give them greater self-determination, ending with a ringing appeal:

What we ask of America is not charity, not paternalism, even when benevolent. We ask only that the nature of our situation be recognized and made the basis of policy and action. In short, the Indians ask for assistance, technical and financial, for the time needed, however long that may be, to regain in the America of the space age some measure of the adjustment they enjoyed as the original possessors of their native land.

The Chicago Conference was, undoubtedly, a remarkable achievement – perhaps never before, and certainly not since the end of the 'Indian Wars', had so many disparate groups come together on their own initiative and united behind a common strategy – but it also exposed some of the rapidly widening divisions in Indian America. Although the final statement was carefully worded to play on non-Indian sympathies and avoid giving offence, many older Native Americans, cowed by a lifetime of threats from BIA officials, feared that even such a mild-mannered gesture of independence might provoke government reprisals. Some younger Indians, on the other hand, felt that the conference had not gone far enough. '... We looked on,' one of them recalled. 'We saw the "Uncle Tomahawks" fumbling around, passing resolutions, and putting headdresses on people. But as for taking a strong stand they just weren't doing it.' Leaving Chicago frustrated, the young radicals promptly organized their own, more outspoken, National Indian Youth Council.

During the remainder of Kennedy's brief presidency and the first turbulent years of the Johnson administration, the difference of approach focused primarily on the pressing issue of Native American poverty. There was no question that conditions in most Indian communities were appalling: a series of studies in the early 1960s revealed that more than 90 per cent of their housing was substandard; their infant mortality rate was more than twice the national average; their incidence of preventable diseases such as tuberculosis, meningitis and dysentery exceeded the general population's by anything up to a hundred times; their average age of death was forty-three years; and, with unemployment running between 40 per cent and 80 per cent, their average family income was only around 20 per cent of their Anglo-American neighbours. When NCAI delegates presented a petition to President Johnson in 1964, however, they still felt obliged to couch their concerns in terms which – with its echoes of the sentimental 'Great White Father' imagery used by generations of Euro-American treaty-makers – seemed calculated to disarm and flatter:

We are thankful that the great policies and programmes of our late, beloved, fallen President, John Fitzgerald Kennedy, will go forward under your administration. We again express our deep sorrow and grief for our late Chief, known to our people as Chief High Eagle...

We are delighted that you are going forward with President Kennedy's programmes and that you desire to make his hopes for the American Indian come true. You remembered us in your State of the Union message and this gave heart to all our people. Now, in aid of your programmes we should like to bring to your consideration our thoughts on some of our problems.

The rhetoric of the NIYC, by contrast, while no less emotional, was a good deal blunter. Members of the Youth Council – and other Indians – joined the Poor People's March on Washington in the summer of 1964, and its President, Mel Thom, a Paiute from Nevada, explicitly outlined the real anxieties gnawing at Native Americans in a (to some ears, frighteningly) forthright address to the Capital Conference on Poverty in Washington in 1964. While committing the Youth Council to 'joining in a concerted effort to remove the causes of poverty that destroys life among our people ... [and] continues to eat away at our existence,' he forcefully pointed out that Native Americans were not prepared to become more prosperous at the cost of losing their identity:

We must recognize and point out to others that we do want to live under better conditions, but we want to remember that we are Indians. We want to remain Indian people. We want this country to know that our Indian lands and homes are precious to us. We never want to see them taken away from us ...

Many of our friends feel that the Indian's greatest dream is to be free from second-class citizenship. We as youths have been taught that this freedom from second-class citizenship should be our goal. Let it be heard from Indian youth today that we do not want to be freed from our special relationship with the Federal Government. We only want our relationship between Indian Tribes and the Government to be one of good working relationship. We do not want to destroy our culture, our life that brought us through the period in which Indians were almost annihilated.

We do not want to be pushed into the mainstream of American life. The Indian youth fears this, and this fear should be investigated and removed. We want it to be understood by all those concerned with Indian welfare that no people can ever develop when there is fear and anxiety. There is fear among our Indian people today that our tribal relationship with the Federal Government will be terminated soon. This fear must be removed and life allowed to develop by free choices. The policy to push Indians into the mainstream of American life must be re-evaluated. We must have hope. We must have a goal. But that is not what the Indian people want. We will never be able to fully join in on that effort.

For any programme or policy to work we must be involved at the grassroots level. The responsibility to make decisions for ourselves must be placed in Indian hands. Any real help for Indian people must take cultural values into consideration. Programmes set up to help people must fit into the cultural framework . . .

Indian tribes need greater political power to act. This country respects power and is based on the power system. If Indian communities and Indian tribes do not have political power we will never be able to hang on to what we have now . . .

Partly in response to these demands, President Johnson promised to put 'first Americans first' in his attempt to create a 'Great Society'. In the face of stiff opposition from the Bureau of Indian Affairs, his administration made Native Americans eligible for assistance under the new Economic Opportunity Act, the main legislative weapon in the War On Poverty. The OEO's Indian budget was small – only $4 million in the first year – but it extended the tribes' access to resources and agencies that were not dominated by the BIA, and allowed them, often for the first time, to take initiatives that reflected their *own* vision of their needs and priorities. The result was an explosion of excitement in communities across 'Indian Country'. At the Standing Rock Sioux reservation, for instance, a total of $600,000 was given for a whole range of projects, including the establishment of a model tribal cattle ranch to teach ranch management; Headstart educational schemes in isolated rural communities, a programme designed to increase the involvement of old people in tribal life and a course in tribal politics. The local Sioux Headstart director said: 'Nothing like this has ever happened here before. We were never given the chance.' The Indian OEO director for the Makah tribe in Washington State was equally enthusiastic: 'It's the most exciting thing that's happened out here for years. We are really doing something by ourselves, for ourselves.'

The War On Poverty not only improved material conditions on many reservations, it also helped to breed a new hope and self-confidence among people whose experience had taught them to view the future with dread. Tribal leaders were able to go to Washington when they, rather than a BIA superintendent, wanted, and to develop personal relationships with officials in a host of different federal departments. They learnt how to write grant applications, to administer large sums of money, and even, on occasion, to bend the rules. The Sioux lawyer, Philip S. Deloria, recalls that:

> ... the OEO had a legal prohibition against construction. All it could do was remodel – tear down a wall for a Headstart classroom – but it could not build a bridge, a road, or a house. Roger Jourdain, of Red Lake [a Chippewa community in Minnesota], secured money for a training programme for carpenters, plumbers, and electricians, with a half million dollars budgeted for 'training materials.' Remarkably the 'homework' looked a lot like houses, and both the Red Lake people and the Red Lake sawmill benefited immeasurably.

But many Native Americans nonetheless had serious misgivings about the War On Poverty. Progress was hampered both by continuing bureaucratic restrictions – many proposals were rejected as 'unfeasible' and then rewritten by 'experts' until, as one leader said, 'the tribe says it isn't what they wanted. And of course it doesn't work.' – and a chronic shortage of funds. By 1966, the annual allocation for Native American projects was still only $12 million, or about $30 per reservation Indian – only a fraction of the amount that would have been required for long-term economic development. (By way of comparison: Congress estimated that $4.5 *billion* would be required to revitalize Appalachia, an area smaller than 'Indian Country'.) Even with the limited sums available, the government showed a marked preference for short-term, largely cosmetic projects: as Harry Peltier, the tribal OEO director on the Chippewa Turtle Mountain reservation, complained:

> We have been given more than a million dollars. We have a payroll of two hundred to two hundred and fifty people. We have sixteen projects. And what happens when it all ends? We will be lucky to have created four jobs.
>
> Instead of giving all that money, like welfare, why couldn't they let the tribes put it in capital investment? But no! They wouldn't let us do that. So we train people for jobs that won't exist. Our people are

in such a state of depression they would jump on any bandwagon that offered hope. But the government feeds the wagon before the horse.

On many reservations, moreover, much of the money, almost inevitably, ended up in the pockets of a relatively small tribal élite, creating or exacerbating tensions and resentments between families and factions.

But the most profound anxiety was that, ultimately, the War On Poverty would prove to be just another phase in the war on 'Indianness'. 'War has been declared on our condition,' said Mel Thom.

> To many of us poverty is a way of life. We do not like to be miserable, but our poor conditions have preserved a way of life for a while. Is this just stepping up efforts to absorb us into the mainstream of American life?

This unease grew, in part, from a fear that the Great Society could ultimately turn out to be just a kind of back-door Termination. By treating Native Americans just like other 'deprived' minorities, the War On Poverty might further blur the distinction, in the public mind, between Indians and other ethnic groups, and end up destroying by stealth the special legal status that Watkins and his followers had failed to demolish by a full-scale frontal assault. (In case this seems unduly paranoid, it is important to remember that Congress had taken the decision to 'free' Native Americans from 'all federal supervision and control' barely a decade before, just at the point when the New Deal had lulled them into believing that the United States was finally prepared to accept them as a permanent feature of American life.)

Although, as the Poor People's March demonstrated, the young radicals were willing to make a common cause with other disaffected minorities – some of them, in a half tongue-in-cheek acknowledgement of the Black Power movement, began saying that their aim was 'Red Power' – they were therefore also determined to stress the Indians' uniqueness. In an acute comparative analysis of 'The Red and the Black', Vine Deloria Jr. pointed out that Native and African Americans had sharply contrasting historical experiences, reflecting the very different ways in which they had been perceived by Europeans. While the Indian was an exotic 'wild animal' who had to be tamed by 'civilization', the black was an inferior 'beast of burden' who must be kept in his place:

> The white man adopted two basic approaches ... He systematically excluded blacks from all programmes, policies, social events, and economic schemes ...
>
> With the Indian the process was simply reversed ... Indians were ... subjected to the most intense pressure to become white. Laws passed by Congress had but one goal – the Anglo-Saxonization of the Indian ...
>
> The white man forbade the black to enter his own social and economic system and at the same time force-fed the Indian what he was denying the black. Yet the white man demanded that the black conform to white standards and insisted that the Indian don feathers and beads periodically to perform for him.

Because of these fundamental differences, Deloria and the other young radicals knew that the language of 'Civil Rights', which black leaders like Martin Luther King were using to try to win greater protection and opportunity for their people, could be invoked, as it so often had before, to justify *depriving* Native Americans of their identity and their remaining lands and resources. It is no coincidence that what one prominent Sioux described as 'the main thrust of anti-Indianism in this country' has come from an organization called the National Interstate Congress on Equal Rights and Responsibilities.

The NIYC's strategy was to highlight and reassert the Indians' rights as separate nations who had given up the very ground on which the United States was built and who were legally protected by solemn treaties. This, they argued, differentiated Native Americans from everyone else, and meant that they should be helped as a matter of right rather than of charity. As the radical tribal chairman Robert Jourdain put it:

> Where did you get the money for your government programmes? And your riches? From us! You acquired the richest resource we had. It was our land that made you rich.
>
> You are not giving us anything. You are merely returning a finger of sand for all that you have taken. But you act like you were doing us a kindness.

As a first focus for their campaign, the Youth Council chose the issue of tribal fishing rights in the northwest states of Oregon, Washington and Idaho. In these areas, fish had always been – and to a large extent remained – not only the staple food for peoples such as the Makah, the Yakima and the Tulalip, but also one of the central *motifs* of their cultures, and under the nineteenth-century treaties by which they had surrendered the bulk of their territory, the federal government had guaranteed that the Indians could continue to fish in their 'usual and accustomed' places. This right had been gradually eroded by the state authorities, however: in 1929, for example, the Quinault of Washington State had been barred from fishing at Peacock Split on the Columbia River so that their fishing rights could be leased to the Baker's Bay Fishing Company for $36,000 a year. Now, as a result of damming, pollution and large-scale commercial operations, the stock of fish in the region was drastically depleted, and the states had introduced conservation measures which they insisted must be applied equally to native and non-native people. When the tribes protested, the authorities replied that, under Public Law 280, passed during the Termination era, states had gained the right to extend their authority over Indian communities. 'The treaty must be broken. That's what happens when progress pushes forward,' said the director of State Fisheries in Washington.

In February 1964, following a court ruling in the State's favour, elders of the Makah tribe asked the NIYC to become involved in the dispute. The Youth Council immediately challenged the view that native fishermen were a threat to the survival of the trout and salmon on which their peoples had depended for thousands of years. 'It wasn't the Indians who killed off the buffalo,' they pointed out. 'The Indians do have conservation laws.' The real problem, they claimed, was not Native Americans but commercial fisheries:

> Salmon runs must survive Japanese, Russian, Alaskan, and Canadian fishermen before they reach our Northwestern streams and rivers. Upon entering Washington water, the salmon must pass through flotillas of commercial fisheries and sportsmen. At the end of the line are the Indians.

Determined that 'Justice [should] no longer be prostituted to the growing demands of non-Indians fishing and commercial interests upon fisheries resources,' the Youth Council resolved: 'We will stand with the tribes on the riverbanks.'

The NIYC response was to launch a campaign of civil disobedience. By continuing to fish in the 'usual and accustomed grounds' and defying the state authorities to arrest them, Native Americans would, they hoped, draw public attention to the problem and force the federal government to act in defence of its own treaties. It was, they knew, a potentially dangerous strategy, but 'the survival of the tribes' was at stake. According to Mel Thom:

> In the beginning the Indians just watched. The riverbanks were crowded. It was tense . . . You could feel the hostility build up against the game wardens. The authorities, the people with the law, were really mad at us for being there.
>
> We knew the game wardens would make arrests. They did. This was not going to be a cowboys-and-Indians story.
>
> And then a funny thing happened. The Indians began to enjoy it. They were happy to see some direct action. Then the tenseness broke. You would see kids running back and forth on the riverbanks and laughing.
>
> And some of the Indians took out their cameras and began taking pictures of the game wardens. Most times you see white people taking pictures of Indians, but this time it was Indians taking pictures of *mad* white people. That made them madder. It was our turn.
>
> You could feel there was a squaring off. [It was] the first time in recent history that we were publicly demonstrating what we privately felt.

The NIYC campaign helped to spark a new mood in 'Indian Country'. Fish-ins erupted throughout the Northwest, leading to scores of arrests and bringing Native Americans from across the United States – at one gathering, there were more than a thousand people from fifty-six tribes – into the area to support the beleaguered fishing peoples. At the same time, hundreds of non-Indians, including Marlon Brando and the black comedian Dick Gregory, publicly demonstrated their solidarity with the Indians by joining the protests and risking imprisonment. Finally, in 1966, the federal Department of Justice announced that since its treaties with Native Americans were 'solemn obligations of the government,' it would 'defend, on request, individual Indians, who fish in accordance with the treaty and tribal regulations, in the event they are charged, by a state, with violation of its fish and game laws.'

It was a remarkable, unprecedented victory: indisputable proof that what one NIYC member called 'the first full-scale intertribal *action* since the Indians defeated General Custer on the Little Big Horn' had been an extraordinary success. There was, however, something deeply paradoxical about it. The NIYC could justly claim to have waged probably the most effective Indian campaign against enforced assimilation in the twentieth century, yet their very achievement was, in some respects, a measure of just how far the forces of assimilation had already reshaped Indian America. Most of the members of the Youth Council had grown up at a time when a host of different factors – increased contact between Native and non-native Americans during the war years and the Relocation era, the spread of radio and TV, and, above all, the growing impact of public education – had combined to break down the isolation of Indian communities as never before. The leaders, almost without exception, were college-educated professionals – Mel Thom, for example, worked as an engineer with the Federal Aviation Authority before returning to his reservation to become the unpaid tribal chairman – whose sure-footed political skill reflected, in part, their familiarity with the structures they were attacking. Their increasing tendency to define themselves not only as members of specific tribes but also as 'Indians', their ability to play on Euro-American stereotypes of the native, and the jagged, satirical humour with which they lampooned their opponents all showed just how far non-Indian concepts had started to colonize their understanding of themselves and the world.

The 'New Indians', as the author Stan Steiner famously dubbed them in 1968, were only too painfully aware of these internal contradictions and the threat they posed to Native American cultural survival. In a moving testimony in 1967, one of the most outspoken leaders, Clyde Warrior – a member, ironically, of the small Ponca tribe, whose story ninety years before had fuelled the first great campaign for the 'liberation' of the Indian – gave a perceptive and prescient insight into the progressive Americanization of his people's sense of reality:

Fifty years ago the federal government came into our communities and by force carried most of our children away to distant boarding schools. My father and many of my generation lived their childhoods in an almost prison-like atmosphere. Many returned unable even to speak their own language. Some of them returned to become drunks. Most of them had become white haters or that most pathetic of all modern Indians – Indian haters. Very few ever became more than very confused, ambivalent and immobilized individuals – never able to reconcile the tensions and contradictions built inside themselves by outside institutions. As you can imagine, we have little faith in such kinds of federal programmes devised for our betterment nor do we see education as a panacea for all ills. In recent days, however, some of us have been thinking that perhaps the damage done to our communities by forced assimilation and directed acculturative pro-grammes was minor compared to the situation in which our children now find themselves. There is a whole generation of Indian children who are growing up in the American school system. They still look to their relatives, my generation, and my father's to see if they are worthy people. But their judgement and definition of what is worthy is now the judgement most Americans make. They judge worthiness as competence and competence as worthiness. And I am afraid me and my fathers do not fare well in the light of this situation and judgement. Our children are learning that their people are not worthy and thus that they individually are not worthy. Even if by some stroke of good fortune, prosperity was handed to us 'on a platter' that still would not soften the negative judgement our youngsters have of their people and themselves. As you know, people who feel themselves to be unworthy and feel they cannot escape this unworthiness turn to drink and crime and self-destructive acts. Unless there is some way that we as Indian individuals and communities can prove ourselves competent and worthy in the eyes of our youngsters there will be a generation of Indians grow to adulthood whose reaction to their situation will make previous social ills seem like a Sunday School picnic.

It was their experience of 'modern America' and its destructive effects that convinced the young radicals that they were involved in a life and death struggle – 'this is a real war . . .' said Mel Thom. 'No people . . . ever has been exterminated without putting up a last resistance.' – and, simultaneously, taught them how to fight it. Like the early nineteenth-century 'mixed-blood' Cherokees who had argued that the hope for tribal survival lay in becoming 'civilized', their uncomfortable vantage point gave them a deep insight into the mood of Euro-America. As opposition to the Vietnam War surged and millions of young people started to look for an alternative to 'American' values, they judged, correctly, that direct action such as the fish-ins, which only a decade before would have been unthinkable, could create a groundswell of public sympathy.

In some ways, for all its novelty, the 'New Indians' could be seen as a modern version of the eighteenth- and early nineteenth-century nativist movement. Like Tecumseh before them, the young radicals tried to forge a pan-tribal coalition based on 'high principles derived from the values and beliefs of our ancestors' but adapted to new conditions; like him, they used bellicose rhetoric and assertive tactics which provoked alarm and opposition among the more 'accommodationist' elements in their own community. The Youth Council were able to dismiss many of their critics as 'Apples' – 'red on the outside and white on the inside' – or 'Uncle Tomahawks', who had benefited personally by collaborating with the BIA. Some people, however, genuinely felt that the New Indians' noisy, publicity-seeking behaviour was not 'the Indian Way', while others – understandably, in view of their history – feared that it would create a backlash and allow the United States to resume the Termination policy with impunity. Mel Thom himself conceded:

> Being a conservative people, as they are, the tribal leaders had never had the opportunity to be aggressive. For long they had been dominated and run by the government. So action, direct action, was something they were not sure about. These tribes had never used direct action . . .
>
> The Indian had been stereotyped to act in certain ways; he was not supposed to take direct action, or to picket, or to demonstrate. People were curious to see if the Indians could do these things. So were the Indians!

But – perhaps on the face of it surprisingly – the culturally *most* conservative people generally needed less convincing. Although it is dangerous to generalize and easy to over-simplify – tribes, in practice, are usually a spectrum of views and loyalties rather than a series of clearly defined factions, and individuals can frequently move between one group and another – there was a hard core of 'traditionals' in many communities who, throughout the era of enforced assimilation, had clung stubbornly to their own tribal languages, oral traditions and spiritual beliefs. Descended, in many cases, from the diehards like Crazy Horse and his followers who had held out the longest against the US army in the nineteenth century, they chose to live in isolated settlements remote from the old 'agencies' where the BIA and the tribal government had their headquarters and Euro-American influence was strongest. Because they steadfastly believed that their relationship with the US was still governed by the 'sacred' treaties which their ancestors had signed (and which many of them remembered in remarkable detail), they remained implacably opposed to the Indian Reorganization Act, boycotting elections and viewing the federally elected tribal councils with deep suspicion. Their anxieties about the federal government and the 'progressive' tribal élite were only height-ened by the War On Poverty: why, they reasoned – recalling how Indian Claims Commission awards had been used as a lever to force tribes to accept Termination – would Washington give them huge sums of money except to compromise them?

Many traditional (or 'tribal') people, inured to being ignored or dismissed as backward-looking romantics, saw the burgeoning Youth Council as a beacon of hope.

They had watched, often with mounting despair, as assimilation had sapped the lifeblood of their cultures, making each successive gener-ation more 'American'. The rise of the Red Power movement, with its stress on treaty rights, its reverence for 'the elders' and the 'old ways' and its contempt for the corruption and pusillanimity of many tribal officials, seemed, at last, to be heralding a renaissance. Some viewed it as the long-awaited fulfilment of prophecy: in 1963, for example, Francis Le Quier, the chairman of the Ojibwa Great Council Fire, sent a message 'to the Chiefs and Spiritual Leaders of the Indians of the North and South American Continents':

> This is the day when the Great Spirit calls to all men. This is the day
> our Great Chiefs spoke of . . . This is the day when all the tribes shall

come together and be one nation. This is the day when a new race of
men shall be raised up by the power of the Great Spirit. This is the
day of the Great Justice.

You shall hear the voice of the Owl, the Fox, the Bear, the Coyote
and the Eagle.

Other 'traditionals' were encouraged by protests like the 'fish-ins' to
take 'direct action' themselves. A group of 'full-bloods' in eastern
Oklahoma formed the Five County Cherokee movement and issued a
Declaration that strikingly echoes the millennial language of earlier
cultural revivals:

We meet in a time of darkness to seek the path to the light. We come
together, just as our fathers have always done, to do these things . . .

We, the Five County Cherokees, are one people. We stand united
in the sight of God, our creator. We are joined by love and concern
for each other and for all men . . .

We offer ourselves as the voice of the Cherokee people. For many
years our people have not spoken and have not been heard. Now we
gather as brother and sisters . . .

We do this for the benefit of all Cherokees. We do this as a good
example to all men. Already we have gathered to protect our rights
to harvest fish and game to feed ourselves and our children . . .

When a member of the Five County Cherokees was arrested in 1966
for asserting his right to hunt, hundreds of armed Indians gathered
outside the courthouse, forcing the authorities to take the case out of
Oklahoma's jurisdiction and refer it to a – supposedly fairer – federal
court. Keeping a watchful eye on the trial, Clyde Warrior observed:

We have a Southern social structure in eastern Oklahoma. The only
way you change that structure is to smash it. You turn it over
sideways. And stomp on it. It appears to me that's what will happen
around here. I think violence will come about. And as far as I am
concerned the sooner the better.

❖   ❖   ❖

They call us the New Indians,
Hell, we are the Old Indians,

> *the landlords of this continent,*
> *coming to collect the rent.*
>
> Dennis Banks, Chippewa,
> co-founder American Indian Movement

> *Possibly the only means of being heard was by being vocal and*
> *violent . . . We're being taken seriously.*
>
> Albert White, Chairman, Prairie Island Indian
> Community, Minnesota

> *My parents did not want me to get involved, they weren't active.*
> *They were just struggling to live. When they got involved it was*
> *out of dire need. Their generation was almost at the point of being*
> *beaten into passivity. They would say, 'There's nothing we can do;*
> *government's too powerful.' The defeatism was very strong. One*
> *reason things changed then was that the children of those in*
> *power were resisting.*
>
> Leonard Peltier, activist

> *The movement gave me back my dignity and gave Indian people*
> *back their dignity.*
>
> Len Foster, activist

Clyde Warrior was right: violence did 'come about', although not, perhaps, quite as he expected. (Tragically, he died in 1968.) Over the next few years, the political and cultural landscape of the United States was transformed by a series of traumatic events – mounting losses in Vietnam, the assassinations of Martin Luther King and Robert Kennedy, the ugly collision between police and anti-war protesters at the 1968 Democratic Convention in Chicago – that left the country more fractured and polarized than anyone, even a decade before, could have foreseen. The melting-pot consensus of the Eisenhower era had fragmented into a host of competing identities and ideologies: why should everyone aspire to look like the perfect suburban Anglo family – crew-cut dad, stay-at-home mom and two sporty kids – when even the kids themselves, now at college or dodging the draft in Canada, were rejecting its values and exploring tribalism?

These changes helped to carry the rising tide of Native American activism from the reservations to the cities. By the end of the 1960s, there were perhaps as many as 500,000 Native Americans living in urban areas such as Los Angeles, Minneapolis and Chicago, largely as a result of policies such as Relocation which had been specifically designed to undermine their sense of tribal identity. Even those who seemed outwardly to have assimilated successfully, however, still sometimes found that their appearance and their background provoked hostility, and for thousands more, unable to find permanent homes or jobs and often reduced to drinking on the streets, prejudice and violence were a part of everyday life. To add to the growing confusion and discontent, urban Indians – like their relatives on the reservations – had followed the well-established Native American tradition of military service by volunteering in their thousands to fight in Vietnam, and more and more veterans were starting to return home touched by the general mood of bitterness and disillusion.

For many urban Native Americans, the explosion of pride and self-awareness among other minorities – especially blacks – seemed to offer a way out of their frustration and despair: rather than trying to gain acceptance in the racist, immoral society that had almost exterminated their ancestors and was now waging another genocidal war in Asia, they should return to their ethnic and cultural roots. For most of them, however, this was easier said than done. The children of relocated people, in particular, often had little first-hand knowledge or experience of their parents' background: their sense of who they were came largely from the behaviour of non-native Americans, who classified them – and frequently discriminated against them – simply as 'Indians'. Tribal distinctions were further eroded by the Indian social centres which had sprung up in many cities, where people from many different areas and cultures congregated to try to escape the loneliness and alienation of urban life. Even more than the NIYC leaders, therefore, most young non-reservation Native Americans tended to identify themselves primarily as members of an ethnic group rather than a tribe.

For a variety of reasons, the urban radicals generally found it easier to organize than their reservation counterparts. Living in the cities, they were less hampered both by BIA control and by inter-tribal frictions; they had better access to communications and a more intuitive grasp of how the US system worked; above all, as the former Commissioner of Indian Affairs, Philleo Nash, approvingly observed, their experience had turned them into 'street wise people' who 'understood the amount of leverage that would be obtained by being bad instead of being good.' This growing sense of power led to the creation of a whole spate of local organizations with all-embracing names such as 'American Indians – United' and 'United Native Americans' that reflected the new 'consolidated' Indian perspective. Probably the most influential, in the long term, was the American Indian Movement (AIM), founded in 1968 by two Chippewas, George Mitchell and Dennis Banks, to help the Native American population of Minneapolis. As well as organizing patrols to protect Indians from police brutality, they used War On Poverty funds to establish 'urban alternative' schools, where Native American children who had dropped out of the state system could develop greater cultural awareness and self-respect and learn how to survive in both the Indian and non-Indian worlds.

Their ability to be 'bad' quickly catapulted the urban activists into the national consciousness. In November 1969, a party of seventy-eight Native Americans from some fifty tribes, led by students angry at the lack of opportunity to study and practise their own cultures, 'reclaimed' the abandoned island of Alcatraz 'in the name of all American Indians.' Calling themselves 'Indians of All Tribes', they then invited indigenous people throughout the US, Canada and Mexico to attend a Conference of American Indian Nations. Their aim, they said, was to give 'Indian people . . . a Cultural Centre of their own':

> For several decades, Indian people have not had enough control of training their young people. And without a cultural centre of their own, we are afraid that the old Indian ways may be lost. We believe that the only way to keep them alive is for Indian people to do it themselves . . .
>
> We realize that there are more problems in Indian communities besides having our culture taken away. We have water problems, land problems, 'social' problems, job opportunity problems, and many others . . .
>
> We realize too that we are not getting anywhere fast by working alone as individual tribes. If we can gather together as brothers and come to a common agreement, we feel that we can be much more

effective, doing things for ourselves, instead of having someone else doing it, telling us what is good for us.

So we must start somewhere. We feel that if we are going to succeed, we must hold on to the old ways. *This is the first and most important reason we went to Alcatraz Island.*

We feel that the only reason Indian people have been able to hold on and survive through decades of persecution and cultural deprivation is that the Indian way of life is and has been strong enough to hold the people together.

The occupiers' immediate plan – to build 'a college, a religious and spiritual centre, a museum, a centre of ecology, and a training school' on Alcatraz – came to nothing: the government refused to meet their demands, they were plagued by logistical problems and internal dissension, and when armed federal marshals finally repossessed the island in June 1971 only fifteen Native Americans were still there. Nonetheless, as one of the leaders, Lenada James, modestly puts it:

The protest movement at Alcatraz had positive results. Many individuals were not ashamed to be Indian any more. People who had relocated in the cities were reidentifying themselves as Indians.

The impact was, in fact, galvanic for many Native Americans. During the occupation, hundreds of Indians thronged to the island to join the protest and thousands more were inspired by it. One young man of Indian ancestry, deeply confused about his identity, recalls: 'I was in Vietnam when I heard about Alcatraz. I thought "Right on! That's great what those guys are doing."' He later embarked on a 'personal journey' which led to him readopting a Native American family name and going 'back to my grandfather's culture.' For another urban Indian, Frances Wise:

Alcatraz was a major turning point in my life. For the first time in my life I was proud to be an Indian and an Indian woman. I grew up in an all white area. It was very difficult. You were constantly struggling to maintain any kind of positive feeling, any kind of dignity. Alcatraz changed all that.

During the early 1970s, this new-found pride and militancy fuelled an upsurge of Indian protests across the country, many of them orchestrated by the American Indian Movement, which became a national organization in 1971 and quickly emerged as the most potent voice of Native American activism. AIM's dominance stemmed, in part, from the growing influence of one of its new members, Russell Means, an eloquent, charismatic Oglala Sioux who had already shown his political flair and his genius for publicity by leading demonstrations at two of the most cherished symbols of US culture: Mount Rushmore and the replica of the Pilgrim Fathers' ship, *Mayflower II*. Like many of the NIYC leaders before him, Means argued forcefully that the movement could only legitimately claim to represent the Native American community as a whole if it made the concerns of 'tribal' and 'traditional' people on the reservations, who had done most to keep the 'old ways' alive, its first priority. Although there was some opposition from the old urban leadership, this view increasingly shaped AIM's strategy over the next few years.

There was, without question, a deepening crisis in many Indian communities which spectacular protests like Alcatraz – despite their success in drawing attention to the predicament of Native Americans generally – had done little to highlight or resolve. As well as the chronic problems of poverty, disease, unemployment, inadequate housing and public services, most reservations consisted of poor, low-quality land which, with over-use and growing competition from non-Indians for water and other resources, was becoming progressively more arid and eroded. The BIA, as the Indians' legal trustee, should, in theory, have fought vigorously to protect their rights, many of which were guaranteed by treaty, but in practice – partly because of its susceptibility to corruption and political pressure, and partly because its position within the Department of the Interior gave it a conflict of interest with other agencies, such as the Bureau of Reclamation – it often undermined the tribes by siding with their enemies.

A striking example is the story of a Paiute community at Pyramid Lake on the Nevada–California border, who, under a treaty signed in 1859, received 'first-user' rights to water from the Truckee River. In 1902, however, the Department of the Interior embarked on an irrigation project for non-Indian farmers which diverted water from the river, sharply reducing the level of the lake and threatening the fish on which the Indians depended. By the outbreak of the Second World

War, one species was extinct in the lake, and another, the *cui-cui*, which occurs nowhere else in the world, was struggling for survival.

In 1955, the Bureau of Reclamation persuaded the Secretary of the Interior to authorize the Washoe Project, which involved taking yet more water for non-Indian irrigation schemes. This time, the Paiutes, who before had been too bewildered and frightened to take action, complained to Congress. A decade of inquiries and Task Forces followed, with the Secretary of the Interior exchanging, in dizzying succession, his BIA hat, which made him the champion of the Indians, for his Bureau of Reclamation hat, which made him their opponent. Finally, the Department of the Interior announced that it had modified its plans to 'save' some water for the Paiutes, but that it had no authority to deliver it to them.

Events took a more bizarre turn in 1968, when an Inter-State Compact between Nevada and California agreed that the Indians' allocation of water should be cut back still further and that neither they nor the Department of the Interior could appeal against the decision. When the Secretary of the Interior, briefly on the side of the Indians again, protested, the Governors of California – then Ronald Reagan – and Nevada invited him to meet them in a gambler's cabin cruiser in the middle of Lake Tahoe to sort out their differences. After ninety minutes, they agreed to 'stabilize' Pyramid Lake by draining it another 152 feet – at which point, as one Indian observed, it would be a stable salt-bed.

Other problems arose from the policy of reservation development, which in the 1950s and early 1960s had been hailed as an alternative to endemic poverty and termination but which had, in some places, become a monster. The minority of tribes with rich mineral or fossil fuel deposits, in particular, often found that the BIA had given them appalling advice, encouraging them to sell their resources for far less than they were worth and failing to demand proper environmental safeguards. The Northern Cheyenne tribal council in Montana, for instance, having been told that there would only be a demand for coal for a limited period, were persuaded to sell exploration and mining permits to more than half of their reservation for less than 75 per cent of the market rate at a time (the late 1960s) when energy costs were, in fact, rising. The Department of the Interior's own regulations, moreover, required that a survey of the likely consequences should be made before any leases were sold, but the Bureau failed to carry it out until almost two years *after* the last sale – and then only under immense pressure from Washington. When the study finally appeared it made grim reading, listing, among the possible risks: 'Destruction of Cheyenne culture – the lifestyle of the people,' 'Cheyenne become a minority in their own homeland,' and 'Pollution of all sorts, i.e, human, cultural, air, sound, noise etc.'

These warnings were not fanciful. In 1971, energy suppliers revealed that the exploitation of Cheyenne coal was part of a plan to transform some 250,000 square miles of the northern plains – an area containing 20 per cent of the world's known coal reserves – into a gigantic power station which could fuel the United States for between four and six centuries. A non-Indian city of 30,000 people was envisaged for the Northern Cheyenne reservation (and one of 200,000 for the adjoining Crow reservation), but the BIA did not feel that the magnitude of the project justified making any clauses for the protection of the Indians 'binding upon the lessees.'

The Indians' growing sense of outrage, as the catalogue of BIA abuses began to emerge in the early 1970s, was heightened by a rash of violent racial attacks, which left several Native Americans – including Richard Oakes, one of the leaders of the Alcatraz takeover – dead. When Raymond Yellow Thunder, a 51-year-old Lakota, was stripped naked, forced to dance in front of a group of drunken US army veterans and then murdered in Gordon, Nebraska, at the start of 1972, AIM was finally goaded into action. Led by Russell Means and Dennis Banks, more than 1,000 Native Americans, mostly from the nearby Sioux reservations of Pine Ridge and Rosebud, occupied Gordon and finally succeeded in forcing the authorities to bring the killers to justice – a triumph that made them instant heroes in 'Indian Country' and swelled AIM's membership among 'tribal' people.

For their part, the AIM leaders showed a growing interest in 'traditional' culture. In August 1972, following a Sun Dance at Rosebud, some of them held a momentous meeting with the spiritual leaders Henry and Leonard Crow Dog. One of them later recalled:

> That is actually when the American Indian Movement was first born.
> Because we think that the American Indian Movement is not only an

advocate for Indian people. It is the spiritual rebirth of our nation. It carries the spirituality of our ancient people and of our elder people. So now the American Indian Movement relies very, very heavily on the traditional leaders and the holy men of the various tribes – to give them the direction they need so they can best help the Indian people.

Later the same year, at the suggestion of Robert Burnette, former Executive Director of the National Congress of American Indians, AIM agreed to join other organizations in a spiritual crusade 'under the banner of the Trail of Broken Treaties' and 'proceed to Washington, where we will show the world what Indians truly stand for.' Like Alcatraz, the Trail was an emotional and political turning point for thousands of Indians. As they made their way across the country, the caravans of marchers stopped at reservations to explain their aims and rally support, giving many urban people their first glimpse of the landscape and the community from which their parents or grandparents had been exiled (or had exiled themselves), and many 'tribal' Indians had their first taste of the broader Red Power movement. In her book *Lakota Woman*, Mary Crow Dog records how:

The American Indian Movement hit our reservation like a tornado, like a new wind blowing out of nowhere, a drumbeat from far off getting louder and louder. It was almost like the Ghost Dance fever that had hit the tribes in 1890, old uncle Dick Fool Bull said, spreading like a prairie fire. It even was like the old Ghost Dance song Uncle Dick was humming:

> Maka sitomniya teca ukiye
> Oyate ukiye, oyate ukiye . . .
> A new world is coming,
> A nation is coming,
> The eagle brought the message.

I could feel this new thing, almost hear it, smell it, touch it. Meeting up with AIM for the first time loosened a sort of earthquake inside me.

The evident sincerity of the marchers and their emphasis on 'tribal' issues persuaded many 'traditional' people, including elders and religious leaders, to join them, swelling the Trail of Broken Treaties into an army of Native Americans from the most disparate backgrounds and cultures. In Minneapolis, they held a series of workshops and, despite their immense diversity, were able to agree a twenty-point programme which – in the words of one Native American authority – was 'stamped all over' with 'the mark of the traditional Indian,' stressing the need for 'an honest relationship' between the tribes and the United States based on a respect for treaty rights and a return to the treaty-making process. Frances Wise vividly describes the sense of solidarity and elation as they continued on their way:

> Many of the people with us were like me before Alcatraz. They didn't quite understand what was going on, but they were interested. A lot of people joined us. I remember driving around a freeway cloverleaf outside of Columbus, Ohio. All I could see were cars in front of us and behind us, their lights on, red banners flying from their antennas. It was hard to believe, really. We were that strong. We were really doing something. It was exciting and fulfilling. It's like someone who's been in bondage. Indian country knew that Indians were on the move.

When they reached Washington, however, the atmosphere quickly soured. The government, which from the beginning had been uncertain how to respond – the Assistant Secretary of the Interior had publicly offered to co-operate with the marchers while secretly instructing the Commissioner of Indian Affairs that 'the Bureau is not to provide any funding either directly or indirectly' – had failed either to provide decent accommodation for them or to arrange meetings with the President and other high-ranking leaders. The final straw came when they were refused entry to Arlington Cemetery to honour Native American war dead, on the grounds that they were 'political advocates'. They angrily took possession of the Bureau of Indian Affairs building and, when armed police tried to oust them, barricaded themselves inside with furniture and office equipment. After six days of extreme tension they were at last induced to leave, without bloodshed or legal prosecution and with a promise – temporarily retracted when it transpired that they had taken some documents with them – to investigate and answer their demands. It was not until early the following year, when public and media attention had waned, that the government finally gave a definitive response: declaring the Twenty Points to be impracticable, it rejected them all out of hand.

Although the Trail of Broken Treaties was, in some ways, a tribute to the Native Americans' ability to heal differences and work together, it also revealed a few ominous cracks in their communities. Middle-of-the-road 'tribal' people were sometimes genuinely (if quietly) affronted by the – as they saw it – fundamentalist fervour of 'born-again Indians', who seemed to be reproaching them for abandoning the 'old ways'. As one Sioux put it: 'I don't need some urban activist to come and tell me how to be an Indian. I've always been an Indian. I don't have to put on feathers to prove it.'

A few even muttered that the newcomers weren't 'real' Indians at all, but simply 'hippies', whose romantic conception of native culture had come primarily from non-Indian films and books rather than their own experience.

Some tribal leaders had more practical reasons for fearing the activists. Many of them were closely identified with the increasingly unpopular and discredited BIA: a few had profited from the – frequently secret – sale of leases, and even those who were not personally corrupt often believed that AIM and its followers were inviting disaster by 'rocking the boat.' In 1970, a group of them, openly encouraged by the government, had formed the conservative National Tribal Chairmen's Association to counteract the radicals' influence, and during the BIA occupation several chairmen dutifully accepted an invitation to appear at a press conference to condemn the protestors as 'dissident urban-oriented Indians.' (To their, and the authorities', embarrassment, some of the Trail of Broken Treaties organizers went to the same meeting and denounced them as unrepresentative stooges 'in the hip pocket of the BIA.')

All these tensions came to a head a few months later on the Oglala Sioux' Pine Ridge reservation in South Dakota. In April 1972, Dick Wilson, a right-wing, mixed-blood rancher virulently opposed to the radicals – he once bragged that he would personally 'cut off Russell Means' braids' – and scornful of the predominantly full-blood traditionals, had become chairman of the tribal council, allegedly after buying hundreds of votes with drinks and bribes provided by non-

Indian bootleggers and businessmen. Although he had a reputation as a heavy drinker and a bully, he was supported by local BIA officials, who saw him a useful foil against the increasingly militant and influential activists.

Wilson promptly installed himself as a kind of minor third world dictator, handing out jobs and contracts to family and friends, diverting government funds to his supporters, using a 'goon squad' of armed men to terrorize – and sometimes murder – his opponents and unilaterally suspending the tribal council when it criticized him. The BIA took no steps to end this flamboyant corruption: in fact, when he illegally dismissed the tribal vice-chairman and barred AIM members from attending meetings on the reservation, it gave him an additional $62,000 to provide extra police protection for the BIA building and the tribal headquarters.

Faced with mounting violence and oppression, hundreds of traditionals and other Oglalas formed the Oglala Sioux Civil Rights Organization (OSCRO) to oppose Wilson, and three of the suspended tribal councillors launched impeachment proceedings against him. The hearing was a farce, however: the judge had been appointed by Wilson, who stood behind him, prompting him, and acting as both prosecution and defence. When, unsurprisingly, Wilson won the case, OSCRO held an angry meeting, at which it was decided that AIM should be invited on to the reservation to help overthrow the BIA-backed tribal council and set up a traditional government. Mary Crow Dog remembers arriving with the AIM contingent:

> The scene . . . was peaceful enough. Kids were playing frisbee. Elders were drinking coffee out of paper cups. An old man was telling me, 'What are we to do? If you are with AIM you're a no-good renegade. If you are with Dickie Wilson you're a goddam goon. If you are with the government, you're no Indian at all.' All the old chiefs with the historic great names were there and all the medicine men . . . Only one important traditional man was missing who was too old and sick to attend . . . Contrary to what some of the media said later, the overwhelming majority of those present were Sioux, born and bred on the reservation. Russell Means said a few words which I still remember, though I can't quote them exactly. The drift of his speech was: 'If I have to die, I don't want to die in some barroom brawl, or

in a stupid car accident, but want my death to have some meaning. Maybe the time has come when we need some Indian martyrs.' One old man said something to the effect that he had lived all his life in Pine Ridge in darkness. That the whites and men like Wilson had thrown a blanket over the whole reservation and that he hoped we would be the ones to yank this blanket off and let some sunshine in.

It began to dawn on me that what was about to happen, and what I personally would be involved in, would be unlike anything I had witnessed before. I think everybody who was there felt the same way – an excitement that was choking our throats. But there was still no definite plan for what to do. We had all assumed that we would go to Pine Ridge town, the administrative centre of the reservation, the seat of Wilson's and the government's power. We had always thought that the fate of the Oglalas would be settled there. But as the talks progressed it became clear that nobody wanted us to storm Pine Ridge, garrisoned as it was by the goons, the marshals, and the FBI. We did not want to be slaughtered. There had been too many massacred Indians already in our history. But if not Pine Ridge, then what? As I remember, it was the older women like Ellen Moves Camp and Gladys Bissonette who first pronounced the magic words 'Wounded Knee', who said, 'Go ahead and make your stand at Wounded Knee. If you men won't do it, you can stay here and talk for all eternity and we women will do it.'

The next day, 27 February 1973, a cavalcade of some fifty cars set off for Wounded Knee, passing through the town of Pine Ridge, where 'The half-bloods and goons, the marshals and government snipers on their rooftop, were watching us, expecting us to stop and start a confrontation . . .' When they finally arrived, according to Mary Crow Dog:

. . . we stood on the hill where the fate of the old Sioux Nation, Sitting Bull's and Crazy Horse's nation, had been decided, and where we, ourselves, came face to face with our fate . . .

. . . There were a few snowflakes in the air. We all felt the presence of the spirits of those lying close by in the long ditch [the victims of the 1890 massacre], wondering whether we were about to join them, wondering when the marshals would arrive. We knew that we would not have to wait long for them to make their appearance.

The young men tied eagle feathers to their braids, no longer unemployed kids, juvenile delinquents, or winos, but warriors. I thought of our old warrior societies – the Kit Foxes, the Strong Hearts, the Badgers, the Dog Soldiers. The Kit Foxes – the Tokalas – used to wear long sashes. In the midst of battle, a Tokala would sometimes dismount and pin the end of his sash to the earth. By this he signified his determination to stay and fight on his chosen spot until he was dead, or until a friend rode up and unpinned him, or until victory. Young or old, men or women, we had all become Kit Foxes, and Wounded Knee had become the spot upon which we had pinned ourselves. Soon we would be encircled and there could be no retreat. I could not think of anybody or anything that would 'unpin' us. Somewhere, out on the prairie surrounding us, the forces of the government were gathering, the forces of the greatest power on earth.

They did not have long to wait. Federal forces, alerted that there had been a 'burglary' at Wounded Knee, quickly surrounded the area and sealed it off with roadblocks. The occupiers responded by barricading themselves – and several Sioux and non-Indian residents – into the village.

The siege of Wounded Knee lasted seventy-one days, making it one of the most serious outbreaks of civil unrest in modern US history. Inside the village were hundreds of Sioux and – at various times – members of sixty-four other tribes and a handful of black, chicano and Euro-American supporters who had managed to slip past the government roadblocks; surrounding them, eventually, were more than 300 heavily armed 'goons', National Guardsmen and US marshals from an élite Special Operations Group. On 11 March, having been refused a Congressional investigation of their complaints, the Indians announced at a special ceremony that they were forming a new Independent Oglala Nation and demanded that the tribal council should be abolished and the government should start dealing with them under the terms of the 1868 Fort Laramie Treaty.

Like Alcatraz, Wounded Knee attracted huge media attention and set off a wave of sympathy among Native Americans and radicals across the country. In several cities, Indian and hispanic demonstrators were killed in pro-AIM protests. Supporters airlifted in supplies in small planes, or smuggled them through the cordon around the village. Gradually, though, the government tightened its grip, flying in reinforcements, arresting known sympathizers as they travelled towards the reservation with arms and provisions and using helicopter patrols to deter air-drops. At the same time, there were increasingly intense exchanges of fire, during which two occupiers were killed and one US marshal was seriously wounded. Rather than launch an all-out assault, however – as Wilson impetuously demanded – the federal authorities, only too aware of the political price they would pay if there were more bloodshed, relied on negotiations and a process of attrition to end the siege.

Their patience paid off. At the beginning of May, the occupiers agreed to lay down their arms and leave the village, in exchange for an undertaking that they would be protected against Wilson's regime and that federal representatives would meet them later in the month to discuss the 1868 treaty. The meeting was held as planned, but the government delegation failed to return for a promised follow-up conference two weeks later. Instead, a US marshal gave the hundreds of waiting Sioux a letter from the President's special assistant, which curtly informed them: 'The days of treaty making with the American Indians ended in 1871, 102 years ago. Only Congress can rescind or change in any way statutes enacted since 1871, such as the Indian Reorganization Act . . .'

Appropriately, perhaps, the Wounded Knee siege was the high-water mark of Native American activism. Although the radical movement continued – in 1974, for instance, AIM established the International Treaty Council to try to win recognition of Native American sovereignty from the UN and other nations – it was never again able to attain the same level of public awareness and support. With US withdrawal from the two conflicts – the Vietnam War and the War On Poverty – which had done so much to shape the previous decade, the country gradually drifted towards a more consensual, cautious mood which, once again, subtly but inexorably, altered the way in which Native Americans were seen and saw themselves.

Even when pro-Indian sentiment was at its height – reflected in the huge success of films like *Soldier Blue* and *Little Big Man* – the generalized, hand-wringing concern felt by many people for the 'plight' of Native Americans did not always translate into support for their political demands. As Vine Deloria Jr. records in *God Is Red*, non-

Indians – all too understandably – usually found it easier to identify with the sufferings of dead Native Americans than with the struggles of their living descendants:

> In the next four years it seemed as if every book on modern Indians was promptly buried by a book on the 'real' Indians of yesteryear. The public overwhelmingly turned to *Bury My Heart At Wounded Knee* and *The Memoirs of Chief Red Fox* to avoid the accusations made by modern Indians in *The Tortured Americans* and *Custer Died for Your Sins* ... Each takeover of government property only served to spur further sales of the Brown review of the wars of the 1860s [*Bury My Heart At Wounded Knee*].

Throughout the 1970s, this head-in-the-sand attitude turned increasingly to impatience and irritation. As early as 1972, during the BIA occupation, the *Washington Evening Star* warned:

> Through the years there has been a deep reservoir of public sympathy for the American Indians, but it is bound to be diminished by the atrocious spectacle staged here in recent days. It could be dried up almost totally if there are more such dangerous and destructive acts by Indian extremists.

Almost unnoticed, except by the people most directly affected, the US government took advantage of this more conservative and quiescent atmosphere to embark on a ruthless war against the 'extremists' in AIM and other radical organizations. Federal agents, including a SWAT (Special Weapons and Tactics) team, were despatched to Pine Ridge to support the BIA police and Dick Wilson's 'goons' in a brutal campaign of repression which claimed scores of lives. Using a range of more or less dishonest tactics – in one case, according to the judge, the FBI had 'stooped to a new low' by lying under oath, altering documents and planting a paid spy – federal and state law-enforcement agencies subjected the AIM leaders to systematic harassment, with the result that one or other of them was almost permanently in court or in jail: in the six years following the siege, Russell Means, for instance, faced a total of forty charges, on thirty-nine of which he was acquitted. At the same time, AIM was weakened by a federal agent, Douglass [sic] Durham, who infiltrated the leadership and became Director of Security.

Other Native American leaders, even those who were personally sympathetic to the radicals, were not slow to learn the lessons of the AIM experience: dissidence and political action, beyond certain well-defined limits, would not be tolerated; if you wanted to achieve anything, you must work through the system. The system itself, however, had been modified by the turmoil of the last ten years. Faced by the mounting unrest in Native American communities, the government had established a whole series of Task Forces, Commissions and Inquiries to review policy and find out 'what the Indians want.' One almost unanimous conclusion was that Indians did *not* want Termination, and in 1970 President Nixon, in his Message to Congress on Indian Affairs, declared:

> Because termination is morally and legally unacceptable, because it produces bad practical results, and because the mere threat of termination tends to discourage greater self-sufficiency among Indian groups, I am asking the Congress to pass a new Concurrent Resolution which would expressly renounce, repudiate and repeal the termination policy as expressed in House Concurrent Resolution 108 of the 83rd Congress. This resolution would explicitly affirm the integrity and right to continued existence of all Indian tribes and Alaska native governments, recognizing that cultural pluralism is a source of national strength.

The Nixon and Ford eras brought further encouraging signs of a modest shift in federal policy. In 1970, the government decided that, as a gesture of good faith, the sacred Blue Lake of Taos Pueblo, which had been taken without consultation or compensation in 1906 and which the Indians had been trying to get back ever since, should finally be returned to the tribe. Two years later, Congress passed the Indian Education Act, which gave Native American communities the opportunity to run their own schools and to adapt the curriculum to reflect their own traditions; and in 1975 the Indian Self-Determination and Educational Assistance Act, which allowed tribes, if they wanted, to contract with the government to administer their own federal programmes.

These limited changes fell far short of the wild, exhilarating vision of freedom, sovereignty and rebirth which had inspired the radicals at the fish-ins and on Alcatraz, on the Trail of Broken Treaties and at Wounded Knee, but they did offer a concrete, practical alternative to Termination. All across the country, New Indians, some excitedly, some grudgingly, a few subversively, settled down to the brave new world of Self-Determination – or, as Russell Means put it, 'Self-Administration'.

Epilogue

When Indian bingo games are humming in almost every nook and cranny of our land, stealing the most sacred ritual of the Roman Catholic Church and gathering the white man's coin as quickly as it can reasonably be retrieved, progress is being made. When multitudes of young whites roam the West convinced they are Oglala Sioux Pipe Carriers and on a holy mission to protect 'Mother Earth,' and when priests and ministers, scientists and drug companies, ecologists and environmentalists are crowding the reservations in search of new rituals, new medicines, or new ideas about the land, it would appear as if American Indians finally have it made. Indeed, some tribal chairmen are now well-heeled Republicans worried about gun control, moral fibre, and prayer in schools. In many respects American Indians are looking increasingly like middle-class Americans.

. . . The situation would be perilous indeed were it not for the fact that the white majority spent the past generation tearing down its culture also. A winsome essay in Time *magazine during the summer of 1994 asked the question of how to define things once everything in society is 'hip.' The problem of being 'hip' plays right into our hands. Indians can always become whites because the requirements are not very rigorous, but can whites really become Indians? A good many people seriously want to know. They are discontented with their society, their government, their religion, and everything around them and nothing is more appealing than to cast aside all inhibitions and stride back into the wilderness, or at least a wilderness theme park, seeking the nobility of the wily savage who once physically fought civilization and now, symbolically at least, is prepared to do it again.*

Vine Deloria Jr., *Red Earth, White Lies*

How do we make permanent the understanding that tribes are political entities and a part of the American system? We are more than just unique little cultures. But I do not think that most people or the federal government believe that we are a permanent part of the system. We are tired of the burden of constantly educating the Congress and the government about this basic relationship. We are not like the blacks, Hispanics, or any other ethnic group. We are a permanent part of the political structure of the United States.

LaDonna Harris, Comanche

Many years ago ... our grandparents foresaw ... our future ... [They said:] 'Cities will progress and then decay to the ways of the lowest beings ... Population will increase until the land can hold no more. The tribes of men will mix. The dark liquids they drink will cause the people to fight among themselves. Families will break up: father against children and children against one another.

Maybe when the people have outdone themselves ... [o]ur father, the sun, will not rise to start the day. Then our possessions will turn into beasts and devour us whole.

Zuñi prophecy

During the last quarter of the twentieth century, the Native American world has, arguably, become more contradictory and confusing than at any time in the last 500 years. A swirl of currents and cross-currents, within US society and within Indian communities themselves, has created a picture so complex that – even more intractably than the earlier history – it defies analysis. The perennial urge to simplify, to reduce native people to a repertoire of vivid but childish images – spiritual nature-lover, tragic victim, feckless bum – only adds another layer to the ever-deepening accretions of irony and ambiguity.

As part of a broader effort to encourage greater sensitivity towards minorities 'American Indians' have become 'Native Americans'. Some native people have embraced the new term, seeing it as a weapon against prejudice and 'negative stereotyping', but many others – unknown, apparently, to the sombre liberals who tut-tut and shake their heads when you use the word 'Indian' – still call themselves

'Indians' when they cannot use their own, preferred, tribal name. For thousands, especially on the reservations, it is merely an irrelevance, another solution to the 'Indian Problem' thought up by 'non-Indians' to avoid addressing the real problems of alienation, poverty and dispossession, but others view it as something more sinister: an attempt to magic away centuries of misunderstanding, tragedy and suffering by a simple sleight of tongue. One tribal chairman even suggested to me that its real purpose was to bring about a kind of verbal termination: since all the treaties and laws relating to native people use the word 'Indian', their special legal status would be blurred and undermined by the use of another term.

Certainly, 'Native American', with its assumption that all the immensely varied indigenous societies of the Western hemisphere – who before contact had no concept of being 'natives' of 'America' and never saw themselves as a single, continental population – constitute a homogeneous, 'other' group, is ultimately just as Eurocentric as 'Indian'. Nonetheless, the willingness of millions of non-Indians to retrain themselves to use it, out of an earnest – if sometimes rather fuzzy – desire to avoid giving offence, does suggest that native people, at least in the abstract, are now viewed with greater respect. Striking evidence of this sea change comes from the last three censuses, in which the number of US citizens identifying themselves as 'Indian' soared from just over half a million in 1960 to almost two million in 1990. Demographic research shows that this staggering increase is only partly explicable by high birth rates and lower mortality: much of it stems from a new, more positive climate, in which people of native ancestry, who were previously too ashamed, frightened or confused to admit their background, now feel it is acceptable to 'be Indian.' As Vine Deloria Jr., as barbed as ever, puts it in the recent *Red Earth, White Lies*:

> As whites get more familiar with Indian symbols and beliefs we can expect ... the ... figures to skyrocket beyond belief in the year 2000 and beyond. Indeed, today it is popular to be an Indian. Within a decade it may be a necessity. People are not going to want to take the blame for the sorry state of the nation, and claiming allegiance with the most helpless racial minority may well be the way to escape accusations.

Epilogue

There are other, more tangible signs that US culture has begun to view 'the Indian' in a warmer light. Since the Kiowa–Cherokee N. Scott Momaday won the Pulitzer Prize in 1969 for his novel *The House Made of Dawn*, a whole series of Native American writers and academics – Paula Gunn Allen, Louise Erdrich, Leslie Marmon Silk, Gerald Vizenor and others – have established themselves with books, often with mythical themes, that describe and reflect Indian life. Native American arts and crafts, particularly pottery, jewellery and blankets from the Southwest, are prized by collectors all over the world, and several artists have gained international reputations. The success of *Dances With Wolves* in the early 1990s elevated buckskin, beads and turquoise to high fashion, prompting a spate of articles in glossy magazines about 'the Indian look'. Clearly, after five hundred years, the Euro-American hunger for the wild, exotic, indigenous 'other' is still unsated.

For many Native American groups, the more tolerant atmosphere has brought positive benefits. After years of campaigning, many of the tribes and bands terminated in the 1950s and 1960s have been restored to federal recognition (although the Klamath have still only regained a few acres of their former reservation). Other small, marginalized communities in New England and the Southeast, who had *never* been federally recognized – primarily because their ancestors had surrendered their land not by treaty with the federal government, as required by the Trade and Intercourse Act of 1790, but by more or less fraudulent 'treaties' with colonial or state governments or private individuals – emerged from the shadows to sue the United States for restitution. Some of these cases were dismissed, but several were successful: the Penobscot and the Passamaquoddy of Maine, for example, won 300,000 acres of land, $27.5 million and recognition as 'Indian tribes'. Although this was far less than the 12.5 million acres and $25 billion their lawyers had demanded, it was an important breakthrough for people so inured to discrimination and neglect that they were known as 'the niggers of Maine'.

The proliferation of eastern Indian land claims reflects, in part, the growing number of Native American lawyers, many of whom have joined organizations such as the American Indian Law Resource Center and the Native American Rights Fund (NARF) in order to help native communities turn the 'white man's law' to their advantage rather than being its victims. Among many other causes, NARF, for instance, took up the case of the exhausted and bewildered Pyramid Lake Paiutes and doggedly pursued it through court after court, finally winning a partial victory which – for the time being, at least – seems to have saved the lake. Scores of other lawsuits, to uphold the rights of tribal governments or to secure the return of land, have achieved a success that would probably have been unthinkable two generations ago. At the same time, deep-seated Indian grievances over the despoliation of burial sites and the removal of artefacts by anthropologists and archaeologists have finally been addressed by the Native American Graves Protection and Repatriation Act of 1990, which gives tribes unprecedented powers to reclaim sacred objects and human remains from museums and universities.

Yet these positive developments are paralleled, in many communities, by an equally strong pattern of cultural and economic dissolution. The relentless growth of non-Indian cities and industries, particularly in the arid west and Southwest where most Native Americans live, has bred an ever more intense demand for water, further depleting the already over-exploited rivers and aquifers on which many reservations depend for survival. As the Northern Paiute leader Edward C. Johnson eloquently put it:

> Our natural resources are finite ... The United States is like a big octopus. It has tentacles that are sucking up valuable resources so everybody can live a beautiful life. Indians throughout the West have been subjected to that philosophy. Los Angeles is pulling all the water out of the Owens Valley for its development. And the Indians in Nevada are relegated to a few colonies with no water rights and no land.

Under the 'Winters Doctrine', established by a celebrated case in 1908, the Supreme Court decided that Native Americans who had surrendered land under treaty had a 'prior and paramount right' to enough water to satisfy their 'present and future needs' on their reservations. As the crisis deepened during the 1970s and 1980s, more and more tribes, encouraged by the success of other cases, appealed to the courts to protect their water rights, but many of them quickly learnt that – not surprisingly – it was more difficult to win on an issue which brought them into direct conflict with the vital interests of millions of non-Indians. Often, they found themselves embroiled in cripplingly expensive and nightmarishly slow lawsuits which dragged on for decades as they watched their reservations gradually dying.

Some tribes, such as the Pimas on the Gila River Reservation in Arizona, have already seen the land they painstakingly irrigated for centuries turn to dust. Scores of others are perilously poised on the brink of disaster. For them, the gains of the last three decades are largely irrelevant, unless and until the water question is resolved: no amount of cultural sensitivity – or even returned land – will, in the long term, help communities so parched that the land itself is unproductive and uninhabitable. As the Governor of San Felipe Pueblo, Frank Tenorio, said in 1978:

> There has been a lot said about the sacredness of our land which is our body; and the values of our culture which is our soul; but water is the blood of our tribes, and if its life-giving flow is stopped, or it is polluted, all else will die and the many thousands of years of our communal existence will come to an end.

Under President Reagan, tribes were urged to abandon their attempts to protect their water rights through litigation and instead make pragmatic, 'government to government' compacts with the state authorities to settle the issue. Although this compromise yielded quicker results and was less costly, it often left them with far less than they had been demanding. By abandoning the protection of their treaties, moreover, they were leaving themselves open – in the view of some lawyers – to demands for further concessions in the future. Traditionals sometimes suspected that the malign hand of termination was surreptitiously at work, eroding the tribes' special federal relationship and prodding them further into the US system under the flattering guise of treating them as 'governments'.

In other ways, too, the Reagan administration, for all its emollient rhetoric of 'respect' and 'partnership', undermined tribal autonomy and increased the pressure on Native Americans to assimilate. It drastically cut back federal funding, the main source of revenue for tribal governments, and declared that the panacea for Indian poverty was to be 'private enterprise'. Since there was little Native American 'private enterprise' to speak of in Indian communities, this effectively meant attracting non-Indian companies to the reservations, thereby re-opening them to the same forces that had consistently marginalized, exploited and impoverished Indians in the past.

A few Native American groups had already tried to tame, or at least harness, the corporate monster: in 1975, for instance, in the wake of the revelations of BIA incompetence, a coalition of twenty-five western tribes with mineral and fossil fuel deposits had established the Council of Energy Resource Tribes to try to secure better prices and more effective safeguards for the development of their resources. Many of them, however, were unprepared for the collision with the fiercely competitive ethos of free-market capitalism, which only aggravated the growing cultural tensions within their own community. Johnson Holy Rock, a former President of the Oglala Sioux Tribe and a wise and perceptive interpreter of Indian life, explains:

> Our people are caught in a clash of values. A lot of our economic problems is, we don't understand money. I've been on this planet seventy-two years and I still don't understand money.
>
> Our society was always based on the barter system. And that's still what we understand. You can give $1000.00 to a man on the street and he doesn't know what it will buy. His friends gather round, they all want to borrow from him. And someone'll end up selling something of much less value, a beat-up old car that's worth $250.00, maybe. We don't understand the money that's paid for the object of our desire.
>
> In olden days, young men aspired to be great hunters, great warriors, great athletes. Bringing home game had prestige. Today, there's no more buffalo herds to chase. And the car has become a prestige item. The value is unimportant as long as that object of prestige is acquired.
>
> We just don't know the system. And nobody's trained us. But beyond that, if you go deeper back into the culture, you just can't deny a fellow-tribesman if he's in dire straits. You can't be hard like a white man and turn your back and walk away. You have to give your shirt off your back or give him your last blanket or whatever. Because of that we're pretty poor business people . . .
>
> I buy and sell cattle for a living, but from time to time some

fellow-tribesman'll put pressure on me. And one part of me says, no,
don't be free and easy with that money, that belongs to you and the
family. And another part of me says: give it to him. You'll have some
more cows, and those cows'll have more cows, what's money? And
I'm at war with myself inside.

These tensions run beneath the surface even in those communities
that seem to have adjusted most successfully to private enterprise. The
chairman of one prosperous Southwestern tribe which, with its own
thriving tourist complex and timber mill, is often held up as a model of
Indian 'progress', told me that, even more than their long-running
water rights case, his people's most profound problem was that: 'We
are a small, collective society, where people aren't encouraged to push
themselves forward. And we are surrounded by the most aggressively
individualistic society in the world.'

(As if to prove the point, he then took me across to the school gym –
laid out as a basketball court, like school gyms across America – for the
end-of-year Commencement ceremony. Among the speakers was a
young woman from the community, a graduate of the school herself,
who had left to embark on a successful career in a large US city. Using
her own life as an example of what could be achieved through hard
work and ambition, she gave her listeners an inspirational homily –
'Nothing can stop you if you believe in yourself'; 'Go for it!'; 'Believe in
your dreams' – that came straight out of US soap operas and self-help
manuals and must have collided head-on with the values they had
absorbed from their grandparents.)

The ultimate example (to date) of Native American communities
adapting themselves to the demands of US culture is the rash of casinos
and bingo halls that have sprung up across 'Indian Country'. Because
Indian land is under federal jurisdiction, tribes can run gaming
operations even when gambling is illegal or restricted in the states
adjacent to their reservations, thus attracting thousands of eager
punters who would otherwise have to travel hundreds of miles to have
a flutter. Since businesses on federal reservations are exempt from
taxation – except by the tribe – moreover, they can often make
phenomenal profits. The most celebrated case is probably that of the
Mashantucket Pequots of Connecticut, a tiny community descended

from the remnants of the once-powerful Pequot confederacy that was almost exterminated by English settlers in the seventeenth century. Having successfully sued the government for recognition as an 'Indian tribe', they have used their new-found status to build the biggest casino in America.

In many places, the impact of the casinos has been perhaps the most disruptive force since the allotment policy. Their sheer scale gives them an overwhelming presence, like a skyscraper in the middle of a village (an almost literal description in some cases), allowing them to create a disproportionately vast bridgehead for Euro-American culture. The sudden arrival of thousands of visitors and millions of dollars in previously impoverished – and often isolated – communities struggling to preserve their values and their cohesion finally destroys the fragile equilibrium between different groups, leading, in several instances, to outright civil war.

On the Mohawk reservation at Akwesasne, for instance, gambling (and smuggling across the US–Canadian border) have created an immense gulf between rich and poor and inflamed the centuries-old debate about what it means to be Mohawk. Anti-casino 'Traditionals' accuse the opposing 'Warriors' of being seduced away from their culture by American materialism, while the Warriors claim the Traditionals have been brainwashed into submission by American power: by exploiting the Euro-American addiction to gambling and smoking, they argue, they are merely continuing the old struggle to protect and sustain their communities by other means. During the 1980s, this increasingly acrimonious conflict finally erupted into a series of violent confrontations, arson attacks and even murder which forced the traditional leadership to ask state troopers to intervene – a bitter humiliation for people who have so consistently asserted their sovereignty and independence, and stark evidence of how far their authority had been undermined by the encroaching influence of modern America.

Even Indians who see gaming operations as a legitimate activity – the erosion of their land-base and government cutbacks, after all, have left many tribes with few viable alternatives – are sometimes concerned that, in the long term, they may prove counter-productive. Native Americans, they know, are trapped in a perennial Catch-22: if they appear to live up to their stereotype as 'poor', 'lazy' and 'dependent on welfare', they are seen as a drain on the hard-working American taxpayer and provoke calls for the government to stop featherbedding them; if, on the other hand, they show some initiative and visibly prosper – as the experience of the Five Civilized Tribes and of terminated peoples like the Menominee testify – outraged citizens promptly demand that their reservations should be dissolved and they should be 'treated just like anyone else.' Historically, therefore, success – and some of the casinos, allegedly, have been profitable enough to earn that ultimate accolade of success, Mafia involvement – can be as dangerous as failure. As the Sioux lawyer Philip S. Deloria points out:

> ... anyone who wonders whether termination is still alive need only ask whether a separate Indian political and legal existence will be tolerated in this country if Indians are no longer poor or viewed by the majority as being culturally distinct. Clearly that is not going to happen ...
>
> Indian governments are ... subjected to a different status than other governments. There are not constant reviews of the demographic status of all the little countries in Europe that are frequently compared in size and population with Indian tribes. No one asks whether Monaco and Liechtenstein are sufficiently culturally distinct from neighbouring countries to justify their continued existence. Unlike that of Indian tribes, their political status is taken for granted.

It was, in part, the realization of how vulnerable they were to the vagaries of fashion and political opinion that prompted the 1970s radicals to press, unsuccessfully, for 'the human needs and aspirations of Indian tribes and Indian people' to be removed altogether 'from the workings of the general American political system' and for the treaty-making process to be reinstated. Their fears have been justified by subsequent events. Less than a decade after President Nixon had explicitly renounced the termination policy, a new bill was introduced to Congress – unsuccessfully, on this occasion – which would have resulted in the US virtually abrogating all its treaty obligations. Non-Indian sportsmen, angry that Native Americans can still, under treaty, exercise hunting and fishing rights denied to them, demand 'equal rights and opportunities' and display 'Save Wildlife – Kill an Indian!'

bumper stickers. James Watt, Secretary of the Interior under Ronald Reagan, called Indians 'social misfits' whose homelands were 'examples of the failure of socialism' and said he would like to 'liberate' them. In Moscow, in 1988, Ronald Reagan himself, answering a question about Native Americans, revealed a startling degree of ignorance:

> Let me tell you just a little something about the American Indian in our land. We have provided millions of acres of land for what are called preservations, or the reservations I should say. They, from the beginning, announced that they wanted to maintain their way of life as they had always lived, there in the desert and the plains and so forth, and we set up these reservations so they could and had a Bureau of Indian Affairs to help take care of them, at the same time we provide education for them, schools on the reservations, and they are free, also, to leave the reservations and be American citizens among the rest of us, and many do. Some still prefer, however, that early way of life and we've done everything we can to meet their demands on how they want to live. Maybe we made a mistake. Maybe we should not have humoured them in that wanting to stay in that kind of primitive lifestyle. Maybe we should have said: 'No, come join us, be citizens.'

Native Americans are, understandably, disturbed by the conflicting signals they receive from US society, by the intertwined strands of sentimentality and contempt, yearning and resentment, hostility and po-faced political correctness that co-exist, sometimes even within the same individual. As Vine Deloria Jr. put it in a television interview in 1990:

> Americans are too schizophrenic ... They want Indians to be just like everybody else, no reservations at all, and they want reservations where there are colourful Indians with feathers that they can go visit in the summertime. And when you tell them that that's inconsistent, they say: 'I don't know why.' Each one of them thinks they've got an Indian princess in their background and they're friends with us, and these are deeply held attitudes. There's no way in the world, other than lobotomies, that you can get that out of their minds.

It is not surprising that some tribal leaders, working against this unsettling backdrop and keenly aware of their limited room for

manoeuvre, seem sometimes to be trying to pull off the impossible
trick of appearing reassuringly similar and reassuringly different at the
same time. On ceremonial occasions, they pander to the infantile, not-
quite-real expectations of Euro-American culture – in which the rare
news reports of Native American stories still tend to be given headlines
like 'Indians on warpath' – by donning 'tribal' regalia (almost invariably,
now, the Plains Indian feather war bonnet) and talking gravely about
the 'Great Spirit' and 'Mother Earth'. In their day-to-day dealings with
government agencies and companies, however, they have had to learn
how to discuss 'business plans' and 'contracting for services' with the
aplomb of a corporation lawyer.

Some older and traditional Native Americans see the ability to walk
this tightrope as something more sinister than consummate political
skill. The younger people, they fear, are not merely adept at *playing*
the Indian of European fantasy but have actually *become* him: after
centuries of acculturation, the Euro-American idea of what an Indian
ought to be has finally supplanted the sense of who they really are.
The main culprit, they feel, is television, which carries the seductive
promise of 'the American Way of Life' to even the most isolated
community, and the school system. To quote *Red Earth, White Lies*
again:

> Nothing is calm beneath the veneer of Indian country, and it may be
> that we are seeing the final absorption of the original inhabitants in
> the modern consumer society. The push for education in the last
> generation has done more to erode the sense of Indian identity than
> any integration programme the government previously attempted.
> The irony of the situation is that Indians truly believed that by
> seeking a better life for their children through education, much could
> be accomplished. College and graduate education, however, have
> now created a generation of technicians and professionals who also
> happen to have Indian blood. People want the good life and they are
> prepared to throw away their past in order to get it.

The story of the Passamaquoddy of Maine offers a poignant object
lesson. With their court victory in 1980, they were lifted out of obscurity
and transformed into substantial landowners and entrepreneurs. With
the federal services for which, as a legally recognized 'Indian tribe',

they were now eligible, came new, well-funded schools – which promptly set about demolishing the culture which they had preserved for centuries as a poor and disregarded minority. The education system is, unquestionably, helping a minority of Passamaquoddy children to become 'technicians and professionals', but it is leaving many more confused, frustrated and with all the classic problems of low self-esteem and under-achievement. Wayne Newell, a tribal member who works in one of the schools, sadly observes:

What the current educational model does is alienate you from who you are . . . I'll give you a good example in this community. You know they say, yes, we should teach the native language in the school, and we do, but the proportion of time teaching the native tongue to the children, the writing system and the dictionary, is one tenth what is spent on English. If we put it on a fifty-fifty scale it'd be great, but people are so afraid, including Indian people, to take that risk because somehow they'll be deprived of English and God help them if they can't speak English . . .

To witness the dying of your language on a daily basis is a really painful experience . . . It's really painful. And I don't think it's possible for people to really understand unless they're in this predicament.

The Passamaquoddy experience is only an intense form of what has happened in tribes across the country. Hundreds of miles away, on Pine Ridge, Johnson Holy Rock tells a similar story:

My grandson doesn't understand when I talk to him in my native tongue. [A long time ago], Thomas Jefferson made a prophecy, I look at it as a prophecy, because he said: these people must not live separately from our society. One day they must become a part of the mainstream of American society . . . They're getting close, they're getting close. Our native language is dying . . . I heard one of our young men say publicly: no one can ever take my culture from me, that's mine forever, and I thought to myself, that young man can't even speak our native tongue. In his mind he still had his culture but in reality part of his culture had already been painlessly dissected, he didn't know it and that's where we are today.

A generation ago, Clyde Warrior warned that educating Indians to see the world through Americans eyes and judge themselves by American standards would lead to problems that 'will make previous social ills seem like a Sunday School picnic.' He was right. As the indices of physical hardship – communicable diseases, infant mortality, poor sanitation – slowly decline in many Native American communities, evidence of a spiritual and psychological crisis grows, with soaring rates of drug and alcohol abuse, suicide (particularly among teenagers), homicide, family violence and 'accidental' death. More and more, the problems of poor, alienated and demoralized communities across America are seeping into Indian Country, beamed in on television or brought home by tribespeople returning from the cities. Many Indian parents and grandparents complain that they can no longer control their children, who on some reservations are forsaking their clan and family affiliations to form gangs modelled on the black and hispanic brotherhoods of Los Angeles and Chicago. According to one tribal policeman, Sergeant Juan Arvizu of the Salt River Pima police, the already tattered social fabric is unravelling with alarming speed: 'Three years ago, drive-by shootings in our community were unheard of. Now we are talking about murders, we are talking about drive-by shootings, carjackings, burglaries and thefts, drug trafficking and weapons violations.'

These changes go to the heart of perhaps the most fundamental – and certainly the most sensitive – issue facing Native Americans today: Who, and what, is an Indian? Although there was never a single, absolutely clear-cut European definition, most Euro-Americans – despite notable exceptions, from Richard Pratt to John Collier – have tended to see it, above all, as a matter of 'blood'. For a society whose answer to the 'Indian Question' has almost always been to try to abolish the Indian, this criterion has obvious advantages: Native Americans are only a tiny minority, and if their identity is based solely on their genes they will probably, through intermarriage, eventually vanish without trace into the 'mainstream'. A stark illustration of this thinking came during the Senate hearings on the Indian Reorganization Act in 1934, when John Collier was suggesting that the government should recognize anyone of quarter Native American ancestry as Indian. The chairman of the committee, Senator Burton K. Wheeler, insisted instead that the minimum 'quantum' should be a half 'degree of blood', on the grounds that: 'What we are trying to do is get rid of the Indian problem rather than add to it.'

Most Native American peoples, on the other hand, historically defined themselves not by 'race' but by custom: you belonged to a society, essentially, because you, and its other members, knew you did. Physical kinship was important, because your ancestry – in particular, generally, who your mother was – determined your place in the network of extended families and clans, but it was a far subtler and more complex matter than the brutally simple logic of 'blood quantum'. It was, in fact, possible for someone biologically quite unrelated to be inducted into the community and to acquire 'relatives' by ritual, as the number of 'white Indians' – settlers kidnapped and adopted by Native Americans – during the colonial period testifies. Many notable, and unquestionably 'Indian', Native Americans have, in fact, technically been 'mixed-bloods': the Comanche leader Quanah Parker, for example, was the son of a white woman.

In this century, however, the issue of race has become an ugly and painful running sore in some tribes. During the boarding school era, when 'whiteness' was seen as the ultimate ideal to which Native Americans should be aspiring, 'mixed-blood' children sometimes tried to prove how much 'whiter' they already were by taunting full-bloods as 'dumb Indians'. As adults, the ties of the 'mixed-bloods' to non-Indian society and their generally greater fluency in English then helped them to take many of the most prominent positions in tribal government, which, in some cases – such as Dick Wilson on Pine Ridge – they used to benefit themselves and their relations at the expense of the poor and marginalized 'full-blood' families. (It could be argued that the 'full-bloods' also, to some extent, took advantage of the 'mixed-bloods' by using them as a barrier against the outside world.) The full-bloods responded by showing their superior knowledge of the native language and oral tradition at tribal meetings, and denouncing the 'mixed-blood' élite as 'not real Indians.' 'Only a full-blood can be completely Indian,' one full-blood told me. 'A three-fourths blood is three-fourths Indian, a half-blood is half-Indian, and so on.'

'Mixed-bloods', especially those who, over the last forty years, have been increasingly keen to identify themselves as 'Indian', dismiss this as 'white man's thinking': why, they ask, should any native person accept an arbitrary, culturally alien criterion which only helps Euro-America to define the Indian out of existence? While this is, indisputably, a valid argument, however, it is also true there *is* an increasing practical connection in many communities between 'degree of Indian blood' and 'degree of Indian culture'. Quanah Parker's mother, captured as a child and brought up in a Comanche world, *became* a Comanche: today, by contrast, the disparity between the tribal community and the immensely powerful culture surrounding it means that the arrival of a non-Indian in an Indian family almost invariably increases the already enormous pressure on its members to become *American*. Very few non-Indian spouses, for instance, however culturally sympathetic and aware they are, now learn to speak their partner's native language: as a result, their children will almost certainly grow up hearing English not only at school and on television, but also – predominantly, if not exclusively – at home.

The figures for intermarriage give an indication of just how widespread this process is. While only about 1 per cent of white Americans and 2 per cent of black Americans marry partners of another race, by 1990 more than 50 per cent of married American Indians had non-Indian spouses. If this trend continues, according to one authoritative estimate, the number of Native Americans with 50 per cent or more of 'Indian blood' – Wheeler's threshold for being 'Indian' – will decline from around 87 per cent in 1980 to only about 8 per cent in 2080.

Will the 92 per cent with *less* than a 50 per cent 'blood quantum' still be 'Indian'? If 'Indianness' is not a *racial* category, how can it be defined? Is it a question of living in a tribal community? More than 50 per cent of all Native Americans are now urban. Is it a question of practising a 'traditional' tribal culture? Fewer than 23 per cent of all Indians now speak a native language at home. A more useful and widely accepted answer, used recently to defuse a bitter dispute about who could claim to be an authentic 'Indian' artist, is to say that 'an Indian is someone who is recognized as a member of a recognized Indian tribe.' But even this definition has problems: a child whose mother's tribe is patrilineal and whose father's tribe is matrilineal, for instance, may not belong to either, even though he or she may be biologically of pure Indian ancestry, live in a tribal community and speak a native language.

And it excludes growing numbers of people who identify themselves as Native Americans, who *feel* Native American, but who have no direct connection with a recognized tribe at all.

What muddies the water still further are the tens of thousands of New Age Euro-Americans who, while young Indians are abandoning their myths and dances for television and gang warfare, have turned to shamanic drumming and sweat lodges for an answer to the mystery of life. There are times when it can seem that being 'Native American' has become little more than a matter of sensibility and consumer choice, with a kaleidoscope of competing factions, each claiming that *they* know what it is to be a 'real' Indian.

These are complex, intractable and perhaps, ultimately, unanswerable questions, relating not only to the long and tragic encounter of Europeans and indigenous Americans but to how all of us, in a world which seems increasingly to challenge our sense of identity and the stories we tell about ourselves, try to make sense of our lives. It would be quite wrong, though, to believe that the tumultuous history of the last five centuries has finally dwindled to a post-modern conundrum. There are still hundreds of communities of people scattered across North America who know that they are 'Indian' and that they are caught in a gruelling, day-in-and-day-out battle for physical and spiritual survival. Their struggle, they feel – however dazed and confused the eyes through which they see it – remains the same as their ancestors': to hold on to what is left of their land and resources and to the vision which animates their relationship with each other and with the world.

In tribes throughout the United States, there are strong prophetic traditions about what will happen if this battle is lost. Scores of apocalyptic legends survive, warning of burning skies, poisoned waters and the self-destruction of human society if Euro-Americans continue to despoliate the earth. The Hopi believe that failure to 'save the Hopi Way of life' will lead to imminent global destruction. Some of the most startling predictions are the twenty-seven prophecies of Skanientariio, an eighteenth-century Iroquois holy man (who once preached to Thomas Jefferson):

> In the future our people will see a form of transportation that will not be pulled by a horse or pushed by anything ... They will see

things flying in the sky above us made of metal ... There will be a
day coming when you will see the trees start dying from the top
down: the rivers will become unfit to drink or swim in, and the fish
will float on the top of the waters ... [Y]ou will see a day coming
when we will no longer be able to carry on our ceremonies, for our
children will not be able to speak their own language. It will be at
this time that all the great changes of the earth will take place ...

It is difficult not to interpret stories like this anthropologically, as
semi-conscious warning signals or alarm calls thrown out by cultures
which, at some level, know they are dying. I have met elderly Indians
in several communities who have told me, almost eagerly, of dreams or
visions they have had of impending apocalypse, as if they feel that only
the end of the world can save them now. But I think it is also important
to understand them both as expressions of the Indian world view – in
which 'Progress' is seen not as a joyful march onwards and upwards
towards ever-greater prosperity and freedom, but as a blasphemy against
the Creator who put us here and taught us how to live – and as a critique
of our own culture. In the light of our own anxieties – about nuclear
waste and global warming, about the ability of science to rescue us –
there can be few people who could read the warnings of ecological melt-
down, of death by pollution or epidemic or holocaust, without a *frisson*.

Yet even the predictions of doom are not the last word – at least, not
yet. Even now, even here, there are counter-currents. 'Indian Country'
is stirring, in ways that are still difficult to describe and discern.
Thousands of Native Americans are returning to ceremonies like the
Sun Dance and flocking to inter-tribal pow-wows to dance, sing and
strengthen family and social ties. In the cities they are regrouping,
forming new alliances and affiliations – nothing new, as the pre-contact
flux of tribal mergers and confederacies and secessions suggests – and
relearning old traditions such as the sweat lodge. Most of the 'traditions', it must be said, come from the Plains culture, but, as the
horse-based Plains culture itself testifies, native societies have always
adapted and innovated and borrowed from each other.

On many reservations, there are also distinct signs of a local
renaissance. In the hills of South Dakota, some Sioux families, quietly,
unobtrusively, are keeping their children from school until they are

fluent in Lakota. A number of Iroquois communities, convinced, as one of their spokesman puts it, that their language 'is the soul of the Iroquois nation' and that 'Without it, we do not have a nation, because there is knowledge . . . that does not translate into English,' have started 'survival' schools to immerse their children in their own language and culture. The traditional Mohawk Bear Clan chief Tom Porter and a group of followers have left the bright lights and casinos of Akwesasne and moved to a plot of land in the Mohawk Valley – part of the tribe's original homeland from which they were expelled in the eighteenth century – to found a kind of Mohawk Utopia, in which everyone lives according to Deganawidah's Great Law. In one or two communities, even the apparently intractable divisions between 'traditional' and 'progressive', 'full-blood' and 'mixed-blood' have healed, giving way to a new spirit of unity.

In 1986, the Onondaga traditional chief, Oren Lyons told a conference:

> We will determine what our culture is. It has been pointed out that culture constantly changes. It is not the same today as it was a hundred years ago. We are still a vital, active Indian society. We are not going to be put in a museum or accept your interpretation of our culture. I hope that what I have said will be taken with the respect with which it was presented . . .
>
> . . . we continue to survive. Our chief council is composed of respectable and dignified men. They are profoundly endowed with the spirit of nationhood, freedom and self-determination. When we travel about and meet with the elders from the other different nations and peoples, we find our friends.
>
> I cannot speak for anybody but the Six Nations of Iroquois, but I can tell you that we have children who believe that they are Onondagas. We have longhouses that are full of our young people. We have a lacrosse team called the Iroquois Nationals that competes with Canada, the United States, England and Australia.
>
> It is a fact that a small group of people in the northeast have survived an onslaught for some 490 years. They continue their original manner of government. They also drive cars, have televisions, and ride on planes. We make the bridges that you cross over and build the buildings that you live in.

So, what are we? Are we traditionalists or are we assimilated? If you can get away from your categories and definitions, you will perceive us as a living and continuing society. We believe that the wampum and the ceremonial masks should be at home. We will continue our ceremonies. We have the right to exist and that right does not come from you or your government.

Since Europeans first arrived in the 'New World', they and their descendants in the Western hemisphere have been trying to snare the American Indian in a whole set of rigid, simplistic 'categories and definitions', and the American Indian has been confounding and eluding them. Native Americans have not died out 'like snow before the sun', nor have they 'vanished' into the melting pot of 'civilization'. Their experience over the last five centuries has been a story of almost unimaginable pain and suffering, but also of extraordinary transformation and rebirth. The wily, shapeshifting, contradictory, heroic trickster, whom many contemporary Indians regard as the key *motif* of Native American culture, will surprise us again.

Sources and Further Reading

Note

There is an immense literature on North American native people, ranging from mainstream (and often rather conservative and unimaginative) academic writing to polemics and wide-eyed books about spirituality. In order to create as complete a picture as possible, I have drawn on a wide variety of published – and a few unpublished – historical and ethnographic works, as well as making extensive use of Native American oral tradition and autobiographies and the transcripts of my own conversations and interviews with Indian people. What follows is a lightning guided tour through the main sources for each chapter, together with some suggestions for further reading. Wherever possible, I have recommended easily available texts with their own bibliographies.

General books

One of the first – and still one of the most influential – American historians to start presenting a more informed and sympathetic view of Native Americans in the 1950s and 1960s was Alvin M. Josephy Jr. His painstakingly researched and densely packed *Indian Heritage of America* (London: Jonathan Cape, 1972) is still probably the most authoritative single-volume synthesis of archaeology, ethnology and history available to a general reader.

Both Angie Debo's *A History of the Indians of the United States* (Norman: Oklahoma, 1970; reprinted 1989) and William T. Hagan's *American Indians* (Chicago, 1979) offer straightforward historical overviews. The Debo sometimes has a slightly dated feel to it, but it is informative, passionate and lively. The *Atlas of the North American Indian* by Carl Waldman (New York: Facts On File, 1985) provides a succinct historical summary and an invaluable series of maps.

For ethnography, the twenty-volume *Handbook of North American Indians*, edited by William C. Sturtevant (Washington, DC: Smithsonian Institution; various dates), remains the most comprehensive and authoritative source. Harold Driver's *Indians of North America* (University of Chicago Press, 1979) offers a scholarly anthropological summary in one volume, although its organization and relentlessly academic tone makes it easy to see why many Native Americans find mainstream anthropology alien and perverse.

A pioneering scholar in the field of American Indian studies was D'Arcy McNickle, a member of the Flathead tribe who trained as an anthropologist. His *Native American Tribalism: Indian Survivals and Renewals* (New York: Oxford University Press, 1973) gives a brief, very accessible account of the historical and political forces which have shaped, and continue to shape, the experience of native North Americans. His legacy lives on in the D'Arcy McNickle Center for the History of the American Indian at the Newberry Library in Chicago, which has probably done more than any other institution to encourage serious research in this area. *Indians in American History* (Arlington Heights, Illinois: Harlan Davidson, 1988), edited by the Centre's current director, Frederick E. Hoxie, offers an excellent introduction to some current academic issues in Native American history.

There are few general collections of American Indian oral history: most books, understandably, focus on particular peoples or areas. For a flavour of the oral tradition, *American Indian Myths and Legends*, selected and edited by Richard Erdoes and Alfonso Ortiz (New York: Pantheon Books, 1984), gives a good cross-section of Creation accounts, Trickster tales etc., and one or two oblique but startling Native American stories about the arrival of Europeans. There is also a brief and illuminating Introduction by the editors.

Prologue

Most of the quotes from participants in the 1990 Wounded Knee Ride are taken from my own interviews on the Pine Ridge reservation in South Dakota, where I was working on a two-part documentary, *Savagery and the American Indian*, for BBC Television.

I: ORIGINS

1. This is How It Was: Two Views of History

Books that helped me to write this chapter include *Myths and Legends of California and the Old Southwest*, collected by Katharine Berry Judson (first published 1912; reprinted by Bison Books, University of Nebraska Press, 1994), from which the Shastika creation account is taken; Alan Watts' *The Way of Liberation: Essays and Lectures on the Transformation of the Self* (New York: Weatherill, 1983); *God Is Red* (New York: Delta Books, 1975) and *Red Earth, White Lies: Native Americans and the Myth of Scientific Fact* (New York: Scribner, 1988), both by Vine Deloria Jr.; and *Stolen Continents: The Americas through Indian Eyes Since 1492* (New York: Houghton Mifflin, 1992), by Ronald Wright. The anthropological texts referred to and quoted from are: Harold E. Driver's *Indians of North America* (2nd Edition; Chicago: University of Chicago Press, 1969); Peter Farb's *Man's Rise to Civilisation: As Shown By the Indians of North America From Primeval Times to the Coming of the Industrial State* (London: Secker and Warburg, 1969); and *Primitive Culture: Researches into the Development of Mythology, Philosophy, Religion, Art and Custom* by Edward B. Tylor (London: John Murray, 1871). The Le Jeune quote (p. 10) is from 'Le Jeune's Relation' in Reuben Gold Thwaites' 73-volume *The Jesuit Relations and Allied Documents* (1896; reprinted New York 1959).

The Tewa anthropologist Alfonso Ortiz wrote extensively about Pueblo culture and is widely quoted in Chapter Seven. The extract I use here (p. 12) is taken from 'Through Tewa Eyes: Origins': *National Geographic Magazine*, October 1991).

The Lakota creation account is taken from an unpublished manuscript by the Lakota scholar Charlotte Black Elk. The quote from N. Scott Momaday (p. 7) comes from an interview with the author in 1990.

Writing about Native American spirituality and cosmology tends to veer between dry, academic reductionism and open-mouthed New Age eagerness. The standard *The Religions of the American Indians* by Ake Hultkrantz (Berkeley and Los Angeles: University of California Press, 1979) is informative but unimaginative; Ruth Underhill's *Red Men's*

Religion: Beliefs and Practices of the Indians North of Mexico (Chicago: University of Chicago Press, 1965) seems to me – for all its un-politically correct title – to have a more intuitive and sympathetic understanding of its subject. The two Deloria books mentioned above remain, in my view, the best introduction to an American Indian perspective on the issues raised here.

2. Contact

The quotes about Columbus (p. 16) come, respectively, from Samuel Morison's *Christopher Columbus, Mariner* (London, 1956) and from 'Tabor Currents – Current news for Alumni, parents and friends of Tabor Academy', November 1994. The Collis quote (pp. 17–18) is taken from *The Vision of Glory: the Extraordinary Nature of the Ordinary* (London: Penguin Books, 1975).

The debate over aboriginal population is immensely contentious and far from resolved. In discussing it, I have drawn heavily on Francis Jennings's *The Invasion of America: Indians, Colonialism and the Cant of Conquest* (New York, 1976), which includes a vigorous (and some would say intemperate) critique of Mooney and Kroeber, and on Russell Thornton's more sober *American Indian Holocaust and Survival: A Population History Since 1492* (Norman: Oklahoma, 1987), which offers probably the most widely-accepted and scholarly overview of the subject and an excellent bibliography.

The quote from John Snelling (pp. 24–5) is taken from *The Elements of Buddhism* (Shaftesbury, Dorset: Element Books, 1990). Trickster tales can be found in several collections of Native American stories, including *American Indian Myths and Legends* (eds. Erdoes and Ortiz) and *Tales of the North American Indians*, edited by Stith Thompson (new edition, Bloomington, Indiana: Indiana University Press, 1966). The Chippewa writer and academic Gerald Vizenor has written extensively on the Trickster theme, in novels such as *The Trickster of Liberty: Tribal Heirs to a Wild Baronage at Petronia* (Minneapolis, 1988) and *Hotline Healers* (Hanover: NH, 1997); in the screenplay *Harold of Orange* (1983) and in some difficult but rewarding non-fiction.

The Innu quote (pp. 25–6) comes from my own interview with the hunter Pien Penashue in 1993, when I spent some weeks in Innu hunting camps in Labrador working on the BBC television documentary, *The Two Worlds of the Innu*. The concept of 'Animal Masters' is discussed in Ruth Underhill's *Red Men's Religion*; Ake Hultkrantz's *Belief and Worship in Native North America*, ed. Christopher Vecsey (Syracuse, 1981); and several works by the ethnologist Frank Speck. Calvin Martin's *Keepers of the Game: Indian-Animal Relationships and the Fur Trade* (Berkeley, 1978) offers a controversial view of how the belief in Animal Masters affected the behaviour of Native Americans in the colonial period.

The quotes from the late Nanepashemet (pp. 27 and 38–9), who at the time was Research Associate at the Plimoth Plantation Museum in Plymouth, Massachusetts, came from my own interview with him in 1990.

For the section on medieval notions of 'the Savage' and the quest for the Earthly Paradise both Bernard Sheehan's *Savagism and Civility: Indians and Englishmen in Colonial Virginia* (New York: Cambridge University Press, 1980) and H. C. Porter's *The Inconstant Savage: England and the North American Indian, 1500–1660* (London: Duckworth, 1979) were a rich source of information. Ronald Wright's *Stolen Continents: The Americas through Indian Eyes Since 1492* (New York: Houghton Mifflin, 1992) gives a brief, immensely readable account of the Spanish conquest of Mexico and Peru; for early European/Native American contacts further north, see Neal Salisbury's invaluable *Manitou and Providence*.

II: INVASION

3. Northeast: One

The opening quote (p. 43) from Wahunsonacock appears in *Native American Testimony. An Anthology of Indian and White Relations: First Encounter to Dispossession*, edited by Peter Nabokov (New York: Harper Torchbooks, 1979). The Freneau poem is quoted in Brian W. Dippie's *The Vanishing American: White Attitudes and U.S. Indian Policy* (Kansas, 1982).

For the discussion of East coast Native American societies, their relationship with the land and the way they were viewed by the first

European explorers and settlers, I drew heavily on three books: Neal Salisbury's *Manitou and Providence*; William Cronon's innovatory (and beautifully written) *Changes In the Land: Indians, Colonists, and the Ecology of New England* (New York: Hill and Wang, 1983); and Francis Jennings's *The Invasion of America: Indians, Colonialism and the Cant of Conquest* (New York: W. W. Norton, 1976). Jennings also provides a good account of the debate over the scale and nature of Indian warfare. For a more detailed examination of the fur trade, see H. A. Innis's *The Fur Trade in Canada: An Introduction to Canadian Economic History* (Toronto, 1964).

On the impact of European diseases, as on aboriginal population, Russell Thornton's *American Indian Holocaust and Survival: A Population History Since 1492* (Norman: Oklahoma, 1987) is a good starting point. The broader issue of the influence of the Americas on the rest of the world and *vice versa* is explored in *The Columbian Exchange: Biological and Cultural Consequences of 1492* by Alfred W. Crosby (Westport: Connecticut, 1972) and in Jack Weatherford's idiosyncratic and engaging *Indian Givers: How the Indians of the Americas Transformed the World* (New York, 1988).

Although there are plentiful primary sources, relatively little seems to have been written on the early history of the Virginia settlement. For much of the material I drew on here I am again greatly indebted to Bernard Sheehan's succinct and elegant *Savagism and Civility: Indians and Englishmen in Colonial Virginia* and to H. C. Porter's *The Inconstant Savage: England and the North American Indian, 1500–1660*. For a painstakingly researched and wonderfully readable case study in the history of relations between colonists and an East coast Native American people, see James H. Merrell's *The Indians' New World: Catawbas and Their Neighbors from European Contact through the Era of Removal* (Chapel Hill, 1989).

4. Northeast: Two

The opening quote (p. 72) is taken from William S. Simmons's *Spirit of the New England Tribes: Indian History and Folklore, 1620–1984* (Hanover, NH: University Press of New England, 1986), a fascinating collection of the surviving oral traditions in New England native communities.

For my account of Indian/English relations I have drawn heavily on Francis Jennings's *The Invasion of America: Indians, Colonialism and the Cant of Conquest* (New York: W. W. Norton, 1976) – which some critics consider too polemical and hostile to the colonists – and Neal Salisbury's *Manitou and Providence*, although Alden T. Vaughan's *New England Frontier: Puritans and Indians, 1620–1675* (Boston, 1965), which follows most earlier historians by taking a more sympathetic approach to the English, was also a useful source. The quotes from Captain John Mason (pp. 90–92) are taken from his *A Brief History of the Pequot War*, first published in 1736 and republished in 1966 as No. 23 in the March of America Facsimile Series (Ann Arbor, Michigan). For a brief, clear modern account of the 'Pequot War', see Chapter Two in *Now That The Buffalo's Gone: A Study of Today's American Indians*, by Alvin M. Josephy, Jr. (Norman: Oklahoma, 1984).

5. New York and the 'Ohio Country'

There is a substantial literature on the Iroquois, particularly on their myths and legends and on the political and social structure of the *Hotinonshonni*. For general background, Dean R. Snow's *The Iroquois* (Cambridge, Mass: Blackwell Publishers, 1994), which combines ethnography with a straight-forward archaeological and historical narrative, proved invaluable. Both Francis Jennings's *The Ambiguous Iroquois Empire: The Covenant Chain Confederation of Indian Tribes from Its Beginnings to the Lancaster Treaty of 1744* (New York: W. W. Norton, 1984) and the Iroquois chapters in Ronald Wright's *Stolen Continents: The Americas through Indian Eyes Since 1492* (New York: Houghton Mifflin, 1992) were rich sources of historical material.

The Iroquois oral tradition is enormously rich and varied (there are more than forty different recorded versions of the origin account alone), and it is imposssible for a book of this scope to do more than hint at its power, range and beauty. The origin account (pp. 99–101) has been adapted from the version that appears in Dean Snow's *The Iroquois*, while the start of the Peacemaker story (p. 103), which was too long to quote in its entirety, is taken from *Traditional Teachings* (North American Indian Travelling College, 1984). For further reading, *Myths and Legends of the New York State Iroquois* by Harriet Maxwell Converse, ed. and annot.

Arthur C. Parker, first published 1908, reprinted 1981 (New York State Museum Bulletin 125, Albany, NY), probably remains the single most authoritative and comprehensive source, although some of the language now sounds rather quaint and flowery. For an Iroquois perspective on Native American–European history, I am indebted to *Wampum Belts*, by Te-ha-ne-tor-ens (Akwesasne Notes: Mohawk Nation, 1972), a fascinating (illustrated) description of some of the patterned belts in which the *Hottinonshonni* recorded important events.

The quote from Lewis Henry Morgan is taken from his 1851 classic *The League of the Ho-de'-no-sau-nee or Iroquois*, reprinted 1991 (North Dighton, Mass: JG Press), which offers valuable insights not only into Iroquois society but also into the origins of social science. For further evidence of the impact of the *Hotinonshonni* on American cultural life, see Edmund Wilson's *Apologies to the Iroquois* (reprinted 1992; Syracuse).

For a detailed (if idiosyncratic) study of how American Indians were caught up in European imperial conflicts, see Francis Jennings's *Empire of Fortune: Crowns, Colonies and Tribes in the Seven Years War in America* (New York: W. W. Norton, 1988). John Demos's gripping *The Unredeemed Captive: A Family Story from Early America* (New York, 1994) looks at the same issue through the personal experience of one family. Kenneth M. Morison's 'Native Americans and the American Revolution: Historic Stories and Shifting Frontier Conflict' in *Indians in American History*, edited by Frederick E. Hoxie (Arlington Heights: Illinois, 1988) interestingly contrasts colonial and Indian understandings of the War of Independence; *The American Revolution in Indian country: Crisis and diversity in Native American communities* by Christopher G. Calloway (1995) gives a painstakingly researched account of the impact of the War on native people, although it arguably takes too sanguine a view of Britain's intentions towards Indians.

Anthony F. C. Wallace's *The Death and Rebirth of the Seneca* (New York: Vintage Books, 1972) gives a detailed account of one Iroquois people's decline before and during the American Revolution and their subsequent struggle for survival and spiritual renewal.

For contemporary Iroquois perspectives on the issues of land rights and sovereignty, see 'Traditional Native Philosophies Relating to Aboriginal Rights' by Oren Lyons, in *The Quest for Justice: Aboriginal Peoples and*

Aboriginal Rights, edited by Menno Boldt and J. Anthony Long (Toronto, 1985); and 'The Sovereignty and Land Rights of the Houdenosaunee' by Irving Powless Jr., in *Iroquois Land Claims*, edited by Christopher Vecsey and William A. Starna (Syracuse, 1988).

6. Southeast

Perhaps because the experience of the 'Five Civilized Tribes' has captured the imagination of generations of Americans, a vast amount has been written about them, and the sheer mass of titles available can be daunting. James Mooney's pioneering *History, Myths and Sacred Formulas of the Cherokees* (reprinted 1982: Nashville, Tennessee) is still probably the most useful source for Cherokee ethnography and offers, in addition, a useful historical summary. For general history, I also drew heavily on three other books: the Cherokee chapters in Ronald Wright's *Stolen Continents: The Americas through Indian Eyes Since 1492* (New York: Houghton Mifflin), particularly for the early period; Debo's *A History of the Indians of the United States*, which is especially good on the 'Five Civilized Tribes' (Debo's own speciality); and Grace Steele Woodward's *The Cherokees* (Norman: Oklahoma, 1963), which – although its tone now seems rather old-fashioned and paternalistic – is strong on the background to the Removal era. John Ehle's more recent *Trail of Tears: the Rise and Fall of the Cherokee Nation* (New York: Doubleday, 1988) has a more popular, less academic feel but is thoroughly researched and informative. Both *The Cherokee Indian Nation: A Troubled History*, edited by Duane King (Tennessee, 1978), and *Cherokee Removal: Before and After*, edited by William L. Anderson (Athens: Georgia, 1991), offer some interesting re-evaluations and new insights.

For a detailed study of the removal process, see *Indian Removal: The Emigration of the Five Civilized Tribes of Indians* by Grant Foreman (revised edition, Norman, Oklahoma, 1986). For an in-depth account of the evolution of US Indian policy generally, Francis Paul Prucha's comprehensive two-volume *The Great Father: The United States Government and the American Indian* (Lincoln: Nebraska, 1984) is the standard work.

The excerpts from the Cherokee oral tradition (pp. 132–3; pp. 137–8; pp. 142–3) are taken from *A Cherokee Vision of Eloh'*, edited by Howard L. Meredith and Virginia E. Milan, translated by Wesley Proctor (Indian

University Press, Bacone College, 1981). For a Cherokee perspective on more recent events, see *Nations Remembered: An Oral History of the Five Civilized Tribes, 1865–1907*, edited by Theda Perdue (Westport: Connecticut, 1980). The quote from Speckled Snake on p. 157 appears in *Touch the Earth: A Self-Portrait of Indian Existence* (New York, 1971).

By way of contrast, *The Removal of the Choctaw Indians* by Arthur H. DeRosier Jr. (Knoxville: Tennessee, 1970) and Angie Debo's *The Rise and Fall of the Choctaw Republic* (Norman, Oklahoma, 1934) describe the experience of another, less well-known 'Civilized Tribe', while John R. Finger's *The Eastern Band of Cherokees: 1819–1900* (Knoxville: Tennessee, 1984) tells the story of those Cherokees who managed to avoid removal. For the more recent history and current situation of the remaining Southeastern Indians, see *Cherokee Americans: The Eastern Band of Cherokees in the Twentieth Century*, also by John R. Finger (Lincoln: Nebraska, 1991) and *Indians of the Southeastern United States in the Late 20th Century*, edited by Anthony J. Paredes (Tuscaloosa: Alabama, 1992).

On nativism, I am indebted to Gregory Evans Dowd's perceptive *A Spirited Resistance: The North American Indian Struggle for Unity, 1745–1815* (Baltimore, 1992) and to R. David Edmunds's *Tecumseh and the Quest for Indian Leadership* (New York, 1984). On the experience of 'white' captives adopted into Native American communities, see the chapter on 'The White Indians of Colonial America' in James Axtell's illuminating *The European and the Indian: Essays in the Ethnohistory of Colonial North America* (New York, 1981).

7. Southwest

I must start by acknowledging my deep debt to two books: to Alfonso Ortiz's remarkable *The Tewa World: Space, Time, Being and Becoming in a Pueblo Society* (Chicago, 1969), for its extraordinary study of Tewa society and for a detailed text of the Tewa creation and migration account, on which my own more condensed version (pp. 183–4; pp. 185–6; and p. 187) is based; and to Ramón Gutiérrez's brilliantly written *When Jesus Came, the Corn Mothers Went Away: Marriage, Sexuality and Power in New Mexico, 1500–1846* (Stanford: California, 1991), for its vivid and original description of the relationship between the Pueblos and the

Franciscan missionaries sent to convert them. There are no obvious alternatives to either of these works: without them, this chapter could not have been written in its present form.

For additional background on Pueblo culture and history three other books were especially helpful: Joe Sando's *Pueblo Nations: Eight Centuries of Pueblo History* (Santa Fe: New Mexico, 1992); *The Pueblo Indians of North America*, by Edward P. Dozier (Prospect Heights: Illinois, 1983); and *New Perspectives on the Pueblos*, edited by Alfonso Ortiz (Albuquerque: New Mexico, 1972). For material about Hopi migrations and culture I am indebted to *Book of the Hopi*, by Frank Waters (New York, 1970).

For the general history of Indian/non-Indian relations in the area, Edward H. Spicer's standard work, *Cycles of Conquest: The Impact of Spain, Mexico and the United States on the Indians of the Southwest, 1533–1960* (Tucson, 1962), was invaluable. Henry F. Dobyns' 'Indians in the Colonial Spanish Borderlands', in *Indians in American History*, edited by Frederick E. Hoxie (Arlington Heights: Illinois, 1988), gives a useful brief introduction to the subject and a good bibliography.

The Tohono O'odham myth quoted at the start of the chapter appears in *American Indian Myths and Legends* (eds. Erdoes and Ortiz). The Pima account of Casa Grande (p. 178) was given to me verbally by Eleanor Whittier on the Gila River reservation in Arizona in 1993. The Zuñi oral tradition concerning Father Juan Greyrobe (p. 204) appears – together with other fascinating material in the newspaper 'Zuñi History: Victories in the 1990s' published in 1991 by The Institute of the North American West in Seattle, Washington: I am grateful to Andrew L. Othole, Cultural Preservation Co-ordinator at the Pueblo of Zuñi, for bringing it to my attention. The statement by the Governor of Taos (pp. 205–6) is quoted in Debo's *A History of the Indians of the United States*.

8. The Far West

Considering the scale of what happened there, comparatively little has been written about the European invasion of California. Jack Forbes's *Native Americans of California and Nevada* (revised edition; Happy Camp, California, 1993) is a good overview, particularly strong on the later period and with useful bibliographies and appendices. It has some striking contemporary quotes, including those from H. H. Bancroft (p. 229), J. Ross Browne (p. 238) and Horace Bell (p. 236). For a modern Indian study of the Spanish missions, see *The Missions of California: A Legacy of Genocide*, edited by Rupert Jeanette Henry Costo (San Francisco, 1987).

The California Indians: a Source Book, compiled and edited by R. F. Heizer and M. A. Whipple (revised edition; Berkeley, California, 1971) is an invaluable collection of ethnography, anthropology, archaeology and historical writings from a wide range of different authors. Thornton's *American Indian Holocaust and Survival: A Population History Since 1492* gives a scholarly account of the genocide of Californian Indians – the matter-of-fact tone makes it all the more appalling – and is the source of the Maidu song at the start of the chapter and the Luiseño song (p. 220).

The other Indian quotes come from a number of different sources. Janitin's account of being captured and enslaved on (pp. 222–3); Lucy Young's reminiscence of her grandfather's dream (pp. 226–7); the narrative of the Stone and Kelsey killing (pp. 229–30) and Chief Joseph's surrender speech (p. 242) all appear in *Native American Testimony. An Anthology of Indian and White Relations: First Encounter to Dispossession*, edited by Peter Nabokov (probably the best and most imaginative general collection of Indian testimony available); the quote from the Wintu origin legend and the *Song of Waida Werris* (p. 219) are in Jeremiah Curtin's *Creation Myths of America* (originally published 1899; reprinted London, 1995), which also contains an illuminating introduction; and Sara Winnemucca's recollection of first seeing 'white' men (p. 226) comes from *Life Among the Piutes: Their Wrongs and Claims* by Sara Winnemucca Hopkins, first published 1883, reprinted Reno, Nevada, 1994. Lauren Bomellyn's quote (p. 214) and his account of the Tolowa massacre (pp. 231–2) are taken from the transcript of my own interview with him in 1990.

I am very indebted to *The Destruction of California Indians: A collection of documents from the period 1847 to 1865 in which are described some of the things that happened to some of the Indians of California* (1974; reprinted Lincoln, Nebraska, 1993), a fascinating and unusual book which introduced me to a great deal of unfamiliar material and is the main source for most of the contemporary newspaper accounts and military reports I quote.

For the discussion of the development of 'scientific' racial theories and the impact of Darwinism I drew heavily both on Brian W. Dippie's *The*

Vanishing American: White Attitudes and U.S. Indian Policy (Lawrence: Kansas, 1982), from which many of the relevant contemporary quotes are taken, and on Robert F. Berkhofer Jr.'s excellent and succinct *The White Man's Indian: Images of the American Indian from Columbus to the Present* (New York, 1978).

As I suggest in the text, the story of the Nez Percés has received, proportionately, far greater attention than the experience of their neighbours further south. There is a good summary of the causes and the course of 'Chief Joseph's War' in Angie Debo's *A History of the Indians of the United States*; for greater detail, see Alvin M. Josephy's monumental *The Nez Perce Indians and the Opening of the Northwest* (abridged edition; Lincoln, Nebraska, 1979) – from which I take Old Chief Joseph's deathbed speech – which also has an excellent bibliography. The quote from *Hemene Moxmox* (Yellow Wolf) (p. 240) is from the vivid and moving *Yellow Wolf: His Own Story*, by Lucullus V. McWhorter (first published 1940; reprinted Caldwell, Idaho, 1991). I am also indebted to the late Joe Redthunder, a descendant of the Joseph band who in 1993 gave me a fascinating oral account of the war and his ancestors' long retreat towards Canada.

The description of Ishi (p. 244) comes from *Ishi in Two Worlds: A Biography of the Last Wild Indian in North America* by Theodora Kroeber (Berkeley, California, 1961), a readable, straightforward and sometimes moving account by A. L. Kroeber's widow. The extracts from T. T. Waterman (pp. 237 and 245) appear in 'Ishi, the Last Yahi', in *The California Indians: a Source Book* (see above).

9. The Great Plains

In part, perhaps, because of its importance in American popular culture, there is a considerable literature on the 'War for the Plains', although much of it displays little interest in, or (except in a very generalized way) empathy for, the experience of the Native Americans involved. Probably the best mainstream academic account is Robert M. Utley's *The Indian Frontier of the American West, 1846–1890* (Albuquerque: New Mexico, 1983). Dee Brown's hugely successful *Bury My Heart At Wounded Knee: an Indian History of the American West* (London, 1971) has been criticized both by historians and by some Indians for giving a simplistic, over-romantic view of Native Americans, but it is thoroughly researched, readable and informative. I am indebted to it for some of the material quoted in my account of Little Crow's War. For background to the later conflicts in the northern plains I also referred to James C. Olson's *Red Cloud and the Sioux Problem* (Lincoln: Nebraska, 1975) and Robert M. Utley's *The Last Days of the Sioux Nation* (New Haven, 1963). For a brief survey of the Ghost Dance movement and suggestions for further reading, see *American Indian Holocaust and Survival: A Population History Since 1492* by Russell Thornton.

The quote on p. 249 is from *Struggle for the Land: Indigenous Resistance to Genocide, Ecocide and Expropriation in Contemporary North America* by the Native American writer Ward Churchill (Monroe: Maine, 1993), which takes a critical look at the 'buffalo commons' idea and proposes a far more radical solution to the economic problems of the Plains. The description of the buffalo-hunting Querechos (p. 251) comes from *The Eyes of Discovery: the Pageant of North America as seen by the First Explorers*, by John Bakeless (New York: 1950).

The description on pp. 263–4 of the smallpox epidemic among the Mandan by the artist George Catlin is taken from his *Letters and Notes on the Manners, Customs and Conditions of the North American Indians* (two volumes; originally published 1844; reprinted New York, 1973). Modern scholars have accused Catlin – with some justice – of romanticizing native people, but much of his writing seems to me to be not only sympathetic but perceptive. Compare his descriptions of Indian life, e.g., with those by the historian Francis Parkman in the almost contemporary *The Oregon Trail* (1849; reprinted New York, 1950).

For historical, archaeological and ethnographic background to the Cheyennes, I am indebted to George Bird Grinnell's classic *The Cheyenne Indians: Their History and Way of Life* (two volumes; first published 1923; reprinted Lincoln, Nebraska, 1972). Most of the Cheyenne oral tradition I quote is taken from the moving and fascinating *Cheyenne Memories* by John Stands In Timber and Margot Liberty (Lincoln: Nebraska, 1972).

The Sioux quotes come from a number of different sources. Standing Bear's description of the hunt (pp. 256–7) and the quotes about fighting 'the whites' (pp. 276–7) appear in *The Sixth Grandfather: Black Elk's Teachings Given to John G. Neihardt*, edited by Raymond J. DeMallie (Lincoln, Nebraska, 1984), a rich source of oral material drawn from interviews with Black Elk and other 'old men' in the 1930s. The excerpts from 'The Gift of the Sacred Pipe' (pp. 257–8) are taken from *The Sacred Pipe: Black Elk's Account of the Seven Rites of the Oglala Sioux*, edited by Joseph Epes Brown (Norman, Oklahoma, 1953; reprinted London, 1973). The epigraph from Black Elk at the start of the chapter is from *Black Elk Speaks* by John G. Neihardt (London, 1974). The contemporary quotes by Black Elk's great-granddaughter, Charlotte Black Elk (pp. 284–5) are from a series of interviews I recorded on the Pine Ridge reservation in 1990 for the BBC TV two-part documentary *Savagery and the American Indian*.

The Iktome story (pp. 261–2) appears in *American Indian Myths and Legends* (eds. Erdoes and Ortiz) and Frank Fool's Crow's explanation of the Sun Dance (p. 259) in Thomas E. Mails's *Sundancing at Rosebud and Pine Ridge* (Sioux Falls: South Dakota, 1978). The quotes from Luther Standing Bear (p. 260) are from his remarkable *Land of the Spotted Eagle* (first published 1933; reprinted Lincoln, Nebraska, 1978), a brilliant and eloquent reflection on his own life and the collision between the Sioux and Anglo-America.

The destruction of Indian Territory during and after the Civil War does not seem to have received the same attention as the removals of the 1830s, but Angie Debo's *A History of the Indians of the United States*, Theda Perdue's *The Cherokee* (New York, 1989) and *The Indians in Oklahoma*, by the Cherokee scholar Rennard Strickland (Norman: Oklahoma, 1980) all offer brief overviews. For more detailed works, see the bibliographical essays by William L. Anderson in *Cherokee Removal: Before and After* and by Rennard Strickland in Morris L. Wardell's *A Political History of the Cherokee Nation, 1838–1907* (reprinted Norman, Oklahoma, 1977).

On changing views of 'the Indian' and the evolution of government policy, I am again indebted to *The Vanishing American: White Attitudes and U.S. Indian Policy* by Brian W. Dippie and Robert F. Berkhofer Jr.'s *The White Man's Indian: Images of the American Indian from Columbus to the Present*.

III: INTERNAL FRONTIERS

10. *Kill the Indian to Save the Man*

For the background to the assimilation policy and the boarding-school system, I am especially indebted to two books, Frederick Hoxie's *A Final Promise: The Campaign to Assimilate the Indians, 1880–1920* (Lincoln: Nebraska, 1984) and *Education for Extinction*, by David Wallace Adams (Lawrence: Kansas, 1995). Again, both Robert F. Berkhofer Jr.'s *The White Man's Indian: Images of the American Indian from Columbus to the Present* and Brian W. Dippie's *The Vanishing American: White Attitudes and U.S. Indian Policy* were also invaluable. Most of the quotes from politicians, bureaucrats and educationalists appear in these four works, although Theodore Roosevelt's robust defence of 'the civilized nations of the Indian Territory' (p. 322) is taken from *The Indian and the White Man*, edited by Wilcomb E. Washburn (New York, 1964).

American Indian Policy in the Twentieth Century, edited by Vine Deloria Jr. (Norman: Oklahoma, 1985), provides an overview of some of the most important issues in Indian policy since the end of the 'Indian Wars' and gave me some useful insights when I was writing this and the ensuing chapters. For a more detailed and systematic study of federal policy, again see *The Great Father: The United States Government and the American Indian* by Francis Paul Prucha.

The quote from Quanah Parker at the beginning of the chapter (p. 289) appears in Angie Debo's *A History of the Indians of the United States*, and Red Cloud's complaint (p. 293) in *Red Cloud and the Sioux Problem* by James C. Olson. Standing Bear's testimony (p. 294) is taken from *Native American Testimony. An Anthology of Indian and White Relations: First Encounter to Dispossession* (ed. Peter Nabokov). All the passages from Luther Standing Bear (no relation) are again from *Land of the Spotted Eagle*. (For an interesting contrast – and a fascinating story in its own right – see Charles Alexander Eastman's *Indian Boyhood* (1902) and *From the Deep Woods to Civilization: Chapters in the Autobiography of an Indian* (1916). Eastman, a Santee Sioux whose family fled from Minnesota after Little Crow's War, did not see a 'white' person until he was sixteen, but later trained as a doctor – an achievement that seemed to support the assimilationists' belief in the 'civilizability' of Indians.) As in the previous chapter, the quote from John Stands In Timber (p. 307) comes from *Cheyenne Memories* by John Stands In Timber and Margot Liberty and the quotes from Charlotte Black Elk (pp. 308–9) from my own interviews in 1990. The same series of interviews is the source for the boarding-school reminiscences (pp. 317–18).

I am again indebted to Frank Waters' *Book of the Hopi* for the story of Loloma and Yukioma and for the Hopi quotes (p. 310). Don C. Talayesva's experiences (pp. 318–20) are recorded in *Sun Chief: The Autobiography of a Hopi* Indian, edited by Leo W. Simmons (first published 1942, reprinted New Haven, 1970), perhaps the most outstanding of a series of remarkable native autobiographies produced during the 1930s and 1940s. See also, for instance, *Son of Old Man Hat: A Navajo Autobiography*, recorded by Walter Dyk (first published 1938, reprinted Lincoln, Nebraska, 1967).

The quotes (p. 305) from the participants at the Indian Territory councils are taken from Angie Debo's *A History of the Indians of the United States*. In describing the later history of Indian Territory I have drawn heavily on another work by Debo, *And Still the Waters Run: the Betrayal of the Five Civilized Tribes* (first published 1940; republished Princeton: NJ, 1991), which is the source of most of the Native American quotes concerning the dissolution of the Five Civilized Tribes.

11. New Deal and Termination

In writing the section on Collier and the Indian New Deal, I am indebted to several works. *John Collier's Crusade for Indian Reform, 1920–1945* by Kenneth R. Philp (Tucson, 1977) is an invaluable account of Collier's life and career, particularly strong on the political background to the Indian New Deal; while two books by Collier himself, *Indians of the Americas: The Long Hope* (New York, 1947) and *From Every Zenith: A Memoir and Some Essays on Life and Thought* (Denver, 1963); convey a strong sense of his passion and visionary zeal (as well as his sometimes impenetrably florid writing style). For its account of Indian policy in the pre-Collier era – and the excerpt from Walter M. Camp's report (p. 331) – I am grateful to Frederick Hoxie's *A Final Promise: The Campaign to Assimilate the Indians,*

1880–1920 (Lincoln: Nebraska, 1984). Brian W. Dippie's *The Vanishing American* was again a source of valuable background information and some excellent quotes, including Ernest Thompson Seton's on pp. 344–5.

The Nations Within: the Past and Future of American Indian Sovereignty by Vine Deloria Jr. and Clifford Lytle (New York, 1984) was extremely helpful, particularly in its analysis of the Indian Reorganization Act and its detailed description of Collier's 'Indian Congresses', from which I took the quotes from the Rev. C. Aaron (p. 346) and Mitchell Red Cloud (p. 351). The texts of the Pueblos' appeal against the Bursum Bill and their 'Declaration to ... the People of the United States' appear in Joe Sando's *Pueblo Nations: Eight Centuries of Pueblo History* (Santa Fé: New Mexico, 1992). Most of the other Native American quotes are taken from *Indian Self-Rule: First-Hand Accounts of Indian-White Relations from Roosevelt to Reagan*, edited by Kenneth R. Philp (Salt Lake City: Utah, 1986), an unusual and immensely helpful collection of views and reminiscences from some of the key figures in American Indian politics and administration over the last sixty years. I am indebted to Dr. Floyd O'Neill, Director Emeritus of the American West Center at the University of Utah, for bringing it to my attention (and, indeed, giving me a copy!).

Indian Self-Rule is also the source for the quotes at the start of the section on Termination. For the background to Termination, both *The Nations Within: the Past and Future of American Indian Sovereignty* by Vine Deloria Jr. and Clifford Lytle and *American Indian Policy in the Twentieth Century*, edited by Vine Deloria Jr., were again very helpful. 'The Evolution of the Termination Policy', by Charles F. Wilkinson and Eric R. Biggs, in *American Indian Law Review*, vol. V, no. 1, was also a useful source.

My account of the Klamath termination draws on a number of documents, including two unpublished papers which I must gratefully acknowledge: 'The Klamath Tribe: An Overview of Its Termination', by Kathleen Shaye Hill; and 'Identification of Selected Problems of Indians Residing in Klamath County, Oregon – An Examination of Data Generated Since Termination of the Klamath Reservation', a doctoral thesis by Charles Crane Brown. The exchanges between Boyd Jackson and Senator Arthur V. Watkins (pp. 363–4) are taken from the record of the Senate and House Subcommittees on Indian Affairs for February 1954. The quotes from Chuck Kimbol (p. 365) and Gordon Bettles (p. 366) are from a series of my own interviews with tribal members in 1985.

12. The New Indians

For the discussion of the emergence of Native American activism in the 1960s I am indebted to several works. Alvin M. Josephy Jr.'s *Red Power: The American Indians' Fight for Freedom* (New York, 1971), an invaluable documentary record of the period, is the source for the opening quotes from Clyde Warrior (pp. 370–71) and Mel Thom (p. 371) and for the extracts from their speeches. The quotes from Vine Deloria Jr. (pp. 376–7 and p. 384) are taken from his book *Custer Died For Your Sins: An Indian Manifesto* (1970; reprinted Norman, Oklahoma, 1988), whose mix of breezy humour, irony and anger make it perhaps the definitive statement of Indian radicalism in the 1960s. The quote from Earl Old Person (pp. 377) appears in Angie Debo's *A History of the Indians of the United States* and those from Helen Peterson (pp. 373–4) and Philip S. Deloria (p. 382) from *Indian Self-Rule: First-Hand Accounts of Indian-White Relations from Roosevelt to Reagan*, edited by Kenneth R. Philp (Salt Lake City: Utah, 1986). Most of the other Native American quotes in the first section are taken from Stan Steiner's indispensable *The New Indians* (New York, 1968), an outstanding account of the early days of the movement that still seems fresh and exciting after thirty years. My choice of Steiner's title for this chapter is an acknowledgement of my deep debt to him.

For additional information I am again grateful to *The Nations Within: the Past and Future of American Indian Sovereignty* by Vine Deloria Jr. and Clifford Lytle. Alvin M. Josephy Jr.'s *Now That The Buffalo's Gone: A Study of Today's American Indians* (Norman: Oklahoma, 1984) gives an excellent short account of the struggle for fishing rights in the Northwest and a detailed bibliography. I am indebted to the same book for its invaluable chapter on the rise of the American Indian Movement and the violence on the Pine Ridge reservation in the 1970s, from which I take the quote about the 'birth' of AIM (pp. 398–9) and the excerpt from the letter (p. 405).

The epigraph from Dennis Banks is taken from *Lakota Woman* by Mary Crow Dog, with Richard Erdoes (New York, 1991), which is also the source for Crow Dog's reminiscences of Wounded Knee in the latter part of the chapter. The quote from Albert White (p. 392) appears in *Indians in Minnesota*, by Elizabeth Ebbott (Minneapolis, 1985). The quotes from Leonard Peltier, Len Foster and Frances Wise appear in 'American Indian Ethnic Renewal', by Joane Nagel, in the *American Sociological Review*, 1995, vol. 60 (December: 947–965), pp. 958–9. Lenada James's comments on Alcatraz (p. 395) are taken from *Indian Self-Rule: First-Hand Accounts of Indian-White Relations from Roosevelt to Reagan*, edited by Kenneth R. Philp, which contains a range of views and recollections of Indian activism.

For an interesting interpretation of the Five County Cherokee movement, see 'New Militants or Resurrected State? The Five County Northeastern Oklahoma Cherokee Organization' by Albert L. Wahrhaftig and Jane Lukens-Wahrhaftig in *The Cherokee Indian Nation: A Troubled History*, edited by Duane H. King (Knoxville: Tennesse, 1979).

Several recent books examine the Sioux' continuing struggle for the recognition of their treaty rights and the return of the Black Hills – see, for example, Peter Matthiessen's *In the Spirit of Crazy Horse* (New York, 1984); Ward Churchill's *Struggle for the Land: Indigenous Resistance to Genocide, Ecocide and Expropriation in Contemporary North America*; and *Black Hills/White Justice: The Sioux Nation Versus the United States 1775 to the Present* by Edward Lazarus (New York, 1991). For the government campaign against AIM, see *Blood of the Land: The Government and Corporate War Against the American Indian Movement* by Rex Weyler (New York, 1982). Jimmie Durham gives a brief but thoughtful insider's view of AIM in his book *A Certain Lack of Coherence: Writings on Art and Cultural Politics* (London, 1993).

Epilogue

The quotes from LaDonna Harris, Edward C. Johnson, Philip S. Deloria and Oren Lyons are all taken from *Indian Self-Rule: First-Hand Accounts of Indian-White Relations from Roosevelt to Reagan*, edited by Kenneth R. Philp. The excerpt from the Zuñi prophecy is from *The Zunis: Self-Portrayals*, by the Zuni People, translated by Alvina Quam (Albuquerque: New Mexico, 1972). The Iroquois prophecy (pp. 425–6) is recorded in *Traditional Teachings* (North American Indian Travelling College, 1984).

The quote from Governor Frank Tenorio (p. 414) appears in *The Native American Almanac: A Portrait of Native America Today* by Arlene

Hirschfelder and Martha Kreipe de Montaño (New York, 1993). The quotes from Johnson Holy Rock and Wayne Newell and the excerpt from the interview with Vine Deloria Jr. are all drawn from my own conversations with Native Americans recorded in 1990.

Sergeant Juan Arvizu's comments (p. 422) are quoted in a newspaper article by Seth Mydans, 'Teen gangs stalking Indian reservations', published in *The Plain Dealer*, 19 March 1995. The quote from President Ronald Reagan is taken from a transcript of BBC TV News for 31 May 1988.

For data on Native American intermarriage and language loss, I am again indebted to 'American Indian Ethnic Renewal', by Joane Nagel, in the *American Sociological Review*, 1995, vol. 60 (December: 947–965), pp. 958–9, as well as to Russell Thornton's *American Indian Holocaust and Survival: A Population History Since 1492*.

Peter Matthiessen's *Indian Country* (London, 1986) gives a readable account of some of the political and environmental problems faced by American Indian communities. For a more up-to-date (and sometimes more critical) analysis of the situation, see *Killing the White Man's Indian: Reinventing Native Americans at the End of the Twentieth Century* by Fergus M. Bordewich (New York, 1996). *The Native American Almanac: A Portrait of Native America Today* by Arlene Hirschfelder and Martha Kreipe de Montaño (New York, 1993) is a patchy but useful single-volume compendium of information about contemporary American Indians. For the *feel* of contemporary Native American life, see the work of novelists and poets such as Sherman Alexie, Louise Erdrich, Joy Harjo, Thomas King, N. Scott Momaday, Louis Owens, Leslie Marmon Silko, Lucy Tapahonso and Gerald Vizenor.

Permissions Acknowledgements

Every effort has been made to contact all copyright holders. The publishers would be happy to rectify any omissions at the first opportunity. Grateful acknowledgement is made to the following publishers for permission to reproduce copyrighted material.

Raymond J. DeMallie, *The Sixth Grandfather: Black Elk's Teachings Given to John G. Neihardt*. Lincoln, Nebraska: University of Nebraska Press, 1984.
For Standing Bear's description of the buffalo hunt on pp. 256–7 and the two quotes about Indian warfare on pp. 276–7 and 277.

Howard L. Meredith and Virginia E. Milan (editors), *A Cherokee Vision of Eloh'*, translated by Wesley Proctor. Indian University Press, Bacone College, 1981.
For the epigraphs on pp. 132–3, 137–8 and 142–3.

Kenneth R. Philp (editor), *Indian Self-Rule: First-Hand Accounts of Indian-White Relations from Roosevelt to Reagan*. Salt Lake City, Utah: Howe Brothers. The Institute of the American West, Utah State University, 1986.
For the Reifel quote on pp. 345–6, the Costo quote on p. 346, the San Carlos Apache quote on p. 355, the Savilla quote on p. 357, the three epigraphs on pp. 358–9, the Helen Peterson quote on p. 374, the Philip S. Deloria quote on p. 382, the La Donna Harris quote on p. 410, the Philip S. Deloria quote on p. 418 and the Oren Lyons quote on p. 427.

Leo W. Simmons (editor), *Sun Chief: The Autobiography of a Hopi Indian*. New Haven: Yale University Press, 1970.
For the quotes on p. 319 and the first two quotes on p. 320.

Dean R. Snow, *The Iroquois*. Cambridge, Mass: Blackwell Publishers, 1994.
For the Iroquois Creation Story on pp. 99–101; and the matrilocality quote on pp. 101–2.

John Stands In Timber and Margot Liberty, *Cheyenne Memories*. Lincoln, Nebraska: Bison Books, University of Nebraska Press, 1972.
For the Sweet Medicine story on pp. 249–50, the excerpts from the Cheyenne origin story on pp. 253–4, pp. 254–5 and p. 255, the quote about disease on pp. 262–3, the description of the Sand Creek Massacre on pp. 273–4 and the second quote on p. 307.

Luther Standing Bear, *Land of the Spotted Eagle*. Lincoln, Nebraska: Bison Books, University of Nebraska Press, 1978.
For the quote on p. 260, the epigraph on p. 303, the first quote on p. 307, the quote about schooling on pp. 313–5, the quote about returned students on pp. 320–1 and the epigraph on p. 330.

Mary Crow with Richard Erdoes, *Lakota Woman*. New York: Grove/Atlantic, 1991.
For quotes from Mary Crow Dog on p. 399, pp. 402–3, and pp. 403–4 and for the epigraph from Dennis Banks on pp. 391–2.

Richard Erdoes and Alfonso Ortiz, *American Indian Myths and Legends*. New York: Pantheon Books, 1984.
For extracts from Montezuma and the Great Flood on pp. 172–4 and The Coming of Wasichu on pp. 261–2.

Alvin M. Josephy (editor), *Red Power: The American Indians' Fight for Freedom*. New York: McGraw-Hill, 1971.
For the quotes from Clyde Warrior on pp. 370–1 and p. 388 and the quotes from Mel Thom on p. 371 and pp. 380–1.

Index